HERITAGE STUDIES

This is the first volume specifically dedicated to the consolidation and clarification of Heritage Studies as a distinct field with its own means of investigation. It presents the range of methods that can be used and illustrates their application through case studies from different parts of the world, including the UK and USA. The challenge that the collection makes explicit is that Heritage Studies must develop a stronger recognition of the scope and nature of its data and a concise yet explorative understanding of its analytical methods.

The methods considered fall within three broad categories: textual/discourse analysis; methods for investigating people's attitudes and behaviour; and methods for exploring the material qualities of heritage. The methods discussed and illustrated range from techniques such as text analysis, interviews and participant observation, to semiotic analysis of heritage sites and the use of GIS. Each essay discusses the ways in which methods used in social analysis generally are explored and adapted to the specific demands that arise when applied to the investigation of heritage in its many forms.

Heritage Studies is a seminal volume that will help to define the field. The global perspective and the shared focus upon the development of reflexive methodologies ensure that the volume explores these central issues in a manner that is simultaneously case-specific and of general relevance.

Marie Louise Stig Sørensen is Senior Lecturer in Archaeology at the University of Cambridge, where she has coordinated the postgraduate degree in Archaeological Heritage and Museums since 1990. Her interest in heritage focuses on identity, especially nationalism, gender and how the sense of belonging is formed. Her publications include *Gender Archaeology* (2000).

John Carman is University Research Fellow and Senior Lecturer in Heritage Valuation at the University of Birmingham. Among other areas, he is particularly interested in sites of past conflict as places of memory. His publications include *Archaeology and Heritage* (2002) and *Against Cultural Property* (2005).

HERITAGE STUDIES

Methods and Approaches

Edited by
Marie Louise Stig Sørensen and John Carman

Routledge
Taylor & Francis Group

LONDON AND NEW YORK

First published 2009
by Routledge
2 Park Square, Milton Park, Abingdon, Oxon, OX14 4RN

Simultaneously published in the USA and Canada
by Routledge
711 Third Avenue, New York, NY 10017

Reprinted 2010

Routledge is an imprint of the Taylor & Francis Group, an informa business

© 2009 Marie Louise Stig Sørensen and John Carman for selection and
editorial matter;
individual chapters, their contributors

Typeset in Garamond 3 by
Saxon Graphics Ltd, Derby

British Library Cataloguing in Publication Data
A catalogue record for this book is available from the British Library

Library of Congress Cataloging in Publication Data
A catalog record for this book has been requested

ISBN 13: 978-0-415-43184 -2 (hbk)
ISBN 13: 978-0-415-43185-9 (pbk)

CONTENTS

CONTENTS

ILLUSTRATIONS

TABLES AND TEXT BOXES

NOTES ON CONTRIBUTORS

Charlotte Andrews is a doctoral candidate in Heritage Studies with the Department of Archaeology, University of Cambridge, with support from the Bank of Bermuda Foundation Sir John W. Cox Scholarship. Between her Masters of Philosophy (MPhil) in Archaeological Heritage and Museums from Cambridge and her BA in Anthropology from Barnard College of Columbia University she spent five years as Curator at Bermuda Maritime Museum. Her doctoral dissertation explores maritime heritage in Bermuda with the aim of offering an expanded conceptualisation of heritage, with implications for museums – and maritime museums and Bermuda's museums specifically – using heritage ethnography as a specialised research method. Following completion of her PhD, she hopes to rejoin the heritage sector in her native Bermuda.

Ian Baxter is a senior lecturer in the Cultural Business Group at Glasgow Caledonian University and Associate Director of the Caledonian Heritage Futures Network. He trained as an archaeologist, and has spent twenty years working with a variety of heritage and tourism organisations throughout the UK. He was a lead consultant supporting the establishment of English Heritage's Heritage Counts programme and has also supported Historic Scotland's Scottish Historic Environment Audit programme. His academic research and consultancy focuses on heritage policy development, methodologies for establishing heritage 'values', and historic visitor attraction management. He is a member of a number of professional committees including the ICOMOS-UK Cultural Tourism Committee, the UK Heritage Research Group (UK-HRG), the National Trust for Scotland's Archaeology and Economic & Community Development Advisory Panels, and English Heritage's Research Advisory Panel. He is also the editor for the Policy Research Notes section in the journal *Cultural Trends*.

John Carman is Research Fellow in Heritage Valuation at the Institute of Archaeology & Antiquity, University of Birmingham. After a career in commerce he gained his PhD from Cambridge University in 1993, having researched the place of law in heritage management in Britain. After a number of years based in Cambridge, where he taught on the MPhil course in Archaeological Heritage and Museums, he moved to his current post in Birmingham. He published the results of his PhD research as *Valuing Ancient Things: Archaeology and Law* (1996) and is the author of *Archaeology and Heritage: An Introduction* (2002) and *Against Cultural Property* (2005), and co-author with Patricia Carman of *Bloody Meadows: Investigating Landscapes of Battle* (2006). He is also a member of the Editorial Board of the *International Journal of Heritage Studies*.

Patricia Carman is a historian, archaeologist and qualified teacher, and co-Director with John Carman of the Bloody Meadows Project, which was initiated in 1998. She is also co-author of *Bloody Meadows: Investigating Landscapes of Battle* (2006).

Paola Filippucci is a lecturer in Social Anthropology at Murray Edwards College, Cambridge, with a background in both social anthropology and archaeology. She has long-term research interests in the perception and politics of the past and of heritage in Europe, and has been investigator on several major international interdisciplinary projects in Europe, such as the European Union project 'Environmental Perception and Policy-Making: Cultural and Natural Heritage and the Preservation of Degradation Sensitive Environments in Southern Europe' and the EU-funded CRIC project *Identity and Conflict: Cultural Heritage and the Re-construction of Identities after Conflict*. Her most recent publications include: 'Archaeology and Memory on the Western Front' in D. Boric (ed.) *Archaeology and Memory* (forthcoming); 'Postcards from the Past: Landscape, Place and the Memory of War in Argonne (France)' in P. Cornish and N. Saunders (eds) *Contested Objects: Material Memories of the Great War* (2009); and 'Memory and Marginality: Remembrance of World War I in Argonne, France' in D. Kaneff, F. Pine and H. Haukanes (eds) *Politics, Religion and Remembering the Past* (2004).

Matthew Fitzjohn is Lecturer in Archaeology at the University of Liverpool. His PhD research at the University of Cambridge addressed issues of identity and landscape in the Iron Age of Greece and southern Italy. An important part of his archaeological and anthropological research is the integration of Geographical Information Systems and Computer Generated Imagery to investigate archaeological data and conceptions of landscape. His publications include: *Uplands of Ancient Sicily and Calabria: The Archaeology of Landscape Revisited* (editor, 2007); 'Equality in the Colonies: Concepts of Equality in Sicily during the Eighth to Sixth Centuries BC', *World Archaeology* 39.2 (2007); and 'Viewing Places: GIS Applications for Examining the Perception of Space in the Mountains of Sicily', *World Archaeology* 39.1 (2007).

Mary-Catherine E. Garden is an archaeologist who has conducted fieldwork in North America, specialising in public archaeology and the exploration of landscapes. She has lectured in the USA and the UK and most recently was a lecturer in Heritage Studies and Associate Director of the Heritage Futures Research Network at Glasgow Caledonian University with responsibilities for local history and heritage societies. She holds degrees in archaeology from the University of Toronto, the College of William and Mary and the University of Cambridge, and has spent many years working with private- and public-sector heritage agencies in North America. Her current research focuses on landscapes of the past and particularly on the role of the heritage site and 'emerging' landscapes of heritage.

Susan Keitumetse has a background in archaeology and environmental science and is currently a Research Fellow in Heritage Tourism. She conducts applied research in the Okavango Delta region of Botswana. Her PhD from the University of Cambridge, Department of Archaeology in 2005 explored the link between sustainable development and archaeological heritage management in Botswana with comparative research in Kenya and the Republic of South Africa. She is a former Rockefeller Foundation Fellow at the Smithsonian Institution, USA, and currently sits on the board of directors of Botswana Tourism Board. Her journal publications include, among others: 'Sustainable Development and Cultural Heritage Resources Management'; 'The Ecotourism of Cultural Heritage Management: Linking Heritage and "Environment" in Okavango Delta Region', *International Journal of Heritage Studies* 15.2–3; and 'UNESCO 2003 Convention on Intangible Heritage: Practical Implications for Heritage Management Approaches in Africa', *South African Archaeological Bulletin* 61.184.

Morag M. Kersel is a postdoctoral fellow at the Joukowsky Institute for Archaeology and the Ancient World at Brown University. She is a former Social Sciences and Humanities Research Postdoctoral Fellow in the Department of Anthropology at the University of Toronto. While in Toronto she conducted research and published widely on the efficacy of cultural heritage law in protecting the archaeological landscape. Kersel received her PhD from the Department of Archaeology at the University of Cambridge, where she studied the trade in antiquities in the Middle East. She currently co-edits with C. Luke the archaeological heritage and ethics section of the *Journal of Field Archaeology* and is a co-editor with N. Brodie, C. Luke and K. Walker Tubb of *Archaeology, Cultural Heritage and the Antiquities Trade* (2006).

Grete Lillehammer is Associate Professor at the Museum of Archaeology, a National Research Centre for Paleostudies and Conservation, University of Stavanger, Norway. She acts as cultural heritage manager and research advisor, and lectures on BA and MA courses in Heritage Studies at the University of

Stavanger. She is also an external examiner in Heritage Studies at the University of Oslo. Her research interests focus on cultural perceptions, landscape conflicts and public attitudes, in particular theory, method and ethics. Among recent publications are: 'The Past in the Present: Landscape Perception, Archaeological Heritage and Marginal Farmland in Jæren, Southwestern Norway', *Norwegian Archaeological Review* 40.2 (2007).

Barbara J. Little is an archaeologist with the National Park Service in Washington, DC and Adjunct Professor of Anthropology at the University of Maryland. She works in public archaeology on issues of public outreach and involvement and on the evaluation and official designations of archaeological places. Recent publications include: *Historical Archaeology: Why the Past Matters* (2007), named an 'Outstanding Academic Title' by *Choice* in 2008; *Assessing Site Significance: A Guide for Archaeologists and Historians*, co-authored with Donald R. Hardesty (2nd edn 2009); *Archaeology as a Tool of Civic Engagement*, co-edited with Paul A. Shackel (2007); and *Heritage of Value, Archaeology of Renown: Reshaping Archaeological Assessment and Significance*, co-edited with Clay Mathers and Timothy Darvill (2005).

Carol McDavid is the Executive Director of the Community Archaeology Research Institute in Houston, Texas, and also serves as adjunct faculty at Rice University and the University of Houston. She holds a PhD in archaeology from the University of Cambridge and serves on the boards of directors of several local history groups and national professional associations. Her publications, community work and research all focus on how archaeologists can make their work more meaningful to the public, and how they can make archaeological research more accessible as a tool for community collaboration and reform. Selected publications include: 'Descendants, Decisions, and Power: The Public Interpretation of the Archaeology of the Levi Jordan Plantation', *Historical Archaeology* 31.3 (1997); 'Archaeologies that Hurt; Descendents that Matter: A Pragmatic Approach to Collaboration in the Public Interpretation of African-American Archaeology', *World Archaeology* 34.2 (2002); 'Beyond Strategy and Good Intentions: Archaeology, Race, and White Privilege', in Barbara Little and Paul Shackel (eds) *An Archaeology of Civic Engagement and Social Justice* (2007).

Catherine Palmer is Principal Lecturer in the School of Service Management (Centre for Tourism Policy Studies), University of Brighton. She has a master's degree in anthropology and sociology of tourism from the University of Surrey and a PhD based in social anthropology focusing on Heritage Tourism and English National Identity from the University of North London. She is a member of the Association of Social Anthropologists and a Fellow of the Royal Anthropological Institute. Her research and publications focus on culture, identity, heritage and tourism, including: 'Royalty, National Identity,

Heritage and Tourism', in P. Long and N. Foster (eds) *Royal Tourism: Excursions around Monarchy* (2008); 'Stalking the Cannibals: Photographic behaviour on the Sepik River', *Tourist Studies* (with J. Lester, 2007); 'An Ethnography of Englishness: Tourism and National Identity', *Annals of Tourism Research* (2005). She teaches on tourism, anthropology and research methods generally and in relation to the MA course in Tourism and Social Anthropology.

Hilary A. Soderland was awarded the Gates Cambridge Trust Scholarship for her MPhil and PhD in the Department of Archaeology, University of Cambridge. Her research interests and publications cross the disciplinary boundaries of archaeology, law, history and heritage. She has been a Visiting Scholar at the American Bar Foundation, Chicago and at the Cegla Center for Interdisciplinary Research of the Law, Buchmann Faculty of Law, Tel Aviv University. She is currently undertaking her Juris Doctorate at Boalt Hall School of Law, University of California-Berkeley. Her museum experience in the USA, the UK and Israel has encompassed archaeology and ethnology curation, accessioning protocol, exhibition preparation and legal compliance. Most recently, she co-edited with George S. Smith and Phyllis Mauch Messenger *Heritage Values in Contemporary Society* (2009). She currently serves on the Society for American Archaeology Repatriation Committee and is co-founder and chair of the Heritage Values Interest Group.

Ulrike Sommer is Lecturer in European Prehistory at the Institute of Archaeology, University College London. She studied prehistory and sociology at Frankfurt University, Germany, where she gained her PhD. After directing the Archaeological Open-Air Museum at Groß-Raden, Germany, she worked on an interdisciplinary research project on the formation of regional identities at the University of Leipzig. She is interested especially in the archaeology of the nineteenth century and its role in the formation of national and regional identities. She is a member of the editorial board of the journal *Public Archaeology* and of the Histories of Archaeology series. She has edited with Sabine Rieckhoff *Auf der Suche nach Identitäten: Volk – Stamm – Kultur – Ethnos* (2007).

Marie Louise Stig Sørensen is a University Senior Lecturer, Department of Archaeology, University of Cambridge. She studied archaeology at Århus University, Denmark, and the University of Cambridge, where she gained her PhD. She coordinates the University of Cambridge MPhil degree in Archaeological Heritage and Museums, and has supervised many PhD students in this field. Her interest within Heritage Studies has mainly focused upon heritage and identity with specific attention on gender and nationalism. Among her publications are: *Gender Archaeology* (2000) and, co-edited with M. Diaz-Andreu, *Excavating Women: A History of Women in European Archaeology* (1998). She is currently the PI on the EU-funded CRIC project *Identity and Conflict: Cultural Heritage and the Re-construction of Identities after Conflict.*

David Uzzell is Professor of Environmental Psychology and leader of the Environmental Psychology Research Group at the University of Surrey. He is currently undertaking research on crime and the environment, risk and human behaviour, the psychology of sustainable development and climate change, and heritage interpretation and exhibition evaluation. He is an International Advisor on the EU-funded CRIC project *Identity and Conflict: Cultural Heritage and the Re-construction of Identities after Conflict*. He edited *Heritage Interpretation*, vols 1 and 2 (1989) and *Contemporary Issues in Heritage and Environmental Interpretation: Problems and Prospects* (1998), with R. Ballantyne. He has been particularly interested in the relationship between heritage and place identity, and introduced the concept of 'hot interpretation' into heritage-interpretation provision. For several years he experienced the sharp end of heritage as a director of a consultancy practice which was responsible for the planning, design and management of heritage-interpretation facilities and services ranging from an A4 leaflet to a multimillion-pound exhibition.

ACKNOWLEDGEMENTS

We are grateful to the British Academy for giving us a grant that allowed a number of speakers to be invited to present papers at the 6th Cambridge Heritage Seminar in 2004. We also want to thank the staff at Routledge, in particular Matthew Gibbons and Lalle Pursglove, for helping with the production of this volume and for their generous patience. We would like to thank Benjamin Morris for his help with proofreading the manuscripts and Katharina Rebay for preparing many of the illustrations. All illustrations, unless otherwise indicated, are the photographs or artwork of the authors.

Part I

SETTING THE SCENE

1

INTRODUCTION

Making the means transparent: reasons and reflections

Marie Louise Stig Sørensen and John Carman

Aims and rationale

The investigation of heritage has become a distinct research area within the Arts and Humanities. We have come to recognise that heritage, in its many different forms, constitutes an influential force in society. We see it expressed, for instance, in the strong links between identity formation and heritage, in the changing valorisation of the tangible as well as intangible heritage, and the increased links between heritage and the leisure society. In response we have seen the development of Heritage Studies as an explicit area of research.

Heritage is a merging interdisciplinary field of study, and its investigation has increasingly been recognised as important by scholars, practitioners (including locally constituted groups and the 'public') and institutions. Investigations of heritage may thus draw on expertise from a range of other disciplines, including anthropology, archaeology, architecture, art, history, psychology, sociology and tourism. Each brings a slightly different focus, whether this is a matter of ontological, epistemological or practical differences, and each has different aims and established routines. The heritage itself may also be understood differently. It may be approached purely as an object of study, or it may be seen as a means of generating income, or as part of political action or sustainable development to engender community spirit and involvement. The concern may be with its regulation or with deciphering its multifaceted characteristics and many roles. Some may see heritage as their inalienable right, while for others it is a construct; yet others see it as timeless and belonging to all.

In different ways and based on a variety of assumptions and practices, heritages play central roles in contemporary societies ranging from definitions of self and claims on identity to being a central income stream through cultural tourism. Clearly such diverse roles, meanings and appearances cannot be captured within a simple terminology but neither can we engage in their studies if it is only the conceptual and theoretical framework that is critically assessed. We also need to engage with the tools – physical, practical and intellectual – that we may employ to study these phenomena. We need to be reflexive, self-aware and critical, sensitive as well as imaginative about how we study heritage. This, moreover, relates to both how we set our intellectual agendas and how we respond to practical challenges. Meanwhile, although methods, of course, have been routinely used in Heritage Studies, there has been little methodological reflection. Heritage Studies has borrowed extensively from other disciplines, but whereas this is a reasonable, indeed a sound tactic, it does not ensure that methods are developed and adapted to the needs of Heritage Studies.

There is a growing number of volumes dedicated the discussion of the phenomenon of heritage generally (e.g. Lowenthal 1998; Smith 2004) and volumes discussing specific topics such as value (e.g. Carman 1996), or branches of heritage activities such as public archaeology (e.g. Jameson 1997; Merriman 2004), or its role in politics, including the creation of nations (e.g. Díaz-Andreu and Champion 1996). There are volumes dedicated to particular sites, such as the Acropolis (Yalouri 2001) or Great Zimbabwe (Ndoro 2001), or to places including museums (e.g. Crooke 2000). But with the exception of discussions of heritage interpretations (e.g. Uzzell and Ballantyne 1998) and the use of questionnaires (Merriman 1991) there is no volume that provides a reflection on and discussion of the range of methods that may be used in Heritage Studies. As a consequence there has been little dialogue about how heritage as a phenomenon can be investigated, and little effort has been given to clarify how our analytical procedures affect and dictate the aims and premises of research and thus shape our understanding. Key concerns that need clarification include recognition of how different methods can be used to investigate heritage, and how interpretations may be constructed from data. As more mature and diversified studies of heritage emerge it is becoming ever more important that the means through which we gain our insights are made explicit and open to scrutiny.

The aim of this volume is to respond to this lack of discussion. It will not provide an exhaustive listing or discussion of the many methods that have been or could be used – such as semiotics, discourse analysis, various forms of interview and participant observations, use of media and computer software, psycho-metric analysis, spatial or material studies, etc. – rather, it will consider and reflect on the need for methodological self-awareness based on a number of specific case studies as well as sharing the insights gained and the solutions selected in each case. Thus, the volume aims to provide a taster of the suite of methods that can be used in Heritage Studies and to illustrate their application through case studies from different parts of the world. The underlying challenge which the volume engages with is that Heritage Studies must develop a stronger recognition of the scope and nature of its data and develop a concise yet explorative understanding of its analytical methods.

The methods to be considered fall within three broad categories: textual/discourse analysis; methods for investigating people's attitudes and behaviour; and methods aimed at exploring the material qualities of heritage. In consequence, the methods discussed and illustrated range from techniques such as text analysis, interviews and participant observation, to semiotic analysis of heritage sites and the use of GIS. Each essay discusses the use of a particular method and how it was adapted to the specific demands that arise when used to investigate a particular dimension of heritage. At the same time, while each essay in its own right provides a significant case study and reflection on methodological development, it is as a collection that their contribution becomes most distinct. Collectively the essays demonstrate the richness of the field: they show the varied dimensions of heritage that call for investigation as well as the wide-ranging and imaginative ways we can meet these needs. The global perspective and varied disciplinary and professional backgrounds furthermore ensure that the authors reflect on the methods to be used in terms of a wide range of countries and contexts. Despite their diversity the shared focus upon the development of reflexive methodologies unites the essays, and the volume aims to explore the question of heritage methodology in a manner that is simultaneously case specific and of general relevance.

Background to the volume

The volume arose out of research activities and collaborations conducted around a number of seminars and workshops in Cambridge during 2002–3 that culminated in the British Academy-sponsored conference *Making the Means Transparent: Research Methodologies in Heritage Studies* in the spring of 2004.[1] This means that substantial feedback and consultation have taken place between many of the authors. The aim of these events was to encourage further research and reflection on the question of heritage methodologies. During the preparation of the volume a number of additional themes were identified, as the field is expanding and methods are being introduced or further refined. In response to this, chapters were solicited from Charlotte Andrews and Matthew Fitzjohn to complement the range of approaches.

The volume is composed of five parts: an introductory part that seeks to outline some of the background to Heritage Studies, three further parts based on the different kinds of dataset that are commonly collected and analysed, and a final part that allows commentary from the perspective of some of the fields from which heritage researchers draw their inspiration. The introductory part provides the necessary context to the volume. In this chapter we outline the background to its production and explain the need for clarification and scrutiny of the methods used to investigate heritage. Chapter 2 provides an outline of heritage as a field of study in order to contextualise the need for methodological reflection and clarity. Chapter 3 helps with this contextualisation by providing a detailed account of the development of public archaeology in the US. Heritage Studies everywhere must acknowledge and respond to the needs of variously composed social groups and to variations in historical trajectories. These needs have been particularly clearly recognised in US heritage discourse and identifying and responding to the needs of different social groups, including descendent communities, are a major concern there. Overall the introductory chapters augment the call for explicit research methodologies within Heritage Studies.

The three parts that follow aim to provide detailed examples of the main research methodologies used in Heritage Studies, how they may become adjusted and implemented in response to specific research objectives and the nature of the data. Cohesion is brought to the parts through their shared focus upon a particular data source for heritage (texts, people and objects/materiality) and the methods that can be used to investigate each of them. Under each theme a range of case studies with their specific reflection and use of methods are presented. The final part consists of commentaries from two experts on social science research methodologies, each representing a distinct disciplinary background (social anthropology and environmental psychology).

Text and heritage

Although a category of 'heritage' can in many ways be described as the result of the production of texts – legal texts, official guidelines and indeed academic literature – there has been very little in the way of specifically textual analysis that has had major impact in the field. Carman's (1996) analysis of law in England – utilising a methodology designed to be exportable to other territories – has largely gone unremarked, despite the significance to heritage scholars of understanding and critiquing relevant regulation. Where textual analysis has been applied, it has most commonly been in looking at popular, journalistic and tourist literature (e.g. Beck 2006). Another approach is exemplified by the recent application of critical discourse analysis to the 'Burra Charter' on heritage management practice in Australia (Waterton et al. 2006).

The essay by Sommer (chapter 6) demonstrates the valuable insights historical sources (exemplified by different types of publications and their contexts) can provide and how they reveal how commonly understood ideas about group identity were constructed as master narratives and how this involved the perpetuation of certain images and connotations. By contrast, Soderland and Baxter (chapters 4 and 5) focus upon the manner in which 'official' texts exert a strong influence on our understanding of the heritage as a contemporary phenomenon. Soderland demonstrates how US conservation law and its development can be examined with the aim of appreciating how the legal understanding of heritage was constructed, while Baxter shows how text can be used to analyse the construction of a modern heritage 'audit' in the UK.

People and heritage

Investigating people and their attitudes is probably one of the methods that has seen most exposure within Heritage Studies, and a few seminal publications can be identified. One is Merriman's (1991) early discussion of the construction and use of questionnaires, which highlighted the difficulty of ensuring the validity of data. Another is Jones's account (2004) of her participant observation work in Scotland concerning the Hilton of Cadboll cross-slab. Her study was not only particularly useful in providing insight into the experience of being a participant observer but also an inspiring example of how to use the interview data in the presentation of the data analysis.

In this volume various approaches to the study of people's attitudes towards, recognition of and expressions about heritage in its different forms are considered. The demanding questions of how value is given and how we can analyse value ascription are illustrated through case studies that discuss and show the use of methods such as interviews and participant observation. The case studies range from assessing ways in which local people's attitudes towards the development of tourist products in Botswana (Keitumetse, chapter 11) can be understood, to the attempt at locating how and when people construct their own sense of heritage and the experience of engagement that fieldwork demands (Andrews, chapter 8). Participant observation is also used as a method for investigating some of the motivations and outcomes for heritage tourism (Palmer, chapter 7), while various forms of interviews and in particular the use of unstructured explorative interview techniques are considered in Kersel's chapter 10, discussing the complexity, including ethical considerations, arising from interviewing those involved in the trade in antiquities in Israel and Palestine. In chapter 9 Sørensen, based on her conversations with farmers about their attitudes to the past and its remains, focuses on interviewing as a journey of discovery and the need to pay greater attention to how we listen. McDavid (chapter 12) is also concerned with participation, but in this case with how one can conduct community archaeology in a way that involves different stakeholders as equal partners. Her essay touches on a number of methods but also includes reflections on what is demanded of the researcher or project manager.

Objects of heritage

Less attention has been given to developing methods for looking at things, monuments or landscapes as heritage. Semiotics is a potential method, but it has proved more suitable to the study of, for instance, museum exhibitions, which through their similarities to texts often provide more evident opportunities for such analysis (Macdonald 2006) than to other parts of the heritage. Two theoretical arguments, Thompson's *Rubbish Theory*, which argued that objects undergo a cycle of value-devaluation and revaluation (Thompson 1979), and Appadurai's (1986) 'social life of things' (or biography of objects) do, however, provide frameworks within which the changing value and roles of objects/things may be tracked and dissected. This has been applied to the field of heritage by, for instance, Carman in his discussion of categories of objects (Carman 1990).

Among newly developing methods we seem to see increased influence from wider society rather than primarily borrowing from neighbouring disciplines. There is, for instance, a distinct influence coming from development concerns, in particular through the use of heritage as a cultural resource and in terms of sustainable development. There has also been a growing involvement with public archaeology, outreach programmes and social inclusion concerns, all of which call for different understandings of what heritage can provide and thus new kinds of analysis. The use of media, in particular new types of software and the internet, is also adding and searching for entirely new qualities, as may be expressed in the idea of 'virtual heritage'. These developments have been outward looking and represent substantial challenges to and opportunities for Heritage Studies, including how it conducts its various kinds of analysis.

The final range of methods therefore brings the subject matter of heritage to the foreground by focusing upon its material existence and forms. This emphasis recognises the contrast between a visitor or user-centred approach and an approach that aims to investigate the possibilities provided by the material nature of various heritage resources, their 'being' quality, and in doing so it calls for a different range of methods than those usually employed in the investigation of heritage. Garden's essay (chapter 15) argues for and demonstrates a cross-fertilisation of methods as it introduces and applies her concept of 'heritagescape'. The 'heritagescape' is a means of investigating qualities of heritage sites that focus on them as material manifestations and particular kinds of places. In a similar vein, Carman and Carman's essay (chapter 16) uses readings of landscape to come to an understanding of the place of historic battlefields in contemporary memory and as particular kinds of places. Lillehammer's essay (chapter 14) draws upon yet other aspects of the material as she uses representation (in the form of drawings) as a medium for gauging reflection upon belonging and attitudes towards landscape heritage. Fitzjohn (chapter 13) demonstrates how some of the layered meanings that different individuals attach to their local cultural landscapes can be investigated and disseminated using GIS.

We propose that all three types of methods represented here – the textual, people-oriented and material – are and should remain important, and that practice-led research as well as basic research benefit from existing side by side and from mutuality of methods and aims. The complexity of what heritage 'is', and the many roles, values and meanings that it may embed, does, however,

8

mean that its study is not a simple matter of copying or borrowing existing methods from other disciplines or practices. There is not a 'one-size-fits-all' method to be identified. Rather, a range of methods will clearly be needed. Heritage Studies' lack of a separate disciplinary identity – existing as it does in an interdisciplinary space – does, however, mean that the field's outline and authority are unclear, making scholars hesitant about commenting beyond their own sphere of expertise. That commentary, the cross-fertilisation in terms not just of ideas but also of how we pursue them rigorously yet imaginatively and with open minds, is, however, urgently needed. We need to share and expand how we reason about the selection of methods and how we understand them when carried out. We need to share experiences about how to analyse the end result, and develop ways of engaging with greater curiosity and openness for Heritage Studies to flourish and the importance of heritage to be better understood and responded to.

Note

1   We are grateful to the many speakers who contributed to making this a remarkable conference, and the graduate students from the Dept of Archaeology, University of Cambridge, who helped organise the event.

Bibliography

Appadurai, A. (ed.) (1986) *The Social Life of Things: Commodities in Cultural Perspective*, Cambridge: Cambridge University Press.

Beck, W. (2006) 'Narratives of World Heritage in Travel Guidebooks', *International Journal of Heritage Studies* 12.6, 521–35.

Carman, J. (1990) 'Commodities, Rubbish and Treasure: Valuing Archaeological Objects', *Archaeological Review from Cambridge* 9.2, 195–207.

——— (1996) *Valuing Ancient Things: Archaeology and Law*. London: Leicester University Press.

Crooke, E. (2000) *Politics, Archaeology and the Creation of a National Museum in Ireland: An Expression of National Life*, Dublin: Irish Academic Press.

Díaz-Andreu, M. and T. Champion (eds) (1996) *Nationalism and Archaeology in Europe*, London: UCL Press.

Jameson, J. H. (1997), *Presenting Archaeology to the Public: Digging for Truths,* Walnut Creek, CA: AltaMira Press.

Jones, S. (2004) *Early Medieval Sculpture and the Production of Meaning, Value and Place: The Case of Hilton of Cadboll*, Edinburgh: Historic Scotland.

Lowenthal, D. (1998) *The Heritage Crusade and the Spoils of History*, Cambridge: Cambridge University Press.

Macdonald, S. (ed.) (2006) *A Companion to Museum Studies*, Oxford: Blackwell.

Merriman, N. (1991) *Beyond the Glass Case: The Past, Heritage and the Public in Britain*, Leicester: Leicester University Press.

——— (ed.) (2004) *Public Archaeology*, London: Routledge.

Ndoro, W. (2001) *Your Monument Our Shrine: The Preservation of Great Zimbabwe*, Uppsala: Department of Archaeology and Ancient History, Uppsala University.

Smith, L. (2004) *Archaeological Theory and the Politics of Cultural Heritage*, London: Routledge.

Thompson, M. (1979) *Rubbish Theory: The Creation and Destruction of Value*, Oxford: Oxford University Press.

Uzzell, D. and R. Ballantyne (eds) (1998) *Contemporary Issues in Heritage and Environmental Interpretation*, London: The Stationery Office.

Waterton, E., L. Smith and G. Campbell (2006) 'The Utility of Discourse Analysis to Heritage Studies: The Burra Charter and Social Inclusion', *International Journal of Heritage Studies* 12.4, 339–55.

Yalouri, E. (2001) *The Acropolis: Global Fame, Local Claim*, Oxford: Berg.

2

HERITAGE STUDIES

An outline

John Carman and Marie Louise Stig Sørensen

Introductory reflection

Heritage Studies now exists as a distinct set of academic practices. The field has been emerging since the 1980s and has developed an ever stronger understanding of its remits and scope, including its relationships to and differences from other disciplines. During this period there has been a dramatic growth in literature dedicated to heritage, and the term 'heritage' is now widely used to label not just academic outputs but also a range of practices, institutions and even products. Concomitant debates about what heritage is and means have occurred regularly. These debates have taken a range of forms, from the UNESCO's declaration in 2003 that intangible cultural products are also part of heritage, to etymological discussions of the word 'heritage', to debates about how the field should be defined. In 2008, for example, a discussion about definition of heritage erupted on the list of the World Archaeological Congress (WAC); apparently this was a concern about terminology, but as with all such discussions underneath the debate about terminology and vocabulary one can discern a clear concern with power and subject. Such debates spring from the newness of Heritage Studies and its attempt at establishing itself as a distinct academic discipline and practice and the associated attempts at demarcating and defining this field. As always, this involves identifying the 'gate keepers' and also the subject matter.

The debates indicate the continuous growth of the field, but also potentially the substantial challenges associated with existing in an interdisciplinary space. Typical of such concerns, the discussions on the WAC list in 2008 were clearly divided between those who questioned the utility of definitions and those who were searching for one. Among the latter, further distinctions could be drawn between arguments taking as their starting point the literate meaning of 'heritage',[1] as if the word itself contains the 'key' to the field, and those arguing that institutions such as UNESCO had (or should have) defined the field. In such discussions, there is a clearly discernible tendency for heritage to be a passive and substantially a physical substance, as in the definition by UNESCO which says, 'Heritage is our legacy from the past, what we live with today, and what we pass on to future generations'.[2] This tendency becomes particularly highlighted in parts of the world where the term 'cultural resource' rather than 'heritage' is used, as the former provides even stronger associations with materiality, ownership and usefulness than the word 'heritage' does. A different approach is to suggest that heritage is an object defined through a set of institutional practices, such as those defined by law or regulations (Cleere 1989: 10; Carman 1996), or a set of practices (Smith 2006). Alternatively, it may be argued that heritage is best understood as a way of interacting with the world when values and associations are used that draw on concepts of heritage. Such definitions do, however, raise questions about whose heritage we are considering; and who is making the definitions. These discussions in themselves tend to become part of the debates and claims over heritage.

We consider all of these debates interesting indicators of the status, state and concerns of the field of Heritage Studies, but nonetheless find that such definitions are unhelpful and that insisting on a clear-cut definition risks constraining and delimiting both analytical efforts and the recognition of particular social scenarios. As one of us (JC) wrote during the 2008 WAC online debate referred to above:

> Surely this proposal [that experts be called upon to offer a once-for-all definition of 'heritage'] misses the point? Such is the diversity of understandings of what '(the) cultural heritage' means that no single definition would be useful – except one that were so vague it would be useless. The 'experts' in the field themselves (i.e. those who research heritage, rather than merely pontificate on it) are not sure what the phenomenon we are dealing with is or how it works. What we do agree is that the heritage is an interesting and important contemporary phenomenon worthy of investigation. For us, the term '(cultural) heritage' is really no more than a convenient shorthand – we are only too aware of its different contexts of use and the different phenomena (material, ideational) it comprises in different parts of the world and for different groups of people. Also, because it is a contemporary phenomenon, any attempt to delineate it also has a tendency to alter it as efforts are made to include a particular heritage (national, regional, ethnic, whatever) within the definition. And that will entail a further redefinition, and so on *ad infinitum*. A more fruitful approach ... is to stop seeking quick and simple fixes to complex problems, to engage with the debates taking place, and recognise the complexity and inherent fluidity of the phenomena we deal with. [Heritage] is too important a field of enquiry to be left to 'experts' who wish to fix it (and thereby kill it stone dead)!
>
> (Carman, email to WAC list, 7 November 2008)

Definitions bring focus and coherence to the field of study, but will also limit and make fixed both what is included for study and what have hitherto been permeable borders towards other academic concerns. We are faced with a conundrum. On the one hand, we appreciate that it is through definitions and agreed terminologies that it becomes possible to have meaningful and constructive conversations and to understand each other. On the other hand, definitions and agreed terminologies censor the field; they, rather than the subject matter, will guide our intellectual engagement and restrict our imagination. We shall therefore use this chapter to outline the history of heritage practice and research as this introduces a reflection of the various ways heritage has been perceived through time. This helps to outline the contours of the intellectual field we are concerned with and how it, in its development, reflects changing needs and abilities both in society at large and within neighbouring disciplines.[3]

Early approaches to heritage

It is difficult to agree on the roots of 'heritage' as a distinct practice and intellectual engagement. Each of the subject areas that may claim heritage as part of its remit will see this history differently. Here we argue that the development during the late eighteenth and early nineteenth centuries of heritage practice and management as public activities marks a distinct qualitative shift in attitudes to the past. It is at this stage that heritage becomes a public concern and its care an expression of the interests and responsibilities of civic societies.

The valorisation of the past that we observe in various earlier societies was of a different kind. The veneration of the past expressed in classical Greece (Miles 2008) or the explicit linkage between past and present seen in the Roman Empire, for example, shown through the reuse of Greek monuments, is often presented as early evidence of an explicit valorisation of heritage. We argue that whereas these, and other examples such as the Chinese emperors' interest in their ancestors (which led them to both excavate burial mounds and instigate large collections of antiquities), are demonstrable early examples of strong interest in the past: they also have characteristics that separate them from later attitudes and practices. The principal difference is that such examples, while demonstrating both an interest in the past and a valorisation of its remains, take different forms and are underwritten by different concerns from what we later identify as heritage practice. There are two obvious characteristics emerging from such apparent early examples which show some of the differences. One is the common tendency for the past to be given a mythical quality or to be treated almost as a realm, a lost time and state of grace. The other is for the remains to be acquired as the personal possession of rising powers, such as the monarchs in medieval Europe or the pope, as they extended their control over resources. King Gustaf Adolf II of Sweden is, for instance, often linked to the emergence of early heritage management as he passed a law in seventeenth-century Sweden declaring

13

all antiquities to be the property of the crown (Cleere 1989: 10). The aim of this law, however, as with many early versions of Treasure Trove law[4] (or other national legislation about precious objects), was to acquire and control objects and to secure their status as part of royal possession (see Hill 1936: 189; Carman 1996: 45–7). A late expression of the individualised interest in the past, and its role in the pursuit of leisure interests, is the phenomenon of the Grand Tour, where it became the done thing for the upper class to travel to Italy (and later Greece) and to explore the sites (Wilton and Bignamini 1996). While there was an interest in the past and its remains, there was no concept of civic duty associated with these activities; it was purely pleasure.

The important difference between these early activities and contemporary ones is that heritage management and practices are now carried out as part of institutional and public concerns and the concept of ownership has changed. Rather than belonging to individuals, heritage became something that was deemed to be held in trust. This change in how the heritage is integrated within society at large has its origins in the late eighteenth and early nineteenth centuries, and many of the structures through which heritage is now managed and recognised were formed then.

The valorisation of the past: nineteenth-century institutions and instrumentalisation of heritage

Whereas one may dispute whether the earlier activities were about heritage rather than an interest in control over resources, it is clear that various relationships changed in the eighteenth century. It is during this century that we see new attitudes towards the heritage becoming expressed. They took the form of, on the one hand, valorisation and interest in heritage *per se* and, on the other hand, a concern with the conservation of the remains of the past. The developments of these changing attitudes are embedded within socio-political tendencies of the time. Moreover, parallel trends can often be found in different parts of the world even if the actual practices (e.g. institutional structure, legal protection, ownership issues) were shaped by differences in local socio-political conditions. This is not the place for a detailed account of these changes, some of which are by now well documented, although a few trends should be mentioned before we move on. The development of museums (together with zoological gardens, botanical gardens and other public-collection enterprises) plays an important role during the period while simultaneously revealing its fundamental interest in the public and its edification (Hooper-Greenhill 1992). The relationship between the development of the national state, nationalism and the growth in interest in the study of the past has also been well documented (e.g. Díaz-Andreu and Champion 1996; Hunter 1996; Kohl and Fawcett 1995). Similarly, the growth of the conservation movement and preservation societies as well as national and local antiquarian or historical societies played an interesting role in changing perceptions of the landscape and in articulating urgency about 'the world we have lost' (Hunter 1996; Olwig 1984; Pearce 2007).

Underwriting these shifts in perceptions and attitudes are two major changes, we believe. One is the development of a distinct public sphere with the associated idea of the public (for detailed discussions of the concept of the public see Carman 2002 and Merriman 2004). In Europe, the political movements during the seventeenth and eighteenth centuries created the preconditions for these changes. In particular, the transformation in concepts of citizens and civil rights arising from the French Revolution and the emergence of the middle class in the wake of the dissolution of the absolute monarchy wrought seminal changes in the political and social landscapes. The public was being educated, edified and civilised, and much was done on their behalf. The emphasis on the public and the casting of society into two partners – the public and the state (now as their guardians rather than formerly the king as their master) – did, however, also create the potential for tension between knowledge producers and consumers, a characteristic that came to dominate much of the heritage debate towards the end of the twentieth century.

The other significant factor is the development of positive values associated with remains of the past. Whereas the positive valorisation of remains from the past by now appears as an almost inalienable aspect of heritage, this has clearly not always been the case. The reason for the development of an explicit and widely held valorisation of the past can partly be found in the impact of industrialisation. During the nineteenth century an interesting and dynamic tension developed between the optimism and future-orientated attitudes articulated in the wake of the industrial revolution and the growing feelings of nostalgia and regret about the world that was disappearing. The effect on the physical heritage could be observed in the devastation of large areas of land due to the pursuit of timber and coal and the consequential destruction of monuments and landscapes. This destruction became a major inspiration for the development of a conservation movement in many areas.

These two tendencies led to the professionalisation of heritage practices, including the development of responsible institutions (such as museums and antiquities services), legal measures and allocations of roles. It also resulted in the creation of new meanings and values, including the need to identify and compare the significance and importance of different kinds of heritage in order to select those deemed to deserve protection. During the nineteenth century engagement with the past therefore developed into two forms: an audience and a professional practitioner. In this development what were formerly antiquarian activities exercised by a small, select and interconnected group of individuals with strong ties to multiple disciplines were replaced by disciplinary activities variously labelled archaeology, Classics, Anglo-Saxon Studies, etc. The care of the past was shaped by and divided between different institutions and specialised disciplines and, rather than a general concern with the past, the practices involved became more narrowly defined and specialised than had been the case before. Whereas this approach to and understanding of the remains of the past had developed from a long history of antiquarian interest that was part of a European mentality, in its professionalised and institutionalised form it became exported to many regions of Asia and Africa as part of colonial administration, with many features still retained today (e.g. Chakrabarti 2003; Ndoro 2003).

These two changes – the development of a role of guardian in terms of the public and the professionalisation of the field – were fuelled by political changes. The nineteenth century in Europe may be seen as the time of the nation state. In the wake of challenges to absolute monarchies new political structures developed, and the nation state was shaped. This political construction was in need of legitimisation and naturalisation, and disciplines such as the emerging field of archaeology could provide this. In the words of the Danish archaeologist J. J. A. Worsaae, archaeology was a 'Supreme nationalistic discipline' (Sørensen 1996; Worsaae 1843).

Heritage management in the nineteenth and twentieth centuries: expansion and consolidation

The institutional involvements together with the distinct practical dimension of heritage management and research meant that it lent itself to expansion, consolidation through professionalism and export. We see this most clearly in terms of the export of heritage practices through colonial administrations and international law. Whereas heritage management was not a primary concern of the colonial powers, most colonial administrations at some point instigated a system of heritage protection – usually in imitation of the 'home' arrangements of the colonising power. During the latter part of the nineteenth century and the first half of the twentieth century, heritage legislation, management systems and practices based on various European models were thus installed throughout many parts of the world. Moreover, even areas not under colonial administration began to import the Euro-American heritage model and having heritage and a national museum became as much a part of a country's national paraphernalia as the flag and the anthem.

The export and increased internationalisation of heritage management may be seen even more clearly in the field of law. Heritage legislation has over the past century evolved from being concerned with ownership, to legislation between the state and the private individual to, from the 1950s onwards, including concerns about international legislation. With regard to the latter, this has not just involved policies produced by international bodies such as UNESCO, but also the expansion of legislation into regulation and collaboration with regard to shared international issues such as the illicit traffic in antiquities, the protection of heritage during armed conflict and international regulation of the maritime heritage. These processes led to the creation of the legal tools and instruments needed to regulate and safeguard the heritage, but in the process we have also opened up the potential gap and incompatibility in attitudes between the traditional 'owners' of heritage and the institutional guardians, and between different knowledge and belief systems.

The 'birth of Heritage Studies'

As a specific field of practice that investigates the role of the past in the present and the various kinds of actions – from governmental institutional practices to individual leisure use and responses – Heritage Studies is a relatively new discipline or field of studies. Its contours and agenda emerged ever more explicit after World War II, but it was first in the 1980s that it became clearly identified. Various things had happened by then to push for this development. One is the political trend, including post-colonialism, which made it possible to recognise new voices and increased appreciation of alternative claims about the past, including challenging controls over access and representations. The other is developments within academia where post-structuralism and post-modernity inspired critique of knowledge claims and authority. For heritage this meant a challenge, for example, to established views about how importance (and thus the status of preservation) is granted. The result was that not only established practices, but also their epistemological basis, were questioned and challenged. Our relationship to and practice of 'heritage' shifted from being a taken-for-granted field of meanings and practices to becoming an area calling out for investigation and analysis aiming to understand how heritage becomes constituted, what it is and does, and how different groups engage with it.

It is during this period that we begin to find publications that may be labelled 'heritage literature' and that the first canonical works were produced. As a way of discerning the development in this literature, we shall comment on some of the main publications and themes that have contributed to shaping this field.

Heritage as an 'industry' and the emergence of debate

The literature of Heritage Studies has been characterised as belonging to one of three main categories: commentary, guidance and research (Carman 2002: 1–4). Although publications offering guidance to practitioners have been with us the longest – the earliest dating from the beginnings of what we would now call 'heritage management' in the nineteenth century – and this is the most prolific category, the field of Heritage Studies may be said to have first really begun with the publication of the first commentaries in the 1980s. In this initial phase, the field comprised developments in several otherwise largely unrelated disciplines through their shared underlying concerns. Although a field of Heritage Studies cannot be said to have existed, the rise of something called 'heritage', which was recognised as such by international agencies (UNESCO 1972), in national legislation (for example seen in the UK in a

17

series of National Heritage Acts from 1980 to the present), by the naming of national bodies such as 'English Heritage', and in the expansion of the museum and other sectors (reported upon by Merriman 1991: 8–10), served to create an object of common and legitimate enquiry.

The years 1985 and 1987 saw the publication of a number of key texts that had immediate and substantial impact on scholars interested in the role of the past in the present. These were all by historians. Lowenthal's *The Past is a Foreign Country* (1985) outlined the differences evident between efforts to preserve objects and places from the past and the study and dissemination of their history. He emphasised the anachronisms involved in the processes of preservation and the purposes that lay behind such efforts – less to do with understanding the past than with economic and political imperatives. Wright's collection of journalistic pieces *On Living in an Old Country* (1985) was a sustained assault on the rise of 'heritage' in Britain at the service of nationalistic politics which presented an image of universal middle-class respectability grounded in property ownership and free enterprise. Together these two works opened up the possibility of a critique of modern uses of the past by looking beyond the presentations of the past to the ideologies reflected by such presentations. Hewison's publication in 1987 of *The Heritage Industry* went a step further by offering an analysis of the emergence of 'heritage' as a response to economic and political decline. Focusing in particular upon dominant forms of heritage presentation – of the country house and the industrial landscape – Hewison took the 'industry' to task for presenting a packaged 'safe' vision of Britain's past unsullied by class division or political unrest. For all of these, as for the historian J. H. Plumb, modernity has meant a rift from a continuously created social world whereby the past becomes merely 'a matter of curiosity, nostalgia, a sentimentality' (Plumb 1969: 14) instead of an integral component of the present. Accordingly, contemporary representations of the past became a retreat from a world of job-loss and imperial decline.

These works and others like them can be characterised as 'commentary' because much of this literature is concerned with defining 'heritage' as something separate from 'history' or the 'real' past, deriving from a position that 'heritage' is a bad thing – or at least inferior to the work of academics and others concerned with a more serious investigation of the past. They treat 'heritage' as the field of popularisation of the past and which is therefore primarily concerned with the issue of representation, particularly in its rather narrow sense of public presentation through museums and heritage centres. These are stimulating arguments – and certainly were at the time of publication – especially because they focused upon the ideological underpinnings of a current phenomenon rather than concerning themselves with issues of accuracy or 'authenticity' of representation. However, they are also grounded less in substantive research than in the perception – if not the biases and preconceptions – of the authors. Initial responses were of a like kind, such as the majority of the papers included in the issue of *Archaeological Review from*

Cambridge (Baker 1988) which was published hard on the heels of Hewison's (1987) book; Baker's volume was notable for being the first collection dedicated to the topic of heritage.

The academic debate sparked by these works and others like them was characterised by attempts to discover what 'heritage' really meant to its recipients. One of the earliest systematic efforts was the work of Nick Merriman, who conducted the first wide-scale investigation of attitudes to the past in Britain. Conducted in the 1980s and published in 1991 as *Beyond the Glass Case*, this work argued against the line taken by Lowenthal, Hewison and others, and indeed against any formulation whereby 'heritage' could be reduced to being a part of a 'dominant ideology'. Instead, Merriman identified different communities who valued different types of past – a monumental, national or global history; or a more personalised, family and genealogical past. Taking the view that one attitude to the past was not more valuable than another, the issue for those responsible for interpreting the past inevitably became one of how to reach those who valued the kinds of pasts not represented in museums and heritage sites. In museology, similar concerns and aims were expressed within the New Museology and reflected in works by, for instance, Pearce (1992, 1995) and Vergo (1989), leading to new research initiatives concerning museums and their roles. Inspired by similar concerns, geographers such as Ashworth and Tunbridge took a new perspective upon the 'historic city' and its preservation and presentation to tourists (Ashworth and Tunbridge 1990; Tunbridge and Ashworth 1996).

Merriman came from archaeology, and archaeology also played other roles in developing Heritage Studies as a discipline. Inspired particularly by developments a decade earlier in the USA (McGimsey 1972; Schiffer and Gumerman 1977; King *et al*. 1977), Cleere's interest in comparing the practices of heritage management in different parts of the world resulted in two key works (Cleere 1984, 1989). Others, such as Gathercole (Gathercole and Lowenthal 1990), Ucko (1987) and Layton (1989a, b), among others, took the lead in recognising the expressly political nature of interpreting the past. While Layton and Gathercole focused especially upon the relations between colonial power and indigenous populations, Ucko addressed the moral and ethical issues surrounding international collaboration in archaeology – especially as it related to the involvement of representatives of oppressive regimes in international meetings of scholars. Out of a division concerning South African membership among organisers of a meeting of the International Union of Pre- and Proto-Historic Sciences to be held in Southampton in 1986 arose the World Archaeological Congress, which champions the involvement of peoples 'without history'. Important work was also emerging out of the USA that would inevitably impact on those developing an interest in issues of interpretation. The work of Leone and his colleagues at Annapolis (Leone 1981; Leone *et al*. 1987; Potter and Leone 1986, 1987) in developing a 'critical archaeology' of capitalism involved introducing site visitors to the methods of archaeologists and the processes of interpretation rather than focusing upon the products of that interpretive process.

Another line of concern about politics and the past focused on how interpretations were shaped within political ideologies. There was a cluster of work investigating the use of the past in nationalism (e.g. Díaz-Andreu and Champion 1996; Kohl and Fawcett 1995) and the abuse of the past by various political regimes, especially Nazi Germany (e.g. Arnold 1990). Although awareness of the political role and potentials of archaeology were not new, as this had been recognised from its early nineteenth-century beginnings, the study of these relationships was now driven by different concerns. In essence, the heritage was being recognised as simultaneously defenceless and open to abuse (e.g. Sørensen 1996) and also as a potentially empowering aspect of social life in terms of, for example, the formation of identity and creating a sense of rootedness.

By about 1990, the main themes of an emerging field – as also represented by the work in this volume – were recognisable. As well as issues of institutional and organisational structure (Cleere 1984), the values to be ascribed to components of the heritage, and how they became attached, were under increasing scrutiny, both from a theoretical and critical standpoint (Tainter and Lucas 1983; Leone and Potter 1992) and from the perspective of those more concerned with issues of practice (Darvill et al. 1987; Schaafsma 1989). Similarly, issues related more closely to public interpretation and outreach were taking a high prominence (Stone and MacKenzie 1990). At the same time, the distinctive trope of publication in the field was emerging: the individual case study. The discourse of 'heritage' is a highly nationalistic and particularistic one ('my' museum, 'my' site, etc.), which tends to limit the capacity for more comparative and generalising approaches. Accordingly, the case study of heritage in a particular context or of particular kinds of heritage which exist within particular contexts has become the norm. The One World Archaeology publications of the World Archaeological Congress – which have done much to promote this field within archaeology – are replete with such case studies. Nonetheless, the first 'generation' of heritage postgraduate students (Carman, Smith, Byrne) finished their PhDs during the early 1990s and introduced comparable analyses to the field and explicit theorising. This was applied widely, including to the role of the law in creating value (Carman), to the question of moral versus legal ownership (Byrne) or to the control over heritage as a means of governing living populations (Smith). Their works surpassed the case-study approach, or rather case studies now became a means of exemplifying and learning rather than the goal. Heritage also began to appear as a regular topic at various international and national conferences, including WAC, the European Association of Archaeologists and the American Anthropological Association (AAA). Heritage Studies had arrived, although the relatively few places offering graduate training meant that the researchers were still pushing against a sense of marginalisation.

Legitimising the study of heritage: going global

Rather than staying in the margin and retaining the sense of commentaries, the field expanded and matured. As we approach the end of the first decade of the twenty-first century, research into aspects of heritage is on the rise, both in academia and beyond. The field is sufficiently young that many of those who played their part in the birth of the discipline remain active within it (Merriman 2004; Ashworth *et al.* 2007), while those who immediately followed them have over the past two decades become established scholars in their own right (e.g. Carman 2002, 2005a; Smith 2004, 2006; Smith and Waterton 2009). Indicative of these changes is the increase in the number of PhDs undertaken in the field (among our authors, for instance, Garden, Keitumetse, Kersel, McDavid and Soderland have all achieved their doctorates since 2000). The first dedicated academic journals emerged during the 1990s: the *International Journal of Cultural Property*, which took a primarily legal approach, first appeared in 1992; the *International Journal of Heritage Studies*, which took a broader view of its profile, started in 1994; *Conservation and Management of Archaeological Sites* in 1995; *Public Archaeology* in 2000; *Web Journal on Cultural Patrimony* in 2006; and the US-based *Heritage Management* in 2008. Within archaeology in particular, journals of a more general kind – the *European Journal of Archaeology* in 1999 and *World Archaeology* in 2002 – have also dedicated issues to heritage research. The twenty-first century has also seen the first general textbooks for students in the field (Graham *et al.* 2000; Blockley and Hems 2001; Carman 2002; Howard 2003) and student readers (Smith 2007; Fairclough *et al.* 2008), consequent upon the emergence and rise of courses at both undergraduate and postgraduate level since the early 1990s. Such degree courses are now to be found across the globe within a range of disciplinary 'homes', from archaeology, history and geography, to commercial and business studies, tourism and marketing.

The rise of heritage as an academic concern had, by the late 1990s, an effect on the institutions responsible for heritage practices. Whereas the earliest phases of Heritage Studies as a field of enquiry saw institutional interest reflected in concerns for training and recruitment, or alternatively as hostility to the entry of academic debate into the work of professionals, the later phases saw an increased interest in the professional sectors in ideas emerging from academic debate. Discussions of areas such as the value of heritage objects, and of the definition and ontology of such phenomena, were increasingly reflected in changes to professional practice, such as in the case of historic landscapes (e.g. compare Darvill *et al.* 1993 with Fairclough 2008), and the potentials of heritage have increasingly become recognised in plans for sustainable development and tourism. Similarly, practitioners were found more willing to enter the academic arena – indeed to consider themselves as part of academia – and make contributions of their own (Clarke 2001; Schofield 2005; Little 2007).

New concerns, partly responding to political challenges and partly to missing elements in existing heritage politics, were also formulated: concerns that involved collaborations with indigenous people or local residents as well as lawmakers and politicians. The question of ownership, which has been a more or less acknowledged tension within heritage management since its beginning, came to the foreground. The rights of indigenous people to decide over their past was intensely debated during this period, and various solutions formulated. The NAGPRA legislation, although a late response in terms of the ongoing discussion, and after less comprehensive legislations and practices were established in both Australia and New Zealand, is seminal in this development (see also Little, chapter 3), as it made far-ranging decisions about owners and ownership. The further repercussions of this legislation on practices and research and on regions outside the USA are still not clear, but it may diversify the role of the human body in humanities research in different parts of the world. Interestingly, and telling of the complex tensions that are contained within Heritage Studies, the contemporary arguments about the need to stop the illicit antiquities market and to develop the necessary legal means of doing so (Brodie *et al.* 2000; Renfrew 2000) were underwritten by the contrasting ideological position that heritage belongs to all rather than to someone. In line with such concerns, we also find an explicit debate about ethics (Vitelli 1996; Scarre and Scarre 2006): what does it mean to take sides and to whom do we (as professionals) owe alliances and what are our responsibilities? Work on representations and interpretation also moved on during these years. The concern with the messages produced via the different heritage media pushed attention towards how such meanings were constructed. There were substantial analyses of how meanings were created within various settings – such as monumental landscapes (Holtorf 2000–7; Gustafsson and Karlsson 2004; Yalouri 2001), or museums (Crooke 2000), or even depictions (Moser 1998) – but also a concern with how meaning and knowledge can be shared and co-produced, e.g. the Kohla project (Evans *et al.* 2009), the Levi Jordan plantation (McDavid 1997) and the 'Community Archaeology in Quseir' project in Egypt (Moser 2003). Connected to this concern was the continuous attention towards the value heritage gains or is assigned. At a theoretical level Carman continued working on the 'instruments' and processes through which such value ascription takes place, including the use of language (Carman 2005b), and the concept of value gradually shifted from being a taken-for-granted quality to being seen as part of socio-cultural processes. At a practical level there were also changes. An important challenge to the priority given to the value of authenticity came from the recognition that this taken-for-granted value was differently perceived in many Asian countries, Japan in particular (UNESCO 1994). This challenge gradually gave rise to changes in international conceptualisation of heritage value, leading in 2003 to UNESCO's declaration on intangible heritage (UNESCO 2003; Ahmad 2006).

Twenty-first century concerns: indigenous and other non-Western cultures, heritage of conflict, climate change

From a taken-for-granted position at the end of the nineteenth century that heritage is about and belongs to the nation, we have reached a point where the concerns and awareness of what constitutes heritage, what roles it plays and what challenges it raises have exploded. We have officially as well as cognitively moved from an object/monument-focused understanding of heritage to being able to recognise the many kinds of cultural products that are part of our construction of heritage and the roles it plays in our lives.

As we learn more and explore further aspects of the role of the past in the present we are discovering new connections and relationships. Heritage in its many forms is deeply entwined with other aspects of our lives whether at an individual or a group level. Recent research has added several strands to the investigation of heritage. Smith has mounted important arguments about the past of disenfranchised groups, in particular the working class (Smith 2006; Smith and Waterton 2009), and means and reasons for outreach programmes and community involvement are being further refined. We are also seeing new areas emerging which reflect a concern with understanding the potentials and roles of heritage in terms of some of the pressing problems the world is encountering. There is thus an explicit interest in understanding the role of heritage in cultural tourism, in particular with regard to development policies for Africa. There is also an emerging awareness of the link between heritage and the environment, in particular climate change, both in terms of how heritage is affected by these changes (Srovel 1998) and in terms of how understanding of heritage may be tacked on to perceptions of a changing world (World Heritage Centre 2006). There is also a growing awareness of the potential role heritage can play in peace-building and processes of reconciliation (e.g. Ashworth and Graham 2005; Moore and Whelan 2007; Price 2007), and the role of the reconstruction of cultural heritage during and after violent conflict is being investigated (Baillie 2009; Viejo Rose 2007). The importance of these links has increasingly been recognised by NGOs and by funding agencies, such as the EU, and the impact of reconstructions on people's sense of belonging, their identity and ability to reconstitute meaningful lives is now being studied (Sørensen and Viejo Rose n.d.).

The need for methodologies

Having developed as an in-between subject and with its practitioners working in academic institutions, governments and 'in the field', Heritage Studies, despite its long gestation and substantial and complex scope, has paid scant attention to methods. This does not mean that methods have not been used, but rather that methods borrowed from a range of disciplines have been imported and the forms and relevance assumed rather than critically assessed.

This is an expected characteristic of an emerging field: specialised purposeful methods cannot exist prior to the formulation of specialised research aims. Critical awareness of methods first emerged within various kinds of market research with regard to heritage, including attitudes among the public, but there has been a lack of methods aimed at exploring issues – for example, approaching such attitudes as worth study in their own right rather than seeing them entirely as indicators of something measurable. Investigations aimed at understanding qualities of heritage and how these affect its roles in its various contemporary settings have only recently started to emerge, and with these a new and needed degree of self-awareness is emerging. This will affect not only the sureness with which we conduct our analysis but also how we assess and disseminate our results.

Notes

1   Such discussions, which are by no means uncommon, seem to forget that whereas heritage exists as an important socio-cultural phenomenon almost everywhere, the word used to describe it varies between languages (e.g. Danish: *Kulturarv*, German: *Kulturdenkmal*, French: *Patrimoine*; Spanish: *Patrimonio*; Swedish: *Kulturminn*). The meaning of the English word 'Heritage' cannot, therefore, necessarily be used to define the field.
2   Whereas the exact wording can differ, other institutions and conventions, such as the Faro Framework Convention on the Value of Cultural Heritage for Society, tend to reproduce the same rhetoric and meaning constructed around ideas about inherited resources and legacies from the past which are held to be of timeless value.
3   This chapter will be biased towards the development in Europe and to a lesser degree in the US; this does not mean that heritage practices have not been exercised in other parts of the world, but it reflects how until a few decades ago this was a field dominated by a Eurocentric view of heritage. Analyses of different forms of early heritage perceptions and practices, rather than the situations encountered in the post-colonial era and in our increasingly globalised world, are still largely missing.
4   Treasure Trove is the ancient doctrine that objects of value – chiefly of gold or silver – that have been hidden in the past and of which the ownership is now unknown, belong to the crown. Whereas in the medieval period it was effectively a tax on the dead, from the nineteenth century onwards it became a vehicle whereby ancient objects would find their way into public collections and involved paying finders a reward equal to the value of the object. In 1996 Treasure Trove was replaced in England by the Treasure Act; versions of it persist elsewhere.

Bibliography

Ahmad, Y. (2006) 'The Scope and Definitions of Heritage: From Tangible to Intangible', *International Journal of Heritage Studies* 12.3, 292–300.
Arnold, B. (1990) 'The Past as Propaganda: Totalitarian Archaeology in Nazi Germany', *Antiquity* 64, 464–78.
Ashworth, G. J. and J. E. Tunbridge (1990) *The Tourist-Historic City*, London: Belhaven.
Ashworth, G. J. and B. Graham (eds) (2005) *Senses of Place: Senses of Time*, London: Ashgate.
Ashworth, G., B. Graham and J. Tunbridge (2007) *Pluralising Pasts: Heritage, Identity and Place in Multicultural Societies*, London: Pluto Press.

Baillie, B. (2009) 'The Wounded Church: War, Destruction and Reconstruction of Vukovar's Religious Heritage'. PhD Thesis, University of Cambridge.

Baker, F. (ed.) (1988) 'Archaeology and the Heritage Industry', *Archaeological Review from Cambridge* 7.2 (Autumn).

Blockley, M. and A. Hems (eds) (2001) *Heritage Interpretation: Theory and Practice,* Issues in Heritage Management series, London: English Heritage.

Brodie, N. J., J. Doole, and P. Watson (2000) *Stealing History: The Illicit Trade in Cultural Material*, Cambridge: McDonald Institute.

Carman, J. (1996) *Valuing Ancient Things: Archaeology and Law*, London: Leicester University Press.

—— (2002) *Archaeology and Heritage: An Introduction,* London and New York: Continuum.

—— (2005a) *Against Cultural Property: Archaeology, Heritage and Ownership*, London: Duckworth.

—— (2005b) 'Good Citizens and Sound Economics: The Trajectory of Archaeology in Britain from "Heritage" to "Resource"', in C. Mathers, T. Darvill and B. Little (eds) *Heritage of Value, Archaeology of Renown: Reshaping Archaeological Assessment and Significance*, Gainesville: University Press of Florida, 43–57.

Chakrabarti, D. K. (2003) *Archaeology in the Third World: A History of Indian Archaeology since 1947*, Delhi: D. K. Printworld.

Clarke, K. (2001) *Informed Conservation: Understanding Historic Buildings and their Landscapes for Conservation*, London: English Heritage.

Cleere, H. F. (ed.) (1984) *Approaches to the Archaeological Heritage*, Cambridge: Cambridge University Press.

—— (ed.) (1989) *Archaeological Heritage Management in the Modern World*, London: Unwin Hyman.

Crooke, E. (2000) *Politics, Archaeology and the Creation of a National Museum in Ireland: An Expression of National Life*, Dublin: Irish Academic Press.

Darvill, T., A. Saunders and B. Startin (1987) 'A Question of National Importance: Approaches to the Evaluation of Ancient Monuments for the Monuments Protection Programme in England', *Antiquity* 61, 393–408.

Darvill, T., G. Gerrard, and B. Startin (1993) 'Identifying and Protecting Historic Landscapes', *Antiquity* 67, 563–74.

Díaz-Andreu, M. and T. Champion (eds) (1996) *Nationalism and Archaeology in Europe*, London: UCL Press.

C. Evans, with J. Pettigrew, Y. Kromchain Tamu and M. Turin (2009) *Grounding Knowledge/ Walking Land: Archaeological Research and Ethno-historical Identity in Central Nepal*, Cambridge: McDonald Institute Monographs.

Fairclough, G. (2008) 'A New Landscape for Cultural Heritage Management: Characterisation as a Management Tool', in L. Lozny (ed.) *Landscapes Under Pressure: Theory and Practice of Cultural Heritage Research and Preservation*, New York: Springer.

Fairclough, G., R. Harrison, J. H. Jameson and J. Schofield (eds) (2007) *The Heritage Reader*, London: Routledge.

Gathercole, P. and D. Lowenthal (eds) (1990) *The Politics of the Past*, One World Archaeology series, London: Unwin Hyman.

Graham, B., G. J. Ashworth and J. E. Tunbridge (2000) *A Geography of Heritage: Power, Culture and Economy*, London: Arnold.

Gustafsson, A. and H. Karlsson (2004) *Plats på Scen. Kring beskrivning och förmedling av Bohusläns fasta fornlämningar genom tiderna*, Uddevalla: Bohusläns Museum.

Hewison, R. (1987) *The Heritage Industry: Britain in a Climate of Decline*, London: Methuen.

Hill, Sir G. (1936) *Treasure Trove in Law and Practice from the Earliest Time to the Present Day*, Oxford: Clarendon Press.

Holtorf, C. (2000–7) *Monumental Past: The Life-histories of Megalithic Monuments in Mecklenburg-Vorpommern (Germany)*. Electronic monograph. University of Toronto: Centre for Instructional Technology Development. http://hdl.handle.net/1807/245.

Hooper-Greenhill, E. (1992) *Museums and the Shaping of Knowledge*, London: Routledge.

Howard, P. (2003) *Heritage: Management, Interpretation, Identity*, London and New York: Continuum.

Hunter, M. (1996) *Preserving the Past: The Rise of Heritage in Modern Britain*, Stroud: Sutton.

King, T. F., P. P. Hickman and G. Berg (1977) *Anthropology in Historic Preservation: Caring for Culture's Clutter*, Studies in Archaeology series, New York: Academic Press.

Kohl L. and C. Fawcett (eds) (1995) *Nationalism, Politics, and the Practice of Archaeology*, Cambridge: Cambridge University Press.

Layton, R. (ed.) (1989a) *Conflict in the Archaeology of Living Traditions*, London: Routledge.

—— (ed.) (1989b) *Who Needs the Past? Indigenous Values and Archaeology*, London: Routledge.

Leone, M. (1981) 'Archaeology's Relationship to the Present and the Past', in R. Gould and M. Schiffer (eds) *Modern Material Culture: The Archaeology of Us*, New York: Academic Press.

Leone, M. and P. B. Potter (1992) 'Legitimation and the Classification of Archaeological Sites', *American Antiquity* 57, 137–45.

Leone, M., P. B. Potter and P. A. Shackel (1987) 'Toward a Critical Archaeology', *Current Anthropology* 57.1, 137–45.

Little, B. (2007) *Historical Archaeology: Why the Past Matters*, Walnut Creek, CA: Left Coast Press.

Lowenthal, D. (1985) *The Past is a Foreign Country*, Cambridge: Cambridge University Press.

McDavid, C. (1997) 'Descendants, Decisions, and Power: The Public Interpretation of the Archaeology of the Levi Jordan Plantation', in *The Realm of Politics: Prospects for Public Participation in African-American Archaeology,* special issue of *Historical Archaeology* 31.3, 114–31.

McGimsey, C. R. (1972) *Public Archaeology*, New York: Seminar Books.

Merriman, N. (1991) *Beyond the Glass Case: The Public, Museums and Heritage in Britain*, London: Leicester University Press.

—— (ed.) (2004) *Public Archaeology*, London: Routledge.

Miles, M. (2008) *Art as Plunder: The Ancient Origins of Debate about Cultural Property*, Cambridge: Cambridge University Press.

Moore, N. and Y. Whelan (2007) *Heritage, Memory and the Politics of Identity: New Perspectives on the Cultural Landscape*, London: Ashgate.

Moser, S. (1998) *Ancestral Images: The Iconography of Human Origins*, Ithaca, NY: Cornell University Press.

—— (2003) 'Community Archaeology in Quseir, Egypt', in L. Peers (ed.) *Museums and Source Communities*, London: Routledge, 208–26.

Ndoro, W. (2003) 'Traditional and Customary Heritage Systems: Nostalgia or Reality? Implications of Managing Heritage Sites in Africa', in E. De Merode, R. Semeets and C. Westrik (eds) *Linking Universal and Local Values: Managing a Sustainable Future for World Heritage*, Paris: World Heritage Centre.

Olwig, K. (1984) *Nature's Ideological Landscape: A Literary and Geographic Perspective on its Development and Preservation on Denmark's Jutland Heath*, London: Allen & Unwin.

Pearce, S. M. (1992) *Museums, Objects and Collections: A Cultural Study*, Leicester: Leicester University Press.

—— (1995) *On Collecting: An Investigation into Collecting in the European Tradition*, Collecting Cultures series, London: Routledge.

—— (2007) *Visions of Antiquity:. The Society of Antiquaries of London 1707–2007*, London: The Society of Antiquaries of London.

Plumb, J. H. (1969) *The Death of the Past*, London: Macmillan.

Potter, P. B. and M. P. Leone (1986) 'Liberation not Replication: "Archaeology in Annapolis" Analyzed', *Journal of the Washington Academy of Sciences* 76.2, 97–105.

—— (1987) 'Archaeology in Public in Annapolis: Four Seasons, Six Sites, Seven Tours, and 32,000 Visitors', *American Archaeology* 6.1, 51–61.

Price, N. (ed.) (2007) *Cultural Heritage in Post-War Recovery*. Papers from ICCROM Forum held on 4–6 October, 2005, Rome (ICCROM Conservation Studies: 6), Rome: ICCROM.Santino.

Renfrew, C. (2000) *Loot, Legitimacy and Ownership: The Ethical Crisis in Archaeology*, London: Routledge.

Scarre, C. and G. Scarre (eds) (2006) *The Ethics of Archaeology: Philosophical Perspectives on Archaeological Practice*, Cambridge: Cambridge University Press.

Schaafsma, C. F. (1989) 'Significant until Proven Otherwise: Problems versus Representative Samples', in H. F. Cleere (ed.) *Archaeological Heritage Management in the Modern World*, One World Archaeology series, London: Unwin Hyman, 38–51.

Schiffer, M. B. and G. J. Gumerman (eds) (1977) *Conservation Archaeology: A Guide for Cultural Resource Management Studies*, Studies in Archaeology series, New York: Academic Press.

Schofield, J. (2005) *Combat Archaeology: Material Culture and Modern Conflict*, London: Duckworth.

Smith, L. (2004) *Archaeological Theory and the Politics of Cultural Heritage*, London: Routledge.

—— (2006) *Uses of Heritage*, London: Routledge.

—— (ed.) (2007) *Cultural Heritage: Critical Concepts in Media and Cultural Studies*, London: Routledge.

Smith, L. and E. Waterton (2009) *Heritage, Communities and Archaeology,* Duckworth Debates in Archaeology series. London: Duckworth.

Sørensen, M. L. S. (1996) 'The Fall of a Nation, the Birth of a Subject: The National Use of Archaeology in Nineteenth-century Denmark', in M. Díaz-Andreu and T. Champion (eds) *Nationalism and Archaeology in Europe*, London: UCL Press, 24–47.

Sørensen, M. L. S. and Viejo Rose (n.d.) *Identity and Conflict: Cultural Heritage and the Re-construction of Identities after Conflict*, http://www.cric.arch.cam.ac.uk/index.php.

Stone, P. and R. MacKenzie (eds) (1990) *The Excluded Past: Archaeology in Education*, London: Routledge.

Stovel, H. (ed.) (1998) Risk Preparedness: A Management Manual for World Cultural Heritage. ICCROM, WHC, UNESCO, ICOMOS. http://www.iccrom.org/pdf/ICCROM_17_RiskPreparedness_en.pdf.

Tainter, J. A. and J. G. Lucas (1983) 'Epistemology of the Significance Concept', *American Antiquity* 48, 707–19.

Tunbridge, J. E. and G. J. Ashworth (1996) *Dissonant Heritage: The Management of the Past as a Resource in Conflict*, Chichester: Wiley.

Ucko, P. (1987) *Academic Freedom and Apartheid*, London: Duckworth.

UNESCO (1972) *Convention Concerning the Protection of the World Cultural and Natural Heritage.*

—— (1994) *Nara Declaration on Authenticity.*

—— (2003) *Convention Concerning the Preservation of Intangible Cultural Heritage.*

Vergo, P. (ed.) (1989) *The New Museology*, London: Reaktion.

Viejo Rose, D. (2007) 'Conflict and the Deliberate Destruction of Cultural Heritage', in H. Anheier and Y. R. Isar (eds) *Conflicts and Tensions,* Cultures and Globalisation series, London: Sage.

Vitelli, K. D. (1996) *Archaeological Ethics*, Walnut Creek, CA: AltaMira Press.

Wilton, A. and I. Bignamini (1996) *Grand Tour: The Lure of Italy in the Eighteenth Century*, London: Tate Gallery Publishing.

World Heritage Centre (2006) 'Predicting and Managing the Effects of Climate Change on World Heritage', http://whc.unesco.org/en/climatechange.

Worsaae, J. J. A. (1843) *Danmarks Oldtid oplyst ved Oldsager og Gravjöje*, Copenhagen: Selskabet for trykkefrihedens rette Brug.

Wright, P. (1985) *On Living in an Old Country*, London: Verso.

Yalouri, E. (2001) *The Acropolis: Global Fame, Local Claim*, Oxford: Berg.

3

PUBLIC ARCHAEOLOGY IN THE UNITED STATES IN THE EARLY TWENTY-FIRST CENTURY

Barbara J. Little

In 1968, Salvage Archaeology was declining and CRM was on the horizon. Today CRM is declining and Public Archaeology is on the horizon.

(Moore 2006: 33)

There is no such thing as 'private archeology'.

(McGimsey 1972: 5)

This is an interesting time to be writing about 'public archaeology' in the United States. The meaning and scope of the term are in flux, driven by practitioners and a wide variety of projects and rhetoric. As the quote by Lawrence Moore suggests, the archaeological landscape is changing. What exactly is on the horizon, however, remains to be seen. As Charles McGimsey strongly argued several decades ago, archaeologists who think they can work without responsibility to the public are fooling themselves.

In this chapter I discuss the historical development of public archaeology in the United States with the primary goal of pointing out some of the techniques used by archaeologists, legislators, members of the public and others. Public archaeology has grown through a mixture of opportunism, strategising and planning; practitioners have both laid out careful plans of action and reacted to events on an *ad hoc* basis. My secondary goal is simply to explore the process of how public archaeology grew in order to understand the current system more clearly.

The techniques used to build and support public archaeology are not the field or laboratory tools traditionally associated with archaeology, but they are every bit as essential to an archaeology that functions in the contemporary world. Of course, this observation applies not only to the United States, but to public archaeology across the world, as readers of this entire volume will readily see.

I observe at least three main categories of public archaeology currently practised by professional archaeologists in the United States. These categories are: (1) cultural resource management (CRM) under public law; (2) outreach and education with the intention to prevent looting and vandalism of archaeological places; and (3) archaeology that aims to help communities or individuals in some way or to solve societal problems. I offer broad overviews of these categories. Professional archaeologists who work in museum settings may also be considered public archaeologists and it might be argued that those who teach in publicly funded institutions are public archaeologists because of the source of their salaries. However, these two categories have long traditions distinct from CRM, and I do not treat them here except insofar as the work of many of our museum and academic colleagues contributes to CRM, public interpretation, community archaeology and civic engagement.

Because these categories are not neatly bounded, they can overlap, and in some cases a single project may contribute to all three categories. I believe, however, that they approximate current reality. Research about public archaeology and its practice (e.g. Krupicz 2000) crosscuts these categories. Also crosscutting and indeed enabling the very existence of public archaeology in any form is public interest in the process and results of archaeology. Although these categories have developed somewhat differently, they are often related. Over the past several decades, one of the major factors in prompting professional outreach to combat looting within the United States, for example, is the increase of looting on public land. Such outreach, however, is not limited to supporting the preservation of sites on public land, but expanded to provide education for appreciating diversity in the past and present and thereby living more tolerantly in a multicultural society. In addition, many methods are shared between the categories.

There is another category of public archaeology that I do not treat in this chapter. That is archaeology done by non-professional archaeologists, both individuals and organisations with an intense interest who practise archaeology. Many avocational or amateur archaeological societies have a long history in the USA, and their formation often predates the establishment of the professionally oriented Society for American Archaeology (SAA) in 1934.

Cultural resource management

Publicly funded archaeology is deeply rooted in scholarly interest in the past and individuals' efforts to create institutions and organisations. Efforts began at least as early as Thomas Jefferson's mound excavations (Hantman and Dunham 1993) and the establishment in 1812 of the American Antiquarian Society (AAS) as an organisation to 'encourage the collection and preservation of the Antiquities of our country, and of curious and valuable productions in

Art and Nature [that] have a tendency to enlarge the sphere of human knowledge' (Chaison *et al.* 1992).

Although the history of such efforts and public interest in archaeology is fascinating, it requires more discussion than there is room for in this chapter. Instead I will skip ahead to the middle of the twentieth century and pick up the story with the heyday of salvage archaeology, before the decline to which the opening quote by Moore alludes. With reference to the AAS and other such societies, it is worth noting the long-standing usefulness of organisations to focus efforts and publish research results. Indeed the number of organisations and journals devoted to archaeology continues to increase. Techniques to support scholarly research, professional identity and the definition of the discipline include the establishment and ongoing administration of professional organisations and their meetings, journals, newsletters, other communication networks and organisational goals.

At the point where I pick up the story there are two major federal laws in place affecting archaeology: the Antiquities Act of 1906 and the Historic Sites Act of 1935. The American Anthropological Association and the SAA were already well-established professional organisations by this time. Salvage archaeology is a term that came about after World War II with the creation of the River Basin Archaeological Salvage Program in 1945. The National Park Service (NPS) in the US Department of the Interior and the Smithsonian Institution jointly administered the programme. This programme focused on salvaging the data from sites that were about to be destroyed through water-control projects such as dams and reservoirs. The direct antecedents of these large-scale projects were the 'make work' projects of the Depression-era New Deal, which funded archaeology in order to put large crews to work during the 1930s (e.g. Lyon 1996; McGimsey 1972: 102–11).

After World War II, in response to planning for a nationwide reservoir system which would flood major river valleys all across the country, archaeologists lobbied for salvaging the threatened archaeological sites. The administrative details changed between 1945 and 1960, but, for the most part, the NPS and the Smithsonian jointly administered the federal salvage programme until 1969 when the Smithsonian ended its direct involvement with the River Basin Survey Program (McGimsey 1972: 102–11).

Because the funding for salvage was insufficient, lobbying for a better system finally resulted in the Reservoir Salvage Act of 1960. Although this Act enabled the Secretary of the Interior to pay for salvage, the funding was never sufficient. Lobbying continued until the passage in 1974 of the Moss-Bennett Bill, which amended the Reservoir Salvage Act and expanded it to cover salvage for any federal project, not only water-control projects, and allowed an agency to budget and spend funds according to the scope of the project.

Archaeologists saw the Moss-Bennett Bill (now more commonly known as the Archaeological and Historical Preservation Act, or AHPA) as critically important with great potential for the 'furtherance of American archaeology' (Wilson 1976: 12).

31

The techniques in these cases, of course, were legislative lobbying and persistence. In some cases within governmental agencies, archaeologists can work through their legislative affairs offices to draft needed laws. In addition, as citizens, archaeologists can review and comment on draft regulations or guidance that pertain to the field by responding to notices that appear in the US Federal Register, which is the official daily publication for rules and notices of federal agencies, as well as presidential documents. (The Federal Register is not to be confused with the National Register of Historic Places.)

Rex Wilson, the Department of the Interior's Departmental Consulting Archaeologist at the time that AHPA was passed, wrote that 'The Federal Government now has an unusually fine opportunity to make a solid impact on American archaeology. In Moss-Bennett we have the legislation we have long looked forward to. We fully intend to make the most of it' (Wilson 1976: 14). In order to 'make the most of it', Wilson made extensive administrative changes in the NPS offices in Washington and across the country to more effectively administer the 'federal archaeology program'. However, thirty years later, McGimsey (2004, 2006) expressed his frustration at the failure of AHPA to develop the kind of national programme envisioned by archaeologists at the time, lamenting the lack of uniform programme development and commitment by federal agencies, as well as the continued public unavailability of most public archaeology reports. He and others expected the NPS to take a strong leadership position to ensure appropriate actions by other agencies and to develop a nationwide contracting programme that would cover even non-federal lands. As Departmental Consulting Archaeologist Francis McManamon (2006) explains, NPS approached archaeology by including it within its historic preservation programmes. Instead of developing a nationwide programme under its direct control (had that even been possible, given the reality of bureaucratic competition among agencies), NPS developed the 1983 Secretary of the Interior's Standards and Guidelines for Archeology and Historic Preservation. The Secretary of the Interior expects agencies to develop and fund their own procedures while adhering to the Standards and Guidelines. Partly due to the NPS approach, the US federal archaeology programme is diffuse and spread among various departments and bureaus, each following the same laws and uniform regulations but doing so through their own policies and priorities.

AHPA expanded the Secretary of the Interior's leadership role in federal archaeology. Beginning in 1976, authorised by this 1974 statute, the Secretary of the Interior, through the Departmental Consulting Archaeologist function of the National Park Service, began to report to Congress on the federal archaeology programme, an activity that raised the profile of the programme. Most of the reports contain specific recommendations. Table 3.1 lists those recommendations by year. In 1976 through 1978 most agencies were unfamiliar enough with their legal obligations that the report recommended that agencies needed to comply with laws and regulations and share information with each other.

Table 3.1 Categorised recommendations to the United States Congress on the Federal Archeology Program 1976-97

Recommendations	Year
Agencies need to comply with laws and regulations	1976; 1977–8
Should coordinate archaeological programme with planning and with National Environmental Policy Act (NEPA) compliance	1976; 1977–8; 1980–2
Use partnerships	1988–90; 1991–3; 1994–5
Improve inventory on federal lands	1985–6; 1987; 1988–90; 1991–3; 1994–5; 1996–7
Evaluate more sites for significance under NRHP criteria	1985–6; 1988–90; 1991–3; 1994–5; 1996–7
Preservation in place	1975; 1976; 1987; 1990–3
Protect sites, especially from looting and vandalism	1985–6; 1988–90; 1991–3; 1994–5; 1996–7
Increase the amount of research on federal lands	1991–3
Proper curation of archaeological material	1976; 1985–6; 1987; 1988–90; 1991–3; 1994–5; 1996–7
Share information among agencies (and public)	1976; 1977–8; 1985–6; 1987; 1988–90; 1991–3; 1994–5
Use and share archaeological paleoenvironmental data	1987
Share information with public audiences	1985–6; 1987; 1988–90; 1991–3; 1994–5; 1996–7
Treatment of human remains	1980–2

Recommendations appear in reports as follows:
1975 (Wilson n.d.a); 1976 (Wilson n.d.b); 1977–8 (HCRS 1979); 1979 (Keel 1981); 1980–2 (Aten 1983); 1983–4 (Carbone and Keel 1986); 1985–6 (Keel *et al.* 1989); 1987 (McManamon *et al.* 1993); 1988–90 (Knudson *et al.* 1995); 1991–3 (Haas 1997); 1994–5 (Haas 1998); 1996–7 (Haas 1999).

Recommendations to coordinate with the National Environmental Policy Act of 1969 disappeared from the report after 1982, although that call has resurfaced more recently within several agencies.

Table 3.1 highlights the ongoing concerns of federal agency archaeologists, including adequate inventory, evaluation, preservation, protection and curation. In 1985 the report began to include recommendations for public outreach, particularly with the goal of combating looting, as seen in the next section. Along with other pressures, such recommendations resulted in the 1988 amendments to the Archaeological Resources Protection Act (ARPA) discussed below. The techniques of public archaeology in this sense of making sure good work is accomplished certainly include all the methods involved in doing professional-quality archaeology in any setting, such as site discovery and excavation. However, further techniques include many different skills pertinent to administration, bureaucratic expertise with budgets and resource allocation, and organisational structure. How programmes are organised matters both for new programmes and for continuing ones.

This 1974 Act continued the salvage archaeology mentality which aimed to excavate as much as possible. Further expansion of the government role in archaeology did not please everyone, for various reasons. Such laws were not always entirely welcome or seen as unmixed blessings. In 1976, for example, Ray Matheny and Dale Berge discussed their fears that all available professionals would be so busy complying with laws that such publicly mandated archaeology would destroy academic research and innovation. Although they complained of excessive governmental control and about the many changes that would be necessary, they state optimistically – and presciently – that 'We are probably clever enough to turn contractual archaeology into a vigorous discipline, but it will require a reorientation of research design' (Matheny and Berge 1976: 4).

University-based archaeology programmes, which were contracted for much of this salvage work, came to rely on such work for their research projects. That situation of federally funded research and the reliance on salvage funds for research raised issues of salvage being done when it was not strictly necessary. Some archaeologists began to call for conservation of the archaeological record, urging that excavation should occur when sites were really going to be lost (Lipe 1974). Such conservation concerns for archaeology were raised in concert with societal concerns for conserving natural resources and with the growing threat to archaeological sites by looters during the 1970s (Reaves 1976). The issue of preservation versus excavation remains important and was always important for Native Americans, whose desire to preserve ancestral places clashed with archaeological interests for generations. For example, Watkins (2000) traces the increase in Native American protests against archaeologists to the publication in 1969 of Vine Deloria's *Custer Died for Your Sins: An Indian Manifesto*. Twenty years of protest, pressure and lobbying eventually led to the Native American Graves Protection and Repatriation Act (NAGPRA). Again, the techniques of legislative lobbying and persistence are important for many of the changes that have occurred within public archaeology.

Other pivotal discussions also occurred in 1974. With funding from the National Park Service, the SAA organised a series of six seminars under McGimsey's direction to examine the changes underway and to discuss the future of archaeology. The Airlie House Report (McGimsey and Davis 1977) summarises the results. The series of seminars included discussions about certification and accreditation, reports, management, communication, law and American Indians, raising issues that continue to be of concern, such as ethics, costs, report publication, preservation, communication and cooperation. Each of these topics requires skills and methods beyond the standard archaeological 'toolkit' of field and laboratory methods.

That same year was an important year for public archaeology in another way. The Ninth Circuit Court of Appeals struck down the Antiquities Act of 1906 as unconstitutionally vague. Following that ruling, legal challenges to the Act increased and it became clear that a new law was needed. The looting and selling of artefacts was increasing and therefore the pressure on public lands was also increasing. As Robert Collins points out, in 1906 a fine of $500 may have been a deterrent but by the mid-1970s a single Mimbres bowl could fetch up to $20,000 (Collins 1980).

When it became clear the Antiquities Act of 1906 was insufficient for prosecuting looting on public land, Congress passed ARPA in 1979. This law revised the earlier statute and established criminal and civil penalties for violations. It also established procedures for issuing permits for testing and excavation, requiring various interagency programme reporting and coordination activities. The 1988 amendments to ARPA strengthened law enforcement and explicitly added agency responsibility for public education, again with the purpose of combating looting.

ARPA recognised tribal interests in archaeology (Downer 2003: 415). The regulations require that a federal land manager notify tribes of any permit that 'may result in harm to, or destruction of, any Indian tribal religious or cultural site on public lands' (36 CFR 7.7(a)). In addition, the agency is to consult when requested and to incorporate agreed-upon stipulations into permits granted (36 CFR 7.7(a)(3)).

Effective techniques connected with this law include not only the lobbying efforts needed to enact it, but the ongoing need to educate attorneys and judges about the value of laws that protect heritage and encouragement to enforce and prosecute. In addition, archaeologists need to understand the law and gain the skills needed to assist crime-scene investigation in cooperation with law enforcement. Consultation skills are also required to work with Native American groups, not only for ARPA but under other important laws as well.

One of the most influential statutes – and the one that ultimately created the CRM industry that came to overshadow salvage archaeology – was the National Historic Preservation Act of 1966 (NHPA). Interestingly, as Hester Davis observes, archaeologists were so involved in getting the 1974 legislation passed that they paid relatively little attention to NHPA (Davis 1996). The other major environmental law of the time was the National Environmental Policy Act (NEPA), passed in 1969. The Department of Transportation (DOT) Act of 1966 is also relevant for historic preservation and public archaeology. Because the conditions set out in Section 4(f) regulations refer to *significant* historic sites, departments of transportation use the NHPA process of determining whether archaeological sites are eligible for listing in the National Register of Historic Places (NRHP). Within that process, significance and integrity are the major elements in determining eligibility.

Congress passed NHPA in response to concerns about the adverse impacts of federal development projects such as urban renewal and highway construction on archaeological sites and historic structures. It established national policy and programmes for preservation by requiring agencies to consider historic properties during development. NHPA created the NRHP, which added properties of local and state significance to the list of places 'worthy of preservation'. Before NHPA, the list of such places included nationally significant places such as National Historic Landmarks designated since 1935 under the Historic Sites Act. NHPA also created the Advisory Council on Historic Preservation and delegated a good deal of responsibility for preservation to the states, creating the State Historic Preservation Offices (SHPO). Not until amendments to the Act in 1992 were Native Americans given rights to adopt SHPO responsibilities on tribal land; the first Tribal Historic Preservation Offices were established in 1996.

NHPA created a framework and a process, but when it was passed it affected only properties that were listed in the NRHP. In 1976, amendments extended the application of Section 106 process to include properties eligible for listing in the NRHP – rather than limiting consideration to properties already listed, as the initial law did. In 1980 amendments added Section 110, which directed federal agencies to assume more responsibility and stewardship for historic properties under their control. The same amendments established Certified Local Governments (CLG) to recognise both local government interest in preservation and Indian tribes' interest as well, opening the door for grants (Watkins 2000: 39) (see Advisory Council on Historic Preservation (2000) for details about amendments to this 1966 preservation law.)

Another legal impetus for public archaeology was the Indian Land Claims Commission, established in 1948, which required tribes to document the maximum extent of their tribal territory before it was taken away. Alan Downer summarises, 'In many cases, tribal archaeological programs, tribal oral history programs, and tribal museums developed from these early efforts' (Downer 2003: 414).

Due to both the amended NHPA and AHPA, the amount of work done as cultural resource management expanded exponentially, particularly after 1976. A rough idea of the difference between the pace of work before and after that year is demonstrated by a comparison of CRM reports submitted annually. For example, the Southwestern Region of the US Forest Service (Green 1977) issued a bibliography of approximately 900 cultural resource reports submitted to the regional office dated any time since the passage of the Antiquities Act in 1906 until January 1977. The bibliography for 1977 (Davis 1978) lists over 600 for that year alone, and the numbers continued to grow.

The change in volume has, of course, created its own challenges, not the least of which is the curation of artefacts and records and the distribution of reports. Indeed, American archaeologists are virtually drowning in success. We have a collections crisis in underfunded repositories that are running out of storage space (e.g. Childs 2004), an information-management crisis, including the burgeoning grey literature of unpublished reports, and incompatible digital databases, when data are available electronically at all.

An important goal for public archaeology is to make results – including collections, associated records, databases and reports – accessible and useful. In 1990, Regulations for the Curation of Federally-owned and Administered Archeological Collections were published in final form (36 CFR 79). These regulations establish definitions, standards and procedures that federal agencies must observe to manage and preserve archaeological collections and associated records from federal projects, although many agencies continue to struggle to comply with the high standards set by these regulations. Techniques for public archaeology must be developed and widely used to manage collections of artefacts and associated records so that the results of archaeological investigation are available for further use.

The year 1990 was important to CRM for further legal reasons as well. The National Park Service issued guidelines to assist states and federal agencies to comply with the Abandoned Shipwreck Act of 1987. One of the most important provisions of the Act was to remove shipwrecks from the Federal Admiralty Court, which tended to treat shipwrecks as commodities lost at sea in need of salvage. The Act allows states to claim and manage shipwrecks for multiple uses, including preservation, public access and recreation (Aubry 1997). Techniques for archaeologists include recognising the legitimacy of multiple uses and sharing access to sites.

The most influential recent law is NAGPRA. Congress passed this law in 1990 to provide for the repatriation of Native American, Native Hawaiian and Native Alaskan human remains and objects of cultural patrimony from federal lands, which are held by federal agencies or museums that receive federal funds. Archaeology in the USA changed deeply after the passage of NAGPRA (e.g. Dongoske et al. 2000; Swidler et al. 1997; Watkins 2000). The techniques needed here included consultation, which was not new to the legal process but became unavoidable under NAGPRA. Archaeologists are continuing to figure out ways to effectively work with descendant and local communities (e.g. Colwell-Chanthaphonh and Ferguson 2008; Little and Shackel 2007).

Public outreach and education combating looting and vandalism

After more than twenty years of effort by its proponents, the Antiquities Act of 1906 was passed into law to combat the looting of sites on federal land, asserting a public interest in antiquities and the knowledge to be gained from them. Section 3 specifies that archaeological collections from public lands have 'permanent preservation in public museums'. Looting and vandalism continued to threaten and destroy sites throughout the twentieth century. However, the auction of the Green Collection of American Indian Art in New York in 1971 and the record prices objects brought created renewed public interest in North American artefacts. In bringing to public attention the connection between the art market and site destruction, Karl Meyer remarked that as a result 'looting, which was already epidemic, spread with fresh intensity' (Meyer 1973 :8).

During the 1970s, as looting was increasing, land managers in the southwestern United States focused on both law enforcement of the Antiquities Act and education in an ongoing attempt to deter looting. Several archaeologists (e.g. McGimsey 1972) issued a strong call for public education as a method of preserving archaeological heritage.

As mentioned earlier, rampant looting and vandalism of sites in the southwestern United States and the unsuccessful use of the Antiquities Act to prosecute looters led to the passage of ARPA in 1979. Although it did provide the legal basis for prosecution, the law alone, of course, could not solve the problem and federal archaeologists formed an interagency working group to study how to combat looting. In the mid-1980s, federal agencies established the Public Awareness Working Group (PAWG) to share information and improve the public's knowledge and appreciation of archaeology. The thinking behind public awareness was that an informed person would be less likely to damage or destroy archaeological remains because he or she would understand their importance.

Increasing calls for public outreach came in concert with legislation. Hester Davis (1976) remarks on the rapid increase in state laws related to CRM in the first half of the 1970s, calling on archaeologists to fulfil their responsibility not only to protect sites in terms of those laws but also to write reports in such a way that people could actually read them. Because state legislators respond to public interest and pressure, Davis calls on archaeologists to respond to the public's actions in calling for state laws to protect archaeological resources:

> We are archaeologists; they are legislators, or district engineers, or TV script writers, or landscape architects. The destiny of the country's archaeological resources is in their hands – how can we pretend to 'manage' the resources, if we neither speak their language nor translate our ideas into their idiom? They have their own job to do; our responsibility, as I see it, is to channel this massive public reaction by means of increased communication.
>
> (Davis 1976: 54)

From the viewpoint of the federal archaeology programme, Francis McManamon summarises the twin goals aimed at combating looting:

More general awareness through public education is needed to persuade Americans that looting diminishes our common heritage and the legacy that they leave to their children and grandchildren. More public programs are needed to provide Americans who want to 'do' archaeology with legitimate opportunities to participate in professionally supervised field, laboratory, and curatorial work. Each of these areas is part of the long term solution to reducing the looting problem. Federal agency archaeology programs will continue to spearhead many of these efforts.

(McManamon 1991: 267)

A number of conferences during the 1980s and 1990s helped set the profession's agenda for public outreach and education to be focused on anti-looting efforts. Peter Wells and others in Minnesota organised a series of three conferences. These were 'Presenting the Past to the Public' in 1987, 'Presenting the Past: Media, Marketing, and the Public' in 1988 and 'Presenting the Past to the Public: History and Archaeology in Schools and Museums' in 1989. Along with the latter conference was a public programme entitled 'Confronting Columbus: Contact and Cultural Diversity in America'. Congressman Bruce Vento, Chairman of the Subcommittee on National Parks and Public Lands, was the first speaker for that public programme, demonstrating a politician's response to popular public interest. The Congressman's participation highlights the technique of advocating with legislative representatives and elected officials and giving them opportunities to demonstrate their commitment in publicly visible ways.

In his description of the conference series, Wells's acknowledgements make it clear that there was active cooperation among individuals in the academy, state government and the federal government (Wells 1991). These efforts crosscut the profession and continue to do so. They are most successful when participants create broad coalitions and partnerships.

In addition, the SAA organised two conferences around the theme of site preservation. 'Saving the Past for the Future' and 'Saving the Past for the Future, II' were held in 1989 and 1994. After the first, the SAA's Public Education Committee (PEC) was established and has remained a standing and active committee. Interestingly, there was a short-lived public education committee of the SAA in the early 1980s that failed to get enough support from the Society to keep it going (Roberts 1995). Clearly the professional organisation recognised the need for public education activities by the end of the decade.

The success of these conferences demonstrates the value of the technique: organise meetings where individuals can think together about a problem or situation, create a plan with goals and methods for achieving those goals, and call on others to join them in working towards an envisioned future. Following through to accomplish the planned goals is, of course, essential.

These public outreach efforts were not simply concerned with campaigns to inform people of the legal consequences of looting on public land, although that component was important. The goals were far more expansive and overlap into a sense of public archaeology as a social force for teaching about multiculturalism and appreciation for other people's histories. Indeed, such education programmes can be good examples of explicit public benefits of archaeology (e.g. Moe 2002; Smardz and Smith 2000). Providing relevant and useful information to educators, often as lesson plans or curriculum guides and support materials, is an important technique for public outreach.

The overall goal here is clear: communicate archaeological work in ways that the public finds understandable and compelling. The techniques range from public service advertising to exhibits to on-site tours to lesson plans for the classroom. Work with volunteers and avocational archaeologists. For places where there is heritage tourism, provide meaningful interpretation to different publics, and both on-site and off-site visitors via electronic and traditional media. Participate in interpretive planning, including design and content for exhibits, writing effective museum labels, outdoor panels and signage, preparing and giving talks, and other services. Work with concessionaires or non-profit partners who run bookshops and gift shops or provide tours and other services to visitors. Create a media plan and work with the media to get adequate and accurate coverage through television, radio and print.

Public archaeology in service to communities and society

Generations of archaeologists have felt strongly the need for the work to be useful, not only to justify continued funding, but also to act as responsible scholars. Richard Ford's 1973 article 'Archaeology Serving Humanity', published in one of the volumes that helped to define the 'new archaeology', makes it clear that the quest for relevance is not a recent invention. It was not only academics who were convinced that archaeology matters. For example, citizens of Alexandria, Virginia, 'have been engaged in the preservation, study and public interpretation of archaeological sites since 1961' (Cressey 1987: 1). In 1975, the city established the first municipal Archaeological Commission in the country, hiring a city archaeologist soon thereafter. In this latter case, the techniques and skills from an archaeologist's point of view are to work within city government at the direction of a public commission. Balancing the needs and interests of volunteers, history enthusiasts, developers, historic preservationists and one's own research interests is a skill that is becoming increasingly important as more archaeologists immerse themselves in community-based work.

As CRM practitioners struggled to define their new field, some archaeologists sought relevance by proposing nationally significant research topics and suggesting that public funding be selectively allocated according to topics of wide public benefit. For New Mexico's public lands under the control of the

Forest Service, for example, Tom King and Fred Plog propose three topics: the rise and fall of civilisation, environmental change and abandonment/depopulation (King and Plog 1983). They summarise their reasoning for believing that these questions will have demonstrable public payoff: 'The first does because its study can enable us to better understand our own society and its future. The second enables us to predict future environmental conditions in the area. The third should elucidate a past event – the depopulation of the area in the 12th through 14th centuries – that could recur in the future' (King and Plog 1983: 5).

The idea of setting national research goals retains some appeal. William Lees and Julia King, for example, call for 'priorities for our national historic preservation program and ... guidelines for all publicly funded archaeology' (Lees and King 2007: 59). In light of such calls, however, I am cautious that a democratic system requires independence and that central authority – especially governmental authority – about ideas and significance or worthiness is not something that I would recommend for the independent future of archaeology (Little 2007a).

The argument for relevance does not require a national research agenda; it does, however, require explicit effort by archaeologists. Direct applicability to environmental issues again has become an important point of focus in the discipline. Charles Redman and his colleagues explain:

> Investigating possible human impacts on ancient environments offers an almost unique opportunity to link insights derived from the past to pressing contemporary issues. Answers to questions on resource extraction, ground cover change, habitat integrity, and soil fertility that interest scholars in a wide range of sister disciplines lie in exactly the kind of data that archaeologists collect and are good at interpreting.
>
> (Redman et al. 2004: 1–2)

For further discussion of contributions of archaeology to ecological conservation see also Minnis (1999); Minnis et al. (2006); Redman (1999); Sabloff (2006, 2008); and contributors to McGovern (2007). One technique for making archaeological practice relevant to the wider society is to explicitly link methods and results with current issues. The public benefits of archaeology can extend to many different constituencies, from ecologists and environmental activists, as the previous examples suggest, to historians, teachers and many kinds of communities (Little 2002).

While acknowledging that community-based and community-controlled projects have been conducted over the course of decades, Yvonne Marshall could say in her introduction to a recent issue of *World Archaeology* that community archaeology was a relatively new development (Marshall 2002). Marshall is referring to public archaeology in which there is community involvement in all parts of a project as a phenomenon that has reached a critical mass. Indeed, there are community archaeology projects all over the world and an increasing number specifically identifying community building and social capital. In addition to the contributors in Marshall's volume, see, for example, the following, including the individual contributions to edited volumes: Anyon and Ferguson (1995); Baram *et al.* (2001); Colwell-Chanthaphonh and Ferguson (2006, 2008); Derry and Malloy (2003); Dongoske *et al.* (2000); Hantman (2005); Hodder (2000); Klesert and Downer (1990); LaRoche (2005); LaRoche and Blakey (1997); McDavid (1997); Mortensen (2005); Muckle (2002); Nassaney (2004); Nicholas and Andrews (1997); Shackel (2005); Shackel and Chambers (2004); Stottman (forthcoming); Swidler *et al.* (1997); Uunila (2005); and Williams and Pope (n.d.).

Every community project needs to employ a range of techniques in addition to the archaeological work itself. An example of one such project designed with both research and public outreach goals is that undertaken in Annapolis, the state capital of Maryland since 1695. In the early 1980s, at the invitation of and with the assistance of the local preservation organisation, Mark Leone initiated 'Archaeology in Annapolis', a research programme with an essential and integrated public programme designed to be immediately relevant to site visitors.

Leone describes the on-site public interpretation in an article for *Museum News* (Leone 1983). In 1987, Leone, Parker Potter and Paul Shackel discuss the full extent of the programme in *Current Anthropology*. They describe the way in which critical theory shaped the project and its desired outcomes:

> We do suggest that a critical archaeology may produce more reliable knowledge of the past by exploring the social and political contexts of its production . . . From its inception, this project . . . aimed at demystifying archaeology, teaching about how a past is constructed, and discovering how the past was used locally so as to understand local ideology and identify the aspects of it that need illuminating.
>
> (Leone *et al.* 1987: 285)

In this project the relevance of archaeology and its value to community is contained not only in the process and the results of excavation and analysis, but also in the ways in which historical knowledge in the broadest sense is formed and conveyed. The technique in this case is to design public programmes, including tours and exhibits, with clear messages and a coherent theoretical basis.

The public programme of the Archaeology in Annapolis project has continued for much of the life of that project. As one of the archaeologists who both directed excavations and gave public tours, I can say that the engagement with visitors over ideas in a local context was both enlightening and inspiring (as well as, admittedly, occasionally disappointing and frustrating). Both Paul Shackel and I have maintained an interest in this thread of public archaeology in our work (e.g. Shackel and Chambers 2004; Shackel 2003; Little 2002;

Little 2007b). This ongoing interest is most explicitly expressed in our edited volume *Archaeology as a Tool of Civic Engagement* (Little and Shackel 2007), in which restorative justice is one of the themes. The goal of the book is to:

> Encourage archaeologists to think about effective ways to participate in the civic renewal movement. The goals of this somewhat loosely defined, yet quite real, movement include community building, the creation of social capital, and active citizen engagement in community and civic life. Although archaeology per se is not usually seen as an explicit part of this movement, there is a role for the discipline to play, particularly as archaeological projects increasingly involve the communities in which they occur and the descendants of the peoples whose lives are the subject of study.
>
> (Little 2007c: 1)

It is worth reiterating the technique of connecting archaeology to contemporary issues; in addition, an engaged archaeology involves looking beyond the discipline itself for ways in which archaeology can contribute to society. Further techniques include communication skills such as those required for directed dialogue, facilitation and negotiation.

Such engaged work fits into the tradition of community archaeology and the aspiration of relevance. As archaeologists recognise different responsibilities to communities, the communities change as well. Although some professional archaeologists have long recognised legitimate interests of Native Americans and worked with tribes, such widespread recognition was forced by the passage of NAGPRA in 1990 (see especially Swidler *et al.* 1997; Watkins 2000). Civil Rights movements in the 1950s and 1960s included the American Indian Movement (AIM) and the genesis of Native critiques of archaeology eventually leading to NAGPRA. However, Native Americans have been asserting their interest in ancestral lands and burials for centuries and in protection of the archaeologically defined past at least since the beginnings of professional archaeology. For example, the first president of the SAA reported on a 1937 resolution by a group of Seneca Chiefs requesting laws to protect archaeological sites. Arthur C. Parker, who was also a Seneca, quotes Henry Sutton, President of the Neighborhood Indian Society of Rochester:

> We, the members of the Indian Neighborhood Society of Rochester, together with our associated friends from the various Indian reservations of New York and Ontario, look with disapproval upon the unskilled and unscientific excavations conducted by commercial relic hunters in the village sites and burial places of the ancient peoples of the first American race. Many of these excavations are on parity with grave robbing for the value of the trinkets recovered thereby. We protest that this work has no justification, that it is robbing America

of the only remaining source of her pre-history and is an uncivilised affront to the memory of our forefathers.

(Parker 1938: 267–8)

Public archaeology involving both Native perspectives and those of professional archaeologists (and, of course, public archaeology done by professional tribal archaeologists) involves different purposes and methods than that which is done without Native input. Contributors to the thematic issue of the *American Indian Quarterly* on 'decolonizing archaeology' (Fall 2006) discuss what it means to practise archaeology from a Native point of view, as does Joe Watkins (2000) in his book *Indigenous Archaeology: American Indian Values and Scientific Practice*. Watkins (2005) proposes that by involving indigenous people in the design and practice of projects, archaeology can add understanding humanity to its purpose. Adding oral tradition and multivocality is an important conceptual and methodological change to standard archaeological practice that is essential to creating an archaeology that takes its descendant 'public' into full account (e.g. Colwell-Chanthaphonh and Ferguson 2006).

Public archaeologists working with indigenous groups need to learn techniques of consultation, negotiation and dialogue as well as oral history (e.g. Whiteley 2002). Community-based archaeology with any group benefits from the same techniques. In this volume (chapter 12), Carol McDavid discusses the methods and purpose of her work within communities in Texas. McDavid and an increasing number of archaeologists are confronting racism explicitly in their work. One highly publicised and important project has raised the consciousness of historical archaeologists in ways similar to the impact of NAGPRA (Colwell-Chanthaphonh 2007). The African Burial Ground project in New York City provides a dramatic case study for civic engagement.

In the early 1990s the US General Services Administration (GSA) contracted for routine investigations to comply with the National Historic Preservation Act in advance of a new federal building at Foley Square in lower Manhattan. Historical maps indicated the location of an eighteenth-century 'Negroes Burying Ground', but consultants working in advance of the construction assumed that any cemetery would have been long since destroyed by subsequent construction. Excavations, beginning in the summer of 1991 and continuing through July 1992, eventually disinterred more than 400 burials. GSA did not anticipate the storm of public controversy that would be unleashed and continue for over a decade.

As Cheryl LaRoche and Michael Blakey describe, 'The dynamics of the relationship and the shape of the project have been determined to a large extent by the relentless determination of the African-American descendent community to exercise control over the handling and disposition of the physical remains and artifacts of their ancestors' (LaRoche and Blakey 1997: 84). Concerned citizens, including journalists, religious leaders, artists, architects, lawyers and many others, came together. The 'constant barrage of petitions, angry rhetoric and community dissension, congressional hearings, professional meetings, lobbying, and political action' changed the project completely and forced the continuing public engagement aspects of the project, from research design, through re-interment, through memorialisation and ongoing public outreach (LaRoche and Blakey 1997: 86). There are several techniques for public archaeology suggested by these cases. One is to study the history of a contemporary issue like racism and participate in dialogues within a community about it. Others include the facilitation and public involvement techniques used by governments and the advocacy and activism techniques used by citizens.

Concluding remarks

I began this chapter by citing Lawrence Moore's prediction about the demise of CRM and the rise of public archaeology. Moore analyses CRM as a business in terms of predictable industry cycles of growth and decline as well as the retirement of the baby boomer generation. He also ties the ultimate diminishment of the field to the shift in value from research (promoted until the mid-1970s) to preservation, which gained ascendancy with the NHPA. He rightly observes that 'A new ethic is emerging that involves Public Archaeology and multivocal interpretive discourse' and suggests that 'The best way to take advantage of these changes is to place young people in new jobs in Public Archaeology' by which he at least means 'more interpretive projects engaging the public' (Moore 2006: 32, 33).

The new ethic to which Moore alludes is perhaps not that new, but it is gaining in influence. At least part of the source in the USA has been the effects of NAGPRA and the amendments to NHPA that greatly expanded the tribal role in the formal preservation process. The meaning of archaeology within government – and the reason that government is concerned about archaeology – has to do with a sense of self and sovereignty. For tribes, as Welch and his colleagues explain, this is a critical relationship in which archaeology plays a central function (Welch et al. 2006).

Throughout the profession, the sense is emerging of the need for a different and broader educational curriculum for archaeologists for changing types of work (e.g. Bender and Smith 2000). Working effectively in public archaeology requires not only knowledge of legal and regulatory structure but also a broad view of how archaeology fits into the public realm. Archaeologists must judge and balance the public benefits of archaeology against other needs and explain the relevance of archaeological work. Techniques common to all types of public archaeology include effective planning and telling compelling stories about our research questions and results, including our results in terms of community building. Our audiences include other archaeologists as well as historians, anthropologists, the media and a broad range of interested publics.

By the late 1980s private companies were conducting the majority of the archaeology done in the United States and archaeologists had to scramble to learn how to run for-profit businesses that also produced professional results (Roberts *et al.* 2004: 2). Currently, CRM is a well-established business with a continuing need to define its relationship with the academy and profession. Roberts *et al.* identify 'One of the most important questions for the new millennium is who will teach tomorrow's contract archaeologists?' (Roberts *et al.* 2004: 12).

However, contract archaeology is only part of CRM. The other part is governmental and the question stands as well, who will teach the skills needed for the broad field of CRM? Archaeologists work in a wide variety of agencies and programmes in federal, tribal, state and local government. Getting archaeology done within a government setting presents challenges connected with overseeing the process, permitting and a variety of regulatory requirements. Particularly on public lands, balancing the mission and priorities of an agency or jurisdiction against the needs of archaeology is challenging. In many government settings, there often is only one archaeologist who must speak for the resources in daily balancing acts to meet the demands of widely divergent constituents and authorities. At the core of government archaeology at any level is the decision-making that balances policy, preservation and mission. This work results in actions that affect archaeological resources in immediate and often irreversible ways.

I selectively have explored the development and context for each of three categories of professional public archaeology in the United States to provide a sense of how they all fit reasonably under the same rubric, relating to each other in both mutually supportive and sometimes contradictory ways. Federal agencies, tribes, state and local governments, professional organisations, individual archaeologists and members of the public have all played roles and often have worked together to change the ways in which public archaeology has developed. The single certain attribute of the future appears to be change.

To recall Matheny and Berge's statement quoted earlier, archaeologists are probably 'clever enough' to turn contractual archaeology into a public archaeology that is engaging and relevant to descendant communities, other social scientists and humanities scholars, and the broader public, but it will require a reorientation of intent.

Acknowledgement

1   Much of the research and writing for this article was done while I was an Ethel-Jane West-feldt Bunting Summer Scholar at the School for Advanced Research on the Human Experience during the summer of 2007. I sincerely thank SAR for that support. I would like to thank the editors for their invitation to the Cambridge Heritage Seminar *Making the Means Transparent: Research Methodologies in Archaeological Heritage Studies*, held in March 2004, and for inviting me to contribute to this book. This chapter is on a different topic than my contribution to the seminar. I would like to thank the editors and Paul Shackel for their helpful comments; I alone, of course, am responsible for errors.

Bibliography

Abandoned Shipwreck Act of 1987 (43 U.S.C. [United States Code] 2101–2106).

Advisory Council on Historic Preservation (2000) *Federal Historic Preservation Case Law, 1966–1996* And: *Federal Historic Preservation Case Law Update, 1996–2000*. A Special Report Funded in Part by the United States Army Environmental Center. http://www.achp.gov/book/COVER1.html (accessed 24 August 2007).

Anyon, R. and T. J. Ferguson (1995) 'Cultural Resources Management at the Pueblo of Zuni, New Mexico, USA', *Antiquity* 69.266, 913–30.

Aten, L. E. (1983) *Archeological and Historical Data Recovery Program*. [FY1980, FY1981, FY1982], Washington, DC: Department of the Interior, National Park Service, Interagency Resources Division.

Aubry, M. (1997) 'Abandoned Shipwreck Act (ASA)', in J. P. Delgado (ed.) *Encyclopedia of Underwater and Maritime Archaeology*, London: British Museum Press. http://www.nps.gov/ history/archeology/tools/laws/ASA.htm (accessed 17 February 2008).

Baram, U., S. L. White and E. Westfall (2001) *Historical Archaeological Investigations of Site #8SO585 in Venice, Florida: The Venice Train Depot (VTD) Excavations of 2001*. Produced for Sarasota County Area Transit.

Bender, S. J. and G. S. Smith (eds) (2000) *Teaching Archaeology in the Twenty-First Century*, Washington, DC: Society for American Archaeology.

Carbone, V. A. and B. C. Keel (1986) *Annual Report to Congress on the Federal Archeological Program FY83 and FY84*, Washington, DC: Department of the Interior, National Park Service, Archeological Assistance Division.

Chaison, J. D., J. B. Hench and C. W. Stoffel (1992) *Under its Generous Dome*, Worcester, MA; American Antiquarian Society. Portions available http://www.americanantiquarian.org/ guidebook.htm (accessed 4 August 2007).

Childs, S. T. (2004) *Our Collective Responsibility: The Ethics and Practice of Archaeological Collections Stewardship*, Washington, DC: Society for American Archaeology.

Collins, R. B. (1980) 'The Meaning Behind ARPA: How the Act is Meant to Work', in Miscellaneous Papers numbers 33 and 34, 1–9. *Cultural Resources Report no. 32*. USDA Forest Service, Southwest Region.

Colwell-Chanthaphonh, C. (2007) 'History, Justice and Reconciliation', in B. J. Little and P. A. Shackel (eds) *Archaeology as a Tool of Civic Engagement*, Lanham, MD: AltaMira Press, 23–46.

Colwell-Chanthaphonh, C. and T. J. Ferguson (2006) 'Memory Pieces and Footprints: Multivocality and the Meanings of Ancient Times and Ancestral Places among the Zuni and Hopi', *American Anthropologist* 108.1, 148–62.

—— (eds) (2008) *Collaboration in Archaeological Practice: Engaging Descendant Communities*, Lanham, MD: AltaMira Press.

Cressey, P. J. (1987) 'Community Archaeology in Alexandria, Virginia', *Conserve Neighborhoods* 69. National Trust for Historic Preservation.

Davis, H. A. (1976) 'The Public and Cultural Resource Management: Reaction and Responsibility', in R. T. Matheny and D. L. Berge (eds) *Symposium on Dynamics of Cultural Resource Management*, USDA Forest Service, Southwestern Region, Report Number 10, 50–5.

—— (1996) 'NHPA and the Practice of Archeology', *CRM* 19.6, 42–4.

Davis, P. (1978) *Bibliography of Cultural Resource Reports Submitted to the Forest Service, Southwestern Region in 1977*, USDA Forest Service, Southwestern Region.

Derry, L. and M. Malloy (eds) (2003) *Archaeologists and Local Communities: Partners in Exploring the Past*, Washington, DC: Society for American Archaeology.

Dongoske, K., M. Aldenderfer and K. Doehner (eds) (2000) *Working Together: Native Americans and Archaeologists*, Washington, DC: Society for American Archaeology.

Downer, A. (2003) 'Native Americans and Historic Preservation', in R. E. Stipe (ed.) *A Richer Heritage: Historic Preservation in the Twenty-First Century*, Chapel Hill: University of North Carolina Press, 405–421.

Ford, R. I. (1973) 'Archaeology Serving Humanity', in C. L. Redman (ed.) *Research and Theory in Current Archaeology*, New York: John Wiley, 83–94.

Green, D. F. (1977) *Bibliography of Cultural Resource Reports Submitted to the Forest Service, Southwestern Region, Through 1976*, USDA Forest Service, Southwestern Region.

Haas, D. (1997) *Report on the Federal Archeology Program FY1991-FY1993*, Washington, DC: Departmental Consulting Archeologist, Archeology and Ethnography Program, National Park Service, US Department of the Interior. http://www.nps.gov/history/archeology/SRC/reportPdfs/1991–93.pdf.

—— (1998) *Federal Archeology Program Report to Congress 1994–1995*, Washington, DC: US Department of the Interior, National Park Service, Departmental Consulting Archeologist, Archeology and Ethnography Program. http://www.nps.gov/history/archeology/SRC/reportPdfs/1994-95.pdf.

—— (1999) *The Federal Archeology Program 1996–1997: Secretary of the Interior's Report to Congress*, Washington, DC: US Department of the Interior, National Park Service, Departmental Consulting Archeologist, Archeology and Ethnography Program. http://www.nps.gov/history/archeology/SRC/reportPdfs/1996–97.pdf.

Hantman, J. L. (2005) 'Colonial Legacies and the Public Meaning of Monacan Archaeology in Virginia', *SAA Archaeological Record* 5.2, 31–3.

Hantman, J. L. and G. Dunham (1993) 'The Enlightened Archaeologist', *Archaeology* 46.3, 44–9.

Heritage Conservation and Recreation Service (HCRS) (1979) *Archaeological and Historical Data Recovery Program 1977–1978*, Washington, DC: US Department of the Interior, HCRS Publication number 15.

Hodder, I. (ed.) (2000) *Towards Reflexive Method in Archaeology: The Example at Catalhoyuk*. Cambridge: McDonald Institute for Archaeological Research and British Institute of Archaeology at Ankara.

Keel, B. C. (1981) *Archeological and Historical Data Recovery Program 1979*, Washington, DC: US Department of the Interior, National Park Service, Interagency Resources Division.

Keel, B. C., F. P. McManamon and G. S. Smith (compilers) (1989) *Federal Archeology: The Current Program*. Annual Report to Congress on the Federal Archeology Program FY 1985 and FY 1986. US Department of the Interior, National Park Service, Departmental Consulting Archeologist and Archeological Assistance Division, Washington, DC. http://www.nps.gov/history/archeology/SRC/reportPdfs/1985–86.pdf.

King, T. F. and F. Plog (1983) 'Introduction', in D. F. Green and F. Plog (eds) *Problem Orientation and Allocation Strategies for Prehistoric Cultural Resources on the New Mexico National Forests*, Cultural Resources Management Report No. 3, 1–8, USDA Forest Service, Southwest Region.

Klesert, A. L. and A. S. Downer (eds) (1990) *Preservation on the Reservation: Native Americans, Native American Lands, and Archaeology*, Window Rock, AZ: Navajo Nation Papers in Anthropology No. 26.

Knudson, R., F. P. McManamon and J. E. Myers (compilers) (1995) *The Federal Archeology Program: Report to Congress for 1988–90*, Washington, DC: US Department of the Interior, National Park Service, Departmental Consulting Archeologist, Archeology and Ethnography Program. http://www.nps.gov/history/archeology/SRC/reportPdfs/1988-90.pdf.

Krupicz, A. S. (2000) 'Be All You Can Be: Evaluating Archaeological Outreach Programs'. MA Report, University of Arkansas, Fayetteville.

LaRoche, C. J. (2005) 'Heritage, Archaeology, and African American History', *SAA Archaeological Record* 5.2, 34–7.

LaRoche, C. J. and M. L. Blakey (1997) 'Seizing Intellectual Power: The Dialogue at the New York African Burial Ground', *Historical Archaeology* 31.3, 84–106.

Lees, W. B. and J. A. King (2007) 'What Are We Really Learning through Publicly Funded Historical Archaeology (and Is It Worth the Considerable Expense?)', *Historical Archaeology* 47.2.

Leone, M. P. (1983) 'Method as Message: Interpreting the Past with the Public', *Museum News* 62.1, 35–41.

Leone, M. P., P. B. Potter and P. A. Shackel (1987) 'Toward a Critical Archaeology', *Current Anthropology*, 28.3, 283–302.

Lipe, W. D. (1974) 'A Conservation Model for Archaeology', *Kiva* 39.3, 4, 214–45.

Little, B. J. (ed.) (2002) *Public Benefits of Archaeology*, Gainesville: University Press of Florida.

—— (2007a) 'What Are We Learning? Who Are We Serving? Publicly Funded Historical Archaeology and Public Scholarship', *Historical Archaeology*, 47.2, 72–9.

       (2007b) *Historical Archaeology. Why the Past Matters*, Walnut Creek, CA: Left Coast Press.

—— (2007c) 'Archaeology and Civic Engagement', in B. J. Little and P. A. Shackel (eds) *Archaeology as a Tool of Civic Engagement*, Lanham, MD: AltaMira Press, 1–22.

Little, B. J. and P. A. Shackel (eds) (2007) *Archaeology as a Tool of Civic Engagement*, Lanham, MD: AltaMira Press.

Lyon, E. A. (1996) *A New Deal for Southeastern Archaeology*, Tuscaloosa, AL: University of Alabama Press.

McDavid, C. (1997) 'Descendants, Decisions, and Power: The Public Interpretation of the Archaeology of the Levi Jordan Plantation', *Historical Archaeology* 31.3, 114–31.

McGimsey, C. R., III (1972) *Public Archaeology*, New York: Seminar Press.

—— (2004) *CRM on CRM: One Person's Perspective on the Birth and Early Development of Cultural Resource Management*, Fayetteville, AR: Arkansas Archaeological Survey Research Series No. 61.

—— (2006) 'The Life and Hard Times of the Archaeological and Historic Preservation Act in Washington, DC: An Assessment 30 Years After', *SAA Archaeological Record* 6.5, 6.

McGimsey, C. R., III and H. A. Davis (1977) *The Management of Archaeological Resources: The Airlie House Report*, Washington, DC: Special Publication of the Society for American Archaeology.

McGovern, T. L. (ed.) (2007) 'In Focus: Archaeology of Global Change', *American Anthropologist* 109.1.

McManamon, F. P. (1991) 'The Federal Government's Recent Response to Archaeological Looting', in G. Smith and J. L. Ehrenhard (eds) *Protecting the Past*, Boca Raton, FL: CRC Press. http://www.nps.gov/history/scac/protecting/html/5g-mcmanamon.htm.

—— (2006) 'National Leadership and Coordination for Federal Archaeology', *SAA Archaeological Record* 6.5, 7–9.

McManamon, F. P., P. C. Knoll, R. Knudson, G. S. Smith and R. C. Waldbauer (compilers) (1993) *Federal Archaeological Programs and Activities: The Secretary of the Interior's Report to Congress {FY1987}*, Washington, DC: US Department of the Interior, National Park Service, Departmental Consulting Archeologist, Archeology and Ethnography Program. http://www.nps.gov/history/archeology/SRC/reportPdfs/1987.pdf.

Marshall, Y. (ed.) (2002) 'Community Archaeology', thematic issue of *World Archaeology* 34.2.

Matheny, R. T. and D. L. Berge (1976) 'Some Problems Pertaining to Cultural Resource Management', in R. T. Matheny and D. L. Berge (eds) *Symposium on Dynamics of Cultural Resource Management*, USDA Forest Service, Southwestern Region, Report Number 10, 1–8.

Meyer, K. E. (1973) *The Plundered Past*, New York: Atheneum.

Minnis, P. E. (1999) 'Sustainability: The Long View from Archaeology', *New Mexico Journal of Science*, 39, 23–41.

Minnis, P. E., B. J. Little, R. Kelly, S. E. Ingram, D. Snow, L. Sebastian and K. A. Spielmann (2006) 'Answering the Skeptic's Question', *SAA Archaeological Record* 6.5, 17–20.

Moe, J. M. (2002) 'Project Archaeology: Putting the Intrigue of the Past in Public Education', in B. J. Little (ed.) *Public Benefits of Archaeology*, Gainesville: University Press of Florida, 176–86.

Moore, L. E. (2006) 'CRM: Beyond its Peak', *SAA Archaeological Record* 6.1, 30–3.

Mortensen, L. (2005) 'The Local Meaning of International Heritage at Copan, Honduras', *SAA Archaeological Record* 5.2, 28–30.

Muckle, B. (ed.) (2002) 'Community Archaeology', *Teaching Anthropology: Society for Anthropology in Community Colleges Notes* 9.1.

Nassaney, M. S. (2004) 'Implementing Community Service Learning through Archaeological Practice', *Michigan Journal of Community Service Learning*, Summer, 89–99.

Nicholas, G. P. and T. D. Andrews (eds) (1997) *At a Crossroads: Archaeology and First Peoples in Canada*, Burnaby, British Columbia: Publication No. 24, Archaeology Press, Department of Archaeology, Simon Fraser University.

Parker, A. C. (1938) 'Indians versus Pot Hunters', *American Antiquity* 3, 267–8.

Reaves, R. W., III (1976) 'Historic Preservation Laws and Policies: Background and History', in. R. T. Matheny and D. L. Berge (eds) *Symposium on Dynamics of Cultural Resource Management*, USDA Forest Service, Southwestern Region, Report Number 10, 15–23.

Redman, C. L. (1999) *Human Impact on Ancient Environments*, Tucson: University of Arizona Press.

Redman, C. L., S. R. James, P. R. Fish and J. D. Rogers (2004) 'Introduction: Human Impacts on Past Environments', in C. L. Redman, S. R. James, P. R. Fish and J. D. Rogers (eds) *Archaeology of Global Change: The Impact of Humans on Their Environment*, Washington, DC: Smithsonian Books, 1–8.

Roberts, H., R. V. N. Ahlstrom and B. Roth (eds) (2004) *From Campus to Corporation: The Emergence of Contract Archaeology in the Southwestern United States*, Washington, DC: Society for American Archaeology.

Roberts, M. E. (1995) 'The Failed Promise of Public Archaeology', paper presented at the Society for American Archaeology. www.timelinesinc.com/michael's_saa_paper.htm (accessed 30 January 2006).

Sabloff, J. A. (2006) 'Susan Kent and the Relevance of Anthropological Archaeology', *Anthropological Papers of the American Anthropological Association*, 16, 151–6.

—— (2008) *Archaeology Matters: Action Archaeology in the Modern World*, Walnut Creek, CA: Left Coast Press.

Shackel, P. A. (2003) *Memory in Black and White; Race, Commemoration, and the Post-Bellum Landscape*, Walnut Creek, CA: AltaMira Press.

—— (2005) 'Memory, Civic Engagement, and the Public Meaning of Archaeological Heritage', *SAA Archaeological Record* 5.2, 24–7.

Shackel, P. A. and E. Chambers (eds) (2004) *Places in Mind: Public Archeology as Applied Anthropology*, New York: Routledge.

Smardz, K. and S. J. Smith (eds) (2000) *The Archaeological Education Handbook: Sharing the Past with Kids*, Walnut Creek, CA: AltaMira Press.

Stottman, J. (ed.) (forthcoming) *Changing the World with Archaeology: Archaeology Activism*, Gainesville: University Press of Florida.

Swidler, N., K. Dongoske, R. Anyon and A. Downer (eds) (1997) *Native Americans and Archaeologists: Stepping Stones to Common Ground*, Walnut Creek, CA: AltaMira Press.

Uunila, K. (2005) 'Using the Past in Calvert County, Maryland: Archaeology as a Tool for Building Community', *SAA Archaeological Record* 5.2, 38–40.

Watkins, J. (2000) *Indigenous Archaeology: American Indian Values and Scientific Practice*, Walnut Creek, CA: AltaMira Press.

—— (2005) 'Artefacts, Archaeologists and American Indians', *Public Archaeology* 4, 187–91.

Welch, J. R., M. Altaha, D. Gatewood, K. A. Hoerig and R. Riley (2006) 'Archaeology, Stewardship, and Sovereignty', *SAA Archaeological Record* 6.4, 17–20, 57.

Wells, P. S. (1991) 'Presenting the Past: A Conference Series Aimed at Public Education', in G. Smith and J. L. Ehrenhard (eds) *Protecting the Past*, Boca Raton, FL: CRC Press. http://www.nps.gov/history/seac/protecting/html/4l-wells.htm.

Whiteley, P. M. (2002) 'Archaeology and Oral Traditions: The Scientific Importance of Dialogue', *American Antiquity* 67.3, 405–15.

Williams, S. and P. Pope (n.d.) 'Findings: How Community Archaeology Creates Social Capital and Builds Community Capacity', produced for the Newfoundland Archaeological Heritage Outreach Program (2000–5). http://www.arts.mun.ca/nahop/SocialCapital.html (accessed 19 January 2007).

Wilson, R. L. (n.d.a) *Archaeological and Historical Data Recovery Program Fiscal Year 1975*, Washington, DC: US Department of the Interior, National Park Service, Departmental Consulting Archeologist.

—— (n.d.b) *Archaeological and Historical Data Recovery Program Fiscal Year 1976*, Washington, DC: US Department of the Interior, National Park Service, Departmental Consulting Archeologist.

—— (1976) 'Response to Public Law 93–291', in R. T. Matheny and D. L. Berge (eds) *Symposium on Dynamics of Cultural Resource Management*, USDA Forest Service, Southwestern Region, Report Number 10, 9–14.

PUBLIC ARCHITECTURE OF THE UNITED STATES

Part II

HERITAGE METHODOLOGIES: INVESTIGATING TEXTS

4

THE HISTORY OF HERITAGE

A method in analysing legislative historiography

Hilary A. Soderland

Introduction

Heritage by its very nature values the past and is concerned with the manner through which the past is constructed in the present. By capturing the essence of past occurrences, the historical dimension of heritage not only documents past production of knowledge but also provides an enduring context within which its changing meanings can be traced. Written records and textual documents attest to how knowledge was created and chronicled, embodying and assimilating the particular values of the time when the history was recorded. Thus, text as an historical resource sheds light on how and why a certain history was created at a given time as well as how it was incorporated into the historical canon. It is in this way that the history of heritage illuminates the interplay among knowledge, text and value.

This chapter discusses the use of archival material in heritage research.[1] Archival documents constitute a primary historical source – a direct record of the past – and bear witness to past manifestations of knowledge. Therefore, an analysis of textual collections contained in archival repositories enables the creation of an historiographical heritage. The emphasis here is legislative archival material and the methods employed in the construction of a legislative history: *a history of heritage*. The specific archives drawn upon are those of the United States government that record the procedures through which federal legislation is enacted, and serve as the textual record for the history of law. These archives are the historical resource from which the history of legislation can be constructed. The legislative history of a law provides a snapshot of the particular time when society's values – whether social, political, economic, ethical, *inter alia* or a combination – were such that law was enacted to encapsulate them.

The methodological principle that underpins the use of archival material in the construction of a legislative history is in this instance applied to the United

States.[2] Its precepts, however, are not limited to any individual nation. National variation in the lawmaking process obviously results in deviations and differences as to how laws are made and consequently as to how the textual record that details the history of law is produced. Variance means that it is not possible simply to apply this method through direct replication but instead to adapt its underlying tenets accordingly when transferred among legal frameworks. Thus, such inherent distinctions in systems of law do not preclude extending the legal-historical methodological approach to understanding and synthesising the archive as a written record for the history of law in diverse national and governmental contexts. Despite the fact that legislatures and legislative systems across the globe are individualised, most legal systems record the lawmaking process through the production of written materials. As a result, the critical examination of those legislative archives can illuminate the historical dimension of heritage.

The chapter begins with a summation (for contextual purposes) of the United States legislative procedure in the making of federal laws. This is followed by an explanation of the source, purpose and scope of the archival materials that constitute the building blocks of the legislative history in the United States. The framework within which these archives are situated is then set forth to explicate the methods devised and employed to interpret the assembly, compilation and assessment of the archive as historical text within the domain of heritage. These two sections provide the information essential to understanding how the concept of heritage is reflected in the legislative histories of law. The final section illustrates the manner through which the concept of heritage is reflected in the legislative history of the 1906 Antiquities Act. As the first United States federal law enacted specifically to address antiquities as its central concern, it set a precedent – serving as the ideological and procedural base – for all subsequent archaeological legislation. The final section delves further into the significance of positing the legislative archive as archaeological artefact. In considering the 'archive as artefact' it presents concluding remarks on the new and dynamic lines of enquiry this methodological approach yields for the field of Heritage Studies.

The United States legislative procedure in the making of federal laws

Inherent in this methodology is an understanding of how laws are made and the intricacies of the legislative process in the system of government under consideration. Since the mechanisms germane to the enactment of law in this case are governed by the extremely complex and multifaceted apparatus of the United States federal legislative system, this section considers only the procedures applicable to the making of a legislative history.[3] It is detailed but essential. It sets forth the particular legislative system, demonstrating how it is both formulated and archived. Then it provides a means through which that legislative archive can be broken down into manageable units for analysis. The templates developed as tools to implement this legal-historical methodological approach are devised in a manner best to denote and evaluate a specific lawmaking process. As a result, these templates are tailored to the United States framework and as such are not directly applicable to another nation or government. Nonetheless, as indicated previously, the tenets underlying this method embrace variance, facilitate the capacity to transcend national borders and accommodate diverse legislative processes that are documented through the production of a written record.

In the United States, the Constitution is the supreme law of the land and has endured as the cornerstone of the legal system since its adoption in 1789.[4] As specified by the Constitution, the powers vested in the governing system are balanced among the three branches of federal government: the legislative (administered by Congress), the executive (under the direction of the President) and the judicial (the court system, headed by the Supreme Court of the United States).[5] Congress is composed of the House of Representatives and the Senate and any given Congress lasts for two years, divided into two sessions. The primary function of Congress is the making of laws. In order for a bill to become law, it must be passed by both houses of Congress in *identical* form and (1) approved by the President; or (2) if the President fails to return it with objections to the body in which it originated within ten days while Congress is in session, it automatically becomes law; or (3) if the President vetoes the bill, Congress can override the presidential veto with a two-thirds majority vote in each house. This process is visually represented in the flowchart shown in Table 4.1. Since there is no single prescribed course for how federal laws are made, or the complicated processes bills undergo to become law, to determine the course of a piece of legislation – its 'legislative history' or development from origination to termination or codification – the proceedings and other material pertinent to any bill must first be collected and analysed.

The construction of a legislative history

A legislative history is constructed through a critical examination of both published and unpublished archival documents. As indicated in the previous section, in the United States context the manner through which a bill becomes law is not predetermined but is formulated upon how a bill is negotiated through the procedures of the federal legislature. Consequently bills follow very different courses and become laws in very different ways. The archived records and material pertinent to any bill similarly take varied forms, and must first be assembled in order to discover the course of a given piece of legislation. Tracing a bill's development from origination to either codification or termination includes documenting when and by whom it was introduced, whether it was considered by Congressional Committees, and if any associated reports, hearings, unpublished material and/or proposed amendments were produced. This identifies what decisions affecting the legislation were made at

Table 4.1 The Legislative Process Flowchart: how a bill becomes a law

**Legislation may begin in either Congressional chamber.
Similar proposals are often introduced in both chambers.**

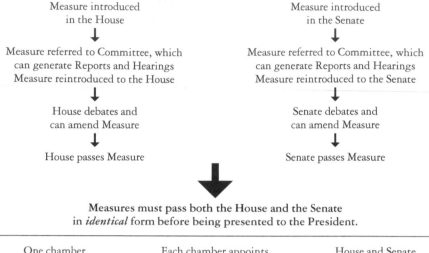

Measure introduced
in the House
↓
Measure referred to Committee, which
can generate Reports and Hearings
Measure reintroduced to the House
↓
House debates and
can amend Measure
↓
House passes Measure

Measure introduced
in the Senate
↓
Measure referred to Committee, which
can generate Reports and Hearings
Measure reintroduced to the Senate
↓
Senate debates and
can amend Measure
↓
Senate passes Measure

**Measures must pass both the House and the Senate
in *identical* form before being presented to the President.**

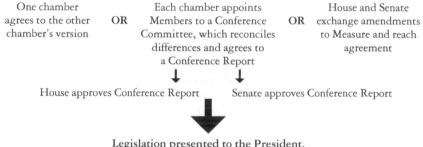

One chamber
agrees to the other   **OR**
chamber's version

Each chamber appoints
Members to a Conference
Committee, which reconciles
differences and agrees to
a Conference Report
↓   ↓

OR

House and Senate
exchange amendments
to Measure and reach
agreement

House approves Conference Report   Senate approves Conference Report

Legislation presented to the President.

President signs Measure
Measure becomes law   **OR**

If President does not
sign Measure into law
within ten days when
Congress is in session,
then Measure becomes law

OR

President vetoes Measure
Measure does not
become law, unless both
chambers override veto
by $\frac{2}{3}$ majority

which stages in the legislative process and enables the creation of the 'history' of a bill and, in turn, the 'history' of a law. Such a method encompasses the context within which a bill becomes law. It also takes into consideration the values and attitudes of the time and how these affected the making of any piece of legislation. The archival resources applicable to the construction of a legislative history are enumerated in Table 4.2.

Table 4.2 The Construction of a Legislative History

---

1. *The Congressional Record Index* (for each Congress)

• List of all Congressional Members – from the House of Representatives and the Senate
• Subject Index (organized alphabetically)
• House Bills Index (organized numerically by bill number)
• Senate Bills Index (organized numerically by bill number)

2. *The Congressional Record* (the proceedings, debates and notations of Congress)

• All relevant pages listed under House and Senate Bills in the Congressional Record Index:
  • Congressional Record – House
  • Congressional Record – Senate

3. *The Daily Digest* (summary of the daily Congressional activity)

• The Daily Digest began in 1947.

4. *Congressional Committee action: House Reports*

• The Congressional Record Index and/or Congressional Record lists accompanying House Reports.*

5. *Congressional Committee action: Senate Reports*

• The Congressional Record Index and/or Congressional Record lists accompanying Senate Reports.*

6. *Congressional Committee action: published Committee Hearings*

• The Congressional Committee Reports function as the citation for accompanying published Committee Hearings.

7. *Congressional Committee action: unpublished Committee Hearings*

• The Congressional Committee Reports function as the citation for accompanying unpublished Committee Hearings.*

8. *Congressional Committee action: unpublished Congressional Committee material* (material referred to or produced by a Committee, including bill files, Committee papers and record books, meeting minutes, correspondence, memoranda, petitions and memorials)

• The unpublished Congressional Committee material must be located by searching paper registers at the United States National Archives in Washington, DC, first by Congress, then by either the House or the Senate and finally by the relevant Committee.

*There are also paper indices of Congressional Committee Reports and Hearings that can be cross-referenced.

The archival resource: the Congressional Record Index

For United States federal law, the initial archival document utilised in the construction of a legislative history is the Congressional Record Index, which for every Congress serves as the guide to all legislative action. Each Index consists of a list of all Congressional members (of both the House of Representatives and the Senate), an alphabetical subject index and a bill index. There are separate bill indices for the House and the Senate, organised numerically by bill number. Thus, the various indices permit research on a particular bill to start from a bill number, the individual Congress member who introduced the bill, or the subject or title of a bill. Cross-referencing among the various indices is prudent in order to ensure that all the applicable bill material is obtained. The information gleaned from the Congressional Record Index is crucial since it furnishes the citations that indicate the precise location of a particular bill in the proceedings of Congress and, in so doing, functions as the foundation from which all subsequent legislative information is built.

The archival resource: the Congressional Record

Corresponding to the Congressional Record Index, there is a Congressional Record for each Congress that documents the proceedings, debates and notations of Congress. It is the verbatim transcript of Congressional activity and is divided into House action and Senate action. Depending on the length of time a given Congress is in session and the length of debate, the Congressional Record can be (and invariably is) voluminous. Thus it would be virtually impossible to locate a particular bill without the references acquired in the Congressional Record Index that specify the exact pages in the Congressional Record that chronicle action on a bill. Utilising these page references, it is possible to trace a bill through Congress first by pinpointing each citation in the Congressional Record, and then by assembling all bill action in a chronological compilation.

The archival resource

The Daily Digest, which began in 1947, is a summary of the daily Congressional activity and is generally bound with the Congressional Record. It supplies a brief overview of the action for each day Congress is convened, and is valuable as a supplement to the Congressional Record.

The archival resource: Congressional Committee action– Reports and Hearings

The chronological compilation of all bill action within a Congress must be examined for mention of the involvement of Congressional Committees.

Congressional Committees are an important stage both in the legislative process (because these bodies wield great control over a bill's future) and in contextualising a bill's legislative history. The Committee structure provides a platform for detailed examination and consideration, for public comment and contribution, and for the expression of dissenting or minority viewpoints. Though both the House and Senate have separate Committees to oversee proposed legislation, there is a great deal of topical overlap, as illustrated in Table 4.3.

Table 4.3 The Congressional Committees

House Standing Committees	*Senate Standing Committees*
• Agriculture	• Agriculture, Nutrition, & Forestry
• Appropriations	• Appropriations
• Armed Services	• Armed Services
• Budget	• Banking, Housing, & Urban Affairs
• Education and the Workforce	• Budget
• Energy and Commerce	• Commerce, Science, & Transportation
• Financial Services	• Energy & Natural Resources
• Government Reform	• Environment & Public Works
• Homeland Security	• Finance
• House Administration	• Foreign Relations
• International Relations	• Health, Education, Labor, & Pensions
• Judiciary	• Homeland Security & Governmental Affairs
• Resources	• Judiciary
• Rules	• Rules & Administration
• Science	• Small Business and Entrepreneurship
• Small Business	• Veterans' Affairs
• Standards of Official Conduct	
• Transportation & Infrastructure	
• Veterans' Affairs	
• Ways and Means	

Joint Standing Committees
• Joint Committee on Printing
• Joint Committee on Taxation
• Joint Committee on the Library
• Joint Economic Committee

Congressional Committees generate two official forms of textual documents, 'Committee Reports' and 'Committee Hearings', both of which are demarcated to either the House or the Senate. Congressional Committee action regarding Reports is indicated in the Congressional Record Index and in the Congressional Record. This is not generally the case for Committee Hearings. There are, however, paper indices (separate from the Congressional Record Index) that list Congressional Committee Reports and Hearings that can be cross-referenced, although the information contained in the Congressional Reports functions as the prime legislative citation for locating related Congressional Hearings.

When a bill is introduced in Congress, it is typically referred to the Committee (and then potentially to the Subcommittee) that has jurisdiction over the subject matter most closely related to the bill. If a Committee articulates its support for a bill, it is ordinarily the Chair who reintroduces the bill to whichever body of Congress from which it was referred, along with an accompanying Committee Report. Committee Reports normally include a statement of the intention and breadth of the proposed bill; an examination of the purpose of each section of the bill; the Committee's findings through examination of the issue(s) at hand (such as information gathered through public hearings); reasons for the Committee's support and recommendation for Congressional approval; explanation of any proposed amendments; and, if applicable, the wording of the current law for which the Committee proposes a change.[6] Committee Reports are 'perhaps the most valuable single element of the legislative history of a law. They are used by courts, executive departments, and the public as a source of information regarding the purpose and meaning of the law' (Johnson 2000: 14).

At this stage in the legislative process, it is important to emphasise that Committee recommendations to Congress, which may or may not include Congressional Committee Reports and/or Hearings, are solely advisory and no change occurs without Congressional approval. Committees, as previously indicated, articulate support for a bill to Congress through the submission of a Committee Report and a statement of support for either the original bill without amendment, the original bill with proposed amendments, or a new bill written by the Committee to incorporate modifications, amendments and/ or annotations the Committee deems fit. Yet even in this consultative role, the extensive information customarily included in Congressional Committee official textual documents provides a wealth of information about the evolution of a bill in its path to become law.

Not all bills referred to Congressional Committee are reported back to Congress (with an accompanying Committee Report) or even reviewed by the Committee. A Committee vote determines whether a bill referred to that Committee will have Committee support as it stands (as introduced in Congress), will warrant Committee action, or will receive no attention or action by the Committee and in effect will be postponed indefinitely. In the latter instance, when the bill referred from Congress is 'tabled' by a Committee, it 'dies' in Committee and never is reintroduced to Congress. Such is the fate of numerous bills in the legislative process. Consequently, there is rarely a negative Committee Report made to Congress since bills without Committee support are simply shelved and never acted upon. The termination of bills in Committee is an appropriate indicator of the power wielded by Congressional Committees in the legislative process.

A further indication of the influence of Congressional Committees is the extent of discretionary latitude in overseeing proposed legislation.[7] Congressional Committees dictate whether the issues presented in a bill are of sufficient stature to warrant further investigation in the form of a hearing. Committee Hearings, which can be 'published' or 'unpublished', are the amalgamation of the verbatim transcript of testimony and evidence presented during the hearing itself in addition to all written material submitted from relevant parties. These data, when taken under consideration by the Committee (in quorum), provide a solid foundation from which the Committee can reach an informed decision vis-à-vis a proposed piece of legislation. Committee Hearings are the principal conduit through which the public can contribute to the legislative process and, in so doing, provide the opportunity for democratic representation. In this respect, these official documents provide a compelling component in the historical contextualisation of a bill within its contemporary society.

The archival resource: Congressional Committee action – unpublished Congressional Committee material

The final archival resource in the construction of a legislative history is unpublished Committee material, which encompasses documents either referred to a Committee through Congressional action or produced by the Committee itself. The amount and extent of unpublished material any Committee receives or produces varies greatly, and, as with most processes involving the making of legislation, the more recent the timeframe the greater the paper trail. Unpublished Committee material can include Committee bill files, papers record books, meeting minutes, correspondence, memoranda, petitions, memorials and other related documents. It is important to note that these categories are typical, but by no means the only ones under which material can be produced by a Committee. Unpublished literature is not listed in the Congressional Record Index and must be located by searching paper registers available only at the National Archives in Washington, DC, looking first by Congress, then by either the House or the Senate and, finally, by the relevant Committee or Subcommittee. Although this material is the most difficult to locate and there is no mechanism to verify that all applicable material has been found, it is extremely useful in situating the legislative history of a bill within its greater societal context.

The archival resource framework

In the construction of a legislative history, locating the relevant textual references within the immeasurable written record produced in the legislative process is only the first step. The task of managing the accumulated textual resource in a consistent methodical manner conducive to study and withstanding scrutiny is critical to both the scope of enquiry and the research results. Therefore, the management strategy devised in this methodology uses a systematic approach to organise and classify this body of archival material.[8] By formatting the legal-historical text of different laws to the same templates – the Legislative History Checklist and the Legislative History Chronological Compilation – the precise course of how bills become laws becomes transparent.[9] Furthermore, each step a bill undergoes in the legislative process is categorised, enabling patterns to be identified and comparisons to be made among and between laws despite temporal variation. Employing this method exploits the archive as resource in order to extract otherwise muted data that can then be used in a constructive synthesis.

This methodology affirms that the particular Congress that passes legislation is of the utmost significance since it provides the legislative milieu that successfully captures the ideals and values of the particular time that enacted law. As a result, while germane bills introduced in prior Congresses can provide a meaningful supplement to the archival material produced by the enacting Congress, it is the legislative history (or histories) of the bill(s) within the enacting Congress that are most instructive.

The archival resource framework: the Legislative History Checklist

The Legislative History Checklist shows the archival material that exists and, in turn, that has been drawn upon to construct a bill's legislative history. Figure 4.1 demonstrates the Legislative History Checklist template with all items accounted for, which is an infrequent occurrence. In the construction of a legislative history, the absence of text at any point is important to note since it exposes a consequential element. Written records or textual documents necessarily are not produced at every potential opportunity and thus what is not present can be as telling as what is present. The degree to which any particular type of material is generated for a bill is testament to how knowledge was created as the bill navigated the legislative process. The Legislative History Checklist supplies a succinct format that orients *potential* archival information to *actual* archival material, summarising what is where in the legislative process and supplying the information upon which the Legislative History Chronological Compilation can be constructed.

---

1. *The Congressional Record Index*
   - ☑ List of all Congressional Members – from the House of Representatives and the Senate
   - ☑ Subject Index
   - ☑ House Bills Index
   - ☑ Senate Bills Index

2. *The Congressional Record*
   - ☑ All relevant pages listed under House and Senate Bills in the Congressional Record Index:
      - ☑ Congressional Record – House
      - ☑ Congressional Record – Senate

3. *The Daily Digest*
   - ☑ Daily Digest pages:

4. *Congressional Committee action: House Reports*
   - ☑ House Report: [Report Number]

5. *Congressional Committee action: Senate Reports*
   - ☑ Senate Report: [Report Number]

6. *Congressional Committee action: published Committee Hearings*
   - ☑ Published Committee Hearing: [Hearing Number]

7. *Congressional Committee action: unpublished Committee Hearings*
   - ☑ Unpublished Committee Hearings: [Hearing Number]

8. *Congressional Committee action: unpublished Congressional Committee Material (bill files; Committee papers, minutes, correspondence, and memoranda; petitions and memorials referred to Committee)*
   - ☑ Unpublished material from the House/Senate Committee [Name of Committee] includes:
      - Bill files
      - Committee Papers and Record Books
      - Correspondence
      - Memoranda
      - Petitions
      - Other Various Related Documents

Figure 4.1 The Legislative History Checklist template

The archival resource framework: the Legislative History Chronological Compilation

The Legislative History Chronological Compilation assembled from the available archival information for any law provides a sequencing framework for its legislative history.[10] By diachronically documenting the course of bills, it shows when Congressional actions affecting each bill occurred and whether the action took place in the House or in the Senate. It indicates when and where a bill terminates or the process through which it becomes law. In illuminating the stages of a bill by tracking its Congressional action (or lack thereof), the Legislative History Chronological Compilation is an invaluable resource in the historiography of a bill and/or a law.

The archival resource framework: conclusion

By compartmentalising the material amassed from archival research, the Legislative History Checklist and the Legislative History Chronological Compilation mitigate the complex structure of the United States legislative system to facilitate the assessment of the convoluted processes bills negotiate to become law. Moreover, these templates display the detailed and subtle narrative of a fertile primary source. They capture the knowledge produced and recorded in the archival texts in legislative histories, in histories of heritage.[11] Such 'histories' do not connote static annals entrenched in the past. Quite the opposite is the case. While constructed in the historical sphere, these 'histories' offer a dynamic forum that embraces the capability to foreshadow future legislation. Thus, the history of a law's heritage reflects the concept of heritage in the United States at the time of codification and provides a platform from which the legislative histories of ensuing archaeology laws can be constructed. In the next section, these templates as methodological instruments are implemented to construct the legislative history of the 1906 Antiquities Act, which elucidates the statute's historiographical heritage and serves to illuminate its continued significance to the fabric of American archaeology.

The legislative history of the 1906 American Antiquities Act

The 1906 Antiquities Act is hailed unequivocally as the foundation stone in the legal preservation and protection of America's archaeological resources. Its legacy, still evident over a century later, is routinely attributed to its foresight and concise yet broad scope. As the first of many federal laws, regulations and standards directing the course of cultural heritage management and historic preservation, the Antiquities Act has left an indelible mark on the American landscape.[12]

Still in effect today, the Antiquities Act has three main provisions: Section 1 imposes penalties for the damage or destruction of 'any object of antiquity' on federally owned or controlled land. Section 2 grants executive proclamation powers to the President to declare national monuments, making a single unilateral action all that is necessary to set aside government land for preservation. Section 3 requires government-issued permits in order to conduct archaeological investigations, excavations or research on federally owned or controlled land, and also stipulates that objects removed from such endeavours are to be cared for permanently in a public facility. The full text of the Act appears in Figure 4.2.

The 1906 Antiquities Act

16 U.S.C. §§ 431-433 • 59TH CONGRESS, 1ST SESSION • JUNE 8, 1906

Be it enacted by the Senate and House of Representatives of the United States of America in Congress assembled,

Sec. 1. That any person who shall appropriate, excavate, injure, or destroy any historic or prehistoric ruin or monument, or any object of antiquity, situated on lands owned or controlled by the Government of the United States, without the permission of the Secretary of the Department of the Government having jurisdiction over the lands on which said antiquities are situated, shall, upon conviction, be fined in a sum of not more than five hundred dollars or be imprisoned for a period of not more than ninety days, or shall suffer both fine and imprisonment, in the discretion of the court.

Sec. 2. That the President of the United States is hereby authorized, in his discretion, to declare by public proclamation historic landmarks, historic and prehistoric structures, and other objects of historic or scientific interest that are situated upon the lands owned or controlled by the Government of the United States to be national monuments, and may reserve as a part thereof parcels of land, the limits of which in all cases shall be confined to the smallest area compatible with proper care and management of the objects to be protected: Provided, That when such objects are situated upon a tract covered by a bona fide unperfected claim or held in private ownership, the tract, or so much thereof as may be necessary for the proper care and management of the object, may be relinquished to the Government, and the Secretary of the Interior is hereby authorized to accept the relinquishment of such tracts in [sic] behalf of the Government of the United States.

Sec. 3. That permits for the examination of ruins, the excavation of archaeological sites, and the gathering of objects of antiquity upon the lands under their respective jurisdictions may be granted by the Secretaries of the Interior, Agriculture, and War to institutions which they may deem properly qualified to conduct such examination, excavation, or gathering, subject to such rules and regulation as they may prescribe: Provided, That the examinations, excavations, and gatherings are undertaken for the benefit of reputable museums, universities, colleges, or other recognized scientific or educational institutions, with a view to increasing the knowledge of such objects, and that the gatherings shall be made for permanent preservation in public museums.

Sec. 4. That the Secretaries of the Departments aforesaid shall make and publish from time to time uniform rules and regulations for the purpose of carrying out the provisions of this Act.

Figure 4.2 The 1906 Antiquities Act

59th Congress

Two bills were introduced in the 59th Congress in 1906 that mandated the protection and preservation of antiquities. Although one originated in the House, H.R. 11016, and one in the Senate, S. 4698, both were entitled 'For the Preservation of American Antiquities.' The extant archival material that has been drawn upon to construct these bills' legislative histories is shown in Figure 4.3, the 59th Congress Legislative History Checklist. The Congressional Record Index and the Congressional Record, along with Congressional Committee Reports and Unpublished Material are the primary historical sources. As indicated, there are no associated Congressional Hearings in the 59th Congress. From the archival information, the chronological compilation in Figure 4.4 assembled for H.R. 11016 and S. 4698 provides the sequencing framework for the Act's legislative history. As is the fate of numerous bills, H.R. 11016 never became law. In contrast, S. 4698 passed the Senate and then the House before securing the Presidential approval that ratified it into law on June 8, 1906.

As illustrated in Figures 4.3 and 4.4, during the 59th Congress there were three key places of engagement for H.R. 11016 and S. 4698 in the legislative process. The Congressional Record merely makes note of when these bills were introduced, referred between Congressional bodies, enrolled and, in the case of S. 4698, approved by the President. In contrast, the Congressional Committee Reports, House Report 2224 and Senate Report 3797, in addition to the House debate and the Unpublished Committee Material, offer insight into the issues and attitudes at the crux of the bill.

59th Congress: House Report 2224

H.R. 11016, introduced by Representative John F. Lacey (R-IA)[13] on January 9, 1906 and subsequently referred to the House Committee on Public Lands, was reported back to the House with amendment on March 12, 1906, accompanied by House Report 2224. Amendments were slight, three inserts in total, and the scope and purpose of the bill remained unaltered. The eight pages of House Report 2224 complement the House Report and House Hearing issued by the same Committee during the 58th Congress. Those earlier materials concerned the enactment of a bill very similar to H.R. 11016 that did not receive action before the end of the 58th Congress and thus died in Committee.[14] House Report 2224 offers justification for the urgent need for legislation. A strong argument to legislate arose when the absence of law in the United States was compared to other nations:

> Practically every civilized government in the world has enacted laws for the preservation of the remains of the historic past, and has provided that excavations and explorations shall be conducted in some systematic and practical way so as not to needlessly destroy buildings and other objects of interest. The United States should adopt some method of protecting these remains that are still upon the public domain or in Indian reservations.
>
> (House Report 2224, March 12, 1906: 1–2)

House Report 2224 also included a detailed memorandum[15] by Professor Edgar Lee Hewett,[16] former President of the New Mexico Normal University at Las Vegas,

---

1906 ANTIQUITIES ACT
59th Congress 1st Session: December 4, 1905 to June 30, 1906

H.R. 11016   For the Preservation of American Antiquities

S. 4698   **For the Preservation of American Antiquities**

1. *The Congressional Record Index*
   - ☑ List of all Congressional Members – from the House of Representatives and the Senate
   - ☑ Subject Index
   - ☑ House Bills Index
   - ☑ Senate Bills Index

2. *The Congressional Record*
   - ☑ All relevant pages listed under House and Senate Bills in the Congressional Record Index:
   - ☑ Congressional Record – House
   - ☑ Congressional Record – Senate

3. *The Daily Digest*
   - ☐ Daily Digest (not published until 1947)

4. *Congressional Committee action: House Reports*
   - ☑ House Report 2224

5. *Congressional Committee action: Senate Reports*
   - ☑ Senate Report 3797

6. *Congressional Committee action: published Committee Hearings*
   - ☐ Published Committee Hearings for H.R. 11016 or S. 4698

7. *Congressional Committee action: unpublished Committee Hearings*
   - ☐ Unpublished Committee Hearings for H.R. 11016 or S. 4698

8. *Congressional Committee action: unpublished Congressional Committee Material (bill files; Committee papers, minutes, correspondence, and memoranda; petitions and memorials referred to Committee)*
   - ☑ Unpublished Material from the House and the Senate Committee on Public Lands includes:
     - • Bill files
     - • Committee Papers and Record Books
     - • Correspondence
     - • Memoranda
     - • Petitions
     - • Other Various Related Documents

Figure 4.3 The 59th Congress Legislative History Checklist

1906 ANTIQUITIES ACT
59th Congress 1st Session: December 4, 1905 to June 30, 1906

59(1) H.R. 11016
January 9, 1906   HOUSE

For the Preservation of American Antiquities
Introduced by Representative John F. Lacey (R-IA)
Referred to the Committee on Public Lands

59(1) S. 4698
February 26, 1906   SENATE

For the Preservation of American Antiquities
Introduced by Senator Thomas Patterson (D-CO)
Referred to the Committee on Public Lands

59(1) H.R. 11016
March 12, 1906   HOUSE

For the Preservation of American Antiquities
Reported back (from the Committee on Public
Lands) with amendment, accompanied by
House Report 2224

59(1) S. 4698
May 24, 1906   SENATE

For the Preservation of American Antiquities
Reported back (from the Committee on Public
Lands) without amendment, accompanied by
Senate Report 3797
Passed Senate

59(1) S. 4698
May 25, 1906   HOUSE

For the Preservation of American Antiquities
Referred from the Senate
Referred to the Committee on Public Lands

59(1) S. 4698
June 5, 1906   HOUSE

For the Preservation of American Antiquities
Reported back (from the Committee on
Public Lands)
Debated
Passed House

59(1) S. 4698
June 7, 1906   HOUSE

For the Preservation of American Antiquities
Enrolled Bill Signed

59(1) S. 4698
June 8, 1906   SENATE

For the Preservation of American Antiquities
Enrolled Bill Signed

59(1) S. 4698
*June 8, 1906   SENATE

For the Preservation of American Antiquities
Approved by President Theodore Roosevelt
Codified into Public Law 59–209

*June 8, 1906 was the date that President Theodore Roosevelt approved the American Antiquities Act;
Presidential approval was not recorded in the Congressional Record until June 11, 1906.

Figure 4.4 The 59th Congress Chronological Compilation

New Mexico, regarding the severity of the situation in the Southwest and the urgency of enacting protective legislation in conjunction with the establishment of National Parks.[17] Hewett's memorandum summarised the past and contemporaneous condition of archaeology in the Southwest[18] and included the map set forth in Figure 4.5. Grouping the archaeological ruins regionally, Hewett documented prior excavation, instances of vandalism and/or looting, and the current status of sites, on both a regional and an individual scale. Hewett deemed the investigation of ruins to be paramount in contributing to scientific knowledge and condemned the increasing vandalism and trafficking in artefacts and the consequent detrimental effects on the interests of science. Reflecting the attitude widespread among scientists of the time, Hewett stated in his memorandum:

> These relics are priceless when secured by proper scientific methods, and of comparatively little value when scattered about either in museums or private collections without accompanying records. No scientific man is true to the highest ideals of science who does not protest against this outrageous traffic, and it will be a lasting reproach upon our Government if it does not use its power to restrain it.
>
> (House Report 2224, March 12, 1906: 3)

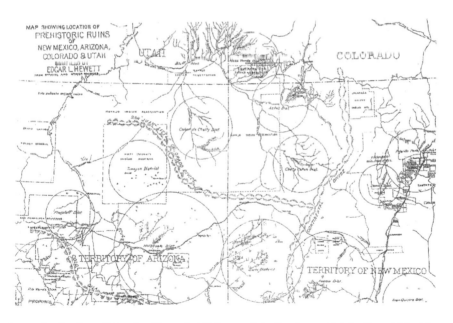

Figure 4.5 Professor Edgar Lee Hewett's 1904 map of the Southwest. Originally published in Professor Hewett's 1904 'Memorandum Concerning the Historic and Prehistoric Ruins of Arizona, New Mexico, Colorado, and Utah, and their Preservation,' this map was reproduced during the 58th Congress for inclusion (as appendices) to House Report 3704 and to the January 11, 1905 House Published Hearing.

This use of a scientific-knowledge justification for the legal means necessary to preserve remains of the past represents a recurring theme in the early efforts to preserve America's cultural landscape. Hewett further justified the need for legislation to protect these regions so that they 'may be a perpetual source of education, and enjoyment for the American people, as well as for travelers from foreign lands' (House Report 2224, March 12, 1906: 2–3).

59th Congress: Senate Report 3797

S. 4698, introduced by Senator Thomas Patterson (D-CO) on 26 February 1906 and subsequently referred to the Senate Committee on Public Lands, was reported back to the Senate without amendment on May 24, 1906, accompanied by Senate Report 3797. Only three paragraphs in length, Senate Report 3797 (which comprises Figure 4.6) is uncharacteristically short. Similar to House Report 2224, the Report produced by the Senate Committee on Public Lands in the 59th Congress followed a more comprehensive review of the issues raised in previous Congresses. Senate Report 3797 proclaimed unanimous Committee recommendation for the passage of S. 4698 and named other entities that had expressed to the Committee their support for S. 4698, including the Archaeological Institute of America, the American Anthropological Association and the Smithsonian Institution.

59th Congress: House Debate

The only debate during the 59th Congress occurred in the House prior to the passage of S. 4698 on June 5, 1906 when the bill was reported back from the House Committee on Public Lands. Centred on the issue of land as public domain, debate was brief and consensus was swift due to the prior discussion of the issues in Congress. At a time when the American people and legislators alike were wary of transferring authority away from the people and to the executive branch, many were opposed to the withdrawal of land from the public for forests or other reserves. This attitude contradicted, and frequently prevailed over, the recognition that there was a compelling need to protect the natural and cultural resources of the nation. This conflict was particularly salient in the West, where public land rights defined livelihood.[19] (For excellent insight into the tumultuous relationships between the Southwest and the East – the people, the institutions, the political agendas – from the 1890s onward see Snead 2001.)

Thus the brevity of debate in the 59th Congress (the Congress that enacted the Antiquities Act) on such a resounding matter clearly indicates previous Congressional focus on the subject. Nevertheless, the debate still symbolised the most enduring and poignant competing ideals that Congress had contended with prior to endorsement. Much of the opposition to bills that advocated the ideals and principles of what became the Antiquities Act was founded on the

59TH CONGRESS,	SENATE.	REPORT,
1st Session.		No. 3797

PRESERVATION OF AMERICAN ANTIQUITIES.

MAY 24, 1906.—Ordered to be printed.

MR. PATTERSON, from the Committee on Public Lands, submitted the following

REPORT.

[To accompany S. 4698.]

The Committee on Public Lands, to whom was referred the bill (S. 4698) for the preservation of American antiquities, having had the same under consideration, beg leave to report it back with the recommendation that the bill do pass.

This measure has the hearty support of the Archæological Institute of America, the American Anthropological Association, the Smithsonian Institution, and numerous museums throughout the country, and in view of the fact that the historic and prehistoric ruins and monuments on the public lands of the United States are rapidly being destroyed by parties who are gathering them as relics and for the use of museums and colleges, etc., your committee are of the opinion that their preservation is of great importance.

The bill is carefully drawn, and the committee are unanimously in favor of its passage.

Figure 4.6 Senate Report 3797

proclamation power granted to the President to remove vast amounts of land from the public domain. This issue, contentious even today, was downplayed in the House debate. On 5 June 1906, Representative Stephens (D-TX) expressed concern that S. 4698 would function in a similar manner to the forest reserve bill 'by which seventy or eighty million acres of land in the United States have been tied up' (House Congressional Record, June 5, 1906: 7888), and would consequently restrict public access and the ability to settle. Representative Lacey assured him that S. 4698 did not sanction the same latitude to restrict land but instead would

73

merely make small reservations [of land] where the objects are of sufficient interest to preserve them. The bill provides that it shall be the smallest area necesstry [sic] for the care and maintenance of the objects to be preserved ... It is to preserve these old objects of special interest and the Indian remains in the pueblos in the Southwest, whilst the other reserves the forests and the water courses.

(House Congressional Record, June 5, 1906: 7888)

After hearing Representative Lacey's reply, Representative Stephens stated that he had no objection to the passage of the bill. There were no objections when asked by the Speaker of the House,[20] so the bill passed the House of Representatives.

59th Congress: unpublished Congressional material

The unpublished Congressional material from the House and the Senate Committees on Public Lands during the 59th Congress relating to H.R. 11016 or S. 4698 includes drafts of bills and letters, statements, and resolutions sent by concerned parties. Since pillaging and destruction of archaeological sites were particularly devastating in the Southwest, much of the unpublished literature advocating the ideals and values of what became the Antiquities Act originated from this region. Constituent groups in Colorado that appealed to the House and Senate Committees on Public Lands during the 59th Congress included the Colorado Cliff Dwellers Association,[21] the Colorado Equal Suffrage Association the Pueblo Business Men's Association, the State Forestry Association and the State Horticultural Society. The letter from the Pueblo Business Men's Association (Figure 4.7) was written four months and six days before the Antiquities Act was passed. As with many other letters of its kind,[22] it called upon the government to reserve land in order to protect objects of the past. The Pueblo Business Men's Association specifically advocated that land be set aside in Mesa Verde, Colorado[23] to protect

relics of a long extinct type of civilization ... [since] [t]here is danger that these wonderful ruins which have attracted the attention of scholars from all over the world, through neglect and spoliation will suffer in their value to this country and also to the scientific world.

(unpublished Pueblo Business Men's Association letter,
February 2, 1906: 1)

The letters from the Colorado State Forestry Association and the Colorado State Horticultural Society called upon Congress to endorse H.R. 11016[24] and to safeguard Mesa Verde 'under the custodianship of the Government' (unpublished Colorado State Forestry Association letter, January 31, 1906: 1). These letters illustrate the

G. L. L. GANN, PRESIDENT.
J. A. BARCLAY VICE-PRESIDENT.

C. B. CRAWFORD, TREASURER.
E. W. PALMER, SECRETARY.

Pueblo Business Men's Association,

ROOMS 115, 116, 117, 118 CENTRAL BLOCK.

PUEBLO, COLORADO. Feb. 2, 1906.

BOARD OF DIRECTORS:
W. L. ANDERSON
J. A. BARCLAY
F. J. BURCH
P. BYRNES
C. B. CRAWFORD
C. W. CREWS
G. L. L. GANN
CHAS. E. GAST
W. F. GREER
F. S. HOAG
J. F. KEATING
GEO. E. KING
WM. E. MEAGHER
GEO. D. MESTON
J. E. PEAIRS
C. B. SCHMIDT
A. SONNEBORN

Senator H. M. Teller,

White House,

Washington, D. C.

Dear Sir:-

This is to certify that at a regular meeting of The Pueblo Business Men's Association held January 5, 1906, the following resolutions were unanimously adopted.

Whereas; There are in the Southwestern part of the State of Colorado, relics of a long extinct type of civilization known as the Cliff Dwellings of the Mesa Verde, and

Whereas; There is danger that these wonderful ruins which have attracted the attention of scholars from all over the world, through neglect and spoliation will suffer in their value to this country and also to the scientific world, therefore be it

Resolved; That the Pueblo Business Men's Association heartily favors and endorses the bill prepared by the Hon. Commissioner of the General Land Office, recommended by the Hon. Secretary of the Interior and introduced by the Hon. H. M. Hogg, a Representative from this State, setting aside a certain tract o land comprising a greater part of the ruins already referred to and known as the Mesa Verde National park and protecting it in the interest of Science and be it further

Resolved; That a copy of these resolutions be sent to Hon. Theodore Roosevelt, President of the U. S. , to Hon. Ethan Allen Hitchcock, Secretary of the Interior , to HOn. Wm A. Richards Commissioner of the General Land Office, to Hon. J. C. Cannon, Speaker of the House of Representatives, to Hon. Henry C. Hansborough, Chairman of the Public Lands Committee of the Senate, to Hon. John F. Lacy, Chairman of the Publid Lands Committee of the House of Representatives and to Colorado's Senators and Representatives in Congress at Washington,

Very truly,

The Pueblo Business Men's Ass'n,

By E. W. Palmer
Sec'y.

Figure 4.7 The Pueblo Business Men's Association, letter, February 2, 1906

grave apprehension on the part of public-spirited citizens that these far-famed ruins, through neglect or spoliation, may be deprived of their value, to the shame of the present generation, the guardians of our great State and Nation and to the bitter regret of posterity.

(unpublished Colorado State Forestry Association letter, January 31, 1906: 1)

In addition to this strong element of support in the Southwest, individuals, institutions and citizen groups all across the United States petitioned and lobbied Congress to enact change. The unpublished accounts of these original documents offer insight, in nuance and phrase, into the values and attitudes of those who advocated the legal protection and preservation of America's cultural terrain.

59th Congress: analysis and conclusion

The Antiquities Act was and remains a milestone in the American preservation movement. Yet the legal culmination of the ideals and values that anchor the law was long and arduous in the making. Paralleling the complex, protracted process of negotiation undertaken by countless statutes in navigating the United States legislature, the realisation of the Antiquities Act did not occur overnight. This landmark legislation coalesced from decades of debate as to how, or under what circumstances, archaeology warranted legal protection. Varied constituents championed divergent interests representing the social, cultural, political and economic spectra of the time. The dedication of various scholars, individual citizens, members of Congress, advocacy groups and intellectual societies was instrumental to the passage of the Antiquities Act. It is an historical examination of the law's immediate Congressional context that reveals the background of the significant issues critical at the legislative stage.

This methodology draws upon archival material to discuss the legislative history of the Antiquities Act. Such archival material – Congressional records, proceedings, Reports and Hearings, debate, and published and unpublished documents – attests to the societal milieu and temporal contextualisation of the law. Examining the legislative material from the 59th Congress not only focuses on the critical issues accorded consideration by the Congress that ratified the Antiquities Act but also underscores the manner in which such issues intersected to figure in the development of law. The enactment of S. 4698 completed a long succession of bills introduced in various Congresses over two decades in an effort to protect and preserve antiquities.[25] As with many bills that become law, prior bills that embodied similar ideas and convictions had originated in preceding Congresses.[26] The first of those bills that dealt with the ideals that were actualised in the 1906 Antiquities Act was introduced in 1882, during the 47th Congress, by Senator George F. Hoar (R-MA). After the embryonic concept was presented to Congress, it was nearly a quarter of a century before it came to fruition. From the 47th to the 59th Congress, bills were put forth intermittently by Congress members sympathetic to the preservation cause. Around the turn of the twentieth century, as the preservation ethic in American society deepened, so did the resolve of its advocates in Congress.

It was by 1906 that the circumstances of the American nation and its representatives in Congress were ready to embrace and champion the ideals of protection and preservation. Thus, in the 59th Congress, when S. 4698 was introduced, it possessed sufficient support to triumph over its opposition.[27] The snapshot of values captured within the legislative history of S. 4698, in tandem with that of H.R. 11016, provides significant testament to the ethos of the day and to the beginning of heritage preservation in the United States. It is the history of the Antiquities Act's heritage that encapsulates the interplay among knowledge, text and value, and thus documents how knowledge was produced and codified into law just over 100 years ago. Within this, the specific and fine-grained testimony of a rich primary documentation is the key to actual insight into how the Antiquities Act came to be created in the way it was, at the time it was. This methodological approach therefore explicates the legislative trajectory that moulded this first federal statute, which pioneered the legal regulation of archaeology and became the platform for subsequent archaeology laws.

Conclusion

Little, if any, debate exists within Heritage Studies that the past is a dynamic construct that changes over time. It is quite paradoxical therefore that the application of methodologies within the heritage paradigm has afforded negligible notice to the ways in which the historical record that documents, records and captures that past is also dynamic. There remains a dearth of methodological approaches that address the processes through which the history of heritage is manifested and encapsulated in the archival resource. The methods devised and applied to the historical dimension of heritage in this chapter concern the place and effect of law.

> Law is a phenomenon of culture and reflects norms of behavioral values ... held by the host culture. Law does not exist independently of those values. ... [It] is a social construct that reflects both modal values held by a population and the relative ordering of those values. Law ... tends to be directional and is a product of the disputes and problems presented to it historically.
>
> (Price 1991: 3, 116)

Law engages the past and as a constant regulatory apparatus not only provides a foundation for change but also serves to link the heritage of the past with that of the present. As a mechanism that temporally traces shifting conceptions of heritage, law offers a vital axis of articulation within the field of Heritage Studies. While '[m]anaging the cultural resources of the modern world takes place within many arenas, frameworks, or contexts ... [t]he cornerstone of cultural resource management, however, lies in a complex of government laws, policies, and implementing regulations' (Hardesty and Little 2000: 7). Just as understanding the role of law in contemporary society is essential, so too is understanding the place of law in the historical realm.[28] An examination of the history of legislation provides a window into the changing conceptions of what tangible and intangible vestiges of the past resources warrant protection and who has the legal standing to participate in that determination. As illustrated by the Antiquities Act, this methodological framework enabled the legislative history of an archaeology law to unfold by illuminating the contemporaneous values and attitudes that affected the context within which a bill successfully negotiated the legislative process. In so doing, this legal-historical approach based on the principle of 'archive as artefact' sheds light on why and how particular representations of the past are accorded a place in history.

In tracing the historiography of archaeology law, it is archival material as an historical resource that forms the foundation of this research methodology. Whereas the utilisation of archives as an historical resource and object of study is commonplace in the discipline of history, it is seldom a method employed in Heritage Studies or one that permeates the discourse of archaeology. This disciplinary demarcation is entrenched in, and perpetuated by, the methodological strictures governing each field. As a consequence, there is often an undue distance and disconnection between 'history' and 'prehistory'. Yet, in spite of this detachment, archival material and archaeological artefacts share many similarities as resources. Archives, like artefacts, are direct records of the past and as such bear witness to the materialisation of past knowledge. An archaeologist analysing an artefact endeavours to extract information about the past just as does the historian analysing text. Traditionally, archaeology has situated the written record (when available) to complement the information ascertained from the material remains recovered in the archaeological process – not as the primary archaeological record. Archaeology is the only discipline dedicated to the recovery, documentation, analysis and interpretation of the pre-recorded human past; the discipline does not depend on a written record. For historical times, the textual record routinely has been viewed as a supplement and not as the primary archaeological resource: translations of cuneiform, Egyptian hieroglyphics and Mayan glyphs and codices have complemented suppositions and conclusions made from the examination of physical finds and artefacts. In contrast, this methodology in the history of heritage contends that material remains are not always the primary element composing the archaeological record. The archaeological record is also captured in text. Therefore, while considering the legislative archive as archaeological artefact is underexplored and far from traditional in archaeology, it is precisely this concept of 'archive as artefact' that situates the written record as primary resource, as object of study and as *the* archaeological record that anchors this mode of enquiry.

This approach does not chart the evolving technical conventions of archaeology (its refinement of techniques of discovery and preservation), but instead considers archaeological study as a construct of laws and values that have attempted to specify how and by whom the material remains of past cultures are to be used and studied. The manner in which such value is ascribed to law, or to a corpus of law,[29] is captured in the construction of a legislative history (or legislative histories). This methodology therefore articulates the process through which the concept of heritage is expressed as well as how it is perpetuated in law.

Situating this legal-historical mode of enquiry within the domain of Heritage Studies analyzes the written text as the object of study, in order to extract information on the past that offers a new and kinetic perspective to an archival resource often viewed as static. If history 'is [a] constructed ... narrative, written and rewritten to suit the needs of the day' (Crawford 2000: 228), then legal texts capture a snapshot of a specific historical instance when the narrative was recorded and of the specific people who did or did not participate in that process. Thus the law provides a lens through which a historiographical heritage is brought to the forefront, and in turn through which the phenomenon of heritage can be historicised. The primary textual resource of the legislative archival material portrays the voices that have defined and redefined conceptions of heritage in the lawmaking process over time, as well as the ways in which such conceptions of heritage have been framed in legal classification. Chronicling the history of law governing archaeological heritage uncovers the historical associations that have culminated in the archaeology of today, and deepens understanding of the active influence infused by such associations in contemporary archaeological heritage.

Notes

1   Whereas archives as research resources and objects of study are elemental to the discipline of history and entrenched in the historical narrative, these primary sources are underexplored in Heritage Studies.
2   In this context, I recognise the seminal work on archaeology, value and the law introduced in the heritage discourse by John Carman in *Valuing Ancient Things: Archaeology and Law* (1996), both as an ideological point of departure and as work that formed the aperture necessary for my own. Through an examination of English law, Carman 'carrie[d] out the first detailed contextual study anywhere of the rise of archaeological preservation legislation, the ideology represented by that legislation, and the manner in which that legislation affects archaeology ... His work was the first effective counterblast to those critics of archaeological heritage management who seek to dismiss it as trivial or dysfunctional' (Carman 1996: viii–ix). In so doing, Carman's research on heritage law broke new ground within the discipline of archaeology. By demonstrating how heritage law can be analysed as text in order to determine its role in defining heritage, Carman identified three key ways in which the law defines heritage objects: selection, categorisation and ascription of value.
3   Aspects of the Congressional system not found in this overview include special resolutions, instances of special privilege, recess authority, motion to discharge a bill, motion to suspend the rules, special circumstances arising in matters of national security, the particulars of voting methods, and reasons for conferences and the significance of conference reports. Similarly, neither the rules and regulations pertaining to the legislative calendars that administer Congressional proceedings (there are five calendars in the House and two in the Senate) nor the role of the Government Printing Office and the Congressional Budget Office in determining how revenue is distributed and the expenditure level allowed to maintain a balanced budget is covered. A detailed account of these procedures, among others, is offered by Charles W. Johnson III in the revised and updated 2000 edition of *How Our Laws Are Made*. See also Brown 1996; Cannon 1920; Deschler 2002; Deschler and Brown 1982; Dove 1997; Hinds 1907; Schneider 1999.
4   Officially adopted on March 4, 1789, the United States Constitution is the oldest written constitution in effect, due predominantly to its simple and flexible framework.
5   In addition to the federal government, there are state and local governments with corresponding jurisdictional authority. Native American Tribes also administer sovereign governments.

6   In addition, Committee Reports can include any relevant executive communications and supplemental information or minority viewpoints submitted by any Committee member(s) within a specified timeframe. An estimated cost assessment of the bill's implementation prepared by the Committee or by the Congressional Budget Office can also accompany a Committee Report.

7   Within the Congressional Committee, the command of the Chair is significant and determinative in whether or not a bill will be considered, given further attention in the form of a Report and/or Hearing, or will be reported out of Committee. These are all decisive steps in the continuation (or termination) of a bill. With the support of the Committee Chair, it is highly unlikely that a bill will 'die' in Committee.

8   Once again, the methodological framework is applied to the United States context. The templates are devised in a manner conducive to apply the legal-historical methodology to this specific system of law. Yet, as previously noted, this does not preclude the ability to transfer or apply the spirit of the approach to other modes of governance (with legislative systems that also produce a written record/legislative archive).

9   These templates display the precise course of *all* germane bills introduced during the Congress that enacted law, not just *the* bill that became law. Because only one bill can become law, all other kindred bills introduced in the same Congress (or, if applicable, in prior Congress(es)) 'die' at some point in the legislative process. Hence, an examination of the templates explicates exactly where and how each bill terminated and offers a wealth of information regarding the bill that became law as well as the bills that 'died.'

10 Given that there is nothing certain or consistent in the legislative history of a law (besides the introduction and subsequent Committee referral), there is no 'representative' template as such. For an example of a Legislative History Chronological Compilation refer to Figure 4.4, which delineates the Legislative History Chronological Compilation for the 1906 Antiquities Act.

11 Whereas the breadth and scope of archival text vary for each piece of proposed legislation, there is virtually always exponentially more material produced by those of more recent time than for those of an earlier date. For instance, bills that became law in the early twentieth century have a modest written record compared to those of the early twenty-first century. (The disproportionate amounts of generated material cannot be attributed to preservation/ conservation shortcomings – which would pertain only to the unpublished literature – but to the vast degrees of difference in the paper trail resulting from the legislative process.) In terms of law governing America's archaeology, the sheer volume of archival documents produced for the 1906 Antiquities Act and the 1916 National Park Organic Act is dwarfed in comparison to that produced for the 1979 Archaeological Resource Protection Act and the 1990 Native American Graves Protection and Repatriation Act. Thus, while the selection of text from an archival corpus poses a methodological challenge regardless of the extent or type of material, it generally is a more elaborate undertaking to synthesise material from more recent statutes.

12 In 1906, the law accorded protection to 'objects of antiquity' or relics of the past prized for their scientific value and potential. Native American human remains were encompassed within this terminology and were considered no different from other artefacts. The contents of Native American graves legally became federal property to be held in perpetuity in public repositories at the discretion of the federal government. This legacy of the Act, seldom considered, persisted for many decades. 'Beginning with the passage of the Antiquities Act in 1906, archaeologists (perhaps unintentionally) began to co-opt the American Indian's unwritten history and material culture. The United States government deemed archaeological and historical sites of past cultures in the United States as worthy of protection for the benefit of the public, but it ultimately developed a permit system that centred protection of the past within the scientific community rather than in the hands of those whose ancestors were responsible for its creation' (Watkins 2003: 275).

13 The letters within parentheses that follow the name of a member of Congress denote first political party affiliation (R stands for Republican and D for Democrat) and then state or

possession of representation (the two-letter abbreviation adheres to the standardised format used by the United States Post Office). For instance, Representative Lacey was a Republican who represented the state of Iowa.

14 In the enactment of the Antiquities Act, there was a great deal of Congressional action during the 58th Congress that helped set the stage for the support in the 59th Congress for the bill that became the Antiquities Act. Since the Congressional material of the 59th Congress makes direct reference to the written records of the immediately preceding Congress, these archival documents provide meaningful supplemental information.

15 Professor Edgar Lee Hewett's 'Memorandum Concerning the Historic and Prehistoric Ruins of Arizona, New Mexico, Colorado, and Utah, and their Preservation' was included in multiple places in the legislative process. It was initially published in 1904 by the United States Government Printing Office as a Circular Relating to Historic and Prehistoric Ruins of the Southwest and their Preservation, which included a preface of two letters: the first dated October 1, 1904 written by W. A. Richards, Commissioner of the General Land Office to the Secretary of the Interior, and the second dated September 3, 1904 written by Edgar Lee Hewett to W. A. Richards. This original publication included an accompanying map (Figure 4.5) and illustrative photographs (no trace remains of the latter). Hewett's memorandum, along with his September 3, 1904 introductory letter, were also included as appendices in two Congressional Committee documents during the 58th Congress: House Report 3704 and the January 11, 1905 House Published Hearing.

16 The advocacy and skilful negotiations of Edgar Lee Hewett, a staunch proponent of antiquities legislation, were instrumental in the realisation of the Antiquities Act.

17 In efforts to safeguard archaeological resources, preservation advocates adroitly maximised the opportunity for success by pursuing their objectives in more than one direction. The call for protective legislation at the federal level was frequently joined by the entreaty to establish National Parks to afford protection for particular areas under siege from looting, vandalism, mediocre and incomprehensive excavation, and overall disregard. Before the National Park Organic Act was codified on August 25, 1916, National Parks and other protected areas, such as National Monuments, were created by singular acts of Congress or by executive proclamations – a piecemeal process that resulted in protected isolated 'islands' throughout the country without uniform administration or funding. (See Carroll 1920 for a discussion of America's earliest National Monuments.) Consequently, prior to the 1916 National Park Organic Act and before the Antiquities Act in 1906 accorded protection at the federal level, it was not uncommon for those active in the preservation movement to propose protection for archaeological sites through National Park designation as well as through a protective federal statute. The history of Mesa Verde, Colorado exemplifies this association well. (McClurg 1930).

18 In the September 3, 1904 letter that prefaced his memorandum, Hewett outlined the sources from which he gathered information and acknowledged the input received from knowledgeable specialists. The contributions of Dr Jesse Walter Fewkes of the Bureau of American Ethnology, Dr Walter Hough of the National Museum, Mr A. F. Bandelier of the American Museum of Natural History and Mr S. J. Holsinger were specifically noted.

19 Arguments of public versus private rights to land and the withdrawal of land from the public domain erupted in Congress with vehemence during the early 1900s. Tension and discord, deeply embedded in the contentious grazing rights issue, triggered major Congressional debate preceding both the 1906 Antiquities Act and the 1916 National Park Service Organic Act.

20 The Speaker of the House is usually the senior member of the majority party and is elected by the House members to serve as the Presiding Officer of the House of Representatives.

21 Founded by journalist Virginia McClurg (1857–1931), the Colorado Cliff Dwellers Association (CCDA) was one of many women's clubs established by middle- and upper-class women throughout the nation to effect change in society through community involvement. Their national platforms, predicated on philanthropic causes and/or the need for legislative reform, advocated mainly welfare, education, public health and other similar humanitarian

services. In Colorado, although women's clubs did not emerge until the early 1880s, these societies espoused the same ideals set forth in the national agenda in addition to activity on the state and local level in 'the preservation and restoration of prehistoric ruins in south-western Colorado' (Beaton 1992: 4).

22 It was common in the 59th Congress for correspondence filed with the Committee on Public Lands to have been copied to all relevant governmental representatives. Letters written by the Pueblo Business Men's Association, the Colorado State Forestry Association and the Colorado State Horticultural Society were copied to the Speaker of the House of Representatives, the Chairs of the Senate and House Committees on Public Lands as well as to all Colorado Congressional representatives. During the 59th Congress, 1st Session, the Speaker of the House of Representatives was Joseph G. Cannon (R-IL), the Chair of the Senate Committee on Public Lands was Senator Henry C. Hansbrough (R-ND) and the Chair of the House Committee on Public Lands was Representative John F. Lacey (R-IA). The Senators from Colorado were Thomas M. Patterson (D-CO) of Denver and Henry M. Teller (D-CO) of Central City. The Representatives from Colorado were Robert W. Bonynge (R-CO) of Denver, Franklin E. Brooks (R-CO) of Colorado Springs and Herschel M. Hogg (R-CO) of Telluride.

23 Located in the isolated south-west corner of Colorado, the archaeological site of Mesa Verde is inextricably linked to the making of the 1906 Antiquities Act. Native Americans occupied the region for more than 1,000 years (from approximately AD 100 to AD 1300) and left the largest, most comprehensive and well-preserved assemblages of cliff dwellings in North America e.g., among many, Arnold 1992; Fewkes 1909, 1911, 1920; Fiero 1988; Nordenskiöld 1893). As evident from the legislative archival material, the Mesa Verde cliff dwellings figured prominently in the American preservation movement, recognised as being 'unique in character and unsurpassed in many ways by any of their kind in the known world, attracting the attention and study of travelers, historians, and ethnologists from every continent' (unpublished Colorado State Forestry Association letter, January 31, 1906: 1). This distinctive quality of Mesa Verde not only has permeated its own history but also has proven a decisive factor in the initial protection of archaeology (Bauer 1991; McNitt 1966; Nordenskiöld 1893). Preservationists, archaeologists, citizen groups and others harnessed the renown of Mesa Verde in conjunction with the exponential increase in the looting of the site with resultant destruction of the archaeological resource as a rationale in the justification for establishing protective legislation. The ideals and attitudes embraced by Progressives and preservation campaign constituents who advocated for the Antiquities Act were aligned with those who supported legislation to protect Mesa Verde itself in the form of a National Park. (See Hays 1999 for a detailed account of the Progressive philosophy and its influential role in the American conservation movement.) As a result, bills were put forth both stipulating the protection of the Mesa Verde environs through National Park status and providing for the legal protection of antiquities. Bills that related to the Antiquities Act or to Mesa Verde frequently were linked both in the legislative process and in the literature produced by those in favour of protection. In fact, the bills that supported these ideals were passed into law within the same month of the 59th Congress. Following the codification of the Antiquities Act on June 8, 1906, the 59th Congress established the Mesa Verde National Park on June 29, 1906, conferring official protection to Mesa Verde through both statutes.

24 At the time these letters were written (on January 31, 1906 and February 1, 1906 respectively) only H.R. 11016, which was introduced in the House on January 9, 1906 by Representative John F. Lacey (R-IA), was under Congressional purview. S. 4698 was not introduced in the Senate until February 26, 1906 by Senator Thomas Patterson (D-CO).

25 A thorough account of the legislative activity that preceded the 59th Congress in 1906 is covered by Raymond H. Thompson in a 2000 special issue of the *Journal of the Southwest* that updates and supplements the history of the Antiquities Act written by Ronald F. Lee, originally published in 1970 by the United States National Park Service (Thompson 2000).

26 This chapter discusses the application of the method in the history of heritage in terms of how it pertains to the enacting Congress – the most critical and indispensable Congressional setting

– for one statute. Alternatively, this methodology can accommodate charting the legislative history for all germane bills prior to the one which was enacted. Materials reviewed utilising the methodological approach in this manner can provide a very thorough and comprehensive representation of how the values underpinning a statute have developed over time.

27 As demonstrated in the legislative history of the Act, by 1906 resistance to the measure principally centred on the basis that it granted excessive control to the federal government to withdraw vast amounts of land for non-commercial use. By 1906, disagreement focused not on the necessity of protective legislation, but rather on the language best defining such protection: it was the *how*, not the *why*, which was the point of contention.

28 Constructing a legislative history offers insights into the purpose for and context from which law arose, was crafted and ultimately was codified. This information additionally can assist in gauging legislative intent, which can be used by the judiciary in the interpretation of law.

29 By further expanding the frame of analysis from one focused on individual and more temporally encapsulated pieces of legislation to one premised on a greater timeframe of legislation enacted to regulate and protect archaeology, a fuller understanding of the emergence, development and complexities of the concept of heritage is possible. A chronological synthesis of legislative histories accordingly offers the temporal contextualisation necessary to delve into how the relationships among law, archaeology and history engender heritage in historical and contemporary contexts, and how heritage in turn rebounds on archaeology, history and law. The 'archive as artefact' thus considers the socio-legal construction of archaeological heritage from both a historical and a contemporary perspective.

Bibliography

Arnold, C. (1992) *The Ancient Cliff Dwellers of Mesa Verde*, New York: Clarion Books.

Bauer, F. (1991) *Gustaf Nordenskjöld: Pioneer Archaeologist of Mesa Verde*, Mesa Verde National Park, CO: Mesa Verde Museum Association.

Beaton, G. M. (1992) 'The widening sphere of women's lives: the literary study and philanthropic work of six women's clubs in Denver, 1881–1945', *Essays and Monographs in Colorado History* 13, 1–68.

Brown, W. II. (1996) *House Practice: a Guide to the Rules, Precedents, and Procedures of the House*, Washington, DC: Government Printing Office.

Carman, R. J. (1996) *Valuing Ancient Things: Archaeology and Law*, London: Leicester University Press.

Carroll, M. (1920) 'The Story of our National Monuments: Historical Introduction' *Art and Archaeology* 10(1–2), 3–6.

Crawford, S. J. (2000) '(Re)Constructing Bodies: Semiotic Sovereignty and the Debate over Kennewick Man', in D. A. Mihesuah (ed.) *Repatriation Reader: Who Owns American Indian Remains?*, Lincoln: University of Nebraska Press, 211–36.

Deschler, L. (1977–2002) *Deschler's Precedents of the United States House of Representatives: including References to Provisions of the Constitution and Laws, and to Decisions of the Courts*, Washington, DC: Government Printing Office.

Deschler, L. and W. H. Brown (1982) *Procedure in the US House of Representatives, 97th Congress: a Summary of the Modern Precedents and Practices of the House, 86th Congress–97th Congress*, Washington, DC: Government Printing Office.

Dove, R. B. (1997) *Enactment of a Law*, Washington, DC: US Senate, http://thomas.loc.gov/home/enactment/enactlawtoc.html (accessed 11 February 2007).

Fewkes, J. W. (1909) *Antiquities of the Mesa Verde National Park, Spruce-tree House (Bulletin 41)*, Bureau of American Ethnology, Smithsonian Institution, Washington, DC: Government Printing Office.

—— (1911) *Antiquities of the Mesa Verde National Park, Cliff Palace (Bulletin 51)*, Bureau of American Ethnology, Smithsonian Institution, Washington, DC: Government Printing Office.

—— (1920) 'The story of our National Monuments: New Fire House, a ruin lately excavated in the Mesa Verde' *Art and Archaeology*, 10(1–2), 44–46.

Fiero, K. (1998) *Balcony House: a History of a Cliff, Mesa Verde National Park, Colorado*, Mesa Verde National Park, CO: Mesa Verde Museum Association in association with the National Park Service, US Department of the Interior.

Hardesty, D. L. and B. J. Little (2000) *Assessing Site Significance: A Guide for Archaeologists and Historians*, Walnut Creek, CA: AltaMira Press.

Hewett, E. L. (1904) *Circular Relating to Historic and Prehistoric Ruins of the Southwest and their Preservation*, Washington, DC: Government Printing Office.

Hinds, A. C. (1907) *Hinds' Precedents of the House of Representatives of the United States, including References to Provisions of the Constitution, the Laws, and Decisions of the United States Senate*, Washington, DC: Government Printing Office.

Johnson, C. W., III (2000) *How our Laws are Made*, rev. edn, Washington, DC: Government Printing Office.

Lee, R. F. (1970) *The Antiquities Act of 1906*, Washington, DC: National Park Service, Office of History and Historic Architecture, Eastern Service Center.

McClurg, V. (1930) 'The Making of Mesa Verde into a National Park', *The Colorado Magazine* 7(6), 216–219.

McNitt, F. (1966) *Richard Wetherill: Anasazi*. Albuquerque: University of New Mexico Press.

Nordenskiöld, G. (1893) *The Cliff Dwellers of the Mesa Verde, Southwestern Colorado; their Pottery and Implements* (D. L. Morgan, trans), Stockholm: P. A. Norstedt and Söner.

Price, H. M., III (1991) *Disputing the Dead: US Law on Aboriginal Remains and Grave Goods*, Columbia: University of Missouri Press.

Schneider, J. (1990) *House Rules Manual*, Washington, DC: Congressional Research Service, Library of Congress.

Thompson, R. H. (2000) 'Edgar Lee Hewett and the Political Process', *Journal of the Southwest* 42.2, 273–318.

Watkins, J. E. (2003) 'Beyond the Margin: American Indians, First Nations, and Archaeology in North America', *American Antiquity* 68.2, 273–85.

Archival materials

Congressional Record, 59th Congress, 1st Session: 4 December 1905 to 30 June 1906.

House Report 2224 at 1–8, *Preservation of American Antiquities (March 12, 1906)*, House Committee on Public Lands, 59th Congress (1906).

House Report 3704 at 1–10, *Prehistoric Ruins on Public Lands (January 19, 1905)*. House Committee on Public Lands, 58th Congress (1905).

Preservation of Prehistoric Ruins on the Public Lands, (Published) Hearing before the Committee on Public Lands, House of Representatives, 58th Congress, 1 (January 11, 1905).

Senate Report 3797 at 1, *Preservation of American Antiquities (May 24, 1906)*, Senate Committee on Public Lands, 59th Congress (1906).

Unpublished Committee Material, Senate Committee on Public Lands, 59th Congress (1906):
Pueblo Business Men's Association, letter of 2 February 1906 to Senator H. M. Teller.
Colorado Equal Suffrage Association, letter of 2 February 1906.
Colorado State Forestry Association, letter of 31 January 1906.
Colorado State Horticultural Society, letter of 1 February 1906.

5

MEANS MAKETH THE END

The context for the development of methodologies to assess the state of the historic environment in the UK

Ian Baxter

Introduction

The role of management within the heritage sector has changed over the past two decades as heritage itself has increasingly been recognised as playing a key role in many crosscutting societal, economic and political arenas. The management of heritage as a resource, a force and a concept has adapted from a traditional administrative paradigm (based on legalistic notions of protection and status within society and space) towards a new public management strategic paradigm, recognising competing stakeholders, product ranges, impacts and alternative models of service provision. At the heart of this change is a greater appreciation of the kinds of relationships, understandings and knowledge we have about heritage, as both a conceptual entity and a set of processes. More fundamentally for the realm of heritage knowledge, the paradigm shift has brought about a growing appreciation of what management of heritage does, rather than what we know *per se* about heritage. This was prompted by the changing ideals of public service (and thus public and governmental management of heritage assets) and has been greatly assisted by the development of methodologies for assessing the state of the historic environment (or heritage resource, see Baxter 2004 for a review of the changing terminology of heritage management). The notion of 'audit', as applied to heritage in England since 2002 with the launch of the 'State of the Historic Environment Report', has not only fulfilled a need for greater public accountability for how taxpayers' money is spent on heritage, but has also begun to bridge the 'old' and 'new' forms of public management of heritage and, more widely, cultural resources. Audit as a mechanism has thus begun to measure what has been achieved by management and additionally to understand what else may be required. In line with these changes, it has become necessary to investigate new facets of the construction of heritage, including the management system itself. This calls for the recognition of a new range of concerns and questions, and concomitant with that searching for new data and developing new methods of analysis. This chapter reflects on how we may analyse these changing circumstances in the management of heritage with particular attention to how we use the concept of heritage auditing to analyse change and impact. It looks at these issues through the specific managerial implications that the devolution of the political/cultural power base in the United Kingdom had for the development of a heritage auditing programme within Scotland. While the data and procedures are specific to England and Scotland, the importance of managerial paradigms and of understanding the roles and methods of audit are of wide general relevance for heritage.

Identifying new concerns: the relationships of heritage and culture in a devolved nation

The change in the political colour of the UK central government in the late 1990s (from Conservative to 'New' Labour), and the bringing about of large-scale devolution of political powers for the UK's nations (the devolution of Wales and Scotland from the United Kingdom), brought the culture of these 'nations', and the management and promotion of their cultures, into the public agenda. Culture, and, within its ambit, heritage, while perhaps the most readily devolved area of political responsibility in administrative terms, is of particular importance to the successful growth and development of devolved areas for a myriad of reasons – not least the politics of identity. Devolution and articulation of cultural identity are intimately linked, evident by the immediate appointment and creation of ministerial posts with cultural responsibility, and major reviews of cultural policies, being instigated in the devolved countries. Scanning cultural policy statements, it can be clearly seen that the heritage's role within the politics of cultural identity and devolution was to provide a firm cultural context, community and physical manifestation of history and a sense of place for the emergent nations within the greater whole of the United Kingdom. There is an abundance of data to show how political and media rhetoric, aspirant articulation of ideals, assertion of status and reflection on history followed the devolution in Scotland in public and professional fora, bringing with it unsaid expectations of the new status that heritage had attained.

Changing relationships between people and their cultures, and governments and their cultural responsibilities, form a subset within the wider global context of quickening cultural change brought about by the forces of globalisation (chapters in Held 2004). These wider competing forces of globalisation and localisation have produced an intersection of fundamental importance for the management and administration of culture and heritage, as the 'experience economy' has developed as the fourth stage of economic change from production to service-based industries (Pine 1999). Scotland, in particular, has seen widespread decline in its once-prevalent production industries, affecting areas from ship-building and engineering to mining and fishing. The country, via public reinvestment and regeneration, has grown its service-based facilities, with the establishment of financial districts in the major cities of Edinburgh and Glasgow, and investment in high-tech facilities in areas such as 'Silicon Glen'. However, great investment and return has also been seen in the focused construction of Scotland as a product and brand – particularly in the form of a tourist location (McCrone et al. 1999) – and its tourist industry has over the past two decades been in competition for the most important industry in Scotland, in terms of Gross Domestic Product and, indeed, global recognition (VisitScotland 2007). Devolution has added to the pace of and desire for this development as a key contribution to Scotland's successful future (Keating 2005). Culture and heritage are major drivers in the Scottish tourism industry, in terms of both motivation to visit the country and actual visitor numbers to sites and attractions by international and domestic tourists, and thus are a major source of economic input for heritage and the wider historic environment of Scotland (VisitScotland/Moffat Centre for Travel and Tourism Business Development 2007). The drivers for the industry to produce unique and authentic experiences fit the wider aspirations for the country's heritage as perceived by the political paymasters at the time of devolution, creating a mix of motivation for developing heritage and cultural relationships in Scotland. It has also resulted in greater public interest and consequentially scrutiny of how and why heritage is managed in the way that it is.

Environmental scanning: the heritage-sector business environment

Where commonality in the broad philosophies and practices of heritage management can be identified as a 'sector', that sector's wider 'environment', in terms of its relationships and influences, needs to be clearly understood. The needs for contextualisation and for establishing the context of managerial practice and its relationships to its business environment are captured by the standard strategic management tool of environmental scanning. This can be used to place heritage in a broadly based 'business' context. Part of that business context influencing the growth in interest in heritage management in Scotland has already been outlined above. Such interest, of course, has equally applied to the continuing (albeit reconfigured) management of the sector within England, and many other areas, but in order to more fully understand the changing business (environmental) context for heritage we need to more readily examine business-sector relationships (public as well as private) that it is a part of in order to identify and define influences and drivers of change in our way of doing things in heritage. Since the creation of a dedicated UK government Ministry for Culture (the Department for Culture, Media & Sport/ DCMS), the cultural and creative industries have coalesced into distinct sectors identified through a combination of internal and external drivers or pressures, strategic direction, their own competitive and collaborative environment, and the market and policy forces driving change in their management and offerings (DCMS 2006a). As distinct sectors, the cultural industries' umbrella has grown to formulate distinctive identities for sectors such as heritage/historic environment, architecture, museums and galleries, tourism, sport and so on. This formulation has seen its own devolved versions within the different nations, and it is therefore the general principles and effects of this formulation that are important here for how we develop methods for the analysis of heritage. In short, there are some generic premises for change within the business of heritage which are important to understand as management 'process'; but there are also unique business-process characteristics which may be defined (in our case) on a geopolitical basis giving rise to distinct types and philosophies of heritage management.

Two key principles have affected development of cultural organisations across the sector and their corporate management. First, competition, meaning that cultural organisations have had to quickly implement or demonstrate best value where it is based on public support in the form of subsidy, and also recognise that under high-level policy direction any particular organisational model should not necessarily be supported as the only delivery vehicle for that service. Competitors, collaborators and alternative/new forms of service have also had to be built into the management strategies for cultural organisations (including heritage). In particular, this has required an internal management shift towards a commercially and competitively competent organisation with core business available to it all the time. Second, a key principle of single-funding streams from governments to cultural organisations has given way to a requirement for organisations to diversify their funding base, partly due to a sustained year-on-year real-cost reduction in direct grants from the public purse. Accounting models that can cope with activities managed and costed on a project basis, and the requirement for performance information to support fund-raising from multiple sources, have also further pushed the development of management information systems within individual organisations (Flynn 2007).

This change in both the internal and external requirements for knowledge and data, in actual fact a greater *understanding* of organisational roles, has been charted across the cultural sector. This should not be seen as a surprising change in the internal and external operational environment, but should be understood as reflecting different kinds of change and perception, as both the policy context and the audience expectation have shifted with great pace. In effect, what can be proposed is that in the past decade, particularly, a combination of economic, social, political and cultural pressures have together produced a requirement for a new set of management paradigms wherein cultural organisations have needed to rethink their roles, activities and implementations faster than ever before (Flynn 2007).

The classic management tool of environmental scanning (mentioned already as a strategic management 'toolkit' for establishing business relationships, influences and drivers, including allies and competitors) shows a similar situation for other comparable cultural sub-sectors and industries, although there are different speeds of change evident within each. Depending on circumstance, these similar drivers of change produce the opportunity and threat of both convergence and competition in aim and approach. This in itself is a further reinforcement of the need for effective and efficient management (the generic term for the 'tools' used to effect change). Perhaps the largest changes have been seen in the fields of sustainability and environment, where, allied to heritage (in the form of natural heritage), we have seen a move to landscape approaches to analysis and management, processes of characterisation, and the requirement for the principles of sustainability to be applied in both provision and consumption of natural heritage products, places and services. Greater linkages have also been made between environment and heritage, both in conceptual understanding and in practical management situations. This is exemplified in the revitalised work of British Waterways in its stewardship and development of the canal and waterways system of Britain (British Waterways 2002; Fairclough and Symonds 1999).

Elsewhere, the arts sector has seen debate over the past five years on the role and relevance of traditional and non-traditional art forms, changing expectations and needs for audiences, opportunities for social wellbeing and health, and the desire to form greater linkages and deliver wider benefits using artistic practices and outlooks. Particularly in the last couple of years, high-level statements (Purnell 2007) outlining new policy direction and aspiration have led to the national public agency supporting the arts to encourage national debate on the arts and its value (Bunting 2007). The debate has attempted to establish the role of the arts and perceptions of it as a sector both within the industry and externally for its users and non-users. At the same time, peer review has been undertaken at national and regional levels to gauge a socio-political understanding of arts and public funding (Bunting 2007).

In the museums and galleries sector, a continuing shift in the philosophy of collecting and presenting items of material culture has also led to renewed debate on the role of the museum and the needs of user groups. Perhaps unsurprisingly, the educative rather than the leisure role of museums and galleries has come under pressure. Greater expectations have also been placed on institutions receiving public money based on their performance in widening their audiences and activities – often played out through the funding agreements and targets negotiated between the funding ministry and the recipient (DCMS 2006b). As a result, methods for measuring performance are being developed. Public engagement with museums and galleries at a local level has, for example, been measured through the programme of local performance indicators (a set of published measures, often agreed across common policy themes or organisational geographic areas of responsibility to establish whether outputs are meeting the aims and objectives: in essence, a results table). 'Engagement' as a policy theme derived from government and aimed at increasing participation of targeted sub-sectors of communities in aspects of public service provision (such as ethnic minorities' or disadvantaged socio-economic groups' use of cultural services) has also begun to be measured at a national level: this has been done via the large-scale socio-cultural 'Taking Part' survey commissioned by the Department for Culture, Media and Sport (DCMS and Office of National Statistics 2007).

Another major comparable sector is that of the built environment, and over the past decade we have seen a number of agendas driven by the recognition of the importance of place management and understanding the effect of spaces and places on communities. Governmental organisations such as the Commission for Architecture and the Built Environment (CABE, in England) and Architecture and Design Scotland have overlapped with the traditional realms of heritage in developing the conceptual understanding of townscapes and streetscapes, 'liveable places', and the form and function of public buildings (CABE and HM Government 2006). The spaces between buildings have not been forgotten either, through shared developments between architecture, planning and heritage bodies in the realms of public park improvements, street management strategies, and demystifying and democratising design processes. Revisions and renewal of processes within the planning system have also been instigated, and review has begun of the system of designation and protection of heritage assets and places. The planning system's aspiration to put planning at the heart of community development – simplifying proce-dures, encouraging greater community and stakeholder input, and the move to e-planning applications and monitoring – has further altered the infor-mation requirements and understandings of places, place-making and the processes of change within the built environment. From these broadening approaches to place and space, not only is new data being produced, but focus is also placed on new ways of interlinking and interpreting data from different themes (e.g. attitudes to risk and the use of public space; impacts of archi-tecture and design on health).

An overarching context for all of the above sectors is the new economic 'industry', which in the UK has been produced by a decade of National Lottery support for culture, heritage, the arts, natural environments and community development. This benefactor, financially the largest supporter, has changed the face of cultural and heritage aspiration and management (Heritage Lottery Fund 2006). A wealth of new requirements and expectations for strategic planning and project management needed to access lottery funding has accordingly impacted on the sector in a significant manner, bringing with it new and wider skills requirements, professional processes and competencies, and again broadening knowledge requirement and production. This has impacted the field of heritage, as the number and range of projects can be collated in databases, and systematic or targeted analyses of the funding and its impact can be conducted, opening up new avenues for heritage research (e.g. Paul Drury Partnership 2007).

Evolution of regional approaches: divergence and continuity

Against the background boldly stated above, the new context for the heritage sector in both England and Scotland brought drivers with a pace of change that the long-established sector had to adapt to in order not to be left behind. As already noted, these changes were spurred in part by the heritage sector realising that its image was tarnished by class connotations, poor service and experiences that were less than engaging, and a lack of transparency in terms of management procedures and impacts and use of public resources. The heritage sector was articulating continual concern that it was unappreciated and did not register on any political radar despite its own perception of importance. The environmental sector, in contrast, having embraced the concept of 'sustainability', had facts and figures available as well as effective advocacy. Indeed, closer to home, the museums sector had embraced change and through its revitalised education and accessibility missions was featuring in policy circles (via both rhetoric and documentation) (Travers 2006). In Scotland, a clear message that the heritage sector needed to get its act together to articulate clearly its own value and its value to others had been sent to the sector in the early stages of the post-devolution period. England had already gone through a similar process as questions were asked about the relationship between politics, funding and an effective sector which could produce clear advocacy messages; the government was pushing the heritage sector to fulfil its potential role according to evidence-based policy-making. Analysing public debates and documents, one can follow the development of this concern. English Heritage commissioned a MORI poll in 2000, as the government began to review its policies for the historic environment, and this was used to demonstrate that heritage mattered to all sections of society, making it vital to address the mixture of perceptions and misconceptions about the sector. In the document *Power of Place* (English Heritage 2000) which followed the poll, the sector published a review of its future. In 2001 English Heritage endorsed the government policy statement in *A Force for Our Future* (Department for Culture, Media and Sport, Architecture and Historic Environment Division 2001), calling for the publication of regular 'State of the Historic Environment' reports by the sector (coordinated by English Heritage) in order to address an information deficit that undermined effective management. One may identify this as the introduction of an explicit audit culture – an explicit methodological change for the sector allowing transparency and comparison in judgement of stated aims and objectives both externally imposed as a public duty for funding support, and internally set as part of organisational strategy. The implicit comparison may be made between private shareholders in an organisation and public stakeholders in a public service-delivery institution.

The first State of the Historic Environment Report (subsequently renamed *Heritage Counts*) was published in 2002, and has been published annually since then (English Heritage and Historic Environment Review Executive Committee 2007). Its evolution from an earlier tourism-focused analysis of heritage management has been considered elsewhere (Baxter 2003), and the rolling programme of reporting performance against indicators and thematic reviews of issues (such as skills, rural communities, volunteering) as they affect the management and protection of heritage in England is now well established.

The establishment of a basis for regularised management information on which broader policy linkages across crosscutting government issues can be built fills a key policy gap for the heritage in terms of articulating its own management and philosophies better. This furthermore creates transparency in application of public investment, and allows commonalities across geopolitical/economic borders to be identified at the same time as it reinforces regionally, demographically or thematically potential solutions or approaches.

Building value via the evidence base

The debate in policy, political, public and organisational contexts on the role, effective protection and provision of heritage services in all their forms has at its heart the concept of value. This is a vital consideration to achieve effective results for investment (not just economic) on the part of communities, in an arena of competing concerns and demands. As an idea, value has been debated in recent years across various parts of the cultural sector, and from different perspectives. A concept with overtly economic connotations has foreseeable application and attractiveness in a business (market-economy) context: for example, establishment of the economic value of cultural objects, and the economic impact of cultural activities in many circumstances, and attention which heritage-specific contexts receive are no exception to this (Snowball 2007; Towse 2003). However, a broader socio-cultural understanding of value has drawn on ideas of cultural capital, as discussed originally by Bourdieu (1984). A contemporary understanding of value as developed and applied within the cultural sphere over the past decade has accordingly, in addition to economic value, considered ideas such as community values, psychological values, and other intangible and tangible benefits that may be gained from involvement in activities deemed to be cultural. Within the particular geopolitical context of devolution within Scotland it becomes clear that further weight is also attached to the value of the institution of government at a devolved level.

The policy-process angle within the values debate lies within the move, already noted, from an administrative to a strategic management paradigm in public services. In the UK (including Scotland) the integral requirement of evidence to develop and test policy has been laid out in *The Green Book: Appraisal and Evaluation in Central Government* (HM Treasury 2003). This document formally sets the framework for testing public value as understood by government where it needs to prioritise spending of tax revenues. It is supported by *The Magenta Book*, produced by the government's Social Research Unit, which provides additional guidance for policy evaluation and analysis (Cabinet Office 2003). The impact of policy directions and implementation of policy processes have an obvious need for constant provision and assessment of information and data, and from this the definitions and consequences of developing value chains have begun to be reassessed over time. Economic and social impacts data and modelling are now a dynamic process supporting policy development, providing new datasets for integration into the policy-assessment and review cycle. Cultural economics has begun to feature more widely within the heritage sector's thinking in the past five years, fitting with a values-based approach adopted to strategic funding directions and conservation management advice from the Heritage Lottery Fund and English Heritage (Clark and English Heritage 2001). This is exemplified by conditions being placed on grants, often requiring shared investment or match-funding, application of business models, and whole-life costing. Indeed, the Heritage Counts programme of research coordinated by English Heritage on behalf of the wider heritage sector in England has benefited from the employment of an economist within the organisation. This kind of post, also established within the Heritage Lottery Fund, is a clear example of the development of the shift within professional heritage practice. Interestingly, the crosscutting nature of the values debate has led to linkages being made recently between environmental economists and the heritage sector, as the wider 'landscape' approaches to heritage have come into the mainstream. The argument for a values-based approach therefore has the notion of defined (positive) 'outcomes' as its quest.

An understanding of the impact of heritage has begun to draw on interdisciplinary skills and approaches, and the concordant information and knowledge sets arising from specialisms. Long-established economic impact modelling, used most clearly at the intersection of heritage and tourism is, for instance, adding considerably to the weight of evidence showing the beneficial role that heritage has in regeneration and property development (Heritage Lottery Fund 2004). While tourist visitor numbers have provided some of the best datasets for the role of heritage in the UK for a number of years (Baxter *et al.* 2001), as the heritage sector has become more sophisticated in its need for understanding its role, then anecdotal evidence and partial data on tourist and local views on the sense of place (and motivations to visit a given place) have also begun to be more readily built into a wider concept of heritage impact research (Baxter 2004).

The sophistication required for the development of the heritage knowledge base, in terms of management information and data, has brought about more complex research needs and research strategy requirements. The established role of the discipline of heritage management has been reinforced using the value debate as a starting point to begin to model the practices, outputs and outcomes of managing the historic environment and heritage assets in particular ways. Such modelling appended to an increase in analytical material and data shows a level of professionalism and purpose that in turn can assist the advocacy process for heritage, moving it up the political agenda, where data can be marshalled and adapted for a multitude of contexts (Baxter 2004). In England, the maturity of the value debate and its relevance for heritage can be seen through the dedicated stream of research from the public policy think tank Demos, which (via funding from the Heritage Lottery Fund) has produced funded-programme-specific and strategic organisational research reports, culminating in a high-profile conference and associated publication on *The Public Value of Heritage* in 2006 (Clark 2006). This conference considered where the values debate was now having a bearing on heritage management decision-making, building on international work such as that previously developed at the Getty Foundation and from the complementary disciplines of cultural economics, natural and built environment (De la Torre and Getty Conservation Institute 2003). Of particular note in the conceptual development has been the modelling of heritage outputs and outcomes and their intrinsic, institutional and instrumental benefits, and the accessible approach of adapting economic/econometric modelling for use in heritage (Accenture and the National Trust 2006; Clark 2006; National Economic Research Associates 2003). The debate over value instigated in England has provided much of the groundwork for the opportunity of greater strategic development for the heritage sector within the home nations by developing a model for enhancing the knowledge base through heritage auditing.

Methodological focus at the core of the heritage business environment

Although the politics of identity were perhaps the noisiest aspects of devolution, the business of running a new country's economy also pushed heritage up the agenda. In a devolved Scotland, the major industries which can contribute to the country's prosperity and social development have quickly come in for review. Apart from the political arena, within the cultural administration arena, the politics of Scotland, Scottish culture and heritage have been intimately tied to an appreciation of the image and brand of Scotland, tourism operational performance, and cultural institutions which have been established with a strong Scottish and Celtic identity (McCrone *et al.* 1999; Ruiz and Scotland Development Department Research Programme 2004). A combination of 'environmental factors' can be identified in the period following devolution. This has established a newly differentiated business context for the sector, and thus new requirements. In particular, the factors and drivers for methodological development have included: a perceived advocacy vacuum, with no identifiable 'organisational champion' for the heritage sector; a need for specific policy in the cultural sector (to cover heritage/historic environment aspirations); new governmental structures and changed organisational responsibilities and reporting mechanisms; a number of *causes célèbres* gaining media and political attention, and thus scrutiny in the new political democratic processes (especially debates in the Scottish Parliament); and onward development and refinement of policy and philosophy elsewhere (most obviously, the nearby counterpart sectors in England and Wales).

A consideration of the required methodological responses to the above came out of a number of questions asked of a newly established (following devolution) Historic Environment Advisory Council for Scotland (HEACS). One was to establish whether there was a need for a 'heritage audit' within Scotland and the way in which this could be taken forward. Further consideration was to be given to the effectiveness of heritage protection legislation and the infrastructure of the heritage sector in Scotland (Historic Environment Advisory Council for Scotland 2004; Jura Consultants 2006).

Interestingly, while in England the heritage auditing programme had established itself by straight away beginning a process of data collection and research, the Scottish approach was to ask further questions of the role of the heritage information and infrastructure base, and the possible underlying methodologies for gathering evidence. Thus methodological development has been usefully placed at the heart of the emergent heritage management processes in Scotland. While HEACS considered the strategic context for government (as a ministerial advisory body), the non-governmental umbrella organisation the Built Environment Forum Scotland (BEFS) undertook its own scoping within the NGO sector, with an allied advocacy campaign that was launched in 2004 under the banner 'The Bigger Picture' (Built Environment Forum Scotland 2004). Within both of these allied investigations, a number of core 'knowledge' issues were evaluated: consideration was given to building on experience within England and international heritage auditing programmes from Australia and Canada; the poor relationship between the sector and the wider cultural sphere perceived in the analysis being undertaken by the government's established Cultural Commission (Cultural Commission 2005) was considered; the applicability of indicator frameworks for measuring the state of the historic environment, as already used in sustainable development and environmental fields, was considered; and the life cycle of properties and places in the relationship between conservation and development was being addressed.

By the end of 2004 HEACS reported to government on the need for a heritage audit within Scotland, recognising within the unique devolved administrative context that a three-staged methodological approach to auditing might be undertaken over a four-to-five-year period to establish a base on which annual reporting might eventually take place and yield useful results. The tripartite approach suggested undertaking a sector-driven audit, an issue-driven audit and a gap-driven audit: each building on the knowledge base and available data (HEACS 2004). During 2005, Historic Scotland, the executive arm of government charged with delivery of heritage management policies, established the internal mechanism within its Policy Directorate to

95

manage the audit process. In 2006 Historic Scotland commissioned the first piece of research within the putative Scottish heritage audit, designed to assess the state of the knowledge base on which an audit could be undertaken. The aim of the research was to identify and catalogue existing historic environment datasets and to assess how fit for purpose these data would be to address key questions about the historic environment. The research was conducted between March and October 2006 (by the author) and used a mixed approach to gathering information, which involved a survey of around 230 organisations, stakeholder interviews, literature reviews and information signposting (identification of data sources and organisations collecting relevant information/analysis). The key issues arising from the study are noted in Table 5.1, which contains the executive summary of the research. Methodologies and data sources, and the requirement for their development, can be seen to be the fundamental requirement on which effective and transparent management can be built.

What has become evident from the research is that despite the positive developments theoretically derived from an 'audit culture', the notion of audit relies on a certain level of available data, and furthermore understanding of the data-management systems in place in order to produce meaningful management information and transparency of performance by organisations. Indeed, in order to perform an effective audit of information, dedicated information needs to be gathered for that purpose: in the case of the initial stages of heritage auditing, this has not been the case in Scotland. Information has been gathered from multiple sources, utilising datasets collected for other purposes, and therefore when heritage audit-related questions are asked of this data it has not been possible to provide answers. The pre-assessment of the heritage management information resource in Scotland, intended as a precursor to actual audit, has therefore shown up an interesting divergence in philosophy and practice for the sector more widely. This is reflected on further below.

Conclusion: data, information and knowledge are not the same things

What has become clear from the rolling programme of heritage audit in England, and the preparations for the Scottish heritage audit, is that the understanding of knowledge-management methodologies and the role they play in strategic management for the heritage sector is still in its formative stages. Despite the existence of published reviews of the interaction of management and archaeology from the mid-1990s (Cooper 1995), there has been a paucity of further work on knowledge management in the broader sense of historic environment management. The evolution of English Heritage (in England) as an organisation and its corporate understanding of the heritage information resource, particularly the recent publication of its research strategy and draft conservation principles, have begun to address this through the creation of its so-called 'virtuous heritage circle' – though this is largely

Table 5.1 Key findings from Historic Scotland data-assessment project (from Baxter 2006)

Existing data and data gaps:

• The Project has been a successful starting point for identifying and evaluating existing information sources for the Audit.

• More than 100 easily accessible datasets have been identified. These data address, in part, key questions about the historic environment.

• In addition, it is estimated that local authorities may hold around 50 useful 'generic' datasets. However, during the course of the Project it was beginning to emerge that not all 32 local authorities hold the same core data.

• As well as obvious datasets, there are many less accessible sources of information which may be useful.

• There are substantial data gaps – particularly about the condition of the historic environment resource and within individual local authorities' information bases.

Fit for purpose:

• Without a fuller understanding of individual organisations' knowledge-management processes, it has not been possible to fully assess how fit for purpose existing historic environment datasets are.

• From the survey of organisations, however, it appears that few individual datasets are completely fit for the purpose of the audit in their current form.

Capacity and participation:

• It has become apparent that there are substantial challenges in the data-gathering process, which will require a flexible approach to working with the sector.

• There appears to be a capacity issue across the sector. During the course of this and other audit-related projects, some organisations found it difficult to provide information and respond to surveys. Therefore, the Audit will need to consider how best to build capacity to fill gaps in information.

• Participation in the written survey was low among some groups, because of capacity issues and a lack of awareness of the benefits of the Audit.

Comparison with English Heritage

• An investigation of the approach by English Heritage (which is a number of years ahead of Scotland in the auditing process) found that, as well as a national manager, they fund a number of local posts to facilitate delivery of the audit at a local level as well as at a national level. They have also made the decision to commission a range of bespoke work that exactly meets their needs.

Conclusions and recommendations

Many of the findings from this Project come as no major surprise. However, things have now moved from the realm of anecdotes to evidence-based facts – which provides a robust basis for the next steps.

Table 5.1 (continued)

The main conclusions and recommendations are:

1: The Project has made a useful start in identifying what data exists, making an initial assessment of how fit for purpose it is, and preparing a baseline database and directory of data resources. However, there are gaps in this knowledge base. There is an opportunity to add to and enhance the database by further focused information trawls and targeted interviews with local authorities to find out more about available data which is known to exist.

   Feedback on the usefulness of the directory of data resources and the database should be gathered. The sector should then agree whether to maintain these resources and the implications of this.

2: Data has been created within the sector by a range of organisations in different locations and for a very wide variety of specific purposes. However, for the purposes of the Audit, many of the datasets as they stand cannot be considered fit for purpose. It is clear that existing data alone will not address all of the key questions posed by the audit – either because data does not exist or it is not fit for purpose.

   Therefore, the audit should develop a research and information-gathering strategy to fill these data gaps. It should also agree whether to adopt a thematic or area-based approach to filling gaps – either independently or in association with compilers of key datasets.

3: There are apparent capacity problems within the sector in responding to requests for information.

   In addressing these, a view needs to be established on whether it is best to build capacity locally or to commission bespoke work to make data available and fit for purpose.

4: The datasets identified within the scope of this Project have been those easiest to access and catalogue. A greater task lies ahead to identify and assess a wider range of datasets and information less readily accessible.

   The audit should consider how useful these other information sources are and how cost-effective it would be to make use of them.

5: There was warm reception to the aspirations of the Audit and widespread support among the sector for a directory of data resources. If the Audit is to successfully share information and secure buy-in from the sector, two-way communication about the aims of the Audit and its usefulness is vital. In particular, it is essential to the success of the Audit to have targeted liaison with local authorities to raise awareness about the Audit, its findings and the benefits of participation.

   Local authorities should be consulted, as major stakeholders in the Audit process, and also as the largest gap in current data provision. This will provide a forum to discuss capacity for providing data and the shared benefits of the Audit.

Table 5.1 (continued)

6: There is a lot of experience within English Heritage, who are undertaking a similar type of audit. In the course of this they are commissioning a range of bespoke research.

Synergies should be sought with the Heritage Counts process in England for efficiencies and effectiveness in research.

7: A fuller understanding of individual organisations' knowledge management processes is necessary to allow a full assessment of how fit for purpose existing historic environment datasets are.

The sector (and specifically the Audit process) should gain a greater understanding of knowledge creation and management processes within organisations which potentially hold historic environment-related information.

---

conceptual in nature at this point in time and is more aligned with strategic intent than operational effectiveness (English Heritage 2006).

An appreciation of knowledge-management and within it the role and function of both data and their concomitant collection and analysis strategies has become ever more vital as the business environment for heritage has forced the sector's hand in both accounting for its performance and justifying support for it. The changing philosophy within public management towards a strategic perspective of evidence-based policy-making has moved the back-office functionality of heritage management operations into the frontline for debate and consideration. Effective management information upon which informed choices (and thus informed conservation (Clark and English Heritage 2001)) can be built cannot rely on second-hand data, or data which have been collected for other purposes. The precursor audit research in Scotland has obviously shown that data pertaining to the management of the heritage resource exist, but that they may not be structured in such a way that they can usefully add to knowledge about the effects of managing heritage. Data and resulting information can be used to measure specific outputs, as has been shown in the first-stage report for Scotland's Historic Environment Audit, but the nucleus of this informs the sector of process rather than outcome (Historic Scotland 2007). A values-based approach advocates an understanding of outcome, but may be stalled unless the methodological philosophy of heritage audit can catch up. The research in Scotland has gone some way to identify this methodological knowledge gap by asking pertinent questions which cut to the heart of management information and the hypotheses about a need to create heritage management knowledge. That the data that we currently have about heritage may provide information about what it is; but not what it does. The devolved context for heritage audit methodologies considered here therefore has wider scope to provide beneficial support for developing philosophies of heritage management through reassessment of the ability to assess our 'business' processes and their transparency.

Bibliography

Accenture and the National Trust (2006) *Demonstrating the Public Value of Heritage*, London: The National Trust.

Baxter, I. (2003) 'Auditing the Historic Environment: Measurements, Datasets and English Heritage's State of the Historic Environment Report 2002', *Cultural Trends* 46, 3–31.

—— (2004) 'From Heritage to Historic Environment: Professionalising the Experience of the Past for Visitors', *Journal of Hospitality & Tourism* 2.2, 5–25.

—— (2006) *Historic Environment Audit: Assessment of Data Quality*, Edinburgh: Historic Scotland.

Baxter, I., English Tourism Council and Glasgow Caledonian University Moffat Centre for Travel and Tourism Business Development (2001) *The Heritage Monitor: The Annual Review of the Historic Environment for Everyone Interested in Conservation, Tourism and Development*, London: English Tourism Council.

Bourdieu, P. (1984) *Distinction: A Social Critique of the Judgement of Taste*, London: Routledge.

British Waterways (2002) *Waterways for People*, Watford: British Waterways.

Built Environment Forum Scotland (BEFS) (2004) *The Bigger Picture: Investing in Scotland's Historic Environment*, Edinburgh: BEFS.

Bunting, C. (2007) *Public Value and the Arts in England: Discussion and Conclusion of the Arts Debate*, London: Arts Council England.

Cabinet Office (2003) *The Magenta Book: Guidance Notes for Policy Evaluation and Analysis*, London: Cabinet Office/HM Government.

Clark, C. M. and English Heritage (2001) *Informed Conservation: Understanding Historic Buildings and their Landscapes for Conservation*, London: English Heritage.

Clark, K. (ed.) (2006) *Capturing the Public Value of Heritage: The Proceedings of the London Conference 25–26 January 2006*, London: English Heritage.

Commission for Architecture and the Built Environment (CABE) and HM Government (2006) *Better Public Building*, London: CABE.

Cooper, M. A. (ed.) (1995) *Managing Archaeology*, London: Routledge.

Cultural Commission (2005) *'Our Next Major Enterprise ...' Final Report of the Cultural Commission (June 2005)*, Edinburgh: Cultural Commission and Scottish Executive.

De la Torre, M. and Getty Conservation Institute (2003) *Assessing the Values of Cultural Heritage: Research Report*, Los Angeles: Getty Conservation Institute.

Department for Culture, Media and Sport (DCMS) (2004) *Review of Heritage Protection: The Way Forward*, London: DCMS.

—— (2006a) *Creative Economy Programme: Evidence and Analysis Final Report*, London: DCMS.

—— (2006b) *Department for Culture, Media and Sport – Sponsored Bodies Funding Agreements – Museums and Galleries 2005/06–2007/08*. http://www.culture.gov.uk/Reference_library/Publications/archive_2006/fa_mandg_0508.htm?contextId={6E27314D-E0EC-4C5B-A175-F667D1F9C1FD} (accessed 31 January 2008).

Department for Culture, Media and Sport, Architecture and Historic Environment Division (2001) *The Historic Environment: A Force for our Future*, London: DCMS.

Department for Culture, Media and Sport (DCMS) and Office of National Statistics (2007) *Taking Part: The National Survey of Culture, Leisure and Sport (Annual Report 2005/2006)*, London: DCMS.

English Heritage (2000) *Power of Place: The Future of the Historic Environment*, London: Power of Place Office.

—— (2006) *Conservation Principles: Policies and Guidance for the Sustainable Management of the Historic Environment (Second Stage Consultation)*, London: English Heritage.

English Heritage and Historic Environment Review Executive Committee (2007) *Heritage Counts: The State of England's Historic Environment 2006*, London: English Heritage.

Fairclough, G. J. and J. A. Symonds (1999) *Historic Landscape Characterisation: 'The State of the Art'*, London: English Heritage.

Fenton, S., C. Swanson and E. L. Scottish (2001) *The Historic Environment*, Edinburgh, Scottish Environment Link.

Flynn, N. (2007) *Public Sector Management*, 5th edn, London: Sage.

Hanna, M. and English Tourism Council (2000) *The Heritage Monitor: A Yearly Analysis of Trends Affecting England's Architectural Heritage – A Vital Tourism Asset*, London: English Tourism Council.

Held, D. (ed.) (2004) *Globalizing World?: Culture, Economics, Politics*, London: Routledge

Heritage Lottery Fund (2004) *New Life: Heritage and Regeneration*, London: Heritage Lottery Fund.

—— (2006) *Our Heritage, Our Future, Your Say*, London: Heritage Lottery Fund.

Historic Environment Advisory Council for Scotland (HEACS) (2004) *Report and Recommendations on the Need for a Heritage Audit in Scotland and How to Take it Forward*, Edinburgh: HEACS.

Historic Scotland (2007) *A Review of Existing Information for Scotland's Historic Environment Audit (SHEA)*, Edinburgh: Historic Scotland.

HM Treasury (2003) *The Green Book: Appraisal and Evaluation in Central Government*, London: The Stationery Office.

Jura Consultants (2006) *Mapping the Infrastructure of the Historic and Contemporary Built Environment*, Edinburgh: Built Environment Forum Scotland.

Keating, M. (2005) *The Government of Scotland: Public Policy Making after Devolution*, Edinburgh: Edinburgh University Press.

McCrone, D., A. Morris and R. Kiely (1999) *Scotland – the Brand: The Making of Scottish Heritage*, Edinburgh. Polygon and Edinburgh University Press.

National Economic Research Associates (NERA) (2003) *Economic Issues in the Heritage Sector (Report for the Monument Trust)*, London: NERA.

Paul Drury Partnership (2007) *Assessment of the Conservation Outcomes of HLF Funded Heritage Grants Projects*, London: Heritage Lottery Fund.

Pine, B. J. (1999) *The Experience Economy: Work is Theatre and Every Business a Stage*, Boston: Harvard Business School Press.

Purnell, J. (2007) 'World-class from the Grassroots Up: Culture in the Next Ten Years', speech by Secretary of State Rt Hon James Purnell MP at the National Portrait Gallery, 6 July 2007, http://www.culture.gov.uk/Reference_library/Minister_Speeches/Ministers_Speech_Archive/James_Purnell/jamespurnellsos_speechcultureinthenexttenyrs.htm?contextId={C2D4CFB0-CEEB-461F-AB3D-B0A7B008F13B} (accessed 31 January 2008).

Resource: The Council for Museums, Archives and Libraries (2001) *Renaissance in the Regions: A New Vision for England's Museums*, London: Resource.

Ruiz, J. and Scotland Development Department Research Programme (2004) *A Literature Review of the Evidence Base for Culture, the Arts and Sports Policy*, Edinburgh: Scottish Executive.

Scottish Executive (2000) *Creating our Future ... Minding our Past: Scotland's National Cultural Strategy*, Edinburgh: Scottish Executive.

Snowball, J. (2007) *Measuring the Value of Culture: Methods and Examples in Cultural Economics*, Heidelberg: Springer.

Towse, R. (2003) *A Handbook of Cultural Economics*, Cheltenham: Edward Elgar.

Travers, T. (2006) *Museums and Galleries in Britain: Economic, Social and Creative Impacts*, London: National Museum Directors Conference.

VisitScotland (2007) *VisitScotland Corporate Plan 2007–2010*, Edinburgh: VisitScotland.

VisitScotland/Moffat Centre for Travel and Tourism Business Development (2007) *Visitor Attraction Monitor 2006*, Glasgow: Glasgow Caledonian University/VisitScotland.

Welsh Assembly Government (2002) *Creative Future: A Culture Strategy for Wales*, Cardiff: Welsh Assembly Government.

Welsh Assembly Government and Cadw (2004) *Review of the Historic Environment in Wales*, Cardiff: Welsh Assembly Government.

—— (2007) *The Welsh Historic Environment: Position Statement 2006*, Cardiff: Welsh Assembly Government.

6

METHODS USED TO
INVESTIGATE THE USE OF THE PAST
IN THE FORMATION
OF REGIONAL IDENTITIES

Ulrike Sommer

Introduction

This chapter discusses the range of sources and methods that can be used to investigate identity formation in a historical perspective. The discussion is based on research on the formation and changes of 'Saxon identity' in the nineteenth and twentieth centuries.[1] Saxony (with its changing borders) was a middle-sized state in the eastern part of the Holy Roman Empire, an independent kingdom from 1806 to 1918, and a German Federal state from 1918 to 1952 and again after 1990. While the following discussion is specific to this case study, I try to identify a broad range of sources that should be available for any area, just as the approach and methods outlined would be relevant for the study of other kinds of social identity constructions and can be applied to different regions.

The verb most commonly used in connection with heritage is probably 'preserving', but heritage is also created, and is constantly changed according to present-day needs. Heritage, or in a wider sense the past, is created to justify the present, or, more precisely, one specific interpretation of the present and by implication expectations for the future. This past is created by people, and it is created with specific goals. This is not to deny that there is a 'real' past, things that happened before the present moment; but only a tiny portion of past events ever makes it into the recorded or materially preserved past, and only another very tiny proportion of this is used in the creation and reinforcement of group identities.

There are a number of ways of looking at the *process* of identity formation, among which the following may be considered typical:

1   An essentialist paradigm may be used to argue that *the* formation of identity simply happens or had to happen. Key events can then be objectively identified and narrated. This approach would see the national myth as the expression of some inherent fundamental trait of the group being formed.

2   A simplified functionalist top-down model, where a group of people with clear political aims codify a specific history for consumption by the general public.

3   The Three-step model. This model recognises three steps in the formation of identity. These are the specialists collecting the facts, the intermediate organisations that modify the concepts developed by the specialists for mass consumption and, finally, the consumers. This model can be expanded to include different types of specialists, intermediate organisations and consumers, each with different interests. Feedback between the different levels is to be expected. This Three-step model implies a degree of autonomy of the intellectual sphere that is clearly unwarranted. Numerous 'outside' factors impinge on all levels, most prominently the government, both by its control of funding and the direct control of appointments and jobs (sacking of political opponents or 'politically unreliable' people) and by the control of publications (censorship, grants for publication). Economic factors such as the book market and media, levels of private sponsorship, the use of archaeology in tourism, and the perception of archaeology as an obstacle to investment and urban expansion also come into play. Ideological systems and research paradigms with a wider social impact also influence the development and use of archaeological research and heritage perception: such systems include the Christian Church, Darwinism, Marxism, various types of chauvinism and racism, and Christian, Jewish and Islamic fundamentalism. In practice, none of the ideal-type steps are clearly delineated, and, of course, there tend to be a number of different groups at each step, with often radically divergent aims and interests.

4   Latour's Four Horizons model (1989b) has looked at the connections between science and society that are missing from the Three-step model. He has identified four 'horizons', seen as interlocking circles which can guide research into the history of science in a less systemic and less hierarchical manner. The horizons are:

    a   Mobilisation of data. This includes the instruments, technology and procedures needed to make the external world available to scientific research, the techniques and definitions needed for systematic and formalised data collection, and the places used for storing and displaying these data. In the case of prehistory, the horizon would include collections, museums, catalogues, maps, county-inventories and excavations, but also systems of classification and a specialised and generally accepted terminology.

b   Self-constitution. This concerns the definition of the research field as a separate subject, the criteria for inclusion in this field as well as the creation of university chairs, societies, associations and research institutions.

c   Alliances. This refers to the acceptance of a discipline by and support of outside groups, mobilisation of financial resources to fund the research, laboratories and collections. This includes the arguments needed to appear relevant to these other groups. Latour names the government (bureaucracy and technocracy), the army, industry and educational bodies as key elements.

d   Representation or staging. This includes public relations, the many ways a discipline presents itself, its aims, results and methods, to the public.

e   Cohesion. This core element refers to the way these factors are connected into a coherent whole.

In the following, the Three-step model is used as an organising principle for the discussion, without implying any hierarchy, primacy of production or directionality between the three levels.

Collecting the facts

The sources used for the study of the formation of Saxon identity, and discussed here in detail, were mainly textual. Other sources, in particular pictorial sources such as historical paintings, illustrations in scientific volumes, popular treatises and historical novels, would also be another useful avenue of research into the formation of different kinds of identity (see Mitchell 2000 for an English example), and could be used to consider questions such as: who and what is depicted, in what context, how far does actual archaeological research influence the illustrations, which key moments are identified in the past, who is acting and how does this relate to the written sources? There has not been much research into the nineteenth-century tradition of historical paintings in terms of identity formation, although there are some recent studies of illustrations and their ideological context (e.g. Jud and Kaenel 2002; Molyneaux 1997; Moser 1998). Postcards, pictures in popular illustrated magazines and cheap calendars give an indication of popular knowledge and appreciation of actual monuments, the way they are depicted and the mechanisms for the selection of 'relevant' monuments (e.g. Köhnke 2001). Likewise, actual examples of material culture form another much neglected source. Some analyses of statues and monuments (Nipperdey 1968; Tacke 1995; Dörner 1995) have appeared, but museum buildings, the layout and presentation of museum exhibitions, replicas and reproductions, and attempts at restoring/recreating prehistoric and early historic monuments (Ahrens 1990) offer a wide scope for further exploration. The methodology is as yet somewhat underdeveloped, though much can be learned from architectural studies or the history of art.

The study of past identity formation is beset by the uneven nature of sources. The sphere of the producers/specialist is normally the one best documented. For the nineteenth and early twentieth centuries, the period considered here, there is a plethora of sources for the scholarly point of view: published books and articles, as well as scholarly discussions of individual sites and authoritative accounts of the local, regional and national history. The actions of governing bodies are also well documented in the form of official decrees and laws as well as (more or less) detailed instructions for their implementation. Parliamentary discussions of the issues and petitions relating to them are conserved in official archives. In addition, after the enactment of the law for the protection of ancient monuments and the foundation of the Antiquities Services and the Service for the Protection of Ancient Monuments (or similar administrative bodies), one can find lists of monuments, records of excavations and finds in the archives of various institutions. While under direct governmental control, these bodies also acted as intermediate institutions, transmitting the research of specialists to both the general public and to government officials, and developing an institutional dynamic of their own. Their institutional history tends to be very well documented in archival material, and numerous institutional histories have been published (normally in connection with some anniversary). While these publications may contain useful facts, it should be recognised that they constitute the official origin myth of the institution in question and analyse neither the social, political and ideological context nor the institutional dynamics mentioned above. They tend to present a typical 'ahistorical history' (Latour 1989a: 783), anachronistically written from the point of present-day interests and ruling paradigms. Moreover, in the context of the radically changing political regimes of Central Europe, they tend to gloss over or omit potentially embarrassing time periods. Memoirs of scholars and politicians are another contemporary source which has not been extensively looked into, although M.-A. Kaeser (2002, 2003) has shown how a detailed analysis of a single biographical source can be used to unravel a complex network of scientific and political interdependencies.

Intermediate organisations

The role of intermediate organisations is also relatively well documented. Intermediate organisations that were influential in identity construction are, for example, antiquarian and historical societies and the educational system. Other 'multipliers' may be authors of historical novels, painters and illustrators, producers of local histories and organisers of historical pageants, and journalists. In the time period in question, the clergy together with local teachers often acted as multipliers. With both leisure time and a position of local authority they were often used by professionals to obtain data – part of a tradition of questionnaires from the antiquarians onwards of collecting data about local customs, dialects, superstitions or antiquities. The work of anti-quarian societies tends to be well documented, as most of them published detailed proceedings, and there are numerous surveys listing these bodies. Catalogues of their collections and libraries, as well as extensive archives, often survive as well.

The history of museums and collections is also quite well documented. In this case study, both the Royal collection in Dresden and the growing number of private collections that developed all over the country during this time were relevant organisations. The existence, and often the content, of the collections can be traced (though it is unclear to what extent short-lived private collections have been recorded). It is, however, difficult to establish any method for measuring their impact: data on the nature of the exhibitions or on the number of visitors, let alone their reaction, are very sparse indeed. Nonetheless, much useful information still slumbers in the archives of individual museums. Penny's (2002) study of German ethnographical museums shows the potential for more detailed case studies. Whereas Roth (1990) provides a general outline of the development of local museums (*Heimatmuseen*), individual studies investigating the local political and social context are still lacking. Detailed pictures of collections or exhibitions are quite rare up to *c*. 1890, and museum displays were (and are) seldom adequately documented. Guidebooks are usually the only sources available about how museums presented their collections, but not only were they only produced for the bigger museums, but they have not often been systematically collected. Newspaper accounts of exhibitions are a valuable source, but are time-consuming to collect if the relevant newspapers have not been digitised.

The general public

Based on the more obvious sources available, we thus tend to know a great deal about what people were told to believe about the past, and the strategies used to 'sell' this interpretation, but often it is impossible to tell who was actually reached by these interpretations and how people reacted to the pictures and narratives offered to them – whether they believed them, ignored them or incorporated them into differing accounts of their own, and if this had any influence on their actions.

For my case study I was not able to locate any sources that relate directly to the popular perception of monuments or reflections on the distant past in general, such as might be found in diaries, letters or essays. They are bound to exist, but as they are probably extremely rare they are of dubious use for gauging general trends. The production of written documents is moreover closely linked to the level of literacy; moreover, mundane factors such as access to writing materials, the amount of leisure-time, an environment conducive to intellectual activities and the initiative of somebody to preserve these documents are essential for their existence. In other words, peasants and workers are extremely unlikely to have left any surviving documents. In 1866, about half the German population were functionally illiterate (Wittmann 1982: 200), and in 1875 about a quarter of the population (Schenda 1970).

My study proceeded from the assumption that the production of texts, pictures and displays is in some way connected to the consumption of these bids for identification, the assumption that the products offered are in some way connected to what the 'consumers' want or at least prefer. At the same time, as the following case study shows, the production of accounts of the past is also in a substantial manner influenced by political and economic conditions, and only by comparing a wide range of different sources can a start be made at untangling the influence of various factors. In the following I shall outline the methods used for the case study of the formation of Saxon identity.

Investigating the construction of narratives

In the creation of group identity, the past commonly plays an important role (Hobsbawm 1997). This might be linked to the belief that a deep past guarantees a long future, proving the strong coherence of the group in question, its prowess in defending its territory and its resilient nature in the face of external threats. The group is seen as optimally adapted to its environment, which it has marked as its own by numerous monuments and other changes wrought on the landscape. Often, though, the origin myth is actually the past of a group not yet in existence, and the past is describing the future anticipated for this group having yet to achieve an uncontested identity (e.g. nationhood) and external recognition.

To investigate these constructions I was thus interested in these questions:

* Why is a particular episode of history/prehistory selected for inclusion in the narrative about the national past?
* How was the selected references to the past made relevant to the present?
* How has this narrative changed through time?
* What happens if there are conflicting accounts?
* How do new master narratives originate and gain validity?

To answer these questions, a cross-section of Saxon archaeological publications, both more 'scholarly' and lay literature, and popular and political texts were perused. Actually, this distinction does not make much sense during most of the nineteenth century, as most antiquarians had to earn their living in a different occupation (if they had to earn their living, that is), and most archaeological work in the later nineteenth and early twentieth centuries was conducted by laymen who were members of historical and archaeological societies. The selected texts were analysed according to criteria taken from critical discourse analysis (Fairclough 1995; van Dijk 1985; Wodak and Meyer 2001). Within the texts, four levels were distinguished:

1   Historical master narrative. A master narrative has been characterised as a coherent narrative with a clear perspective on present or hoped-for political conditions (most commonly the national state), focusing on collective agents (Middell *et al.* 2000 22). Master narratives provide social cohesion and integration between different social/regional groups. According to Rüsen (2002), master narratives supply cultural identity via events in the past. They not only provide cultural identity, but also create and describe difference to other groups (Rüsen 1994). These master narratives change according to social and political context, but they tend to do so rather slowly. A fully fledged master narrative is difficult to dislodge, as it seems to unfold an inherent dynamic of its own, and contravening facts often appear useless against the narrative logic of such a story.

Such narratives can be subdivided into smaller elements. Based on Propp's (1968) study of narrative structures of fairy tales, three further text-elements were distinguished:

2   Motifs. A motif is defined as a self-contained 'scene' that relies on the existence of a master narrative already known to the recipients. The placement and function of these motifs can change; they can be incorporated into a number of different master narratives (see, for example, Eidson 2001; Friedrich *et al.* 2002). Motifs do not necessarily contain any obvious lesson or relate to an important historical event, but they are often narratologically satisfying episodes ('good stories') and are sometimes made into important historical events.

3   Topoi. Topoi, collective symbols and cultural stereotypes are descriptions like 'the dark primeval forests of prehistory'. As especially the studies of Jäger (1993) and Wodak *et al.* (1998) have shown, these topoi are highly significant as bearers of ideologically charged messages. They are part of a web of metaphors connected to collective symbols. 'Percolating Slavonic tribes' is an example of such a highly ideologically laden topos frequently found in the texts analysed.

4   Finally, ephiteta refers to the smallest (but no less important) narrative units used in the text, such as 'warlike Germans' or 'peaceful Sorabians'.

Different narrative elements change at different speeds (*'Ungleichzeitigkeit'*/non-synchronism). Motifs and topoi often persist for a very long time, remaining long after the master narrative they were a part of has disappeared from the published discourse. Motifs normally seem fairly neutral ideologically, although they may carry sublimated messages about what history is, who makes history, gender and social stereotypes etc. Of course, the collective symbols also change through time, although, again, probably on a different timescale than the master narratives. The collective symbols used should therefore also be traced in other fields of discourse. There are also examples where the master narrative was retained and only the ephiteta were changed, 'peaceful Sorabians' became 'cowardly Sorabians' etc. This marks a conscious ideological change, but it is possibly less effective than a new master narrative; it may even be counterproductive as different levels of the text deliver different messages.

Examples of master narrative

Through time, distinctly different master narratives about who the original Saxons were, their origin and how they reached their present homeland have been formulated. These can be identified through analysis of the different sources in terms of master narrative, motifs, topoi and ephiteta. The analysis shows that several origins have been proposed, including Slavs, Celts, Illyrians, a racial mix and Germanic tribes.

The assignment of a Slavic origin serves as an example of such different narratives. Arguments for a Slavic origin were already popular in the eighteenth century. Saxon histories of the eighteenth and nineteenth centuries normally described the Slavs as peaceful, hospitable, true to their words and their spouses, industrious and law-abiding, and of a 'soft, but deep' joyous mind (Hahn 1851). They enjoyed music, cultivation of fields and flocks, and generally improving the land. These descriptions have been collected by Herder and other authors investigating 'national mentalities' (e.g. von Anton 1789; Dobrovský 1784, 1786). This description of the prehistoric/early medieval Slav mentality corresponded closely with the eighteenth- and nineteenth-century Saxon self-image. The Saxons described themselves as industrious, cosmopolitan and cultured, in contrast to their hated Prussian neighbours, whose military successes Saxony could not match. Instead they emphasised cultural values, the arts, trade and industry.

In the analysis it became clear that few of the sources contained a fully fledged master narrative, the texts often relying on other, obviously well-known, texts which are signalled by the use of a number of key topoi. In other instances, a master narrative is either 'not yet' present or is not actively being constructed. The ideological load is then often transported solely by topoi and epitheta. As an analysis of schoolbooks and popular history-books showed (Sommer 2002; Friedrich *et al.* 2002), master narratives, and motifs and topoi even more so, are tenaciously preserved and often even survive political and ideological changes. But whether this reflects resistance by the authors or a rather insidious tenancy of narrative elements is usually impossible to tell.

Methods of ideological appropriation

There are a number of different methods through which a territory can be ideologically appropriated, and of how the past and its relics are used to justify present or future conditions. In this analysis a number of constructions were traced; they were: the dynastic model, the autochthonist model, the argument for continuation in mentality, arguments about general progress, the settler model, the model of conquest, models of continuity and mixture, and finally simple acceptance of the present territory. The dynastic model and the argument about mentality can be used to exemplify the narratives constructed for such ideological purposes.

In the 'dynastic mode' of medieval and early modern times, the unifying factor was the dynasty. The ruling dynasties are normally portrayed as invaders. Autochthony was a characteristic of the subservient peasantry. In some accounts, the Saxons thus traced their descent to stray mariners of Alexander of Macedonia who had run aground at the northern coast of Germany and treacherously slain the native Thuringians with long knives.

A different type of construction is based on the argument that the mentality of the Saxons and the ancient Slavs remained identical even if a direct descent from the Slavs could not be argued. Sometimes the achievements of both people are directly contrasted. While the modern Saxons are better at things, cultivate Borstorf apples instead of woodapples and build houses of stone instead of clay, all main modern economic activities were already anticipated by the ancient Sorabians, whether agriculture, trade, textile industry or mining (Petermann 1881). It is thus a question of related mental predisposition, created by a similar environment rather than ancestral descent, that creates continuity between past and present.

Quantitative data

As already pointed out, it is difficult to decide who, if anybody, believed in these diverse origin narratives and how widely they were known. In the second part of this chapter, I look at some quantitative data that at least give some indication about the importance of the past and the kind and number of people who showed interest in the past and its remains. I was not able to find any sources amenable to statistical analysis that cover the period 1800–2000, and moreover the sources that do exist are often not comparable over longer periods of time. Only by combining many different and (necessarily) disparate sources is it possible to arrive at an approximate picture. The legal protection of ancient monuments is of widely different dates (and extent) in the different German states and seems to be due more to political power-games (or sometimes, as in the case of Mecklenburg-Schwerin, the interest of the local dynasty in protecting their ancestral sites) than to direct popular interest. Mass-reproduced pictures such as postcards and pictures in calendars might be an interesting source, but are difficult to collect in the absence of databases.

Museums and exhibitions

The interpretation of the development of museums is far from straightforward: there are different types of founders and founding bodies, different proportions of the actual collection devoted to different periods, and different presentations and curatorial aims. Museums and school collections were certainly important at the time, but they are difficult to reconstruct. Only rarely are pictures of the exhibitions preserved, and the arrangement of objects and the content of the boards and labels are almost never recorded.

Antiquarian societies

Antiquarian societies were important in the collection and preservation of the past remains which played a significant role in the formation of identity. It is, therefore, important to understand more of their history. The number and changing names of antiquarian societies can be used to gauge the intellectual climate of the time. For Germany the sources used were Klüpfel (1844); Heimpel (1963); the library catalogue of the Römisch-Germanische Kommission des Deutschen Archäologischen Instituts; Walther (1845), and the website http://www.scholarly-societies.org. Unfortunately, most of these societies did not have a single purpose. The older societies were often learned societies interested in 'everything' or dedicated to general improvement in the spirit of the late Enlightenment (Nipperdey 1972; Döring and Nowak 2000). Most were dominated by the aristocracy, and most did not even survive the end of the Old Empire. The societies founded after 1815 commonly mix anti-quarian and historical research and were dominated by the rising bourgeoisie, similar to other societies dedicated to communal reading, singing, education, charity and social reform. Nipperdey (1972) sees this new type of societies as the training grounds for a modern democracy, and indeed they came under heavy official suspicion and supervision after the failed revolutions of 1830 and 1848. Anthropology (including ethnography and physical anthropology) became popular after 1860. After the turn of the century, the preservation of the countryside (*Heimat*) was becoming increasingly important, with societies arguing for nature conservation, the preservation of scenic countryside and villages, but also for rural festivities and customs (see Schaarschmidt 2004). The economic disaster accompanying the loss of the First World War, espe-cially the hyperinflation that lasted until 1923, led to the collapse of many societies, loss of publishing opportunities and the disappearance of the tradi-tional middle classes who had been the main members of antiquarian and historical societies. From 1933, with the fascist dictatorship, societies for genealogical research and 'racial hygenics' (*Rassehygiene*) became common.

Detailed statistics about the development of membership of societies can often be created; but this should not be seen as a good proxy for general interest in history or prehistory as societies were routinely joined by members of the local elites who did not necessarily take an active part. The number of members present at the annual general assemblies or publishing in the society's journal might be a better indication of actual interest. Closer analysis shows that many antiquarian or historical societies were dominated by the higher or middle bourgeoisie, with peasants and workers almost completely absent. It is only by about 1875 that artisans and clerical workers appear among the members in antiquarian societies in Germany. Whether this represents the genuine distribution of interest, or rather class-based or financial obstacles, is difficult to establish.

Publications

The number of publications on prehistory can also be used to gauge the interest in the subject though, of course, this is not directly related to the number of readers. In Germany scholarly studies were commonly published in German after 1800, when only 4 per cent of all published books were still in Latin, as compared to 58 per cent between 1600 and 1700 and 27.7 per cent in 1740 (Martino 1990: 4). There was a substantial increase in the reading public in the 1790s, and already by 1800 there were numerous complaints about 'Lesesucht', an 'addiction to reading', taking hold of even such unlikely people as common musketeers, traders' apprentices and milkmaids, keeping them from useful work and making them discontent about their natural place in society (Martino 1990: 8). Still, the level of literacy stayed low. In Prussia, where compulsory primary schools had been introduced in 1717, about 20 per cent of the male population (recruits) remained illiterate in 1850. Of course, reading out loud for others was quite common and was actively encouraged by educational societies, but anything save broadsheets, agricultural calendars or religious pamphlets was beyond the means of a peasant or artisan until about 1870.

In the late eighteenth and early nineteenth centuries lending libraries were the most important source for reading matter for all but the upper echelons of society (Martino 1982, 1990). Lending libraries were mainly analysed in terms of their literary impact (such as the popularity of individual authors), but they can also shed light on the popularity and the number of readers of prehistoric publication.

The number of archaeological publications per year can also be informative. There is a very reliable bibliography of prehistoric publications in Saxony (Bierbaum 1957, 1969), which covers the period from 1518 to 1957. According to this there is a more or less even output between 1700 (before that publications are too sparse and irregular to merit this kind of analysis) and 1819 and a steep general rise after the end of the Napoleonic wars. The following period, 1820–1918, shows a number of sharp fluctuations, but a much higher average. The period between the end of the First and the end of the Second World War is characterised by an uninterrupted rise in the number of publications from 1919 to 1925, with an absolute peak in 1926 (536 publications) and an average of 176 publications per year. These data cannot, however, be taken as a direct indication of an increased interest in archaeology. An increase in the population (the inhabitants of Saxony grew from 1.8 million in 1850 to 2.4 million in 1870 (Wittmann 1982: 193)), the increased number of literate and educated people, the widening social range of the members of antiquarian societies (with their journals as outlets for archaeological articles) and the widening range of publication possibilities (especially the increased numbers of daily papers and their weekend glossy magazines) all have influenced these data.

There are other limitations with this kind of data. The figures cannot be interpreted as directly related either to the number of articles and books produced or to the number of readers. Data on print runs are notoriously difficult to obtain, and, again, reveal little about the number of books actually sold. As most historical and antiquarian societies had libraries and a lively book-exchange, publications tended to circulate quite widely and quickly. In addition, summaries of books and important articles would be presented at the meetings and sometimes be published in the proceedings, again widening their impact in a way that is difficult to quantify.

Political events significantly influenced the production of printed texts, and they are important to identify. For this case study, the Napoleonic wars (1813–14) and the Prussian occupation of Saxony after the defeat of Napoleon and his allies in the Battle of Nations at Leipzig in 1814 left a visible mark on publications in general and on Saxon archaeological publications in particular. All historical treaties were censored (Ziegler 1982; Breuer 1982); historians and antiquarians were politically suspect as a matter of course. That science and philosophy had politically immediate consequences was accepted not only by radical journalists and editors like Georg Herwegh (Pepperle 1989), but also by the reactionary Prussian king Wilhelm IV, who took steps to eradicate this dangerous 'dragonseed'. Still, political propaganda was expressed as a matter of fact in historical and archaeological treatises (Sommer 2007). In the aftermath of the German revolution of 1848 we see a steep decrease in both archaeological publications (monographs and articles) and historical novels (Projekt Historischer Roman, http://www.uibk.ac.ar/germanistik/histrom/) and it was not until 1876 that the pre-revolutionary level of publication was regained. In the 1850s this was almost certainly due to political repression, the ban of academics from universities, the exile or emigration of a number of authors, and the above-mentioned censorship and self-censorship. This coincided with a generation change among the antiquarians.

The increase of publications after 1869 can be linked to a new school of anthropological archaeology in Germany, linked to the figure of Rudolf Virchow (1821–1902). He founded the Germany Society of Anthropology, Ethnology and Prehistory (DAG) in 1869, strongly influenced by the International Conferences on Anthropology and Prehistoric Archaeology (CIAAP) in operation since 1865 (Kaeser 2002; Kaeser and Babes (forthcoming)). This school was connected to research into the antiquity of man and biological evolution, and represented a type of prehistory that was international rather than regional or national in scope. The foundation of the DAG led to a spate of foundations of local societies and a renewed interest in prehistory that was borne by anatomists and other scientists rather than by historians.

The turn of the century saw another generational change, with the concomitant death of Virchow in 1902 and the professionalisation of physical anthropology that meant that ethnic ascription by craniometry was gradually given up and the links to prehistoric archaeology broken. The general *fin-de-siècle* atmosphere of doubt and loss of confidence in nineteenth-century ideas of progress was connected in Germany with an increasing nationalist climate, a struggle for a 'place in the sun', colonial achievements, an arms race against France and England and the expectation (or indeed anticipation) of a European great war. The increasing industrialisation and urbanisation led to the first nature-conservation movements that were often linked to an increasingly reactionary ideology. Archaeology became part of the *Heimatbewegung*, although the number of archaeological articles published in journals of walking and mountaineering societies and in journals of the *Heimatbewegung* is low and normally superficial.

The loss of territories under the Versailles Treaty and the perceived threat by nationalist movements in the new post-war countries led to increasingly nationalist publications. Saxony was suddenly projected into the position of a 'frontier-state' against Czechoslovakia and Poland. Archaeology was increasingly used for directly political purposes. The rise in publications after 1933 is almost certainly due to the direct patronage of prehistoric research by the new rulers. The promotion of prehistory can be traced in other areas as well. For example, the number of German chairs in prehistory grew from one in 1927 to eighteen in 1943. New institutions were founded (e.g. Ahnenerbe der SS (Kater 1974), Reichsbund für Vorgeschichte), and prehistoric research was increasingly funded by quangos (Notgemeinschaft für Deutsche Forschung/ DFG). There was certainly direct state control, although it is difficult to establish how this affected local publications. Paper was rationed in 1943 (Schulz 1960), but some popular periodicals were produced until 1944, which indicates their propaganda value.

Popular publications

Popular accounts of history/prehistory can be taken as an indication of a wider interest in the past. Popular accounts of archaeology started in about 1880, closely connected to cheaper methods of printing and a wider distribution of printed products (Martino 1990). There are two main waves of popularisations, one starting about 1885 and ending with the First World War, and the second starting in 1925 and continuing to 1945. Newspapers often only announce a find, while the supplements contain features treating the subject in depth, often illustrated and written by the local teacher or amateur archaeologist. The stories often seem to have been kept, as they reappear much later as part of village chronicles, in tourist leaflets or on the internet.

The proportion of archaeological features in non-archaeological periodicals such as tourist or mountaineering societies, publications for 'home and family' and popular science journals is also interesting. In Germany this proportion drops sharply after the First World War, as their function was taken over by journals for popular archaeology or popular archaeology and folk studies

(*Volkskunde* or *Volkheitskunde*). The latter were primarily founded after 1933 and were controlled by Nazi party organisations.

Within this time period historical novels were loathed by antiquarians, who denounced 'the exaggerated perusal of novels, journals and other ill-advised pastimes' (Preusker 1841: 4). Still, they give an indication of public interest in the past, and we know that they were also read by the 'lower orders'. The genre enjoyed some popularity from the 1880s onwards, slumped slightly after the First World War and had a peak during the Nazi dictatorship, after which it never recovered its former popularity.

History on homepages

In order to look at long-term trends in the development of archaeological narratives, I looked at the official homepages of Saxon villages and towns: 159 official homepages were studied; of these only twenty-four homepages had no information on history. Most pages quoted the first written source as the earliest evidence of the settlement, whereas others mentioned local folktales. The data made it possible to investigate these claims further. For instance, the claims that a town had a medieval origin could be further divided according to whether this referred to German settlers, to local Slavs, or a mixture or a succession of Slavs and Germans. More interesting, however, was the master narrative and the wording of the more extensive accounts on these homepages. Some texts, or rather parts of some texts, could be traced back to the 1880s, many had their roots in the late 1920s and 1930s, and others reproduced local histories from the German Democratic Republic. As in the schoolbooks (Sommer 2002; Friedrich *et al.* 2002), qualifying verbs were sometimes changed or words with an obvious ideological load were dropped, but the core of the story remained unchanged.

Archaeology, be it prehistoric finds or monuments, does not really play any substantial role in any origin story, even if the settlement is traced back to prehistory. Any find can demonstrate venerable antiquity: the exact dating is of almost no interest, as 1,000 years or 10,000 years both simply denote 'very old', and glaring misdates are not that rare. These results show that it is important to have an ancient past, but what kind of past does not seem to matter so much, at least at this local level. To fix the finds in public consciousness a narrative context is needed. Once created, these narrations show a considerable, almost frightening, persistence, surviving several changes of the political and social systems. Old narratives are rarely discarded, but instead integrated into the new stories, even if this does not make for a very convincing story.

Connecting the strands

So how does this all connect? Obviously, numerous facets of the use of the past and different spatial, temporal, ideological and social levels are involved. One important, though frequently repeated, point is that the archaeological find or monument cannot be viewed in isolation. Archaeological texts, illustrations and presentations are part of a network of meanings that is never fully expressed in the archaeological sphere alone. Parts of these meanings are probably irrevocably lost, as they were never recorded. At the same time, the representation of the past is heavily overdetermined, and parts of this web can probably be retrieved from other contexts.

I argue that only a combination of quantitative and qualitative data will enable attempts at tracing and unravelling this network of meanings. There are, on the one hand, microscopic details to be uncovered, and, on the other hand, a very coarse data-structure to be investigated – both are extremely time-consuming to collect. Any attempt to reconstruct a grand whole may be bound to fail, either by descending into 'Whig history' and anachronisms or by getting lost in minute details and never producing a narrative of even remote interest to others. As other contributions in this volume show, this is a problem not only for historical studies in the area of Heritage Studies. The integration of micro- and macro-level research will probably always produce a bad fit, an insufficient approximation to a complex reality we are still part of. In a way, this is part of the conclusion: beware of smooth and satisfying stories – they always lie! The gap should not be smoothed over – it points the way to the possibilities and necessities of further research.

Methodologically, I would argue for a creative approach to the selection of sources, casting the net as wide as possible. Any historical study needs detailed knowledge of the period in question, and is probably best done as part of a collaborative project – I certainly would never have started this project all on my own. As the collection of serial sources is extremely labour-intensive, this should be done with an eye on sharing work and making it available for others. With increasing digitisation, a whole range of new sources becomes available; the work of Stephen Briggs (2007) on the archive of *The Times* is a good example. Both linguistics and sociology make increasing use of specialised software for the quantitative analysis of texts, which should be useful for Heritage Studies as well. Catalogues and collections of digitised pictorial sources have also become increasingly available.

In conclusion, I would argue for setting clear aims and agendas, a distrust of smooth narratives, a trenchant source criticism and the creative use of new sources. Only a broad range of quantitative data and the cooperation with other disciplines will give us the chance to achieve a tentative grasp on past processes of heritage appreciation and its political scope.

Note

1   Part of the research was conducted in the Collaborative Research Centre 417 under the title 'The construction of identities on a regional scale, the example of Saxony', funded by the DFG, German Research Foundation.

Bibliography

Ahrens, C. (1990) *Wiederaufgebaute Vorzeit: archäologische Freilichtmuseen in Europa*, Neumünster: Wachholtz.

Anton, G. von (1789) *Erste Linien eines Versuchs über der alten Slawen Ursprung, Sitten, Gebräuche, Meinungen und Kenntnisse*, in P. Nebo (ed.) (1976) *Gottlob von Anton, Erste Linien eines Versuchs über der alten Slawen Ursprung, Sitten, Gebräuche, Meinungen und Kenntnisse*, Bautzen: Domowina.

Berding, H. (ed.) (1996) *Nationales Bewußtsein und kollektive Identität*, Frankfurt: Suhrkamp.

Bierbaum, G. (1957) 'Land Sachsen, Teil 1 und 2: Vom 16. Jahrhundert bis gegen Ende des 19. Jahrhunderts', in M. Jahn (ed.) *Bibliographie zur Vor- und Frühgeschichte Mitteldeutschlands*, vol. 2. Abh. sächs. Akad. Wiss Leipzig, Phil.-hist. Klasse 48/2, Berlin: Akademie.

―― (1969) 'Land Sachsen, Teil 3a: Gegen Ende des 19. Jahrhunderts bis über Mitte des 20. Jahrhunderts, Land, Bewohner, Kultur, Zeitabschnitte', in M. Jahn (ed.), *Bibliographie zur Vor- und Frühgeschichte Mitteldeutschlands*, vol. 2. Abh. sächs. Akad. Wiss Leipzig, Phil.-hist. Klasse 55/1, Berlin: Akademie.

Breuer, D. (1982) *Zur Geschichte der literarischen Zensur in Deutschland*, Heidelberg: UTB.

Briggs, S. C. (2007) 'The Narrative from Antiquarianism to Archaeology in *The Times* 1785–1900', Lecture at the conference 'Locality and Place in the History of Archaeology', London Institute of Archaeology, 28 March 2007.

Dijk, T. A. van (ed.) (1985) *Discourse and Literature: New Approaches to the Analysis of Literary Genres*, Amsterdam: J. Benjamins.

Dobrovský, J. (1784) *Historisch-kritische Untersuchung, woher die Slawen ihren Namen erhalten haben*, Abhandlungen einer Privatgesellschaft in Böhmen zur Aufnahme der Mathematik, der vaterländischen Geschichte und der Naturgeschichte 6, Prague, 1–280.

―― (1786) *Ueber die Begräbnißart der alten Slawen überhaupt, und der Böhmen insbesondere*, eine Abhandlung, veranlaßt durch die bei Horim im Jahr 1784 auf einer ehemaligen heydnischen Grabstätte ausgegrabenen irdenen Geschirre, Abhandlungen der böhmischen Akademie der Wissenschaften, Prague, 333–59.

Döring, D. and K. Nowak (eds) (2000) *Gelehrte Gesellschaften im mitteldeutschen Raum (1650–1820)*, part 1, Abh. d. Sächs. Akad. d. Wiss. zu Leipzig. Philol.-hist. Klasse 76/2, Stuttgart: Hirzel.

Dörner, A. (1995) *Politischer Mythos und symbolische Politik: Sinnstiftung durch symbolische Formen am Beispiel des Hermannsmythos*, Opladen/Wiesbaden: Westdeutscher Verlag.

Eidson, J. (2001) 'Ländergröße ist nicht immer Länderglück: zur Konstruktion sächsischer Geschichte und Identität in der Landesgeschichtsschreibung des 19. und frühen 20. Jahrhunderts', *Jahrbuch des SFB 417* 1, 90–119.

Fairclough, N. (1995) *Critical Discourse Analysis: The Critical Study of Language*, London: Longman.

Friedrich, C., U. Sommer and M. Middell (2002) 'Der prachtliebende Kurfürst und sein ränke-voller Rat auf dem falschen Weg für das vielgeliebte Sachsen – Geschichtsbilder in sächsischen Lehrbüchern im 19. und 20. Jahrhundert', in H.-W. Wollersheim, M. Moderow and C. Friedrich (eds) *Die Rolle von Schulbüchern für Identifikationsprozesse in historischer Perspektive*, Leipziger Studien zur Erforschung von regionenbezogenen Identifikationsprozessen 5, Leipzig: Universitätsverlag, 161–213.

Giesen, B. (ed.) (1991) *Nationale und kulturelle Identität: Studien zur Entwicklung des kollektiven Bewußtseins in der Neuzeit*, Frankfurt: Suhrkamp.

―― (1999) *Kollektive Identität: Die Intellektuellen und die Nation*, Frankfurt: Suhrkamp.

Hahn, F. (1851) *Die zweite sorbische Grenzmark in ihrer Entstehung, ihren Folgen und Ueberresten*. Variscia, Mittheilungen aus dem Archive des voigtländischen Alterthumsforschenden Vereins 5, Greiz: Selbstverlag des Vereins, 63–8.

Heimpel, H. (1963) *Geschichtsvereine einst und jetzt. Vortrag gehalten am Tag der 70. Wiederkehr der Gründung des Geschichtsvereins für Göttingen und Umgebung 19.11.1962*, Göttingen: Vandenhoek und Ruprecht.

Hobsbawm, E. (1997) *On History*, London: Weidenfeld & Nicholson.

Holtorf, C. (2005) *From Stonehenge to Las Vegas: Archaeology as Popular Culture*, Walnut Creek, CA: AltaMira Press.

Jäger, G. (1982) 'Die Bestände deutscher Leihbibliotheken zwischen 1815 und 1860', in R. Wittmann and B. Hack (eds) *Buchhandel und Literatur: Festschrift für Herbert G. Göpfert zum 75. Geburtstag am 22. September 1982*, Wiesbaden: Otto Harrassowitz, 247–313.

Jäger, S. (ed.) (1992) *Wie kritisch ist die kritische Diskursanalyse? Ansätze zu einer Wende kritischer Wissenschaft*, Münster: Unrast.

—— (1993) *Kritische Diskursanalyse: eine Einführung*, Duisburg: Duisburger Institut für Sprach- und Sozialforschung.

Jud, P. and G. Kaenel (eds) (2002) *Lebensbilder – Scènes de vie: actes du colloque de Zoug (13–14 mars 2001)*, documents du Groupe de travail pour les recherches préhistoriques en Suisse 2, Lausanne: Groupe de travail pour les recherches préhistoriques en Suisse.

Kaeser, M.-A. (2002) 'On the International Roots of Prehistory', *Antiquity* 76, 170–7.

—— (2003) 'La science vécue : les potentialités de la biographie en histoire des sciences', *Revue d'Histoire des Sciences Humaines* 8, 139–60.

Kaeser, M.-A. and M. Babes (forthcoming) *Archéologues sans frontières*, Lisbon: UISPP.

Kater, M. (1974) *Das 'Ahnenerbe' der SS 1935–1945: Ein Beitrag zur Kulturpolitik des Dritten Reiches*, Stuttgart: Deutsche Verlags-Anstalt.

Klüpfel, K. A. (1844) 'Die historischen Zeitschriften und Vereine Deutschlands', *Zeitschrift für Geschichtswissenschaft* 1, 518–59.

Köhnke, K. C. (2001) 'Ein konstruktivistischer Heimatbegriff?', *Jahrbuch des SFB 417* 1, 137–47.

Latour, B. (1989a) 'Pasteur und Pouchet. Die Heterogenese der Wissenschaftsgeschichte', in M. Serres (ed.) *Elemente einer Geschichte der Wissenschaften*, Frankfurt: Suhrkamp, 749–89.

—— (1989b) 'Joliot: Geschichte und Physik im Gemenge', in M. Serres (eds) *Elemente einer Geschichte der Wissenschaften*, Frankfurt: Suhrkamp, 869–903.

Martino, A. (1982) 'Lektüre in Wien um die Jahrhundertwende (1889–1914)', in R. Wittmann and B. Hack (eds) *Buchhandel und Literatur: Festschrift für Herbert G. Göpfert zum 75. Geburtstag am 22. September 1982*, Wiesbaden: Otto Harrassowitz, 314–95.

—— (1990) *Die deutsche Leihbibliothek: Geschichte einer literarischen Institution (1756–1914). Mit einem zusammen mit Georg Jäger erstellten Verzeichnis der erhaltenen Leihbibliothekskataloge*, Wiesbaden: Otto Harrassowitz.

Middell, M., M. Gibas and F. Hadler (2000) 'Sinnstiftung und Systemlegitimation durch historisches Erzählen; Überlegungen zu Funktionsmechanismen von Repräsentationen des Vergangenen', *Comparativ* 10.2, 7–35.

Mitchell, R. (2000) *Picturing the Past: English History in Text and Image 1830–1870*, Oxford: Clarendon Press.

Molyneaux, B. L. (ed.) (1997) *The Cultural Life of Images: Visual Representation in Archaeology*, London, Routledge.

Moser, S. (1998) *Ancestral Images: The Iconography of Human Origins*, Ithaca, NY: Cornell University Press.

Nipperdey, T. (1968) 'Nationalidee und Nationaldenkmal in Deutschland im 19. Jahrhundert', *Historische Zeitschrift* 206, 529–85.

—— (1972) 'Verein als soziale Struktur in Deutschland im späten 18. und frühen 19. Jahrhundert', in H. Bookmann *et al.* (eds) *Geschichtswissenschaft im 19. Jahrhundert, Beiträge zur historischen Forschung in Deutschland*, Göttingen: Vandenhoeck & Ruprecht, 1–44.

Penny, H. G. (2002) *Objects of Culture: Ethnology and Ethnographic Museums in Imperial Germany*, Chapel Hill: University of North Carolina Press.

Pepperle, I. (1989) 'Einleitung', in I. Pepperle (ed.) *Einundzwanzig Bogen aus der Schweiz, herausgegeben von Georg Herwegh*, Leipzig: Reclam, 6–63.

Petermann, K. (1881) *Geschichte des Königreichs Sachsen mit besonderer Berücksichtigung der wichtigsten culturgeschichtlichen Erscheinungen für den Unterricht in vaterländischen Schulen*, Leipzig: Julius Klinkhardt.

Preusker, C. B. (1841) 'Über Dorf-Bibliotheken und Lesezirkel', *Allgemeiner Anzeiger und Nationalzeitung der Deutschen, Gotha* 211, 6 (August).

—— (1841–1944). *Blicke in die vaterländische Vorzeit. Sitten, Sagen Bauwerke, Trachten, Geräthe aus dem heidnischen Alterthume und christlichen Mittelalter der sächsischen und angränzenden Lande für gebildete Leser aller Stände*, Leipzig: Hinrichs.

Propp, V. (1968) *Morphology of the Folk-tale*, American Folklore Society, Bibliographical and Special Series 9, Austin: Texas University Press.

Roth, M. (1990) *Heimatmuseum: zur Geschichte einer deutschen Institution*, Berliner Schriften Museumskunde 7, Berlin: Gebrüder Mann.

Rüsen J. (1994) *Historische Orientierung. Über die Arbeit des Geschichtsbewusstseins, sich in der Zeit zurechtzufinden*, Köln: Böhlau.

—— (2002) *Geschichte im Kulturprozess*, Cologne: Böhlau.

Schaarschmidt, T. (2004) *Regionalkultur und Diktatur: Sächsische Heimatbewegung und Heimat-Propaganda im Dritten Reich und in der SBZ/DDR*, Cologne: Böhlau Verlag.

Schenda, R. (1970) *Volk ohne Buch: Studien zur Sozialgeschichte der populären Lesestoffe, 1770–1910*, Frankfurt: Vittorio Klostermann.

Schulz, H. F. (1960) *Das Schicksal der Bücher und der Buchhandel*, Berlin: de Gruyter.

Sommer, U. (2002) 'Die Darstellung der Vorgeschichte in sächsischen Geschichtsbüchern des 19. Jahrhunderts', in H.-W. Wollersheim, M. Moderow and C. Friedrich (eds) *Die Rolle von Schulbüchern für Identifikationsprozesse in historischer Perspektive*, Leipziger Studien zur Erforschung von regionenbezogenen Identifikationsprozessen 5, Leipzig: Universtitätsverlag, 133–60.

—— (2007) 'The Freedom of the Woods: Antiquarian Landscapes and Politics', *Bulletin of the History of Archaeology* 17.2, 31–41.

Tacke, C. (1995) *Denkmal im sozialen Raum: Nationale Symbole in Deutschland und Frankreich im 19. Jhdt*, Göttingen: Vandenhoeck & Ruprecht.

Virchow, R. (1886) 'Gesamtbericht über die von der deutschen anthropologischen Gesellschaft veranlaßten Erhebungen über die Farbe der Haut, der Haare und der Augen der Schulkinder in Deutschland', *Archiv für Anthropologie* 16, 275–475.

Walther, A. F. (1845) *Systematisches Repetitorium über die Schriften sämtlicher historischer Gesellschaften Deutschlands*, Darmstadt: Historischer Verein für das Großherzogthum Hessen.

Wittmann, R. (1982) *Buchmarkt und Lektüre im 18. und 19. Jahrhundert: Beiträge zum literarischen Leben 1750–1880*, Tübingen: Niemeyer.

Wodak, R. and M. Meyer (eds) (2001) *Methods of Critical Discourse Analysis*, London: Sage.

Wodak, R., R. de Cillia and M. Reisigl (eds) (1998) *Zur diskursiven Konstruktion nationaler Identität*, Frankfurt: Suhrkamp.

Ziegler, E. (1982) 'Zensurgesetzgebung und Zensurpraxis in Deutschland 1819 bis 1848', in R. Wittmann and B. Hack (eds) *Buchhandel und Literatur: Festschrift für Herbert G. Göpfert zum 75. Geburtstag am 22. September*, Wiesbaden: Otto Harrassowitz, 185–220.

Part III

HERITAGE METHODOLOGIES: INVESTIGATING PEOPLE

7

REFLECTIONS ON THE PRACTICE OF ETHNOGRAPHY WITHIN HERITAGE TOURISM

Catherine Palmer

Introduction

In this chapter I reflect upon the methodological issues involved in research designed to explore how meaning is made through tourism. Embedded within an anthropological framework, the research taken as a case study here focused on the relationship between heritage tourism and English national identity through an ethnographic investigation of three heritage sites: Battle Abbey, Hever Castle and Chartwell (Palmer 1999). In what follows, I discuss the original aims of the research, the research strategy and its implementation in order to illustrate the wider methodological issues that arise.

My epistemological focus then and now is understanding how knowledge is constructed through experience of the world, whether consciously in terms of a purposeful desire to seek out knowledge or unconsciously through the mundane, taken-for-granted activities of daily life such as working, shopping or going on holiday. In the context of such activities, the form of knowledge generation I am concerned with pertains to issues of identity and belonging, and specifically to the cultural dynamics or processes by which identity is constructed, mediated and understood through visiting places of historic interest. A focus on heritage is instructive since the heritage is a significant resource and structural component of tourism. It is also an important part of culture because of its association with the notion of inheritance, of something of value handed down for safe keeping from one generation to the next (see Lowenthal 1998). Given that my overarching aim is to explore how individuals make sense of the world, through their experiences of it, then encounters with the heritage can shed light on how sense-making in the present is structured in relation to the past.

The link with anthropology, specifically social anthropology, is clear, since anthropology is concerned with understanding the world through the social and cultural structures that individuals use to organise, guide and give meaning to their lives: structures such as work, play and faith (Delaney 2004; Hendry 1999; Herzfeld 2001). Tourism, as one aspect of 'play', requires individuals to engage with the world and in so doing frames the way in which people think and feel about what being in the world actually means, about who they are, about identity and belonging. Social anthropology is, therefore, rightly interested in how meaning is made through tourism, an interest that has generated a substantial body of knowledge from a variety of different perspectives (see Andrews 2004; Cohen 2004; Edensor 1998; Graburn 1983; MacCannell 1989; Moore 1980; Nash 1996; Palmer 2005; Selwyn 1996; Smith 1989; Tucker 2003). Tourism matters because it is one of the defining activities of the modern world, shaping the ways in which people relate to and make sense of the world, Self and Other.

The significance of tourism and tourists to social science can be traced back to MacCannell's seminal work *The Tourist: A New Theory of the Leisure Class*, which set out to present a critique of tourism as a feature of modernity. MacCannell argues that anthropology's focus on less technologically advanced societies should be redirected towards modern mass leisure generally, and to tourism in particular because '[o]ur first apprehension of modern civilization, it seems to me, emerges in the mind of the tourist' (1989: 1). To this end MacCannell sets out to record and analyse tourist behaviour by following groups of tourists sightseeing in Paris. Sometimes he joins in their activities, while at other times he observes from afar either by watching what takes place or by reading primary and secondary accounts about tourism and tourists. For MacCannell, tourist attractions represent a typology of structure capable of giving access to the thought processes of modern peoples – and so by following tourists 'we may be able to come to a better understanding of ourselves' (1989: 5).

In line with MacCannell, my interest in tourist behaviour is not in the direct impact of that behaviour on destinations and their inhabitants, but in what this behaviour can tell us about ourselves, specifically in this instance ourselves as a nation, as possessing a national identity. A perspective that sees identity as being socially constructed through experience of the world necessitates a focus on culture given that culture is key to understanding the mind of the tourist. Moreover, accessing and interpreting the cultural dynamics that underpin the creation and maintenance of identity requires a methodological framework suited to understanding the experience under investigation: tourists visiting heritage attractions. In this sense, tourists are a form of 'society' within a specific social context – tourism – albeit a society that is highly mobile and in which membership is fluid, temporally contingent, and determined both by location and purpose. Understanding tourism in this way fits well with Berger and Berger's claim that: 'Society is our experience with other people around us ... It serves as the context for everything else we experience, including our experience of the natural world and of ourselves, because these other experiences are also mediated by and modified for us by other people' (1976: 13). The concept of 'tourist society' enables the act of tourism to be visualised as a totality capable of investigation and analysis from a variety of different perspectives, including that concerned with the culture of tourist society, namely social anthropology.

Context and foundations

Anthropology's focus on the interpretation, or representation, of culture is largely (but not exclusively) addressed through ethnography as both method and monograph. As method, ethnography is employed when the aim of the research is to understand the ways in which individuals make sense of their everyday life: '[t]he ethnographer participates, overtly or covertly in people's daily lives, watching what happens, listening to what is said, asking questions; in fact collecting whatever data are available to throw light on the issues with which he or she is concerned' (Hammersley and Atkinson 1983: 2). Ethnography thus entails a 'family of methods' (Willis and Trondman 2000: 5) of which participant observation is merely one of the ways in which data are gathered. Other complementary methods are frequently employed in order to support and 'flesh out' data generated in this way, such as the interviewing of key informants, and the analysis of textual and visual sources. However, participant observation remains a key part of anthropological fieldwork, serving 'as distinctive method and professional rite of passage' (Willis and Trondman 2000: 4).

Ethnography concerns itself with understanding lived experience from the insider's perspective (Geertz 1973; Van Maanen 1988), but although it is uniquely suited to studies of tourism and tourists it remains largely underemployed in these respects, although there are exceptions in Andrews (2004), Cole (2004) and Tucker (2003). The issue of time is certainly a factor here, in terms of a traditional view of ethnographic fieldwork in which one or two years spent in the field living with the local inhabitants is almost the minimum time required. Wolcott queries this basic assumption, however, by asking: '[m]ust an ethnographer *always* spend months and months in the field in order to claim ethnographic validity?' (1999: 197, original emphasis). Clearly the investigation of culture through lived experience requires a certain amount of time, not just because of the complexities involved but also because decisions about time spent in the field are rarely straightforward. The research questions, the nature, purpose and fieldwork location/s, issues of context and history and of intimacy and distance in terms of the social, cultural, economic and linguistic differences between the researcher and the researched all influence 'time' in the field.

Time is particularly significant for research into the impacts of tourism, since both the effects of tourism and tourist attitudes towards these effects are not fixed in time (Wilson 1993). The research discussed here adds another dimension to the issue of time, since tourists on day trips to heritage attractions are characterised by fluidity and flow: each day, indeed each morning and afternoon, often comprises different individuals and groups. Although individuals come and go in all societal groupings, day trips to places of interest are marked by the transitory composition of visitors at the given location. While there are certainly tourism activities where a core group of recognisable individuals can be observed over a period of time – for example cruise-ship passengers, package tourists staying at one hotel for the duration of their holiday, or guided tours – at heritage sites it is not always possible to observe a core group of people day after day, month after month. Tourists visiting Battle Abbey, Hever Castle and Chartwell are not a community, at least not in the 'traditional' sense as illustrated by the contributors to Cohen's (1982a) book on British rural cultures or the work of such as Okely (1983) and Scheper-Hughes (1979).

Indeed, each day at a historic site brings a different set of people, so a disciplinary dictum of a year spent in the field is not necessarily the most appropriate rule for an ethnographic study of tourist behaviour. In addition to the factors noted above, the importance of time with regard to ethnographies of tourist attractions is largely seen in terms of seasonality, days and times of the week, as these factors affect the composition of tourist 'society' on an ongoing basis. Hence judgements of what is enough time to be spent in the field should instead be based on considerations such as data saturation, the number and range of fieldwork locations, and what Wolcott (1999) refers to as a 'matter-of-fact' attitude to time – where too much time in the field is as bad as too little. Scholars of tourism should therefore not allow the issue of time to deter them from employing ethnography as a method, since it can help to uncover significant 'knowledge' in terms of how meaning is made through tourism.

In reflecting upon the three sites of heritage tourism discussed here, Marcus's (1995, 2007) call for multi-sited ethnography offers much food for thought. A traditional ethnographic lens would focus on one tourist attraction and offer a thorough and detailed analysis of embedded practice. However, if I had focused my attention on only one site, then no matter how instructive such a lens would have been it would have resulted in a singular view of identity, a view based upon the historic period depicted at the particular site. Yet the different sites offer multiple versions of identity that cut across time and space. For example, my three sites are in different locations and represent different periods of history – and hence differing perspectives of Englishness. So, although not without its own methodological challenges (see Scarangella 2007), a multi-sited approach enabled me to uncover connections, perspectives and relationships that would have been missed had I focused on only one site (see Palmer 2005).

As noted earlier, what anthropologists actually 'do' in the field is immerse themselves in the life of those individuals or groups with whom they are concerned, as a means of understanding the insider's world-view. Immersion is, however, an intimate act (Herzfeld 2001), and it is not always desirable or even possible to separate the researcher from those individuals under investigation, as Kotsi (2007) illustrates in her work on the experiences of tourists and pilgrims at Mount Athos in Greece. Greek by birth, she describes her ethnographic position as being that of a native anthropologist close to and familiar with the culture under investigation. Such a position caused her to reflect upon what it meant to be Greek, a woman and a member of the Orthodox Church. So although ethnography requires the researcher to maintain a stance that is uncritical of the behaviour and activities observed, while at the same time remaining open to elements that cannot be codified at the time of the study (see Baszanger and Dodier 1997), there is a balance to be struck between intimacy and distance. As Scheper-Hughes acknowledges in response to the controversy generated by her ethnography of mental illness in rural Ireland:

> the real dilemma and contradiction was this: How can we know what we know other than by filtering experience through the highly subjective categories of thinking and feeling that represent our own particular ways of being – such as the American Catholic-school-trained, rebellious though still ambivalently Catholic, post-Freudian, neo-Marxist, feminist woman I was in my initial encounter with the villagers of Ballybran.
>
> (Scheper-Hughes 2000: 127)

The issues Scheper-Hughes raises provide the focus for a book entitled *How Do We Know? Evidence, Ethnography, and the Making of Anthropological Knowledge* (Chua et al. 2008a). Here the contributors discuss the relationship between anthropological evidence and knowledge generation, illustrating the role of the anthropologist in *creating* rather than merely discovering knowledge. As the editors argue, anthropological knowledge is 'the product of a historical, social, and personal assemblage which includes not only the ethnographer's person, but also one's intellectual background, institutional demands, conceptual genealogies, and relational quirks within and beyond the field' (Chua et al. 2008b: 17). Ethnographies of tourism are an interesting example of the above, since many anthropologists are also tourists, and some may even take employment in tourism as a means of gathering data (see Bruner 1995). The ethnographer-tourist has a very real dilemma when considering Scheper-Hughes's point about the effect of subjectivity on knowledge, since the experience of being a tourist – of experiencing the very things that form the focus of investigation – colours the view from above as well as that from within (indeed, the reverse is often true as I have sometimes found it hard to switch off the ethnographic eye when on holiday). Within tourist studies the issue of positionality is increasingly being recognised in terms of its influence on the collection and analysis of data, particularly in situations when the focus is upon cultural particularities or experiences with which the researcher is familiar (see Kotsi 2007; Pritchard and Morgan 2003; Morgan and Pritchard 2005). In these cases I was not able to distance myself from my own position as a female, WASP, ethnographer-tourist who describes herself as both English and British; indeed, I did not even seek this distance since '[t]he ethnographer is an element within the field as well as its "observer"' (Atkinson 1990: 158).

The ethnographer's role in creating rather than merely uncovering knowledge is discussed in a variety of ways in Chua et al. (2008a). In the introductory chapter the editors argue that although it is acknowledged that 'how we know' is deeply entrenched in 'who we are', much still needs to be done as anthropologists must acknowledge their role in creating and not merely uncovering the evidence upon which anthropological knowledge is based (Chua et al. 2008b: 17). As Scheper-Hughes again illustrates:

> Like poetry, ethnography is an act of translation and the kind of 'truth' that it produces is necessarily deeply subjective. ... Our task requires of us only a highly disciplined subjectivity. There are scientific methods and models appropriate to other ways of doing anthropological research, but ethnography, as I understand it, is not a science.
> (Scheper-Hughes 2000: 132)

The cultural translation of people's lives is not, therefore, a neutral act, since acts of translation and interpretation are shot through with issues of power and control. A researcher has a duty therefore to be critical and self-questioning about what he or she uncovers and to adopt a rigorous approach to the relationship between theory, data and interpretation (Herzfeld 2001; Moore and Sanders 2006). Theory is fundamental to both the collection and interpretation of data, providing a context within and against which data can be examined (Herzfeld 2001; Willis and Trondman 2000). Indeed, whatever methods are employed, data require a framework within which they can be analysed: '[o]ne cannot simply observe. A question such as "What is going on here?" can only be addressed when fleshed out with enough detail to answer the related question, "In terms of what?"' (Wolcott 1999: 69).

In considering the relationship between heritage tourism and Englishness, my approach to Wolcott's first question of 'what is going on here?' encompassed three broad areas. First was the tourism industry's use and reliance upon culture, upon the material and symbolic resources of the nation's heritage as a means of defining and promoting Englishness. Second was the symbolic transmission of identity, how each site communicated identity through aspects of the nation's cultural heritage – in other words, the social mechanisms by which identity was conveyed. Third were the ways in which individuals, as tourists and employees, experienced and understood a particular site. The theoretical framework required to address these areas, and thus Wolcott's second question, is primarily found within those disciplines and fields concerned with the study of nations, nationalism and national identity (see Anderson 1991; Bhabha 1990; Connor 1993; Gellner 1983; Kedourie 1960; Smith 1983, 1986, 1991). Of particular relevance were studies linking the theory of nations and the emergence of national consciousness to the experience of identity in everyday life (see Billig 1995; Cohen 1982b; Palmer 1998). Several key issues highlighted by the literature proved to be particularly useful while investigating the social and cultural dynamics at play in visiting heritage attractions. Issues such as the role of the imagination, of feeling and of sentiment, of kinship and community, and of power and agency in constructing a particular interpretation of Englishness were important (cf. Palmer 2005).

From theory to method

Given that the primary focus of the study was the cultural representation of Englishness, the symbolic display of 'ourselves', this involved analysing the ways in which individuals experienced the display of culture, the natural and physical landscapes, and the material and visual artefacts. Such aspects enable the cultural particularities of a people to be communicated and understood (or misunderstood). How people respond to such cultural markers, how they behave, what they say and what they do when confronted by them is important for understanding the cultural transmission of identity, because 'it is through the flow of behaviour – or, more precisely, social action – that cultural forms find articulation' (Geertz 1973: 17).

My overall aim, then, was to access the mind of the tourist as a way of understanding 'what is going on here' in terms of identity. Ethnography enabled me to immerse myself in the world of the tourist and to explore issues of meaning and interpretation by uncovering the thought processes behind visitor reactions to each site. The range of methods furthermore allowed me to search for patterns and themes in visitor thinking, and to understand how visitors conceptualised 'Englishness'. Billig has argued that "[i]deology is to be discovered in those patterns of common-sense thinking which cut across class, age and gender distinctions. This means looking for commonalities in what is said. And just as importantly ... in what is not said' (1992: 19). Hence I was seeking an anthropologically derived 'common-sense' response to each site, although it is acknowledged that 'common sense' as a framework for understanding is not common to all cultures, being as it is context-specific (Herzfeld 2001).

Drawing upon Geertz's (1973) interpretive approach to culture, a key feature of the research methods was the identification and analysis of the structures of signification within the three sites. Battle Abbey, Hever Castle and Chartwell represent specific social settings within which individuals interact with themselves and with others. It was through the observation and recording of such interactions that the visitors' 'conceptual world' was accessed.

Accessing the tourist mind

Given the above, the methods I employed were: the analysis of the particular historic context, in the review and analysis of books, archival sources, documents, guides and other relevant material (published and unpublished) relating to the three sites; tape-recorded interviews with key people associated with the sites, such as employees, managers, members of related associations and relevant individuals from the organisations that owned the sites; observation of visitors at different times taking into account seasonal factors, days and times of the week, with written notes about visitor behaviour and overheard 'conversations'; and, lastly, tape-recorded interviews with visitors. I interviewed site employees 'on the job': in their offices, during communal tea breaks, just prior to opening, or in the 'gaps' between tourists coming and going. I spoke to some staff only once, though I engaged with others in on-off conversations during the research period. I spent around four to five months at each site over an eighteen-month period. The range of methods not only generated a rich amount of data but also enabled data-source triangulation to support the analysis and interpretation of my findings:

> data-source triangulation involves the comparison of data relating to the same phenomenon but deriving from different phases of the fieldwork ... This is very time consuming but, besides providing a validity check, it also gives added depth to the description of the social meanings involved in a setting.
>
> (Hammersley and Atkinson 1983: 198)

The characteristics of each site affected where the visitor interviews took place. The Battle Abbey heritage site is an outdoor site encompassing the ruins of Battle Abbey, hence there was space to interview people as they wandered around the site. No interviews were carried out inside Chartwell or Hever Castle for two reasons. First, their respective managers did not wish visitors to be approached, as this may have detracted from their visit, and second, it would have undermined my anonymity and compromised my observations of visitor behaviour inside and outside the properties. At Hever Castle, visitor interviews were restricted to certain areas, again to minimise any disruption to visitors. Interestingly, this was not the only restriction I encountered at Hever: I was not permitted to interview employees as the management felt this would take them away from their duties around the site. Such access issues highlight the fine line anthropologists have to tread when searching for insights into the thinking of others, a line that requires flexibility and a willingness to adapt to the context of the research setting (see Van Maanen 1988; van Meijl 2005). The interviews with tourists were conducted primarily as conversations, my intention being to put my informants at their ease and so increase the possibility of obtaining information that may more readily indicate patterns of 'common-sense' thinking, underlying feelings, assumptions and beliefs. Cohen provides a useful illustration of what took place:

> The proper ethnographic interview is a conversation in which ethno-graphers risk the appearance of naivety and ignorance in order continually to satisfy themselves that they have understood what is being said ... the conversations ... are instruments ... for stripping away the ballasts of expectation and assumption.
>
> (Cohen 1984: 226)

These visitor interviews highlight a number of issues when taking Cohen's claims alongside Scheper-Hughes's call for 'highly disciplined subjectivity'. The appearance of naivety and ignorance worked well both as a strategy for delving deeper into what people said or did not say, and as a means of enabling them to work through their reactions to the site. That said, I was continually 'on guard', watching for interesting snippets of conversation that could be developed further, or for issues I had not expected or considered to be covered in my conversations with tourists. A conversation is a two-way process, however, and although I was mindful of the need for disciplined subjectivity this was not something the tourists considered at all, for understandable reasons. Hence I was often asked questions in return, questions about my experiences and understanding of a particular site. My dilemma was whether to say exactly what I thought and risk influencing the visitor's own reactions, or 'hide' my real views behind bland statements of interest. In the end I found the latter response hindered conversation while on many occasions the former actually enabled a deeper investigation of what was being discussed.

Moreover, when confronted with questions they have not expected or prepared for, people tend to respond more instinctively than if they are given advance warning of what is to come. In such situations the responses are arguably more 'honest', as the visitor does not have time to think of what might be considered a 'suitable' reply, or of what the researcher may be 'looking for'. In general, my informants were well able to articulate their experiences and thoughts within a conversation that allowed for differing views to be explored by all parties. Having said that, though, a researcher should not 'lose' him or herself so completely that self-questioning gives way to complicity; one useful tactic is 'to make the question "lead" in a direction opposite to that in which one expects the answer to lie and thus avoid the danger of simply misleadingly confirming one's expectations' (Hammersley and Atkinson 1983: 115–16).

I made observations of visitors as they toured each site and notes about their behaviour and conversations overheard. This 'unannounced' participatory stance enabled me to be part of the heritage 'experience' while at the same time witnessing the social and cultural dynamics of visitor interaction with the site. One of the problems with observation is validation: the question of what is chosen to be observed versus what is not chosen (or even noticed), due to the observer's own fallibility or biases of world-view, age, gender, sexual orientation or faith. Adler and Adler (1998) suggest that multiple observers can address these concerns, but this is not always possible, particularly with the kind of research discussed here. Although I was the only observer in an academic sense, I was not the only observer in the field. Site employees and managers are also observers by virtue of working at the sites; they too notice what visitors do and remain acutely aware of visitor reactions and preoccupations since they have to respond to questions about a site. At the two sites where I was allowed to talk to employees they proved invaluable in this regard.

Covert observation does raise ethical concerns. Without entering into a lengthy discussion of these concerns (see Adler and Adler 1998; Denzin 1970; Hammersley and Atkinson 1995; Punch 1998; Scheper-Hughes 2004), one interesting illustration of the dilemmas, the implications and the effectiveness of covert research is provided by Dan Rose's research into black American street life. Rose (1990: 11) argues that his 'ethically painful' decision to undertake covert research fundamentally changed his assumptions about the practice of ethnography, because the reality of covert fieldwork did not sit easily with the theory learnt from books and from the classroom. His experiences caused him to question the corporate academic culture that governs what is acceptable methodological practice. Lugosi makes a similar point when discussing his ethnography of a suburban bar by arguing that the covert–overt debate is not best served by 'a culture of denigration that treats all our untruths as professional misconduct' (2006: 555), since the reality of fieldwork can mean that concealment is sometimes both necessary and unavoidable. My approach to the issue here is in line with that adopted by Denzin: 'I take the stance that justifies "unannounced", disguised research methods. If we are not permitted to study things that people wish hidden then sociology will remain a science of public conduct based on evidence and data given us by volunteers' (Denzin 1970: xiii). Furthermore, Sugden's (2002) investigative ethnography of the deviant subcultures feeding off and into international football illustrates the importance and value of covert research into 'things that people wish hidden'.

For myself, a guiding principle remains that of harm to subjects: would my observations, my analysis or presentation of my findings harm the people I had been observing? Given the character and purpose of my research I would argue no, though I recognize Hammersley and Atkinson's (1995) point that what constitutes harm is a matter of judgement and may well be contentious. Even so, I was mindful of protecting my subjects, of maintaining anonymity: while I noted generalities such as gender and estimated age, no other personal details were sought or recorded. I was not interested in divisions between demographically 'identifiable' people but rather in the many, varied and complex ways in which identity is experienced through culture.

That said, I was interested in nationality insofar as it revealed itself through what people said when visiting a particular site. As my notes made no mention of personal variables other than age and gender, it was and still is impossible for any individual to be identified. Public culture publicly displayed is a legitimate concern of anthropology, and the observation of a publicly accessible activity such as tourism is essential if we are to understand how knowledge is created through tourism. Such a position does not mean that public settings are immune from ethical protocols, given that they are populated by private citizens, but rather highlights the wider point that there is no 'one size fits all' ethical position, particularly for covert observation. The purpose and context (disciplinary and methodological) of any research are key influencing factors. Again, the overarching issue is the balance between harm to subjects and the advancement of knowledge; as Adler and Adler argue, the pursuit of knowledge must 'be fettered by a sensitivity to the rights of unknowing others' (1998: 102–3).

The practice of ethnography

Although my ethnography included an analysis of the many sources (published and unpublished) necessary for locating the sites within an appropriate historic context, I do not discuss this aspect of the methodology here. Rather, I focus on the methods adopted at the three sites: what has been referred to as the messy business of qualitative fieldwork (Jamal and Hollinshead 2001; Ritchie *et al.* 2005). In this respect it is worth bearing in mind Denzin's (1970) observation that the theory of research does not always relate to its practical application, since fieldwork is far from an idealised process where theories fall into place once the data have been gathered. Indeed, reflection may cause a researcher to doubt previously published interpretations of their data (see Greenwood 1989; Salzinger 2004), while a particular method may lead to unexpected and unintended outcomes for both the researcher and the research participants. For example, Weeden's focus-group research into ethical tourism resulted in a revelatory moment for some participants 'when for the first time they felt a personal responsibility for the impact of tourism' (2005: 188). Practical considerations taken in the field often require the researcher to change tack or to modify her or his behaviour in collecting data or interviewing (see Cole 2005; Lugosi 2006). Although my research did not involve my living or working with a community or group in the traditional sense of 'living with', it still presented practical difficulties that at times caused me to suffer from what Rose (1990) has described as the maddening frustration of ethnographic fieldwork.

Like any field site, the characteristics of each site affected the process of observation. Chartwell and Hever Castle present the visitor with buildings to visit and rooms to wander through, so observations of visitors could be made as they toured inside each structure. There are also extensive grounds surrounding both properties, where visitors could again be observed. As noted earlier, Battle Abbey is an outdoor site consisting of the ruins of Battle Abbey, the surrounding fields upon which the Battle of Hastings (1066) was fought, and a gatehouse exhibition about issues of history and archaeology. Hence, the visitor experience of Battle Abbey is quite different to that of the other two sites.

When observing 'what is going on here' it was not possible to follow every visitor or group of visitors, or to record every overheard conversation. Nor was it possible to ask visitors their age, so, as stated above, I had to make an educated guess. Age is a particular issue at Chartwell, where the typical visitor profile signals the predominance of older visitors attracted to the house due to its connection with Winston Churchill and the Second World War. So I needed to ensure that as far as possible I observed visitors of all ages by constantly checking my notes and by being careful to observe visitors such as children, adolescents and people who appeared to be under the age of forty-five to fifty. The checking and rechecking of what is being recorded is vital for assessing whether something is being missed or whether preconceptions are merely being confirmed. I frequently took 'time out' to review what I was recording and to read through my captured 'conversations', so that I could actively search for alternative or differing examples. Such periods of reflection also proved useful during the visitor interviews, since they often suggested potentially fruitful lines of questioning. As noted earlier, the site employees were extremely helpful, providing me with accounts of visitor behaviour and reactions, and frequently asked questions.

The influence of gender on understandings of identity is an important avenue of research but this was not the purpose of my investigation. So when recording my observations, I took note of gender insofar as it enabled me to identify groups of men, women or mixed groups, and to distinguish between individuals when speaking. While the gender of the speaker could be noted, the nationality of the speaker could not always be assured in this way. However, as with gender I was not interested in nationality *per se*, but as identity is influenced by the view of the 'Other' the reactions of non-English people were important. Although it is not possible to determine whether someone is English through observation alone, common sense can be applied by listening to what is being said.

As with any ethnography the notebook is an indispensable part of the ethnographic routine. Mine was no exception, since I used it to record my own thoughts as well as the overheard conversations. As people wandered through Chartwell and the fortified manor house that comprises Hever Castle such conversations manifested in different ways. Some people said little or even nothing, while others were so deep in conversation as to appear oblivious to their surroundings. Indeed, naturally occurring speech in these settings is not usually a sustained monologue but rather a few words here and there, then a pause while individuals read from guidebooks, examine information boards or simply study a particular room or artefact before resuming their conversation. Moreover, people do not always converse logically and their expressions often resemble 'thoughts out loud' rather than actual conversations. Conversations may appear disjointed and can end abruptly or even move to different and often seemingly unrelated topics. The challenge for the ethnographer is to capture as much of the 'conversations' and comments as possible while staying alert for what may be happening at the periphery.

The interviews took place in the grounds of each site. However, visitors to Battle Abbey wandered around the site with a greater degree of serendipity than at the other sites. The difficulties of dealing with such a situation are discussed by Ireland (1990) in his study of Land's End in Cornwall. Here Ireland interviewed visitors at specific locations derived by dividing the site into four areas, so as 'to replicate as far as possible, the exploratory behaviour of the visitor after leaving the car park' (1990: 35). A similar strategy was adopted both at Battle Abbey and for the grounds at Chartwell. As already stated, the locations for the interviews at Hever Castle were prescribed by the manager, who chose the main thoroughfare for visitors going to or from the castle. Although the above reflects a more structured approach to the interviews, I was acutely aware of this 'serendipitous' nature of tourist behaviour. Clearly, visits to heritage attractions are structured by elements such as signage, guidebooks, paths and site employees (see Garden, chapter 15), but visitors also wander around a site in their own fashion, through either naive or purposeful ignorance of such signage. So although certain areas provided a focal point for interviews and acted as key locations from which to observe visitor behaviour, my own wanderings enabled me to access visitors I may not otherwise have encountered.

Data gathered by means of observation and interviews certainly illustrate the messiness of qualitative research. However, 'mess' should not be viewed pejoratively but rather as an apt description of lived experience – both of the group or society being investigated and of the ethnographer. Cultural contexts are not neatly organised into clearly identifiable categories. They are complex, disorganised and disjointed arenas into which a researcher tries, sometimes in vain, to bring about a form of ordered meaning no matter how contingent. In attempting to make sense of visitor behaviour, our interpretations of what we observe and record are necessarily incomplete, since exceptions to the rule can always be found. As Geertz puts it, rather like the chips of a kaleidoscope, socially constructed knowledge and the meaning made from lived experience form and reform in a variety of shapes and patterns:

> for, as in a kaleidoscope, one always sees the chips distributed in *some* pattern, however ill-formed or irregular. But, as in a kaleidoscope, they are detachable from these structures and arrangeable into different ones of a similar sort.
>
> (Geertz 1973: 353, original emphasis)

Conclusion

While the above discussion illustrates some of the methodological and practical aspects of ethnography, it also highlights the value of ethnography as a method for investigating tourist behaviour and the spaces, places and contexts in which it is found. Tourism is a complex cultural phenomenon, yet too often studies of tourism employ methodologies that lack the subtlety and reach needed to scratch beneath the surface when a question such as 'what is going on here?' addresses tourist attractions. This chapter's focus on one particular study illustrates that ethnography is well suited to address the complexities inherent in this question. Moreover, when focusing on heritage tourism, there is much to be gained by adopting a multi-sited ethnographic approach that seeks to uncover relationships between aspects of the heritage rather than singular interpretations of particular heritage spaces. The complex nature of tourism presents an interesting challenge for any researcher given the earlier observation that many anthropologists are themselves tourists. The ethnographer-tourist label highlights van Meijl's (2005) point about the multiple identities required of the researcher in the field as a way to reconcile the irreconcilable demands of ethnographic research. My experiences at the sites discussed here certainly reflect a blurring of the lines between the researcher and the researched. As already noted, I was participating in the experience of touring the sites and was thus aware of my own emotions and thoughts. However, Rose (1990) stresses that the author's voice and emotional reactions should not be excluded, as they too require consideration and analysis. As Hammersley and Atkinson illustrate, '[t]here is, then, a constant interplay between the personal and the emotional on the one hand, and the intellectual on the other. Private response is thus transformed, by reflexive analysis, into potential public knowledge' (1983: 166–7).

To conclude, while there are unique challenges to be faced when the subject of investigation is the researcher's own cultural milieu, it is at times necessary to turn the familiar on its head, to deliberately make it unfamiliar in order to rethink preconceived or taken-for-granted assumptions and knowledge. To this end, ethnography as a method should be more widely employed to uncover and to question the knowledge generated through interpretations of the past.

Bibliography

Adler, P. A. and J. H. Adler (1998) 'Observational Techniques', in N. K. Denzin and Y. Lincoln (eds) *Collecting and Interpreting Qualitative Materials*, London: Sage, 79–109.

Anderson, B. (1991) *Imagined Communities: Reflections on the Origin and Spread of Nationalism*, 2nd edn, London: Verso.

Andrews, H. (2004) 'Escape to Britain: The Case of Charter Tourists to Mallorca'. PhD Thesis, London Metropolitan University.

Atkinson, P. (1990) *The Ethnographic Imagination*, London: Routledge.

Baszanger, I. and N. Dodier (1997) 'Ethnography: Relating the Part to the Whole', in D. Silverman (ed.) *Qualitative Research: Theory, Method and Practice*, London: Sage, 8–23.

Berger, P. L. and B. Berger (1976) *Sociology: A Biographical Approach*, Harmondsworth: Penguin.

Bhabha, H. K. (ed.) (1990) *Nation and Narration*, London: Routledge.

Billig, M. (1992) *Talking of the Royal Family*, London: Routledge.

—— (1995) *Banal Nationalism*, London: Sage.

Bruner, E. M. (1995) 'The Ethnographer/Tourist in Indonesia', in M.-L. Lanfant, J. B. Allcock and E. M. Bruner (eds) *International Tourism: Identity and Change*, London: Sage, 224–41.

Chua, L., C. High and T. Lau (eds) (2008a) *How Do We Know? Evidence, Ethnography, and the Making of Anthropological Knowledge*, Newcastle: Cambridge Scholars Publishing.

—— (2008b) 'Introduction: Questions of Evidence', in L. Chua, C. High and T. Lau (eds) *How Do We Know? Evidence, Ethnography, and the Making of Anthropological Knowledge*, Newcastle: Cambridge Scholars Publishing, 1–19.

Cohen, A. P. (ed.) (1982a) *Belonging: Identity and Social Organisation in British Rural Cultures*, Manchester: Manchester University Press.

—— (1982b) 'Belonging: The Experience of Culture', in A. P. Cohen (ed.) *Belonging: Identity and Social Organisation in British Rural Cultures*, Manchester: Manchester University Press, 1–17.

—— (1984) 'Informants', in R. F. Ellen (ed.) *Ethnographic Research: A Guide to General Conduct (Research Methods in Social Anthropology 1)*, London: Academic Press, 223–9.

Cohen, E. (2004) *Contemporary Tourism: Diversity and Change*, Oxford: Elsevier.

Cole, S. (2004) 'Shared Benefits: Longitudinal Research in Eastern Indonesia', in J. Phillimore and L. Goodson (eds) *Qualitative Research in Tourism:. Ontologies, Epistemologies and Methodologies*, London: Routledge, 292–310.

—— (2005) 'Action Ethnography: Using Participant Observation', in B. W. Ritchie, P. Burns and C. Palmer (eds) *Tourism Research Methods: Integrating Theory with Practice*, Wallingford: CAB International, 63–72.

Connor, W. (1993) 'Beyond Reason: The Nature of the Ethnonational Bond', *Ethnic and Racial Studies* 16.3, 373–89.

Delaney, C. (2004) *Investigating Culture: An Experiential Introduction to Anthropology*, Oxford: Blackwell.

Denzin, N. K. (1970) *The Research Art in Sociology: A Theoretical Introduction to Sociological Methods*, London: Butterworth.

Edensor, T. (1998) *Tourists at the Taj: Performance and Meaning at a Symbolic Site*, London: Routledge.

Geertz, C. (1973) *The Interpretation of Cultures*, New York: Basic Books.

Gellner, E. (1983) *Nations and Nationalism*, Oxford: Basil Blackwell.

Graburn, N. H. H. (1983) 'The Anthropology of Tourism', *Annals of Tourism Research* 10.1, 9–35.

Greenwood, D. J. (1989) 'Culture by the Pound: An Anthropological Perspective on Tourism as Cultural Commoditization', in V. L. Smith (ed.) *Hosts and Guests: The Anthropology of Tourism*, Philadelphia: University of Pennsylvania Press, 171–86.

Hammersley, M. and P. Atkinson (1983) *Ethnography: Principles and Practice*, London: Routledge.

—— (1995) *Ethnography: Principles and Practice*, 2nd edn, London: Routledge.

Hendry, J. (1999) *An Introduction to Social Anthropology: Other People's Worlds*, Basingstoke: Macmillan.

Herzfeld, M. (2001) *Anthropology: Theoretical Practice in Culture and Society*, Oxford: Blackwell.

Ireland, M. J. (1990) 'Come to Cornwall, Come to Land's End: A Study of Visitor Experience at a Touristic Sight', *Problems of Tourism* 8.3–4, 33–53.

Jamal, T. and K. Hollinshead (2001) 'Tourism and the Forbidden Zone: The Undeserved Power of Qualitative Inquiry', *Tourism Management* 22, 63–82.

Kedourie, E. (1960) *Nationalism*, London: Hutchinson.

Kotsi, F. (2007) 'Mirroring the Anthropologist: Reflex-ions of the Self', paper presented at the Association of Social Anthropologists' annual conference 'Thinking Through Tourism', London Metropolitan University, 10–13 April 2007.

Lowenthal, D. (1998) *The Heritage Crusade and the Spoils of History*, Cambridge: Cambridge University Press.

Lugosi, P. (2006) 'Between Overt and Covert Research: Concealment and Disclosure in an Ethnographic Study of Commercial Hospitality', *Qualitative Inquiry* 12.3, 541–61.

MacCannell, D. (1989) *The Tourist: A New Theory of the Leisure Class*, 2nd edn, New York: Schocken.

Marcus, G. (1995) 'Ethnography in/of the World System: The Emergence of Multi-sited Ethnography', *Annual Review of Anthropology* 24, 95–117.

—— (2007) 'What is at Stake – and is Not – in the Idea and Practice of Multi-sited Ethnography', in H. L. Moore and T. Sanders (eds) *Anthropology in Theory: Issues in Epistemology*, Oxford: Blackwell, 618–21.

Moore, A. (1980) 'Walt Disney World: Bounded Ritual Space and the Playful Pilgrimage Center', *Anthropological Quarterly* 53.4, 207–18.

Moore, H. L. and T. Sanders (2006) 'Anthropology and Epistemology', in II. L. Moore and T. Sanders (eds) *Anthropology in Theory: Issues in Epistemology*, Oxford: Blackwell, 1–21.

Morgan, N. and A. Pritchard (2005) 'On Souvenirs and Metonymy: Narratives of Memory, Metaphor and Materiality', *Tourist Studies* 5, 29–53.

Nash, D. (1996) *The Anthropology of Tourism*, Oxford: Pergamon.

Okely, J. (1983) *Changing Cultures: The Traveller-Gypsies*, Cambridge: Cambridge University Press.

Palmer, C. (1998) 'From Theory to Practice: Experiencing the Nation in Everyday Life', *Journal of Material Culture* 3.2, 175–99.

—— (1999) 'Heritage Tourism and English National Identity'. PhD Thesis, University of North London.

—— (2005) 'An Ethnography of Englishness: Experiencing Identity through Tourism', *Annals of Tourism Research* 32, 7–27.

Pritchard, A. and N. Morgan (2003) 'Mythic Geographies of Representation and Identity: Contemporary Postcards of Wales', *Tourism and Cultural Change* 1.2, 111–30.

Punch, M. (1998) 'Politics and Ethics in Qualitative Research', in N. K. Denzin and Y. Lincoln (eds) *The Landscape of Qualitative Research: Theories and Issues*, London: Sage, 156–84.

Ritchie, B. W., P. Burns and C. Palmer (2005) 'Introduction: Reflections on the Practice of Research', in B. W. Ritchie, P. Burns and C. Palmer (eds) *Tourism Research Methods: Integrating Theory with Practice*, Wallingford: CAB International, 1–8.

Rose, D. (1990) *Living the Ethnographic Life*, London: Sage.

Salzinger, L. (2004) 'Revealing the Unmarked: Finding Masculinity in a Global Factory', *Ethnography* 5, 5–27.

Scarangella, L. (2007) 'Multi-sited Ethnography and the Anthropological Study of Tourism', paper presented at the Association of Social Anthropologists' annual conference 'Thinking Through Tourism', London Metropolitan University, 10–13 April 2007.

Scheper-Hughes, N. (1979) *Saints, Scholars, and Schizophrenics: Mental Illness in Rural Ireland*, Berkeley: University of California Press.

—— (2000) 'Ire in Ireland', *Ethnography* 1, 117–40.

—— (2004) 'Parts Unknown: Undercover Ethnography of the Organs-trafficking Underworld', *Ethnography* 5, 29–73.

Selwyn, T. (ed.) (1996) *The Tourist Image: Myths and Myth Making in Tourism*, Chichester: Wiley.

Smith, A. D. (1983) *Theories of Nationalism*, 2nd edn, London: Duckworth.

—— (1986) *Ethnic Origin of Nations*, Oxford: Blackwell.

—— (1991) *National Identity*, London: Penguin.

Smith, V. (ed.) (1989) *Hosts and Guests: The Anthropology of Tourism*, 2nd edn, Philadelphia: University of Pennsylvania Press.

Sugden, J. (2002) *Scum Airways: Inside Football's Underground Economy*, Edinburgh: Mainstream Publishing.

Tucker, H. (2003) *Living with Tourism: Negotiating Identities in a Turkish Village*, London: Routledge.

Van Maanen, J. (1988) *Tales of the Field: On Writing Ethnography*, Chicago: University of Chicago Press.

van Meijl, T. (2005) 'The Critical Ethnographer as Trickster', *Anthropological Forum* 15.3, 235–45.

Weeden, C. (2005) 'A Qualitative Approach to the Ethical Consumer: The Use of Focus Groups for Cognitive Consumer Research in Tourism', in B. W. Ritchie, P. Burns and C. Palmer (eds) *Tourism Research Methods: Integrating Theory with Practice*, Wallingford: CAB International, 179–90.

Willis, P. and M. Trondman (2000) 'Manifesto for Ethnography', *Ethnography* 1, 5–16.

Wilson, D. (1993) 'Time and Tides in the Anthropology of Tourism', in M. Hitchcoch, V. T. King and M. Parnwell (eds) *Tourism in South-East Asia*, London: Routledge, 32–47.

Wolcott, H. F. (1999) *Ethnography: A Way of Seeing*, London: AltaMira Press.

8

HERITAGE ETHNOGRAPHY AS A SPECIALISED CRAFT

Grasping maritime heritage in Bermuda

Charlotte Andrews

Heritage as ethnographic object

Given that the burgeoning field of Heritage Studies does not yet offer a set of established methodologies to choose from, researchers are challenged, but also free, to employ novel lines of enquiry towards our aim of a more complex and satisfying understanding of heritage. I therefore imposed a distinct course upon my doctoral study of maritime heritage in Bermuda, and, by way of this experience, gleaned insight into the pursuit of heritage as an ethnographic object of study. This chapter draws on my research journey in order to explicate this method, which I suggest be termed 'heritage ethnography'. The methodological reflection that follows is intended to be purposive but not prescriptive, suggesting approaches and skills distinct to heritage ethnography without assigning it a restrictive and counterproductive paradigm. I aim to show that heritage ethnography is not a mechanistic or replicable method but a specialised research attitude and sensibility – indeed, a kind of craft.

Heritage ethnography consciously targets heritage as a 'social experience' (Herzfeld 1997), 'communicative practice' (Dicks 2000) or 'cultural process' – in short, something people 'do' (Smith 2006). This interpretation of heritage is relatively specific with respect to both the enormity of today's heritage domain and the associated indiscriminate use of the term 'heritage' that makes it 'something of a floating signifier' (Weiss 2007: 414). The intangible heritage-making explored with this method is heavily bound up with the production of meaning, identity and social value – all concepts central to wider understandings of culture. Yet, heritage ethnography necessarily brackets heritage away from other cultural phenomena by maintaining its relationship with memory and history, even if in subtle, unexpected or liberating ways that break with the narrow definition of heritage as 'the use of the past in the present'. This concentration on heritage reflects the ever-expanding scope of ethnography and its recent disciplinary trend to focus on specific, abstract objects of study, and, conversely, sits in contrast with traditional ethnographic methods that claim comprehensive study of a culture. This qualitative-ethnographic mode of study, entailing fieldwork to closely observe people in their social worlds and employing corresponding modes of analysis and writing (Baszanger and Dodier 1997), responds to heritage being culturally situated. This approach shifts the gaze from the academic to the actual, from heritage as an intellectual concept to heritage as an experience. Yet heritage ethnography remains an exploratory endeavour that seeks a deep and sensitive understanding of heritage towards generating and refining theory.

This question of what constitutes heritage as an experience remains one of the most significant tensions within the heritage paradigm, and is central to establishing heritage ethnography as an explicit method. The underlying premise of the ethnography highlighted here is that heritage is a 'knowable reality' (Knell 2007: 1), or in other words, concrete, credible data that can be detected and interrogated via fieldwork. As an exercise in assemblage, heritage ethnography uses a kind of archaeological sensibility to pick up, contextualise and juxtapose fragments of heritage in order to conceptually explore and model the phenomena.

Still, the method is highly subjective. The work is not making absolute claims about heritage, but, much like post-processual practices of archaeology and history, makes inferences about evidence that is often ambiguous or piecemeal. Our data may be empirical but it is not simply 'given' or 'taken'. It is 'capta' in the sense of being actively sought after and determined (Chippindale 2000: 1). Just as my analysis originates from heritage, so too is heritage created by and in the research process. This subjectivity is demanded by the nature of ethnography as a unique interaction between researcher and context, as well as ethnography being a constructed narrative or textual artefact used to answer academic questions and explore concepts (Clifford 1988). The subjective nature of the work is owed in equal measure to the inherent renewability (Holtorf 2005) or 'active texture' (Burch 2005: 227) of heritage itself. Labelling the method an *ethnography* stresses the basis of the work in reality but does not deny its subjective nature or analytic intention.

The 'rise in ethnographic approaches that aim to understand the nature of heritage and how the past is constituted and utilised in the present' (Smith 2006: 5) has occurred over the past decade, and is now manifest in an array of work on identity, memory, place, communication, performance, historicity, archaeology and material culture. Heritage ethnography is also implicit in much heritage practice, given the 'insistently public nature of archaeological sites and museums' (Meskell and Pels 2005: 23) and that 'heritage professionals use ethnography, interviewing and qualitative research on a daily basis to inform their work' (Kersel 2006: 17). In spite of these predecessors, the development of heritage ethnography remains nascent, having not yet grown from a subconscious or standby method to one that breathes independently and is purposefully chosen. Nor has Heritage Studies reoriented to duly consider heritage ethnography as a central philosophy and method. Thus my undertaking of heritage ethnography was a matter of synthesising existing approaches.

The following approach borrows from generic qualitative and ethnographic methodologies and broader social theory. Particularly in light of the immaturity of heritage ethnography, these outlooks are helpful to its customisation. Choosing appropriate methods was not, however, a matter of uncritical adoption or predetermining my path. Rather, the various methods borrowed were themselves shaped by being posited within heritage ethnography. The fact that heritage ethnography, or another term with the same idea behind it, has not previously been coined attests to the immaturity of the method. My coining of this term may appear to be a semantic move for staking out the territory of the genre; however, my intention is to suggest a divergence from other ethnographies and to foster an explicit and consistent language and collective research identity for the area of study.

A narrow conception of heritage as an ethnographic object has been a major hindrance to the development of heritage ethnography as a method and to the conceptualisation of heritage generally. Identification and critique of an 'Authorised Heritage Discourse' (Smith 2006) – principally as it is produced and naturalised through academic interests, heritage management and museum praxis – has become sophisticated and reflexive, giving us a platform from which we may further expand the conceptualisation of heritage. Yet most heritage research remains tethered to sites and initiatives that are relatively straightforward, stable and safe, keeping the concept deployed in only narrow and familiar ways. Work gravitates to political, intellectual or custodial concerns. Heritage that promotes authenticity and sustainability over time and space or that which creates or conveys consensus and legitimacy is well represented. Studies centred on particular events, conflicts or crises are often touted for the way they bring both theoretical and social issues into stark relief but nonetheless reflect only certain – often highly discursive or historicist – understandings of heritage. Identified or valorised tourism, museum, archaeological and historic sites are standard subjects, and established and cohesive narratives often ground and delimit heritage research. Appreciation of the integration, or even indistinguishability, of tangible and intangible aspects of heritage is mounting (Smith 2006) but there is still disproportionate attention paid to materially manifest heritage. While these topics and approaches are all valid and valuable research interests, they reinforce 'structural logics' (Weiss 2007) that delimit both the academic conceptualisation and the actual use of heritage, and convey the false impression that current scholarship is indicative of the scope of the phenomena – when it remains, in fact, extremely partial.

A content scan of major heritage research journals[1] corroborates this propensity and reveals a corresponding lack of heritage topics that are less tethered or stabilised, indicating a research culture with an aversion to risk. This orientation is also indicative of a widespread assumption of public deficiency towards heritage that underlies many well-intentioned yet self-serving, patronising, and ultimately alienating, outreach and education initiatives. Grassroots heritage,[2] for lack of a better term, receives relatively scarce attention despite its personal, everyday and unmanaged phenomena which are arguably more meaningful to its users. A grassroots orientation can expand our repertoire of known heritage uses and the theoretical idioms used to understand them, making our heritage conceptualisation and corresponding practice more well rounded. Such grassroots heritage is obtained by working

> from the ground up and determin[ing] the markers and substances of heritage from grassroots priorities and values ... it is quite possible that a community will have a much more comprehensive and integrated sense of the connections between past and present.
>
> (Chambers 2004: 204)

> from the bottom-up (from direct contact with those who engage with it) rather than from the 'top down', in terms of evaluating how heritage relates to and is controlled by larger, abstract entities like 'the state' and/or the 'nation'.
>
> (McClanahan 2004: 8–9)

My heritage ethnography had such a grassroots orientation with a concentration on the more everyday and personal heritage of individuals and communities. The intention is to give grassroots heritage the attention it deserves and to promote it as a viable object of study. All the same, I do not mean to perpetuate a simplistic grassroots-authorised dichotomy that implies that the former is more valid or 'authentic' and that the latter is 'tainted' or ideologically driven. Such heritage uses are highly integrated, especially with the influential role of the professional and academic sector in defining, creating and promoting heritage. My 'bottom-up' data consistently challenged the desire to isolate and preserve a more 'organic' state of heritage, in that any search for unadulterated heritage irrevocably alters it. Any claim to certify heritage '100 per cent organic' is patently untrue, and denies the constructed nature of all heritage, no matter its orientation or scale. Therefore this work distinguishes grassroots heritage but does not falsely or dangerously separate it from its broader cultural structures.

Although both heritage ethnography in general and my project in particular are not instrumentalist *per se*, the work does have an applied dimension insofar as it ought to turn on real-world problems outside academia (Rabinow 2008). My concern is the alienation of heritage sectors and museums from their local communities. I therefore seek to triangulate and integrate my data and ideas with heritage praxis, and within this praxis to museums specifically. I am interested in how we might sustain a heritage-oriented way of thinking and working within daily curatorial practice, while remaining realistic about the inevitable institutional constraints of such an approach. Keeping practice intact in the work serves to hone the theory produced and challenge the ethics practised, yet, importantly, the methodology and object of study are not over-determined by practice. Mindful of the heritage practitioner, this work demonstrates the value of 'the space to reflect, and explore in depth ... the space to rethink and to interrogate their policy and practices, and to see the value of engaging with theory and abstraction' (Young 2002: 207).

To develop heritage ethnography overall, it is necessary to develop ways of exploring heritage 'in the wild'. Those of us exploring such grassroots heritage need a better sense of what we are after, how we manage these data and then integrate the knowledge gained 'back' into more mainstream heritage practice and discourse. This support is needed in terms of a philosophy, curiosity or attitude rather than a set of fixed guidelines, thereby enabling researchers to continuously build this distinct methodology through personalised research experiences. Awareness of the ways we negotiate and produce our ethnography is essential to exploring an abstract object like heritage that often feels at once too easy and too difficult to grasp. In the hope that my experience may provide some useful guidance to other researchers, the two sections that follow recall in detail the ways I conceptualised maritime Bermuda as my case study, and heritage as an ethnographic object within it.

Framing the heritage field

Boundedness is crucial to successful ethnographic work. Like most social researchers, I used a case study to circumscribe my unit of analysis to a workable scale and purposeful data sample (VanWynsberghe and Khan 2007). My first step was to focus on my community of interest, Bermuda.[3] Though case study often implies comparison, I approached the Island[4] as a single case, avoiding juxtaposition with ostensibly 'similar' regions such as Caribbean states that would spread the research too thin or invite inappropriate interpretation. I sacrificed both the transnational range of a multi-local approach (Marcus 1995, 1999) and bucked the trend of interpreting heritage through processes of globalization (Karp et al. 2006) in order to explore one 'national-cultural imaginary' (Appadurai 1996) in which heritage is domesticated and experienced. Following Daniel, but with a heritage focus, the idea is exemplification, 'not merely to show the manner in which a reality is culturally and historically constituted, but how deeply so' (1996: 14). Just as Bermuda is not a supracultural illustration suggesting a universal meaning set for heritage, neither is it a unique example that melts into relativism (Flyvbjerg 2006). Set within this problem-oriented ethnography, the Bermuda case has wider implications for heritage theory and practice, as well as small-scale community and island studies. The Rev. Alexander Ewing's 1784 assessment of Bermuda is apt: 'Small though this spot is, a great deal of the world can be seen in it' (Hallett 1993: i).

My interest in Bermuda is neither arbitrary nor solely academic, but logical and also personal. Being Bermudian gives me an intimate relationship with my field site, one that is particularly fitting and revealing for grassroots heritage ethnography. I am part of a growing minority of researchers with local knowledge and experience (Colic-Peisker 2004), for whom 'issues of reflexivity are particularly salient' (Davies 1999: 4), with both benefits and barriers arising from my heightened familiarity, partiality and emotion in this home setting. Mine is a 'differential authority' (Clifford 1997a) that distinguishes the research and counters the unhealthy depreciation of local capacity within the heritage fields, especially in small-scale societies like Bermuda. Still, to inflate my familiarity or neutrality belies the Island's pocketed make-up and my hybrid positioning, as Clifford advises:

> No one can be an insider to all sectors of a community. How the shifting locations are managed, how affiliation, discretion, and critical perspective are sustained, have been and will remain matters of tactical improvisation as much as of formal methodology.
>
> (Clifford 1997a: 86)

The most significant of these 'shifting locations' for me are threefold: first, being a white Bermudian in the statistical minority,[5] moving slowly into greater consciousness of my 'unearned skin privilege'; second, being a local heritage practitioner confronting authorised notions of heritage with which I was willingly indoctrinated during my tenure at the Bermuda Maritime Museum (BMM);[6] and third, being a novice researcher arbitrating home concerns with a necessary analytical detachment, through what Jeganathan calls an 'epistemological ethic of disciplined affect' (2005: 151). My 'tactical improvisation' of these positions subverted any inclination to think of myself as objective or non-involved (Colic-Peisker 2004); rather, as a researcher who interacts with my subjects and environment to 'co-construct the world' (Davies 1999), I was challenged to acknowledge and negotiate my 'embedded ethics' (Meskell and Pels 2005). Proportionally, my interactions forced me to step outside myself, to engage in a kind of method-acting where I mediated the understandings and experiences of my subjects. The reflexivity I employed has therefore been carefully measured, so as to allow both my subjectivity and my 'evidence' to determine the heritage emerging through this ethnography.

Heritage in Bermuda proved to be so rich a topic that I required a second case study in addition to my focus on the Island. I assumed this theme would be straightforward for me to identify, but my local knowledge and vested interest offered many possible paths, urged me to address local issues and stressed the import of this choice for research that itself could come to constitute heritage. Ironically, my tenure at BMM only minimally suggested the maritime theme, and its closeness to museum priorities kept me wary. My limited knowledge of maritime history and culture, puzzlement about the obscure nature of maritime museums and a sense that the topic was detached from contemporary Bermuda all enhanced my distrust. So it was only after considerable debate, false starts and reluctance that maritimity emerged as the front-runner.

With the start of fieldwork, however, my reservations dissolved and the appropriateness and efficacy of the theme became self-evident. Any residual ambivalence I retained was due not to an insecurity about maritimity but to an enthusiasm for heritage ethnography in other thematic areas. My revelation that Bermudian[7] associations with the sea could be a viable and compelling research platform coalesced around several attributes that were nonetheless accompanied by certain challenges. The following characteristics are specific to my project, yet indicate the kinds of qualities other heritage ethnographers might look for in shaping and justifying their case-study choices.

Maritimity resonates with Bermuda's diverse community, distinctive environment and half-millennium of history. There was no lack of people, events or material to engage with, nor any contriving of the theme by myself, the local heritage sector or maritime museums. Maritime heritage and culture are a reality in Bermuda, as they are in island, coastal and other communities worldwide. Furthermore, maritimity offers access to a heterogeneous cross-section of Bermuda's diverse racial, socio-economic and generational mix of people. This addresses the paucity of social research that traverses the Island's conventionally represented demographics. As a local, this was not a path of least resistance, but promoted my contact with people, environments and spaces with which I am both more and less familiar. A highly 'uneven gender component' is the maritime theme's representative caveat, with my fieldwork and findings heavily weighted to male informants and masculinities (M. Jarvis, personal communication, 2006). However, the analytic value of this gender bias trumped my representative concerns, besides constructively agitating some of my feminist assumptions.

Despite its demographic skewing towards masculinity, maritimity is relatively neutral and inclusive compared to more divisive or exploitative local themes[8] that close down communication of heritage meanings, are subsumed by dominant discourses, inhibit dissemination of the project, or overwhelm my confidence as a researcher and local practitioner with heightened accountability. This theme invites participation, openness and transparency, and in doing so actually provided access to more politically relevant issues. The fact that maritimity was a relatively comfortable space for me was conducive to practising 'embedded ethics' on one level, but also questionable in terms of the degree to which heritage ethnographers, particularly local ones, ought to be challenged or uncomfortable. I have at least come to recognise this point.

Maritimity applies to both local and global heritage management and museum practice, lending my research an applied dimension. In Bermuda, maritime heritage relates to various organisations and public programmes, dovetailing with BMM's mission and interests. Internationally, the theme directly pertains to maritime museums, a fast-growing but traditional museum sector attempting to reinvent itself for today's increasingly non-maritime societies. Even so, maritimity offers a less obvious, less conscious type of heritage than heritage researchers and practitioners usually gravitate to, one relatively untouched by popular, authorised or commoditised influences. It allows the researcher to glean heritage meanings more obliquely and disrupts the more established disciplinary perceptions of heritage – including dichotomies of natural–cultural, tangible–intangible, landscape–seascape. Maritimity encompasses an array of heritage phenomena and forms that require an open mindset about its scope. The way the Bermuda and maritime interfaces of the case study shift between being independent, interdependent and interchangeable also furnished a dynamic field site and a valuable strand of data.

However, maritimity is also a romanticised topic that seemingly abrades my call for more risk and autonomy in heritage research. It is a theme that runs the risk of not breaking new ground, of treading territory that more contemporary, avant-garde fields and sectors have already. Yet perhaps the traditional attributes of maritimity paradoxically permit a quantum leap for heritage theory and practice, particularly for advancing both small-scale local sectors like Bermuda and less progressive and 'cutting-edge' fields like maritime museums. Being 'behind the times' is not always a bad thing, particularly given the meteoric rise and saturated nature of heritage and museum enquiry. Maritimity addresses theory and practice in specific ways that open up space for alternative ideas.

Despite bounding the Bermuda case study with the maritime theme, I was nonetheless overcome in the field by my topic's enormity. This was particularly so in terms of the diversity of maritime sub-themes – what I call *loci*. These loci vary significantly in scale, with many more specific sites nesting within general sub-themes such as fishing or sailing. All, however, are magnets for meaning, reflecting the pull maritimity exerts on heritage and identity in a more general sense. Conversations spiralled around, meanings became attached to and recurrences chimed with these influential and ascendant areas of local maritimity. While there may not be an infinite variety of maritime loci in Bermuda, there was an incredible variety in constant flux. As soon as I mapped the field, other loci would arise. The fieldwork felt messy, sprawling and incomplete. I was often frustrated by time constraints or missed opportunities. My decision to pursue one locus over another seemed inconsistent and unscientific. Despite the ubiquity of maritimity and my local knowledge, I was never sure if a particular locus would yield data that could be classified as heritage, especially given that I had no preconceived or consistent criteria for such a designation. While these uncertainties are characteristic of ethnographic experience in general, especially in terms of the tendency to bring an idealised idea of fieldwork into the field, I suggest this lack of compass is particularly endemic to heritage ethnography.

My instinct was to hem in the maritime theme, focusing on just one or two loci. I thought if, for instance, I only explore *fishing* or *sailing*, then I might achieve holistic coverage and a sense of totality. As I began fieldwork, I realised few interviewees or events related to such singular loci or provided contained data, nor could I predict what maritime associations would arise. This was especially so given the inseparable nature of many individual mariners and maritime histories, cultures and networks. A field site so sprawling, discordant and overlapping is certainly unmanageable for research seeking comprehensive coverage. However, the objective of conceptualising heritage actually demanded such a scattershot approach to the field, one analogous to Candea's heuristic device of 'arbitrary location':

> The arbitrary location ... is the actually existing instance, whose messiness, contingency, and lack of an overarching coherence or meaning serve as a 'control' for a broader abstract object of study. It is 'arbitrary' insofar as it bears no *necessary* relation to the wider object of study ... the arbitrary location allows one to rethink conceptual entities, to challenge their coherence and their totalizing aspirations ... the arbitrary location is space which cuts through meaning ... The decision to bound off a site for the study of 'something else', with all the blind spots and limitations which this implies, is a productive form of methodological asceticism.
>
> (Candea 2007: 180)

Therefore in order to keep my focus on heritage as an abstract concept and phenomenon, I cast a wide net over maritime Bermuda. I travelled 'unexpected trajectories' and crossed domains following stories, debates, ideas, people, objects and even boats. Inside the Bermuda case study I emulated Marcus's multi-sited ethnography (1995, 1999) and Clifford's 'routes' (1997a, b). My collage-like approach mirrored the narratives of previous exhibitions, films and programmes on Bermuda maritime heritage, suggesting that others have had a similar inclination with this topic. Mirroring the 'memoryscape', a heritage trail based on experimental art concepts of 'fluxus' and 'situationalism' (Butler 2006), I had to work randomly, as I encountered informants and information, frequently scheduling interviews and events whose timing was often beyond my control. I came to embrace unexpected fieldwork events and sources, including serendipitous ones such as the theming of the national Heritage Month 2007 'Bermuda's Maritime Connections'.[9]

The idea was not to cover everything nor overwhelm myself with a cacophony of maritime elements, but to experience maritime heritage as it is experienced individually and collectively by Bermudians: as something fragmentary, uncontained and unpredictable. This diverse and unforeseeable world countered my unhealthy readiness, especially as a museum curator and academic researcher, to break up or consolidate heritage into neat, 'manageable units' (Nakanishi *et al.* 2003). This multi-sited approach, I contend, in turn stimulates a more penetrating analysis and intriguing narrative.

These loci were not arbitrary, interchangeable illustrations onto which meaning is imprinted or attached. Rather, they were contextualised, carefully positioned elements that sustain – in both consensual and contested ways – a unique cultural logic. They were anchors in a fluid and intricate 'network with no centre' (Young 2002) that shifted me away from a museum-centric outlook. Taking a page from recent work that considers the affective power of objects, monuments and landscapes, I understood these heritage sites and markers as '*sui generis* meaning' themselves (Henare *et al*. 2007: 3). Each is a free-standing entity that does not simply 'carry' the meaning invested by heritage users, but emits its own energy.

In all its complexity I was paradoxically able to construe my field site as a 'coherent and convincing entity', much like Garden's recently conceived 'heritagescape' (2006: 397 and chapter 15 below). As a concept, the 'heritagescape' is deliberately designed 'as a means of interpreting and analysing heritage sites as unique social spaces that offer an experience of the past', with a strong orientation to tangible, managed, 'marked-out' spaces that are explicitly designated as heritage. Without wanting to misrepresent Garden's original application and meaning, or confine my thinking to her tight criteria, I borrowed her notion of 'heritagescape' to conceive of maritime Bermuda as a field site.

Autonomous as they may be, these loci also operate in relation to one other, as a web of connections and a set of wider local social meanings that demand the multi-sited approach taken to my fieldwork. Just as a textile's composite texture differs from the individual strands of which it is composed, I experienced a highly integrated field site that is more than the sum of its parts. Much like historians and archaeologists look beyond discrete sites and events, this heritagescape speaks to broader heritage processes. It also speaks to broader race, class and other identity politics that are so familiar yet fixed in local discourse, issues that lie beyond both maritimity and heritage yet are central to their combined use and meaning. Although my non-comparative approach means I cannot support this with data from elsewhere, I believe this interconnectivity is intensified in small-scale communities like Bermuda, exerting greater influence on the ways heritage is manifest and underscoring the need for multi-sited approaches to heritage ethnography.

My sense of interconnection and coherence conceived as a 'heritagescape' would seem to contradict my experience of the field site as a partial and fragmented 'arbitrary location' that is 'perpetually *deferring* closure' (Candea 2007: 179). Yet these qualities co-existed and mutually supported each other in my fieldwork. I collected and collated observations, gaining an increasing understanding of the site, while generating ever more new questions, topics and pathways. Like the metaphorical rhizome (Deleuze and Guattari 1980), the territory I travelled was 'infinitely variegated, fractal, undergoing continuous generation' and thus had to be 'perceived kinesthetically' (Ingold 2008), or through movement. Interestingly, this sense of 'boundedness without closure' strongly parallels, and is intensified by, the experience of studying a small island, where the physical, cultural and spiritual boundaries – such as those between land and sea, or inside(r) and outside(r) – are alternately indefinite and distinguished in ways that complement rather than clash. The kind of field site we study – and Bermuda occupies many different kinds, of which 'island' is one – ought to influence our practice and production of heritage ethnography.

The maritime loci I encountered were more or less perceptible to me in their possible relationship with heritage. This perceptibility seemed to be indicated by my corresponding levels of 'hesitation or non-hesitation'[10] in the field, levels that were related to my preconceptions of heritage and the extent to which I respectively followed or broke with these. Predictably, the most obvious loci for me were those overtly identified and valorised as heritage or designed to evoke memory or imagination of past mariners and maritime eras. While these spaces did not necessarily entail a relationship with 'history' *per se* and were often associated with protection and care of present-day mariners, there was always an element of use of the past or remembrance in their construction. These spaces were also obvious because they tended to be bounded in space and time, associated with specific individuals, events or places. They were highly public and controlled, or manifest in monuments or performances. Examples of such commemorated maritime loci include tributes to Pilot James 'Jemmy' Darrell, an eighteenth-century black Bermudian slave self-manumitted due to his extraordinary navigational skill; 'Figurehead', a public art memorial erected in 2005 in honour of Bermudians 'lost at sea'; and the bestowing of mystical or heroic status to particular people, places and things within the Island that epitomise maritimity and 'Bermudi-anness' such as the late shipwrights Geary Pitcher and Albert 'Bert' Darrell, the east end community of St David's, the elusive rockfish or the endemic cedar wood long used in the construction of local boats.

Loci oriented to everyday maritime experience and culture were consid-erably more faint, with my uncertainty highest in these spaces where the boundary between heritage and culture was blurred. The frequently subtle and intangible characteristics of these loci contributed to my uneasiness that is partly a natural inclination to seek out the clear and articulate, and partly my role as a heritage researcher and practitioner trained to identify more defined and tangible manifestations of heritage. Yet a sense of relevance and signifi-cance of these maritime practices to everyday lives pulled my attention in these directions and encouraged me to open up to more subtle and embodied connections to environment, space, history and self. Aspects of Bermuda's contemporary maritime practices that I encountered include recreational and commercial fishing, piloting (local reef and channel navigation), and the design, building, preservation, restoration, sailing and racing of a variety of boats (Figure 8.1).

In the field, I was particularly attracted to loci that heralded maritimity as a social remedy. A dysfunctional public education system, lasting racial inequity and tension, inter-generational disconnect, the breakdown of family structures

Figure 8.1 Traditional Bermuda fitted dinghy racing, one of Bermuda's many contemporary maritime practices (photo by the author)

and drifting communal values all factor into a sense of societal 'crisis' in Bermuda at this time. Bermudian youth – those 'at risk' and 'disenfranchised black males' in particular – are seen as the greatest casualties of this situation and are thus the target beneficiaries for positive change. In the urgent search for remedies to this 'crisis', both existing and new maritime youth-development initiatives have come to the fore as promising mechanisms for fostering identity, self-esteem and social and racial reconciliation. Maritime youth-development initiatives such as the Bermuda Sloop Foundation's sail-training programme aboard the *Spirit of Bermuda*, Waterwise and other youth sailing programmes (Figure 8.2) and the Bermuda Sea Cadets Corps, which promotes seamanship and naval tradition, are loci loaded with equal parts cautious aspiration, optimism and seriousness.

Although my ethnography was oriented to grassroots heritage, my field site also included more authorised maritime loci: in terms of both various professional and public maritime heritage institutions and representations, and the individual and community engagements with them. Bermudian relationships with these authorised maritime loci were less often positive or active than dissonant, communicating the cleavage between grassroots and authorised maritime heritage – but also reflecting their co-dependence. Among these authorised loci, I gave special attention to BMM, not only because of my prior association and the associated

151

Figure 8.2 Optimist dinghy sailor participating in Waterwise, one of Bermuda's maritime youth-development initiatives (photo by the author)

ways I brought it into the field with me, but because it was such a prominent and contested feature of the Bermuda maritime 'heritagescape'.

Notwithstanding the inclusion of more authorised maritime loci throughout my fieldwork, I mentally conceptualised the field along the above-mentioned three dimensions: memory and commemoration, live culture, and social remedy. That this division aligns with a past–present–future nexus frequently associated with heritage is, I think, both coincidental and not. The notions of continuity and inheritance that are pronounced in the acts of looking backwards, living in the moment, and projecting aspirations and fears for the future were simply one way of conceptualising the field, but were also an evident structure in my field site. Yet as there is no standard index, loci will differ for every case study. The complexities I experienced in siting maritimity in Bermuda demonstrate that the field site in which we conduct heritage ethnography is more than a decorative backdrop that simply puts things into 'context'. It is a space that actively reveals and constitutes heritage. It is determined by the 'routes' we as heritage ethnographers gravitate towards, often in connection with our positioning as individuals, but also affected by the field-site composition. We must recognise that our conceptualisation of heritage begins with the ways we travel and determine our field site, taking responsibility for this in our encounters and writing.

Handling heritage data

Whereas the previous section is more of a panoramic vista, this section zooms in on the ways I identified and qualified maritime heritage in Bermuda. Once I saw my field site as 'an explicitly "partial" and incomplete window onto complexity' (Candea 2007: 167), I began to recognise the ways I was in fact practising 'bounding, selection and choice' at each stage of my fieldwork. Throughout my nine months of 'home-work', I questioned and qualified what data were prudent to collect and analyse. This entailed readjusting my gaze to locate heritage as live culture, resisting impulses to confine heritage to a relationship with the past and trusting unexpected sources as heritage-rich. I isolated and defined the heritage data I was looking for, but also excluded what became assigned as irrelevant or superfluous, as Candea underlines:

> to be explicit about the necessity of leaving certain things 'out of bounds' ... by turning what feels like an illicit incompleteness into an actual methodological decision, one which the ethnographer reflects upon and takes responsibility for.
>
> (Candea 2007: 174)

Some potential data sources simply did not make the cut. Either the maritime connection was too weak or obscure, or there was no perceptible relationship with heritage. With my grassroots gaze, I remained oriented to less articulate forms of heritage but still needed a grip on my data. In my daily choices of inclusion and exclusion, I was mirroring the work of the heritage practitioner who is employed to make value judgements and consequential rulings. The difference was that I was doing this in a space less dictated by institutional demands and convention, or in tune with community interviewees and context. Plus, I had the space and time to be more reflexive about these choices, a luxurious position compared to the often fierce daily constraints of professional heritage work.

Constructing a heritage ethnography through immersion in a few people's daily lives, in the hopes of catching their uses of maritime heritage, was neither practical nor culturally appropriate in Bermuda. Instead, I employed methods that gave me a fast-track into Bermudian maritime heritage use: one-on-one or small-group interviews, and participant observation at community events. These complementary methods allowed me to tap the experiential, performative, verbalised, discursive and intuitive aspects of heritage. I accessed what people do, say, think and care about – which may or may not be linked.

In total, I conducted 120 formal interviews with 135 people, a fraction of the Island's population,[11] especially in terms of the much smaller number of identifiable maritime heritage users, but an enormous amount of qualitative data. Interview duration was dependent on the energy, speed, coverage and saturation of conversation. I met interviewees at sites familiar and meaningful to them, such as their home, family homestead, old neighbourhood, dock or boat – locations where they might access significant images or things. Some meetings took place at my oceanside cottage, a stimulating venue for maritime memory and imagination. As there can be valuable data in both what interviewees say and how they say it, I encouraged them to use their own words, style and expressions. And because heritage is often performed non-verbally, I encouraged expression in ways other than through words, with body language, mapping, drawing, visiting, performing and handling objects of significance.

My participant observation proved far more extensive than anticipated. I had attended around fifty maritime events by the close of fieldwork. This component of my heritage ethnography did not merely supplement my interviews, but was a major aspect of data collection that enhanced the overall quality of my interpretation. I used a different skill set from my interviews for this public field engagement. This included navigating the unspoken rules and etiquettes of different social networks, practising quiet observation and contemplation, staging strategic interventions and conducting short, informal interviews. Events ranged from the obvious to the hidden, some with easy access or clear relevance and others rife with hurdles and mystery in terms of access to or knowledge about them. Boat races and prize-givings, public commemorations, film screenings, religious and secular services, ventures and voyages aboard various vessels and random acts of seafaring all fell into my observational mix. Participant observation and formal interviews occasionally merged, such as when I accompanied Bermudian pilots on the helm of cruise ships as they navigated Bermuda's channels and reefs or joined commercial fishermen on their daily run out to 'the Banks', offshore reef formations, and the subsequent onshore cleaning and selling of the catch.

I supplemented my interviews and participant observation with the study of documentary and media sources, including newspaper and magazine articles, private and public documents, films, publications and archives. I asked myself, was it appropriate to mix live ethnographic data with dated material originally produced or intended outside my fieldwork? Yet I could not isolate my observational data from these supplemental sources: they were themselves valuable carriers of heritage meaning, in addition to being helpful sources of methodological guidance. For instance, materials from the 'Bermuda Connections: Maritime Arts' archive[12] and BMM's exhibit, collections and research files were especially useful for their conscious maritime-heritage content, as well as aiding my efforts to clarify my work against oral-historical and museological approaches. Though counterintuitive to a sense of grassroots heritage, this documentary study was a form of engagement that complemented my interviews and participant observation. As heritage has a natural propensity to be expressed through a variety of sources, this amalgam of data permits fuller understanding of our ethnographic object.

I tracked most interviewees and events by word of mouth, using existing local knowledge and networks arising as I travelled the field site. I treated the ways I tracked interviewees and events as data in themselves, while simultaneously being mindful of the ways my interventions reinforced or altered those networks. In an effort to relinquish some control over my interviewee selection, I identified a portion of my interviewees by blind recruitment, via an open call for participants in local media. The few respondents I had were still vetted, however, as there was a need to be discerning in all my interviewee and event selection. Being 'local', I had to work especially hard to retain this agency, balancing respect for the suggestions I received with resistance to pressures and obligation. As my research was often interpreted as an oral-history study, it was often suggested (sometimes forcefully) that I interview older or expert informants with accumulated knowledge or memory – especially those regarded as maritime 'heroes' or 'tradition-bearers'. My appreciation of the urgent need in Bermuda for oral-history collection battled with my desire to obtain data from younger informants, who are often regarded as deficient in historical knowledge, memory and heritage. That said, I did not deliberately avoid older or seasoned informants as they clearly too had a great deal to offer, both in themselves and as stimuli for others. The range in ages of my interviewees testifies the extent to which an inter-generational study was achieved.

Before commencing fieldwork, I prepared an interview guide: a script of questions based on normalised idioms on which our current model of heritage is based. The idea was to structure my interviews and analysis, and in so doing to promote accuracy and credibility of data, avoiding 'distortion'. I also intended to use it as an *aide-mémoire* in the intimate and sometimes intimidating interview atmosphere, helping retain my focus and flow (Kersel 2006).

However, my early interviews constantly deviated from this script. They were messy, non-linear and multi-layered. I had to keep conversations going while making some sense of the heritage meanings that arose. A script also conflicted with my decision to eschew a hypothetical framework in favour of a person-centred approach, so early into fieldwork I abandoned the interview guide. Henceforth my interviews were largely improvised, only standardised with initial questions as gentle guidance towards core concepts, like Jones's style:

> The interview design was deliberately informal and conversational in style, with interviewees encouraged to use their own language and set their own agendas. At the same time, prompts were used to ensure that certain key themes were always addressed.
>
> (Jones 2004: 8)

This unstructured format does not predetermine so much what will be elicited, nor does it rely on a synthesis across interviewees. Rather, it allows one 'to understand the complex behaviour of members of society without imposing any a priori categorization that may limit the field of inquiry' (Fontana and Frey 1994: 366). My interviews were a shared space of interpretation for both myself and my interviewees, with heritage meanings generated in a constructivist manner by the relationship we forged in the interview itself. This allowed for interesting moments when interviewees came to 'reveal themselves to themselves and were frequently surprised at the result' (Tilley 2006: 17). It was also a space in which one could suspend assumptions and cynicism and open up to the unknown, a treatment suggested for artefact-oriented anthropologies:

> Rather than dismiss informants' accounts as imaginative 'interpretations' – elaborate metaphorical accounts of a 'reality' that is already given – anthropologists might instead seize on these engagements as opportunities from which novel theoretical understandings can emerge ... to show how such moments of ethnographic 'revelation' – in which unanticipated, previously inconceivable things become apparent ... Too often the anthropologists' immediate reaction is to explain away their own surprise with recourse to more familiar conceptions ... What would happen ... if this wonderment were held in a state of suspension so as to resist the urge to explain it away?
>
> (Henare *et al*. 2007:1)

This improvised approach consistently challenged my interviewing skills, heightening my attention and sensitivity. Though each of my interviews was unique, this does not mean they lacked boundaries, agenda or intention. I had to actively determine my heritage criteria, staying attentive to moments of confirmation and challenge by interviewees. Maritimity provided a helpful conversational boundary, hemming us in from broader life histories and knowledge. I moved the conversation to pursue my local issues of interest, pushing my interviewees to explain things in more depth and asking provocative or stealth questions in order to penetrate surface-level understandings. I directed informants to express everyday heritage use that often goes unarticulated.

My agenda was largely realised at an intuitive level, which possibly suggests the level of subconscious heritage that remains at work even in an explicit study of heritage. I often felt a strong sense of 'microcosm', a sense that a single encounter spoke to the full range of heritage meanings that I would eventually articulate in my writing. This was not a deluded longing for holistic logic, but indicative of the ways even a single interviewee or experience can reflect the larger field site and a range of heritage uses. Again, I believe this interconnectivity and coherence is heightened in small-scale spaces, though not in a way that inhibits complexity. Conversely, this sense of microcosm reminded me that the minority view can be highly significant, keeping me restless for new angles and ensuring against trapping myself in the conventions of my own making.

Despite the degree of control I had in interviews, the work often felt counterintuitive, especially in terms of preconceptions shaped by my past museum work. I tried to resist these leanings but then sometimes I believe I went too far in controlling, censoring or ignoring informants' expressions that aligned with such authorised uses. Two areas were particularly challenging in this regard.

The first was the attraction to 'history', linked to the impulse to confine heritage to a relationship with the past, and to achieving greater validation for my ethnographic data. I was often unsure how much historical knowledge to seek from interviewees. I did employ oral-historical techniques encouraging storytelling and remembering in interviews, but did not demand full, linear life histories. While my interviews cannot be considered comprehensive oral histories, they go 'further' than oral history on both a generative and an analytic level. I was careful with how I described my research project, avoiding prescriptive terms like 'heritage' and 'history'. Not having much prior knowledge of local maritime history kept me curious, and, on reflection, facilitated rapport and comfort with some interviewees. Conversely, at times I was embarrassed by my lack of historical knowledge, especially with interviewees who placed high value on this or who insisted I demonstrate it. When informants offered to prepare for their interview, trying to get their knowledge 'right' to align with their idea of mainstream history, I ignored these statements in order to neither encourage nor discourage this preparation. Sometimes interviewees wanted me to research and validate their version of history, a *quid pro quo* I could not offer. My interviews were often supplemented with historical and documentary sources acquired from the interviewee or unrelated sources; though I have been wary not to use them to build a credible history, I recognised how and why interviewees offered them to me, as an expression of heritage in itself. And in my encounters with people, places, boats and objects it was often unclear how much provenance to record, especially when my research intervention seemed to be the main reason such micro-histories came to light.

Second, whereas in my role as a museum curator I tended to focus on the object, positioning the interviewee in relationship to the potential acquisition, I could not allow objects to be the central elements of my heritage ethnography. By association, I had to resist a collections-based urge to encourage people to share or donate objects to BMM, though at times they did seek this option. Yet, I had to allow things to matter in their own right, as they did for my interviewees. Boats – as living, personalised and technological entities – were an especially potent material source for generating maritime heritage meaning.

I employed several methods to document my ethnographic record, including audio, video and photography. While to some extent intrusive, these recording methods formalised interviews, provided an easily retrievable record, and documented gestures and other expressions, complementing my non-discursive interview techniques. My most valuable means of annotation were handwritten fieldnotes, shorthand accounts of my field and interview impressions (Emerson *et al.* 1995). Although I did not allow my note taking or other recording to prevent me from attending to the field moment, I jotted extensive notes during or just after every conversation or event. Beyond a recording mechanism, writing fieldnotes played an important analytic role. They constituted the real-time *in situ* processing of data, the way I listened with a 'third ear', staying alert to arising concepts, areas in need of further clarification, and my tentative ideas and conclusions. Fieldnotes helped me capture heritage meaning as it momentarily came into relief.

Still, my analysis in the field was largely preliminary. I did not take a hard line to it, such as a strict interpretation of 'grounded theory' that urges constant comparison of data throughout fieldwork (Glaser and Strauss 1967). In practice, it was difficult to think too analytically while I was immersed in live culture and 'drowning in data'. I was constantly moving in and around my field site, with little time to reflect critically. Though I feared a slippage between fieldwork and analysis, I aimed to remain attentive to the raw data, allowing a gradual and less forced comprehension of maritime heritage in Bermuda. I stayed close to the original reality being investigated, keeping things close to face value before reflecting, translating and abstracting too much for my academic purpose. Formal data analysis was thus a distinct stage of my project and occurred once I had physically left the field. This was not post-rationalisation but a systematic review of my recorded and remembered field data and experience. My valuable day-to-day field encounters were not wasted or forgotten, but drawn upon in a condensed period of working through my fieldwork archive.

After completing fieldwork, I reread my books of fieldnotes. With each pass through the material I started to sense salient meanings and categories. I also began to realise the enormous amount of analytic material this record contained. In spite of my being highly selective in the act of writing field-notes, each entry covered much ground. Unlike original unedited recordings or full transcripts that do not differentiate their content, and therefore tend not to be fully considered, the succinct nature of fieldnotes ensures the vast majority of their content is highly purposive. Moreover, my fieldnotes did not forgo the exact context of my recordings because I flagged and paraphrased verbatim quotes for easy retrieval. Transcription of my verbal recordings therefore seemed unnecessary, even regressive to me: an approach backed by claims that it is permissible to compromise lengthy transcripts (Gelsthorpe 2007). By working from my original fieldnotes I return to the complexity of the original field encounter, rather than a polished reconstruction that loses the richness of the original material.

It became apparent that I needed a tool to effectively organise and manage my data, and specifically to code, or attach, different 'hermeneutic units' or tags to my textual data, so I turned to computer-assisted qualitative data-analysis software (CAQDAS) to help do this. I began in my programme of choice with just a few interviews and worked diligently to establish their codes, providing an index for further coding that could be followed and impro-vised upon. Indeed, my approach to coding was not mechanistic, synthesising across interviewees or finding patterns or 'regularities'. Rather, it was about capturing the salient points linking the case study and heritage theory.

For all the very helpful tools CAQDAS offered, I heeded the warning of 'the pitfall of reifying coding as analysis' (Bong 2002: 1) and ultimately constructed my argument outside the software, in the act of writing. Writing supplied a creative space for me to abstract, speculate and make analytic leaps. New threads of understanding were spun both in the ways my data bridged with existing heritage theory and failed to do so. As it is with respect to previous findings that my claims are academically contextualised and earn credibility, I plugged theory in as an explanatory force for my analysis. From the ethnographic direction, I re-embedded my observational engagements into my writing in an effort to remain faithful to the encounters I had with people and to unpack heritage meaning, rather than flattening it out. An important aspect of this re-embedding was interpreting heritage as meta-data, as another level of meaning emerging in contextualised fieldwork moments and interviewee expressions. Yet the work was also about articulating clear ideas about heritage, that which is obvious in context yet often fails to get analysed. So as not to sanitise the messy yet revealing process of interacting with raw heritage data, my writing weaves my choices of inclusion and exclusion and feelings of hesitation or non-hesitation. I have aimed overall for my ethnographic description to be supportive and transparent of my methodology and to enunciate the richness of heritage.

Conclusion

Reflecting these efforts in transparency, in this chapter I have tried to testify to the actual engineering and experience of heritage ethnography, one specifically oriented to more grassroots heritage. At the macro level, I discussed my bounding of my case study or field site in less obvious and less comfortable ways that kept heritage – as the abstract object of study – in focus. At the micro level, I examined how I identified and qualified heritage data in the field and the processes by which I transformed my unstructured field data into an intelligible account. While I separated these macro- and micro-ethnographic levels in this narrative for the sake of clarity, I experienced the two as highly enmeshed and simultaneous.

I have emphasised that what constitutes heritage is never clear, but subject to the nuances of every ethnographic experience and discovering meaning *in situ*. I have shown that undertaking a heritage ethnography involves a balance of holding down an unpredictable and recalcitrant object of study while remaining open-minded about its varied uses and unfamiliar workings. I have admitted the uncertainty that accompanied me throughout my project and suggested this sense is to some extent inbuilt into heritage ethnography. I have recalled the way I gradually released my preconceived notions, allowing heritage to confound my expectations and to see the phenomenon more on its own terms. Like the heritage we study, as heritage ethnographers we are 'in a constant condition of metamorphosis' (Burch 2005: 227). Implicit in speaking to this sense of uncertainty is the argument that it should be accommodated, rather than suppressed, so as to allow it to become a 'productive aspect of fieldwork experience' (Candea 2007: 174). This promotion of heritage ethnography as a distinct method is an attempt to better account for the multifaceted nature of heritage as an object of study that makes its conceptualisation so difficult but valuable.

Having encouraged the development of heritage ethnography, I close with an enthusiastic vision for the method's potential as it comes to fruition as a recognised method. First, it must be conceded that heritage ethnography cannot be all things to heritage theory and practice: as is apparent, an array of topics and concepts lies outside its capacity and boundaries, especially given its grassroots orientation. With that in mind, I believe the method has great promise to spill over into heritage research, practice and public use on a broad level. Use of heritage ethnography is likely to increase as the method is a natural extension of the wave of public outreach in heritage and museums that is currently suffering criticism and dilution. The resulting movements towards individuals and communities will reveal an enormous untapped layer of heritage. A refolding of this vast resource into Heritage Studies and related fields has the potential to provide a stronger theoretical framework for the heritage concept and a foundation for more genuinely democratising heritage sectors, museums and research programmes. Heritage ethnography could furthermore be popularised as a tool for a broader array of individuals and communities to use for understanding heritage as *their* experience.

Notes

1 Including but not limited to *International Journal of Heritage Studies, Cultural Trends, Journal of Material Culture, International Journal of Intangible Heritage, History and Anthropology, Memory Studies, Heritage Management.*
2 My use of 'grassroots' is not meant to imply an activist character, nor to constrain heritage ethnography to the small or individual scale of heritage use.
3 Bermuda is situated over 1,000 miles north-east of the Caribbean in the mid-Atlantic. It is the earth's fifth smallest country at 21 square miles (55 square kilometres), but the largest remaining British dependent territory in terms of population, which is approximately 66,000 including guest workers but not tourists.
4 Although commonly referred to in the singular as 'Island', Bermuda's landmass consists of approximately 138 limestone islands, the seven largest of which are linked by bridges.
5 The racial composition of Bermuda – approximately 60 per cent 'black' and 40 per cent 'white and other' – stands in stark contrast to the white majority of the United States and many European countries. Whites in Bermuda nonetheless have a similar sort of 'invisibility' and 'unconsciousness' because of the legacies of racism and racial privilege.
6 From 1999 to 2004, I was Curator at BMM and engaged in curatorial research, exhibition production, collections management, public outreach, fundraising and strategic planning.
7 I use the term 'Bermudian' in an inclusive and liberal manner, versus restricting it only to those with citizenship or genealogical claims.
8 For instance, in an early proposal for my PhD project, I explicitly sought to explore the heritage of slavery and issues of race but was concerned about pursuing this topic so directly, perhaps risking exploitation of informants and forcing the heritage research.
9 Heritage Month (May) is an annual series of events mounted and supported by the Bermuda government through its Department of Community and Cultural Affairs.

10 Prof. Dame Marilyn Strathern used this phrase in a 2008 Writing-up Seminar, Department of Anthropology, University of Cambridge that I attended. She was referring to ethnography generally but it struck a chord with respect to my heritage ethnography.
11 See note 3 above.
12 In 2001 the Smithsonian Folklife Festival, an exposition of living cultural heritage on the US National Mall in Washington, DC, featured 'Bermuda Connections' as one of its three annual themes, with a 'homecoming' restaging held in Bermuda in 2002. The archive of oral recordings, researcher reports and educational materials is held by the Bermuda government Department of Community and Cultural Affairs. 'Maritime Arts' was one of several cultural areas researched, recorded and represented for the initiative.

Bibliography

Appadurai, A. (1996) *Modernity at Large: Cultural Dimensions of Globalization,* Minneapolis: University of Minnesota Press.
Baszanger, I. and N. Dodier (1997) 'Ethnography: Relating the Part to the Whole', in D. Silverman (ed.) *Qualitative Research: Theory, Method and Practice,* London: Sage, 8–23.
Bong, S. A. (2002) 'Debunking Myths in Qualitative Data Analysis', *Forum: Qualitative Social Research,* 3. http://www.qualitative-research.net/index.php/fqs/article/view/849.
Burch, S. (2005) 'The Texture of Heritage: A Reading of the 750th anniversary of Stockholm', *International Journal of Heritage Studies* 11, 211–33.
Butler, T. (2006) 'Doing Heritage Differently', *Rising East Online* 5: http://www.uel.ac.uk/risingeast/archive05/academic/butler.htm.
Candea, M. (2007) 'Arbitrary Locations: In Defence of the Bounded Field-site', *Journal of the Royal Anthropological Institute* 13, 167–84.
Chambers, E. J. (2004) 'Epilogue: Archaeology, Heritage and Public Endeavour', in P. A. Shackel and E. J. Chambers (eds) *Places in Mind: Public Archaeology as Applied Anthropology,* New York: Routledge, 193–208.
Chippindale, C. (2000) 'Capta and Data: On the True Nature of Archaeological Information', *American Antiquity* 65, 605–12.
Clifford, J. (1988) *The Predicament of Culture: Twentieth-century Ethnography, Literature and Art,* Cambridge, MA: Harvard University Press.
—— (1997a) *Routes: Travel and Translation in the Late Twentieth Century,* Cambridge, MA: Harvard University Press.
—— (1997b) 'Spatial Practices: Fieldwork, Travel, and the Disciplining of Anthropology', in A. Gupta and J. Ferguson (eds) *Anthropological Locations: Boundaries and Grounds of a Field Science,* Berkeley: University of California Press, 185–222.
Colic-Peisker, V. (2004) 'Doing Ethnography in "One's Own Ethnic Community": The Experience of an Awkward Insider', in L. Humme and J. Mulcock (eds) *Anthropologists in the Field: Cases in Participant Observation,* New York: Columbia University Press, 82–94.
Daniel, E. V. (1996) *Charred Lullabies: Chapters in an Anthropology of Violence,* Princeton: Princeton University Press.
Davies, C. A. (1999) *Reflexive Ethnography: A Guide to Researching Selves and Others,* London: Routledge.
Deleuze, G. and F. Guattari (1980) *A Thousand Plateaus (Mille Plateaux),* Minneapolis: University of Minnesota Press.
Dicks, B. (2000) *Heritage, Place and Community,* Cardiff: University of Wales Press.
Emerson, R. M., R. I. Fretz and L. L. Shaw (1995) *Writing Ethnographic Fieldnotes,* Chicago: University of Chicago Press.

Flyvbjerg, B. (2006) 'Five Misunderstandings About Case-Study Research', *Qualitative Inquiry* 12, 219–45.

Fontana, A. and J. H. Frey (1994) 'Interviewing: The Art of Science', in N. K. Denzin and Y. S. Lincoln (eds) *Handbook of Qualitative Research*, Thousand Oaks, CA: Sage, 361–76.

Garden, M. C. E. (2006) 'The Heritagescape: Looking at Landscapes of the Past', *International Journal of Heritage Studies* 12, 394–411.

Gelsthorpe, L. (2007) 'Analysing Interview Data', *Joint School Research Programme Workshop*, Cambridge: University of Cambridge.

Glaser, B. G. and A. L. Strauss (1967) *The Discovery of Grounded Theory: Strategies for Qualitative Research*, New York: Aldine Publishing Company.

Hallett, A. C. (1993) *Chronical of a Colonial Church 1612–1826*, Pembroke, Bermuda: Juniperhill Press.

Henare, A., M. Holbraad and S. Wastell (2007) 'Introduction: Thinking Through Things', in A. Henare, M. Holbraad and S. Wastell (eds) *Thinking Through Things: Theorising Artefacts Ethnographically*, Abingdon: Routledge, 1–31.

Herzfeld, M. (1997) *Cultural Intimacy: Social Poetics in the Nation-State*, New York: Routledge.

Holtorf, C. (2005) *From Stonehenge to Las Vegas*, Walnut Creek, CA: AltaMira Press.

Ingold, T. (2008) 'Pathways through the Weather-World: Movement, Flux and Perception', paper presented at the Garrod Research Seminar, McDonald Institute for Archaeological Research, Cambridge.

Jeganathan, P. (2005) 'Pain, Politics and the Epistemological Ethics of Anthropological Disciplinarity', in L. Meskell and P. Pels (eds) *Embedding Ethics*, Oxford: Berg, 147–67.

Jones, S. (2004) *Early Medieval Sculpture and the Production of Meaning, Value and Place: The Case of Hilton Cadboll*, Edinburgh: Historic Scotland.

Karp, I., C. Kratz, L. Szwaja and T. Ybarra-Frausto (eds) (2006) *Museum Frictions: Public Cultures/ Global Transformations*, Durham, NC: Duke University Press.

Kersel, M. (2006) 'License to Sell: The Legal Trade in Antiquities in Israel'. PhD Thesis, Department of Archaeology, University of Cambridge.

Knell, S. J. (2007) 'Museums, Reality and the Material World', in S. J. Knell (ed.) *Museums in the Material World*, London: Routledge, 1–28.

McClanahan, A. (2004) *The Heart of Neolithic Orkney in its Contemporary Contexts: A Case Study in Heritage Management and Community Values*, Edinburgh: Historic Scotland and the University of Manchester North American Foundation.

Marcus, G. E. (1995) 'Ethnography in/of the World System: The Emergence of Multi-Sited Ethnography', *Annual Review of Anthropology* 24, 95–117.

—— (1999) 'What is at Stake – and is Not – in the Idea and Practice of Multi-sited Ethnography', in H. L. Moore and T. Sanders (eds) *Anthropology in Theory: Issues in Epistemology*, Malden, MA: Blackwell, 618–21.

Meskell, L. and P. Pels (2005) 'Introduction: Embedding Ethics', in L. Meskell and P. Pels (eds) *Embedding Ethics*, Oxford: Berg, 1–26.

Nakanishi, Y., H. Soderland, J. Carman, M. C. Garden and M. L. S. Sørensen (2003) 'Conference Report – Making the Means Transparent: Exploring Research Methodologies in Heritage Studies', *International Journal of Heritage Studies* 9, 275–9.

Rabinow, P. (2008) 'On the Anthropology of the Contemporary', Frazer Lecture, University of Cambridge.

Smith, L. (2006) *The Uses of Heritage*, Abingdon: Routledge.

Tilley, C. (2006) 'Introduction: Identity, Place, Landscape and Heritage', *Journal of Material Culture* 11, 7–32.

VanWynsberghe, R. and S. Khan (2007) 'Redefining Case Study', *International Journal of Qualitative Methods* 6, 1–10.

Weiss, L. (2007) 'Heritage-making and Political Identity', *Journal of Social Archaeology* 7, 413–31.

Young, L. (2002) 'Rethinking Heritage: Cultural Policy and Inclusion', in R. Sandell (ed.) *Museums, Society, Inequality*, London: Routledge, 203–12.

9

BETWEEN THE LINES
AND IN THE MARGINS

Interviewing people about attitudes
to heritage and identity

Marie Louise Stig Sørensen

Introduction

The analysis of various aspects of people's attitudes towards the past and how
these are formed constitute a major area of heritage research, and interviewing
is one of the most commonly used methods in such studies. It is, therefore,
important that we explore the use of interviews as a method in heritage research
and the expectations about the insights that this method raises. In particular,
the understanding of interviews as a means of gaining information about
complex and abstract relations, thoughts and feelings should be considered by
heritage researchers and if necessary the method should be adapted to the
needs of the specific research involved, rather than predetermined by its
existing applications and formats. Interviewing as a method is often discussed
separately from its field of application, apparently assigning it a position as
simply a social science method; in practice, however, it is clear that interviews
are both formed and affected by the knowledge and insights that are pursued.
Moreover, it also seems that several features of the interview, such as expectation about what the aims should be and about the proper conduct of the
interviewer, are affected by the different fieldwork traditions that can be found
within the social sciences. For instance, the archaeological use of interviews is
usually framed in terms of the gathering of factual information, whereas the
social anthropological approach towards the interview, whether explicitly
stated or implicitly embedded within how it is performed, often seems influenced by the long tradition of participant observation within this discipline.
This causes the anthropological interview to become a matter of listening:
emphasising the importance of the interviewer actively avoiding influencing

and biasing the conversation, with the role of the interviewer as a listener echoing the tradition of the unobtrusive presence of the participant observer. In contrast, disciplines such as psychology and psychoanalysis are raised on a tradition of 'digging deeper' and of exploring the apparent resistance to questioning. Their approach to interviewing, as discussed further below, often takes the form of an exploration in which the interviewer plays an active role in asking and pursuing questions and responses. Interviews are therefore not just one method shared and approached in the same manner throughout the social sciences. Further still, there are more possibilities and more diversity than are suggested by the coarse distinction between 'quantitative' and 'qualitative' interviewing methods, and it would significantly enhance the field of Heritage Studies if individual researchers were more aware of such differences, feeling confident in their choice of methods and in their ability to adjust or elaborate on existing methods. The methods indicated by the term 'interview' should be thought about as adjustable tools rather than fixed recipes, but the freedom brought with the rejection of fixed methods also creates new demands about being explicit, rigorous and reflexive when one is working through one's methodological positioning.

So far, it has been common practice for studies of heritage to focus on specific aspects of the complex issues being investigated (e.g. Jones 2004; Merriman 1991). Moreover, abstract issues, such as the normative question about attitudes to the past, are often approached in a manner that refers to a range of more or less explicit reactions and engagements without critically reflecting on the interdependences and inter-reliances between them. In effect the complex questions are rarely answered. Heritage (or 'the past') is used as a kind of collective reference to an array of subject matters that range from ideas or concepts to material objects and monuments fixed in landscapes or museums. This apparent vagueness is, however, not necessarily due to a lack of thoughtfulness; at least two major factors may sit behind the lack of analytical precision. The first is that the field of Heritage Studies is still in its formative stage, and thus lacks a clear overview both of its remit and of its tools. It is important to tread carefully at this early stage and not to limit the visions of what is involved though the use of over-determined terminologies and approaches. The second factor is the tendency of there being an insufficient match between the methods explored in these analyses, their aims and the subject area being investigated. It is this latter point, the incongruence between the nature of the subject matter and the expectations of the methods, which this chapter aims to discuss.

Background to case studies: interviewing as part of the Als project

My interest in interviewing as a method for exploring the position (i.e. value and connotations) of the past in the present has arisen out of a project of interviewing local farmers and amateur archaeologists in connection with an archaeological field-survey project which I directed on the Danish island of Als between 1989 and 2003. During these interactions a number of methods were used: formal and informal interviews; one questionnaire sent to people individually; one questionnaire filled out at a cultural centre in connection with other activities; and a large number of informal interviews conducted in situations ranging from standing next to a tractor in a ploughed field to meeting people after lectures. Videotapes and photographs were also used.

The aims of these interviews, and in particular how they shifted during the duration of the project, need to be briefly introduced in order to characterise the knowledge or insights which were pursued. These changes influenced how the encounters were conducted in various ways: they impacted the set-up of the interviews and my perception of my own role as the interviewer. My overall aim, however, is to reflect upon how one evaluates and understands the insights that these encounters may provide and how in turn we have to think about the interviewing process. In particular, I want to reflect upon how interviewing as a method can be used to engage with complex and abstract ideas, such as heritage, in an enlightening and constructive manner rather than one that produces closure. And while I support approaches to interviewing that emphasise the interview as a conversation, I particularly want to focus on how one may learn to listen, or, in other words, 'the art of hearing data' (Rubin and Rubin 1995).

My first collection of information from the farmers in my study area took the form of a simple questionnaire which, in addition to providing information about the archaeological project, asked them (1) whether they would give the project permission to walk on their fields, and (2) whether they had found any prehistoric objects or observed distinct features on the ground (with a list of possible observations given). This questionnaire was followed up by a personal visit if the field was selected for field-walking. The visits included an informal interview about the farmers' finds, the characteristics of the field, their knowledge about prehistory and the landscape, and so on. I was taking notes, and these were at times followed up by drawings and/or photographs, or walking through the fields together. While there were some sensitive issues regarding ownership (i.e. whether finds should belong to the regional museum or to the owner of the field), the situations were, it seemed to me, straightforward, and took the form of the farmer providing me with information that both of us considered interesting and/or valuable. The farmers told me about their finds in response to simple questions, or, in other words, my questions were phrased in a manner that solicited predictable factual information. The straying into other areas of conversation, such as admiring the objects, appeared to be incidental to the main aim of accumulating a richer dataset about finds from the area.

My interest did, however, early on begin to shift towards the farmers themselves and various dimensions of their relationship to the physical remains of the past in the landscape around them. In response to this shift, I conducted a number of more extensive interviews with selected people, who were identified as probably interested in the past since they had large private collections in their homes. I used open-ended interviews structured around a number of themes, such as the physical integration of the objects within the home, and issues of ownership, in particular what happens to collections when the next generation takes over the farm and the former owner moves into a retirement house. Some of the interviews were recorded on video, and others on tapes or through extensive note taking. In addition, throughout all my other interactions with the local farmers I now began to guide interviews beyond information just about finds to questions about their ways of engaging with the finds. Thus I was asking about how the finds were integrated within the architectural features of the home. I was interested in investigating whether there were some correlations between the socio-economic standing of farmers, including their 'cultural capital', and the manner in which the objects were integrated into the domestic setting. I expected that in the larger and socially more significant farms the finds would be placed more dominantly within the home. In these homes the finds were frequently located, for example, in purpose-built structures in the main rooms, or on windowsills and over the chimney piece. In the homes of the farmers from lower social strata the finds would be located in more random places, including in boxes in the barn or in cupboards in the kitchen.

This change in my focus had several effects upon the interview situation. In particular, our respective roles were affected in a manner which to me proved emotionally difficult. I was now turning my informants into the subject of investigation, a change with which I was somewhat uncomfortable as I thought they might not easily comprehend the reasons for my new questions nor necessarily appreciate or agree to being placed as the subject of investigation. I found it difficult to directly ask the questions that I thought were of interest, as I felt they were contrary to the farmers' expectations of me and their perception of my role. I felt that revealing this interest would mean that I, in their eyes, had ceased to perform my assigned role as the archaeologist, as I was enquiring about private matters rather than matters of information. Although this tension is not the focus of this chapter, it must be acknowledged, and it is an issue that is likely to often affect qualitative 'close-up' interview work. I do feel, however, in view of the arguments I make below, that I was at risk of letting this unease distract me rather than using it in a more constructive manner. This may have been because I had become too singularly focused upon my own part of the interaction and my questions, rather than appreciating more fully the important role(s) of the subject.

Towards the end of the project, a further dimension was added to these interviews through a detailed and elaborate questionnaire filled in by people who participated in a sampling of saliva for historical mtDNA analysis. The questionnaire had several open-ended questions, and assistants who were experienced in oral-history work and interviewing were present to advise and help with the filling in of the schema. This interview-questionnaire set-up was entirely stage-set, garnered considerable press coverage and only included individuals who were self-selected on the basis of being interested in finding out more about their ancestors. The experience did, however, resonate with some of my lingering impressions from looking at the videotapes and from various conversations, and it furthered my concern about how to evaluate what the interviewees were saying and why they chose particular expressions and ways of responding.

Approaches to interviewing

All the methods proved useful for collecting data – especially factual information and 'surface' phenomena. By the latter I mean information which comes easily and without much searching on behalf of either the interviewee or the interviewer – such as whether the farmers thought there were any barrows on their field, or whether in their opinion the objects should remain on the farm or be given to the regional museum. The methods, obviously, are not equally good at all things, and they may therefore be usefully employed together, complementing each other, as most textbooks on social science survey methods recommend (e.g. Cresswell 2003). What concerns me most here, however, are the 'cracks'; I am interested in that which seems to fall between the competence or reach of the methods, and which is only discovered and recognised accidentally and informally. I contend that 'between the lines and in the margins' of the information provided there were additional (and at times more pertinent) insights to be gained about how people relate to the past and what that relationship is about. I further suggest that these nuances get lost if we too slavishly follow the data-collecting procedures commonly presented. This is primarily because such strategies are designed around assumptions of a coherent relationship between questions and answers, and presume furthermore that the questions are unambiguous and simple (i.e. that they will be interpreted and understood in the way intended by the interviewer). But neither of these basic assumptions is necessarily correct or warranted regarding investigation of people and their relationship to the heritage.

It is important to recognise that interviews can have different purposes: they can and should aim at different kinds of insights and discoveries, and in turn their form, how they are conducted and, even more significantly, how they are evaluated must respond to such differences. At their extremes, approaches range from empirical or positivist approaches based on the assumption that there is a truth that belongs to the subject and it is the researcher's role to find it, to post-modern approaches, which argue that there is nothing to be understood or interpreted beyond how the subject constructs their particular version of reality (e.g. essays in Gubrium and Holstein 2003). Most common, however, are approaches which aim to produce comparable data between different interviewees and to seek new knowledge and new insights from how different informants respond to similar questions. To be meaningful, these interviews are based on the assumption that the comparative outcome is valuable and that the data can be compared against some shared or basic parameter. The interviews tend to be structured around questions that are shaped around expectations of how the interviewee will respond and what they can inform about. This type of interview has a long history in sociology and anthropology and is also used in marketing research. It has also been used in surveys of public attitudes within heritage studies (Merriman 1991), but when used within this sector there has been a tendency to conflate the aim of producing comparative data and the aim of exploring and discovering particular aspects of heritage. In order to place the data into comparable categories the interviews commonly build assumptions about the results into their design, and the responses are subsequently processed in terms of 'the nearest fit' to the expected outcomes. Such interview methods can be useful, but they are best suited for investigations of phenomena that have predictable relationships to well-known datasets or where there is a solid basis for predicting responses; they tend to be restrictive for explorative engagements.

There are also examples, although fewer in number, of the use of open-ended subject-orientated interviews in heritage studies. Here the responses are not scanned in terms of their match to other results nor directed to fit with a hierarchy of questions, but are used as part of a journey of discovery. Jones, for example, used in-depth qualitative interviewing in her investigation of the meanings and values surrounding early medieval sculpture in a rural setting (Hilton of Cadboll) in Scotland (Jones 2004).

Qualitative interview techniques are often characterised by their lack of control, by being process-orientated, aiming to understand the actor's view and concerned primarily with discovery (Cook and Reichardt 1979). These, however, are all rather vague characteristics. What, for instance, do we mean by 'control', and what is implied by saying we aim to understand the actor's view? The main difference that I want to emphasise and further explore is therefore the question of control. Irrespective of other differences, interviews differ substantially in terms of their desire for control over the answers. This, moreover, is not merely a matter of power relations or of questions being 'open-ended' but also about an interviewer's willingness to take a position about what kind of information or responses are being sought. It is therefore also about the respective status and roles of the interviewee and the interviewer. I argue below that Heritage Studies needs to explore the interviewee-orientated types of interviewing much more substantially than has hitherto been the case. The reason for this is that we still need to explore our potential data. But we need to do this in a manner that is unrestrained by large bodies of assumptions or by hypotheses since many of the themes we need to investigate are still too unknown and uncharted to benefit from a hypothesis-based approach. Hypothesis-based approaches in their specifications and agreed agendas restrict our field and our ability to learn (Fox Keller 2000). Carol Gilligan, a feminist psychoanalyst and writer, whose work is grounded in listening (1982: xiii), has long been concerned with 'people's voices' in the sense of 'something like what people mean when they speak of the core of the self' (1982: xvi). She argues that if we want to discover how another person constructs reality then we cannot use testing or observations as these methods involve interpretation apart from the subject. Rather, following Gilligan's argument, one must interview out of a deep sense of curiosity about the logic or structure that makes the other person think and express themselves in a certain way. The interviewer must ask questions in order to discover how the other person thinks, not how that person's thinking fits their own thinking. Interviewing in that sense can be understood as a method of coming to understand, and it should take the form of a journey of discovery that reaches beyond mere conversation.

Here I shall try to argue for the potentials of this understanding of the purpose of interviewing by applying the basic arguments to some of the problematic elements of my own interviews on Als. The various interactions provided via the Als project often resulted in immediate, factual and guided responses to my questions and probing. I have also, however, received responses that I initially thought revealed that the interviewee did not understand my question, and I have received responses that took different forms from what I expected. It is these latter two observations that I want to try to deconstruct here in order to understand how interviews may be used and how they may challenge us.

Mistaken responses

Initially, I perceived the apparent mismatch between some of my questions and the responses given in terms of incomprehension: they did not understand my question. Further reflection, and guided by discussions of interviewing in other disciplines (especially a presentation by Carol Gilligan[1]) and some of the discussions of feminist methodologies, has made me question this. I suggest that, mistakenly evaluating their responses in terms of my own expectations, I failed to recognise that they had interpreted my question in a manner that did not correspond with my expectations. It was that different understanding that caused their response. Failing to recognise this, I also missed some of the insights into their understanding of heritage which these responses revealed. In particular, I did not appreciate that, to my interviewees, it was not a mistake but their different construction of reality. With hindsight I suggest that I did not pick up enough of the clues about how many of the farmers tended to respond to my generalised or abstract questions about the past or heritage by translating the question into something more specific – such as the stone axe which they had found. They made my question about their relationship to or their thoughts about the past answerable by converting it into a question about tangible objects. I believe a kind of transferral was taking place between the past and the object; it is possible that in such situations the object *is* the past at a more existential level than we usually imply when referring to objects representing or symbolising the past. If this is in fact a common phenomenon then it may reveal important characteristics both about our cognitive abilities to think the past into the present, and about the status that objects can acquire in situations where such linkages are made.

As an extension of this argument it is also clear that the mutual expectations of what the interview intends to accomplish do not consistently match. For example, I had a distinct problem with finding a polite, socially acceptable[2] (i.e. not noisy or intrusive into the private sphere) way of asking people where and in what order or system they kept the archaeological objects within their home.[3] Furthermore, despite my attempts to ask about it, they did not really tell me where and how they normally kept their archaeological objects. Again, in hindsight, the apparent lack of response to my questioning may too easily or too swiftly have been misinterpreted and thus rejected as ignorance, lack of comprehension or resistance to my intrusion rather than thought about and understood as a response to the perceived irrelevance of my questions. Placing this lack of response within the structure of the interviewing process, I now think that in many cases they did not recognise that my question was indeed a question, and I, interpreting this as a brush-off, did not pursue the issue further by finding other ways of questioning or exploring their way of thinking. In not following up on their responses I did not properly explore the interviews as a *process* of discovery.

Again, I think that I initially missed significant clues. In many of these cases, the objects were included within the domestic setting in a manner that made them appear similar to flowerpots and photographs (see Figure 9.1), rather than being there in the domestic setting as an explicit, discursive statement – but my questions did not place them at that level, and my questions probably did not have any resonance with the ways the farmers were thinking about and engaging with their objects. The archaeological finds were frequently used as if they were decorative and pretty objects, and they were found interspersed with other bric-à-brac on windowsills or shelves, but my questions, rather than relating to this, sought answers that were about identity, significance and status. I still believe that these themes are enormously significant, but they will not necessarily be directly verbalised or communicated in response to direct questioning during an interview as they do not resonate with people's own language about these objects. Theirs is a language built around a taken-for-granted view that a stone axe is pretty, worth displaying, and comparable with a flowerpot or a pretty vase; the point being that the value of the objects is deeply embedded within the cultural world-view of the people I interviewed. These views, furthermore, neither are nor need to be made discursively but are rather part of their lived engagement with their world, including its particular history.[4] They did not, I propose, appreciate my question as a question due to its abstract formulation. Meanwhile, it should be appreciated that such a lack of explicit arguments or recognition – rather than diminishing the significance of a connection – can at times reveal the exact opposite, showing how deeply embedded the accepted significance is.

Figure 9.1 Example of the display of prehistoric objects in the home (photo by the author)

The use of poetics

Another observation that has greatly intrigued me is the use of poetic language, the telling of stories and the use of metaphors. As an example, when I once asked a farmer why he thought he wanted to collect and keep the prehistoric artefacts, he replied, 'If you had a rare tree that bore precious fruit, would you not want to keep them?'

Another time, when a farmer was trying to fill in a questionnaire about notions of heritage and its links to ideas of belonging and identity, he approached me. He is a large man, an important farmer, a practical man with big hands that show years of wear. He is an articulate man but may not be used to writing his thoughts down, certainly not about such matters. His body showed his growing frustration with the inability to capture in writing the *story he wanted to tell*. We agreed that he should dictate the story to me, so I wrote it down. Here is the gist of the story that he wanted to tell:

> You know the big trees growing at the long barrows down in the forest? We call them grandfather and grandmother. You see, this is about when my grandfather had to leave the farm because of the draft.[5] He went to live in Canada, and there he collected seeds from the big trees in the forests over there to plant when he could come back again. When he came back, he went down to our forest and planted them there, next to the barrows. When I was a boy, I used to play there, and we called the trees for grandfather and grandmother. Now, I always take my children down to the forest to have picnic with the grandparents. When I sit there, and the roots of the trees that my grandfather brought back

from Canada go straight into the barrow and into the past and the crown is far above me, then it is all connected and it is just right. So we always say we go down to the grandparents, and the trees and the barrows are the grandparents.

(Interview farmer x)

He was not sure I had understood him, as the feelings he tried to convey were to him so powerful and so special that words clearly seemed inadequate. He had, however, conveyed a great deal, and in particular he gave me a potent glimpse of the poetic link a person may find between the past and him- or herself.

But initially I interpreted these responses as a kind of 'short-cut'. I thought they were revealing an inability to rationalise the relationship to the past. I interpreted the use of poetic language and metaphors as a replacement for a more articulated answer – a kind of retreat. Furthermore, having formulated the question in expectation of a certain kind of response, I interpreted the poetic responses as inferior in terms of their informative value. I saw these statements as lacking a certain detachment and ability to be discursive. While they were very powerful responses, in my analysis I did not primarily focus upon what that told me. These were beautiful images and stories, and that, of course, was their primary value and importance – in response to my questions, my interviewees were revealing the depth of their emotional attachment to their past by returning to me a glimpse of something so special that normal use of language could not express it. Rather than limiting their answers by referring to treasure or value, they talked directly to my imagination and assumed I had the ability to empathise with their own. They allowed me to see that for them the most important response to my question was the depth of their emotions.

This is similar but not identical to the use of 'stories' within interviews, as discussed by Rubin and Rubin (1995). They suggest that a story 'communicates a moral, a broad message, or a set of core beliefs ... it may have a more dreamlike quality to it, with a dream's disjunctive connections and symbolic events' (Rubin and Rubin 1995: 25). They also stress how the stories are valuable because they contain points that the interviewee feels strongly about, 'but does not feel comfortable enough to say directly' (26). Symbols and stories are, therefore, thought of as elements of the conversation that are indicative of important underlying concepts or ideas (58). The difference between their discussion of the use of stories and my example is, I suggest, that the poetic stories in this case should not be approached as indicative of underlying ideas; rather the quality of being poetic is in itself *the meaning* sought after, and the change in style conveys this. The importance of language in terms of the power of words themselves has also been pointed out by Fawret-Saada, who, when doing fieldwork on witchcraft in France, had to work through and with language in a different way as the words in themselves were power rather than knowledge or information (2007: 469). In line with this, I suggest that in my own example the words used were in themselves expressions of wonder and emotions rather than primarily revealing information.

The important point emerging from these reflections is, I believe, that with greater openness and awareness about how the use of language itself harbours different moods and stylistic inflections we may greatly improve our understanding not just of how the relationship to the past is placed within a layered sense of reality, but what roles emotions and empathy play in this process.

'Talking with the hands'

Non-verbal communication is often emphasised as a significant aspect of interviewing, and is usually presented as a communication of what people know but cannot say that they know (e.g. Adler and Adler 1994). The importance of paying attention to non-verbal cues that may indicate emphasis and emotional tones is also stressed by some interviewers (e.g. Rubin and Rubin 1995: 7), who also point to the need 'to encourage learning to recognize and then explore words that have rich connotative or symbolic meanings' (21). The non-verbal may even at times be presented as a way of bringing subconscious or non-discursive knowledge into view of the conscious discursive discourse. Such levels of non-discursive knowledge may matter greatly for the exploration of the role of heritage in the present.

One of my recurrent observations when interviewing people (and which was helpfully documented by the use of video in some interviews) was the physical interaction with objects. The archaeological object was not just referred to as a symbol or a presence in the room, nor was it merely looked at. When we were standing looking at, for example, some stone axes laid out on a mantelpiece, the interviewee would reach out to take the objects one by one and handle them, touching, stroking and turning the objects over, feeling them. These gestures were also used to show the objects or to point out details on them; but the non-verbal communication, which in my mind I called 'talking with the hands', did in the main seem to be an entirely separate communication going on in parallel to our ongoing conversation. At times I would find both the interviewee and myself with a stone axe in our hand while we were talking.

Whereas these common situations may reveal subconscious knowledge and should be considered part of the overall communication, as discussions of non-verbal communication suggest, I believe there are also other distinct dimensions to these phenomena. To recognise these we should remember that these are not just any objects, but objects that have stories and in particular distinct memories attached to them. These memories were often vivid and distinct and were being recalled and retold, for example, in accounts of where and when the objects were found. I suggest that the touching of the object is part of that recall. The tangible qualities of the object re-engage the memory of its discovery, in which touching it becomes an act of re-remembering, including a sense of awe, surprise and delight.

In this observation I believe we see yet another aspect of the complex relationship between the present, the prehistoric object and the past. When the interview became engaged with these finds it encountered a very specific dimension (and potentiality) of heritage: the interviewee's relationship to the past became distilled into a very personalised moment of discovery. A corollary of this observation is that these ways of relating to the past are not shared by everyone, as not everyone has had such an encounter, nor even the possibility of it taking place. This has implications for how we should design our investigation of people's attitudes to the past with a greater awareness of how they may encounter it.

Interviews as conversations and discovery

Such in-depth qualitative interviews are difficult to obtain, and they are demanding. The control over the process appears to be relinquished, and insecurity or a lack of clarity about how to proceed can therefore creep in. It is important to understand what is asked of the interviewer and expected of the interviewee, and to recognise that such in-depth open-ended interviews – while powerful and enlightening – are not always either appropriate or possible. It is also important to recognise that whereas the interview may aim to be a conversation with the implied assumption of mutuality, it imposes obligations on the conversation partners that may not be agreed to: the interview may have to take a different form or follow another route if it encounters resistance or is being outmanoeuvred. Robben's discussion (2007) of how seduction, transference and resistance affected the interviewing about violence in Argentina is a powerful and illustrative example of the potential dynamics of an interview. Another aspect has been emphasised by Bourdieu, who points to how the interview may help (or push) the interviewee to objectify him- or herself, and argues that the interview can be an induced and accompanied self-analysis (Bourdieu *et al.* 1999: 615). It is, therefore, important to be wary of relinquishing complete control, as it may well cause harm and could undermine the ability to learn. We should, however, continue to question what we mean by 'control' when interviewing. For this the metaphor of discovery provides a helpful counterpoint to the idea of a conversation, as it reminds us of the purposefulness of the encounter – we interview to learn. This point is helpful in terms of reassigning control, albeit a different kind of control, to the interviewer insofar as it is not necessarily the case that a person can tell their version of reality, or can provide a verbal insight into their world-view without guidance or mediation (whether this involves a transcription or transference or other ways of helping).

Concluding reflections

In response to these experiences and the recognition of the need to 'listen' better, I suggest that sustained discursive reflection about the aims of the heritage interview is necessary. The importance of observing details of body language and other types of non-verbal communication may also be particularly pertinent when interviews venture into such uncharted fields as heritage. Apparent inarticulateness must also be scrutinised, and we need to give more attention towards how comprehensive or open-ended our questions can be if they are to remain part of a meaningful conversation and analysis. We also need to develop more sensitive ways of incorporating and analysing responses that do not match our expectations and to listen for stylistic changes and ruptures in the narrations.

Most importantly, however, we must recognise that when little is known about a phenomenon it is important we make sure that our methods do not dictate what our results will be. For heritage studies to engage meaningfully and in depth with some of its central concerns about the roles of the past in the present, we need to pay more attention to qualitative methodologies and explore them more explicitly. In order to collect rich qualitative data, and to improve on how we explore new links and associations, approaches to interviews that see them essentially as travels of discovery will be helpful. In such approaches, the interviews should aim to become dynamic, for the interaction between the interviewer and the interviewee to become collaborative, and for objects to become mediators of meanings and important signifiers in their own right. It is important to become aware of this dynamic, and to ensure that the interview does not become static. One must continuously try to make sense of, reassess and recontextualise both the interview and the responses generated. This means that interviews are about engagement, and in conducting them one's questions have to invite a response and, if needed, clarification. Carol Gilligan emphasises that interviews should always be based on a willingness to hear and to listen for the something that changes one's way of thinking – and this is maybe the most important thing to remember. We interview out of both a desire to learn and a curiosity about how people see and understand their world.

Notes

1 The influence of Carol Gilligan's work on my thinking is primarily based on a guest lecture ('Conversations about Interviewing') she gave in Cambridge on 2 March 2004.
2 I am Danish and grew up in the area investigated. I did not know any of the people prior to the interviews, but being a 'native', while helpful in many ways, may also have given me an exaggerated sensitivity to local social norms and good manners.
3 I could sometimes observe this myself, but people had often moved the objects from where they were usually kept in preparation for my visit.
4 The area investigated is part of Slesvig-Holstein, the border region between Germany and Denmark, and has a history that has produced a deep sense of nationalism, including explicit uses of the past in identity formation and sense of pride and efficacy (Sørensen 1996).
5 Due to the German occupation of southern Jutland from 1864 until 1920 thousands of young men emigrated to North America to avoid being drafted into the German army.

Bibliography

Adler, P. A. and P. Adler (1994) 'Observational Techniques', in N. K. Denzin and Y. S. Lincoln (eds) *Handbook of Qualitative Research*, London: Sage, 377–92.

Bourdieu, P. *et al.* (1999) *The Weight of the World: Social Suffering in Contemporary Society*, Cambridge: Polity Press.

Cook, T. D. and C. S. Reichardt (eds) (1979) *Qualitative and Quantitative Methods in Evaluation Research*, Thousand Oaks, CA: Sage.

Cresswell, J. W. (2003) *Research Design: Qualitative, Quantitative, and Mixed Methods Approach*, London: Sage.

Fawret-Saada, J. (2007) 'The Way Things Are Said', in A. C. G. M. Robben and J. A. Sluka (eds) *Ethnographic Fieldwork: An Anthological Reader*, Oxford: Blackwell, 465–75.

Fox Keller, E. (2000) *The Century of the Gene*, Cambridge, MA: Harvard University Press.

Gubrium, J. and J. Holstein (eds) (2003) *Postmodern Interviewing*, Thousand Oaks, CA: Sage.

Gilligan, C. (1982) *In a Different Voice: Psychological Theory and Women's Development*, Cambridge, MA: Harvard University Press.

Jones, S. (2004) *Early Medieval Sculpture and the Production of Meaning, Value and Place: The Case of Hilton of Cadboll*, Edinburgh: Historic Scotland.

Merriman, N. (1991) *Beyond the Glass Case: The Public, Museums and Heritage in Britain*, London: Leicester University Press.

Robben, A. C. G. M. (2007) 'Ethnographic Seduction: Transference and Resistance in Dialogues about Terror and Violence in Argentina', in A. C. G. M. Robben and J. A. Sluka (eds) *Ethnographic Fieldwork: An Anthropological Reader*, Oxford: Blackwell, 159–76.

Rubin, H. and I. Rubin, I. (1995) *Qualitative Interviewing: The Art of Hearing Data*, Thousand Oaks, CA: Sage.

Sørensen, M. L. S. (1996) 'The Fall of a Nation, the Birth of a Subject: The National Use of Archaeology in Nineteenth-century Denmark', in M. Díaz-Andreu and T. Champion (eds) *Nationalism and Archaeology in Europe*, London: UCL Press, 24–47.

10

WALKING A FINE LINE

Obtaining sensitive information
using a valid methodology

Morag M. Kersel

Introduction

In the global marketplace for cultural property there are illegal elements at every stage. Individuals clandestinely pillage archaeological sites. The artefacts then move through a series of both legal and illegal conduits to arrive at a salesroom or auction house for sale to private collectors or museums that turn a blind eye to the question of provenance (archaeological findspot). Investigating this movement of artefacts formed the focus of my PhD research (Kersel 2006). This research is both multi-sited and multi-vocal and the ethnographic enquiry had to reflect those realities. In this chapter the methods of investigation will be illustrated through a series of data-collection techniques employed while conducting field research in Israel and the Palestinian Authority (hereafter the PA). Through trial and error during interviews with looters, dealers, collectors, government employees, archaeologists and academics, a methodology was employed to explore the efficacy of legally sanctioned antiquities markets in combating the illegal excavation of archaeological sites and the resulting illicit trade in antiquities.

Framing the debate

At its most elemental there are two sides to the debate over whether to sell antiquities in the marketplace. Those who support the trade in antiquities include dealers, collectors, museums and some archaeologists. They believe that international trade is inherently desirable and support the notion that many, if not most, artefacts are redundant and lack special archaeological significance or even cultural importance for the archaeologically rich nation. Advocates of this position support a legal trade in antiquities, asserting that by making it illegal, the trade is sent underground, creating a black market ensuring both a lack of control and inflated prices. They see parallels to the world of drug and arms trafficking. From this perspective, a legally sanctioned sale of antiquities will put the illegal trade and looters out of business (Marks 1995; Merryman 1995; Pearlstein 1986; Shanks 2001).

On the other side of the debate are those who oppose a trade in antiquities – legal or illegal. Comprised mainly of archaeologists, national governments, some museum employees and cultural preservationists, this group claims a direct causal relationship between the demand for antiquities and the looting of archaeological sites in order to supply that demand. For them the true culprits in the illicit trade in antiquities are the collectors (Elia 1993; Renfrew 1993), for if there were no demand (or no collecting) there would be little or no need for looting. As a result, they favour a total ban on all trade in antiquities in order to protect the world's cultural heritage from destruction.

This debate framed my PhD project. The legally sanctioned market in Israel (see Text box 10.1) was the primary case study for an examination of the market, with a particular focus on understanding the effects its legality or illegality appears to have on site destruction and on archaeological practice in the region. Israel is unique in the region as one of the only countries with a legally sanctioned sale of antiquities (Figure 10.1). An examination of this case study in Israel and its effects on the PA outlined the scope and complexity of the market, situating the view of archaeologists as one among a multiplicity of claims about the use, meaning and value of the antiquities.

In order to understand the trade in antiquities and recognise its effects on the archaeological landscape, it was imperative that I explore the issues, witness the trade, and speak with those directly involved with the production, distribution and consumption of artefacts. Archaeologists, collectors (whether tourists, high-end or museums), dealers, government employees, museum professionals and a group of miscellaneous stakeholders (including architects, conservators, educators and lawyers) – all of whom express a degree of entitlement to the disposition of artefacts – were consulted throughout the course of my research. The fundamental question of whether there was a discernible relationship between the demand for archaeological goods (in the legal market) and looting of archaeological sites to supply that demand guided the enquiry. After arriving at what I thought was a research question that would contribute to the ongoing debate surrounding the disposition of the material remains of the past, the next tasks were to gather data, assess the market, synthesise the results and arrive at some conclusions. Employing a valid methodology was among my biggest challenges. This chapter recounts the travails of an archaeologist in the world of ethnography.

Text box 10.1 Legal trade – how it works

Under current legislation in Israel (Antiquities Law 5738–1978) you can buy and subsequently export archaeological artefacts from dealers licensed by the Israel Antiquities Authority (IAA) if the artefacts derive from collections that predate the 1978 law. Whether the licensed antiquities shop is in the lobby of a high-priced hotel or in a small alley of the Old City, one of its main purposes is the sale of antiquities. Each licensee has to apply, pay a fee and receive approval from the IAA anti-theft unit in order to obtain a licence to deal in antiquities. In each case the licensed shop has to display its licence prominently and comply with the terms of the 1978 Antiquities Law. Whether or not the dealer supplies a 'certificate of authenticity' is entirely up to the individual, but they are required to provide an export licence (issued by the IAA) for any object they sell if the purchaser requests one. The licensed dealer sends a digital image or takes the object to the IAA offices, where the relevant authorities check the ID number and description against the dealer inventory and then issue an export licence. Both the dealer and the IAA keep track of the inventory via a register. The onus is on the purchaser to request an export licence; if no licence is issued then there is no record of the transaction on file with the IAA. This provides the crucial opportunity to 'launder' recently looted archaeological material through the exchange of register numbers. Theoretically a member of the IAA anti-theft unit (those charged with oversight and licensing of the legal market) can walk into any licensed shop at any time and ask to see the dealer register, which they can then check against the store inventory. In practice this is very unlikely because there is only one person assigned to monitor all sixty dealers throughout the country, and this is only one of their duties for the IAA. This results in fractured oversight and very few inspections. From interviews with some sixty representatives from the IAA and the dealing community it is apparent that despite an overt legal façade of artefact registers, licensing systems and regular inspections, there are covert aspects to meeting demand for archaeological artefacts from the Near East.

Arriving at a methodology

Traditional approaches to fieldwork interviews are based on the assumptions that:

1   the interviewer is skilled and can gain and provide access to knowledge, and
2   there is knowledge to be gained.

As a newcomer to ethnography and interviewing techniques, I sought the aid of professionals in the UK and in the Middle East[1] in order to arrive at a standard methodological practice which would provide relevant data to answer the basic questions surrounding the efficacy of a legal trade. The research

Figure 10.1 Licensed antiquities shop sign, Jerusalem (photo by the author)

conducted for this PhD is what Marcus refers to as a multi-sited ethnography – 'an ethnography that moves from its conventional single-sited location, to multiple sites of observation and participation that cross-cut dichotomies such as the local and the global, the life world and the system' (Marcus 1995: 96). Following the global pathway of an artefact through the specific economic activity of the legal market is fundamentally a multi-sited effort. The trade dictates the interview process and participants: looters, middlemen, dealers, archaeologists, collectors, tourists, government officials, lawyers, museum professionals and conservators situated in Israel, Jordan, the PA, the UK and the US. This work is both multi-sited and multi-vocal and the ethnographic enquiry had to reflect those realities.

The methods used for this research project included: the active interview[2] process; ethnographic analysis; participant observation; and semi-structured interviews. As a social process, fieldwork necessitates relational events which are unique to each situation. From designing the research and establishing goals, to collecting and analysing and publishing the data, each aspect of fieldwork is dependent on interaction between the interviewer and the various stakeholders. Fieldwork relationships do not just happen, but are the outcome of negotiation between the social researcher and the actors in the field (Coffey 1999). Following Holstein and Gubrium's (1995) discussion of active interviews the aim of the present methodological practice was to develop a relationship with the various stakeholders in order to gain information about the legal market for antiquities. Consistently I reminded myself that both the interviewer and interviewee are actively constructing a narrative, a new entity or product – the ethnography.

A total of ninety-four interviews were conducted in Israel, Jordan, the PA, the UK and the USA between January 2003 and October 2005. Interviews were carried out in a conversational style in an attempt to acquire a better understanding of the antiquities trade networks. As an active participant in the interview process, my own age, my education, my gender and my background as a Near Eastern archaeologist created possible biases with the potential to influence how each interview was constructed and negotiated.

Formal interviews were semi-structured and initiated by developing what social scientists refer to as an interview guide (deMarrais 2003; Holstein and Gubrium 1995), outlining a series of questions and concerns that I thought would best address the issue of the legal market (see Text box 10.2). The interview guide provides the interviewer with a set of predetermined questions clarifying their goals and the best approach to engaging participants in conversation. Use of the guide varied from one interview to the next, providing the crux of some interviews and remaining virtually ignored during others (Holstein and Gubrium 1995). I tested prototype questionnaires on local (British) stakeholders and professional colleagues. This testing process was not designed to determine the statistical reliability of the questions, but rather to assure that the questions were relevant, that the wording was clear and that none of the questions was too intrusive or offensive to any of the potential participants. For example, early versions of the interview guide used too many technical terms, were jargon-laden, and some of the questions posed to dealers about income generated from the trade were too personal. As a result, some dealers consulted (long-time acquaintances) suggested more appropriate alternative wording.

The futility of conducting questionnaire-style interviews became apparent early on: these often elicited single words or answers of extreme brevity. A much more productive approach was to start with one relevant question – *Do you think there should be a legal sale of antiquities?* Doing so at the outset and then allowing the respondent time to answer, digress, tell stories and then return to the original question at hand evoked more comprehensive answers, additional information and nuance. Questions in the interview guide could be revisited if the conversation flagged or veered away from the subject. The active interview process allowed for flexibility but also kept the researcher on track answering questions and providing information relevant to the overarching thesis topic.

Armed with a purportedly reliable methodology, the next step was to head into the field and to test my hypotheses and the methods. One of the first hurdles in the field was to identify the stakeholders involved with the trade and then get them to agree to meet with me.

Text box 10.2 The interview guide

Profile data sheet

Date _____

Interviewer_____

Site Visit Yes _____ No_____

Name _____

Address_____

Telephone _____

Email _____

Position _____

THE BIG QUESTION: Should there be a legal sale of antiquities in Israel?

A. Selection Criteria

Collector _____Dealer_____Archaeologist_____Looter___Other_____

Near Eastern archaeological focus Yes_____ No_____

Antiquities Yes_____ No_____

Years in the field _____

B. Dealers/Small Businesses

1. Institutional Profile

Type of organisation Profit_____ Non-profit_____

How long in the business _____ years

Family business Yes_____ No_____

Officially sanctioned by the IAA Yes_____ No_____

Officially sanctioned by the Ministry of Tourism Yes_____ No_____

How many employees _____Full time_____ Part time_____

Finance Officer Yes_____ No_____ Full time_____ Part time_____

Stakeholders_____ Board of Directors_____ Shareholders_____

Business computerised Yes_____ No_____

183

Use of a registry system Yes_____ No_____

Profit margin Yes_____ No_____

2. Consumer Profile

Are the buyers generally tourists? Yes_____ No_____

Are the buyers generally long time collectors? Yes_____ No_____

What countries are they from (or what citizenship)? _____

Do you have repeat customers? Yes_____ No_____

How much do they generally spend? _____

How many items do they purchase (per visit)? _____

How often do you sell a "high end" item? _____

Do you do much business online? Yes_____ No_____

If yes, what kinds of items are purchased online, from what countries? _____

How has the recent uprising affected your business?
Less_____ More via the internet_____

Do buyers routinely ask about provenance? Yes _____ No_____

Is there a recent trend for more consumers to ask about provenance?
Yes _____ No_____

Should dealers, shops and/or auction houses be required to provide provenance?
Yes_____ No ____

Do you think licensing dealer schemes would be an effective means of reducing the illicit trade in art?
Yes_____ No_____ Why or Why not? _____

Is the permit/licensing process difficult? Yes _____ No_____

Are there regular inspections by the IAA or the Ministry of Tourism?
Yes_____ No____ If Yes, How Often_____

Where do you get most of your material from? _____

How would you characterise the role of antiquities dealers in the market place?
_____

Do you find market trends occurring according to "block buster shows" at local museums? Yes_____ No_____

Into the field

Identifying stakeholders

The various stakeholders involved with the trade were identified as shown in Table 10.1.

Each stakeholder in the legal trade in antiquities believes that they have a right to possess, or protect, or purvey (or any combination of the three) archaeological artefacts from the region. The looters, who may claim an inherent right to the land and what lies in the soil, may have no perceived cultural affinity to the artefacts in question, but they recognise that middlemen will pay for the material they illegally excavate. Middlemen assert that they are both meeting consumer demand and adding to the economic stability of the PA (where much of the looting takes place) by providing the looters with added income. Dealers in Jerusalem are providing a service by meeting consumer demand. The tourist wants to take home a memento of his or her visit to the area that will serve as a symbol of a past visit to an important, often sacred, place (Dominguez 1986). Museums and institutions with educational mandates have a vested interest in purchasing artefacts, increasing their collections for the purposes of scholarly study and edification of the public. Architects, conservators, educators and lawyers may play a role in the trade, through valuing, conserving, researching or

Table 10.1 Stakeholders in the production–distribution–consumption model in Israel

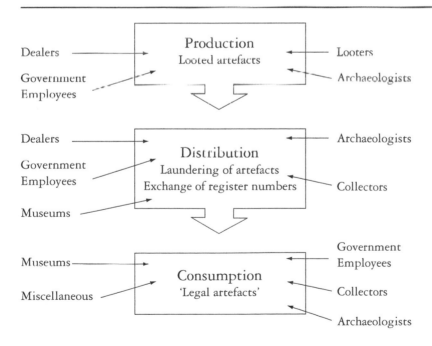

legislative efforts. The government employees of the Israel Antiquities Authority (IAA), the Jordanian Department of Antiquities and the Palestinian Ministry of Tourism and Antiquities are attempting to protect the past for the future, for the benefit of each of their respective publics. Once the stakeholders were identified the next hurdle was convincing people to meet with me.

Gaining access

The problem of obtaining access to data looms large in ethnography. This problem persists throughout the data-collection phase, but is often most acute in initial negotiations during the 'first days in the field' (Holstein and Gubrium 1995). Negotiating access, data collection and analysis are not distinct phases of research, but represent significantly overlapping avenues of investigation. The interviewer can learn from the problems associated with making contact with people as well as from responses to the researcher's approach (Hammersley and Atkinson 1995). Negative responses were often as informative as positive responses.

The strategy of initially contacting people for a formal interview had to be modified within a week of my arrival in Jerusalem. A much more effective approach was to speak with an individual in an informal setting (tea, garden party, sports complex), laying the groundwork for a later, more formal, interview. Essentially the period of September–December 2003 was a series of informal meetings setting the stage for future work with prospective informants.

At times, particularly in the context of participant observation, people selected themselves or others for interview. Many interviewees recommended other potential participants and even offered to provide introductions when necessary. Gatekeepers[3] were often encountered prior to interviewing participants who work in hierarchical sectors (governments, museums). Usually these were powerful people (superiors in the organisational structure) who attempted to select interviewees for my research. Gatekeepers were either genuinely acting in good faith or were attempting to control my access and results. This necessitated a heightened sensitivity on my part to the attempts by others to manipulate the research agenda. Meeting with participants outside their workplace was preferable in order to lessen the influence of institutional power.

Although the suggestions or control of gatekeepers were not always welcome, 'spillage' sometimes proved useful. Active interviews take advantage of informational 'spillage' from one interview to another, using the background knowledge learned from one interviewee to gain further insights from another (Holstein and Gubrium 1995). One dealer stated that some of his 'newly acquired material' came from the Bedouin, who had greater ease of movement throughout the PA and Israel. Subsequent dealers were then asked if they bought any of their material from the Bedouin. Whereas the standardised interview would try to limit informational 'spillage' from one interview to another, active interviewing takes advantage of the growing stockpile of background knowledge that the interviewer collects in prior interviews to pose concrete questions and explore facets of respondents' circumstances that might not otherwise be investigated (Holstein and Gubrium 1995).

After an initial informal meeting or two the individual would usually agree to participate in my study, but in some instances subjects declined to take part. One response to my request for an interview was a polite but firm email: 'I am sorry but I am not a specialist in the matter you are working on.' Another reply was not quite so polite: 'I have nothing else to say on this subject. I can't think why X and Y recommended that you ask me for an interview as far as I am concerned this subject is over and boring and dead. I can't believe that you are conducting PhD research on this, stop wasting my time.' Luckily for my research these two instances were anomalies rather than the norm. A third potential participant readily agreed to meet and we arranged a time and place. I waited for almost two hours, finally concluding that the interviewee had decided against participating. Further attempts to contact the individual were met with silence. In the end I gave up.

Some interest groups were far more reticent to discuss the trade than others. Figure 10.2 illustrates the response rate of the ninety-four respondents in my research. The breakdown of the interviewee populations reflects the hesitancy on the part of looters. I approached fifteen alleged looters and none agreed to

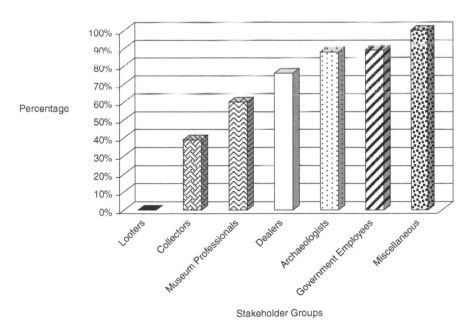

Figure 10.2 Stakeholder groups' response rates

be interviewed for this research (N=0). Only nine of the twenty-three collectors I contacted met with me or allowed me to witness an interaction in an antiquities shop (N=9 or 39 per cent). I achieved a 60 per cent response rate in the museum sphere as six of the ten museum professionals I communicated with agreed to meet to discuss the trade and their museum's acquisition policies. Surprisingly, the dealer community was one of the most willing groups to participate in the study. Thirty-five of the forty-six dealers responded positively to my request for an interview, resulting in a 76 per cent response rate. I naively assumed that they would be the least likely to participate, thinking that as an interest group they had the most to lose – their very livelihoods – by participating. Unsurprisingly the archaeologists, government employees, miscellaneous stakeholder groups (including architects, conservators, educators and lawyers) were the most sympathetic to my research and their rates of participation represent their supportive positions. Twenty-two of twenty-five (88 per cent) archaeologists, seventeen of nineteen (89 per cent) government employees and all five (100 per cent) of the miscellaneous category responded positively to my requests to meet and all graciously provided information on the legal market for antiquities in Israel.

In many cases a key determining factor in participants' positive response was the guarantee of anonymity. None wanted their name included in the study, nor did they want to be quoted, taped or photographed. Of the ninety-four people interviewed only two agreed to be 'on the record' and only one agreed to be taped. One can only sympathise with the reluctance of participants, who were being asked for potentially incriminating information (e.g. where is the archaeological material coming from?). The question then became how does the researcher reciprocate? There was, and is, no real *quid pro quo* in such research. What does this type of research offer potential informants?

Quid pro quo

There must be a shared notion of process of research in order for both the interviewer and the interviewee to benefit from the exchange (Bowler 1997: 66). Ethnographers are usually reluctant to enter into direct market exchanges of money for knowledge, but instead they usually turn to gift exchange. 'Despite all of our writings on the gift, we still tend to treat it as less problematic' (Elyachar 2005: 31) than the exchange of cash for information. I too, was reluctant to pay for information, but in some instances I made purchases of tourist trinkets (bracelets or fridge magnets) as a gesture of goodwill. Elyachar (2005: 31) states that 'when we enter into exchanges with informants, we can become partially absorbed in the social networks that we want to study'; this process of absorption is an important aspect of participant observation necessary to understanding the interviewees' frame of reference. Buying tourist paraphernalia allowed me greater 'access' to the dealer's realm, one of the targeted stakeholders in the trade.

Constructive outcomes were elicited by enlisting the aid of a professor[4] of social anthropology at the Hebrew University and a seasoned programme evaluator[5] who routinely deal with *quid pro quo* issues in interview settings. After many fruitful discussions it was decided that policy change and accountability were what this research could offer most participants, especially to those directly involved with the sale of antiquities and those monitoring such sales (Israeli and Palestinian dealers, collectors and government representatives of both states). On many occasions dealers told me that the licensing requirements enforced by the IAA were a 'huge hassle'. The unannounced visits by the IAA antiquities inspectors, conducted sporadically due to chronic understaffing, impede business for dealers. The dissemination of my research results[6] might result in an overhaul of the current flawed licensing system in Israel, encouraging IAA policy and legislative changes.

Although Israel has a system of legally controlled venues for selling antiquities, the Palestinian Ministry of Tourism and Antiquities banned the legal trade in antiquities in 1996. Given the current situation and the porous borders for artefacts, looting and destruction of archaeological sites in the PA continue unhindered, with the pillaged material often ending up in the Israeli market. The PA Ministry could benefit from the results of this study as policy options are reviewed and instituted in Gaza and the West Bank. All subsequent requests for interviews were framed to appeal to the conviction that by giving a voice to all those who have an opinion on the trade in antiquities, perhaps an equitable protection policy for the cultural heritage of the region could eventually be achieved. But this raises the question of why, in the first instance, would any of the stakeholders agree to meet with me?

Credibility

Gaining access to the various stakeholders in the legal trade of antiquities was not solely determined by a *quid pro quo*, but was also established based on personal credibility. In his research Mackenzie (2005) has stated that he was considered more 'credible' and gained greater access because he was of similar race (Caucasian), gender (male), class (middle) and education level to almost all of the interviewees. My own credibility lay in the fact that I had been an archaeologist in the region for over fifteen years and knew many of the archaeologists and government employees, and through this association was able to gain access to other potential participants.

Cultivating relationships with the dealing and the collecting communities was a more protracted process. This was not surprising because collectors and dealers had potentially 'more to lose' in terms of the possible legal repercussions of information they might provide. I started with some of the most well-known dealers and worked from there. In the Old City in Jerusalem I routinely visited the same shops, drinking countless cups of mint tea and coffee with cardamom in order to cultivate relationships. My interview guide was translated into Arabic[7] and copies distributed to potential participants so that they were able to see the types of questions they would be asked to discuss. A year of fieldwork in the region allowed the investment of time to cultivate relationships in order to gain more information, greater insight and a 'truer response', to borrow a phrase from Chambers.

> [W]here research requires accurate portrayals of stakeholder values or opinions, qualitative ethnographic data have often proven superior to survey data, particularly in cases that involve long-term field exposure and in situations *where informants might feel at risk* or have other reasons to provide incorrect [or misleading] responses, or where their truer responses might develop over time.
>
> (Chambers 2000: 859, my emphasis)

Most informants were at risk either of criticising the government and losing their job, facing criminal charges for dealing in illicit antiquities, or of losing their pride in purchasing an unprovenanced artefact and not asking for the proper documentation. From the outset this element of risk was understood and was incorporated into the research methodology. Once a few interviews were completed in the dealing community, word spread and I could rarely walk down the street in the Old City without someone asking me if I was going to interview them that day.

Attempts to meet with looters during the year were thwarted repeatedly either because of the wider political situation or because of distrust. After I cultivated a very good relationship with one of the dealers in the Old City, he arranged a meeting with a group of organised looters from the PA. After a year and a half, the meeting with the looters was established, but as the day of encounter neared an article appeared in the *Jerusalem Post* (Lefkovits 2005) stating that four looters had been arrested in a night raid by the anti-theft unit of the IAA. The looters I had arranged to meet called off the meeting, perhaps apprehensive about the prospect of what I would be doing with the information I gathered.

Despite these successful inroads into the legal market for antiquities, I continued to worry about the credibility of my research. There is an inherent faith that the results are trustworthy and accurate and that the relationship between the interviewer and the respondent that evolves during the interview process has not unduly biased the account. How could this research be verified without someone revisiting all of the people and places and reinterviewing each and every participant? DeMarrais (2003) states that rigour in design as well as skill in the interview enhance the credibility and trustworthiness of the study, but is this enough?

Ken Polk,[8] a criminologist who routinely deals with the issue of academic truthfulness and accepted methodologies of verifiability, suggested that much research of this type is guided by the 'protection of rights of human subjects'. Under these provisions researchers are required to (K. Polk, personal communication, 2003):

1   notify the subjects – in the form of a plain-language statement – of the nature and purpose of this research,[9]
2   inform them of any risks posed by the research,
3   describe in detail how the informants will be identified, and
4   how and where the data will be stored.

A particular concern for this research was how to preserve the anonymity of informants yet maintain validity of the final results. Providing anonymity is a standard, widely accepted criminological method. The normal procedure is to assure respondents that their data will be treated anonymously and further procedures will be taken to ensure that their identity will not be revealed (K. Polk, personal communication, 2003).

Another way to obviate challenges to authenticity is to provide a written transcript of the interview for participants' annotations (K. Polk, personal communication, 2003). After every interview I provided a transcript and the subject was asked for comments and corrections on any remarks made during the meeting. This tactic proved to be an effective means of acquiring further information on various points. After seeing their words in writing, participants usually elaborated on questions, adding further insights and anecdotes. In only one instance did someone withdraw from the study after reviewing their transcript. In that particular case the subject felt that their comments about their employer were far too inflammatory and could jeopardise their job if any part of what they communicated was published.

Much of the background reading used to anchor this research indicated that ethnographers should always be aware of their 'research selves' and inherent biases. They should err on the side of reflexivity and self criticism when assessing the results and should always take into account the ethical issues associated with their work.

Ethical dilemmas

The Ethical Guidelines for Practitioners of the National Association for the Practice of Anthropology (NAPA)[10] state:

> Our primary responsibility is to respect and consider the welfare and human rights of all categories of people affected by decisions, programs or research in which we take part. However, we recognize that many research and practice settings involve conflicts between benefits accruing to different parties affected by our research. It is our ethical responsibility, to the extent feasible, to bring to bear on decision making, our own or that of others, information concerning the actual

or potential impacts of such activities on all whom they might affect. It is also our responsibility to assure, to the extent possible, that the views of groups so affected are made clear and given full and serious consideration by decision makers and planners, in order to preserve options and choices for affected groups.

(National Association for the Practice of Anthropology, 1988)

While no code of ethics or set of guidelines can anticipate the unique circumstances of individual field research, it was on these guiding principles that I based my research, following the general caveat of 'do no harm'. In the early stages of my fieldwork I used research assistants,[11] who acted on my behalf, asking probing questions of the dealer community and then providing me with the results of their findings. Based on earlier antiquities trade exposés by Lundén (2004) and Watson (1997) I assumed that the dealers would be more forthcoming with 'tourists' (my research assistants) than with me. I presented the results of my initial findings at the 'Making the Means Transparent: Research Methodologies in Archaeological Heritage Studies' conference at the University of Cambridge (the conference from which this volume emanates). During the discussion my presentation elicited much heated response from the seasoned researchers in attendance: my 'undercover' participant observation was deemed unethical. By not providing full disclosure I was in breach of the second rule of the NAPA Ethical Guideline: 'To our resource persons or research subjects we owe full and timely disclosure of the objectives, methods and sponsorship of our activities.' I subsequently revised my research methodology, no longer using 'research assistants' and instead providing each interviewee with an overview of my credentials, the objectives of the research project and the methodology for data collecting as well as a full transcript of the interview.

Another intriguing ethical and moral dilemma encountered as a result of this enquiry was whether researchers should be engaged with clients whose policies or actions might not conform to professional ethical standards or personal standards of morality and law. Does interviewing the various stakeholders implicitly condone particular behaviours? The idea that involvement is better than boycott pervades much of current applied research, but some argue that association is the equivalent of complicity and, as a consequence, recommend that applied researchers excuse themselves from a wide variety of ethically ambiguous situations (see Berreman 1991; Escobar 1991). When incriminating information is received, is it our duty to report it to the respective authorities, potentially compromising any future potential interviews, or even other related studies? How should research proceed under these circumstances? In one example used to illustrate this ethical quandary I was scheduled to meet with a representative of a government institution charged with monitoring the selling of illegal artefacts. This was not a formal interview but an information-gathering session for both parties. In the course of the conversation I related a story of how through unrelated research[12] I was offered genuine material by an unauthorised dealer. Immediately the government employee asked for the name and location of the shop owner, which I declined to provide, noting that to do so might compromise further interviews (the network of antiquities dealers is small and very tightly knit). We were, and still are, at an impasse. In the briefing paper 'Consideration of the Potentially Negative Impact of the Publication of Factual Data about a Study Population on Such Population', Watkins (2000) states that under the AAA Code of Ethics Section III(C)(1), anthropologists are reminded that

> they are not only responsible for the factual content of their state-
> ments but also must consider carefully the social and political impli-
> cations of the information they disseminate. They must do everything
> in their power to insure that such information is well understood,
> properly contextualized, and responsibly utilized ... At the same time,
> they must be alert to the possible harm their information may cause
> people with whom they work.
>
> (Watkins 2000: 1)

Bound by my membership in the AAA, I am obligated to consider the effects of this research on the study population. Additionally, Watkins warns that 'self-censorship by the researcher might be harmful both to the discipline and to the population under study' (2000: 1). In my assessment of the situation both the discipline vis-à-vis my research[13] and the dealer in question would suffer negative effects if I reported the name of the dealer to the IAA representative.

After a year of fieldwork I returned to Cambridge laden with interview transcripts, field notes and musings on my meetings with the various stake-holders. I began my analysis by rereading the primary material, a process that reminded me of the various contexts in which the many interviews took place. I soon realised that parts of what I recorded and compiled were somewhat irrelevant and naive, a realisation that social anthropologists assured me was quite normal. After culling my data I reread the relevant material very closely in order to recapture some of the emotional flavour and interpersonal situa-tions that produced the notes (Bogdan and Taylor 1975). The emphasis in this stage of analysis is on thinking about what is being said, the meaning and the intent of each response — what Strauss (1987) refers to as open coding. Open coding is a constant comparative approach to the data, while axial coding defines common themes in the data, and selective coding reveals the relation-ships between the categories (Glaser and Strauss 1967). All three types of coding were employed in the analysis of the data. One of the dangers of the open-coding stage that social scientists are warned to avoid is the imposition of outside (etic) categories into the coding. Instead the responses should 'speak' for themselves from an insider's (emic) perspective. Interviewers should constantly ask themselves questions of this nature: 'to what extent is this a participant's world view or some composite of my representation of his/her world view?' (Agar 1980: 181). As someone new to the field of ethnography, I constantly reminded myself of these dangers and often consulted with social anthropologists to verify my coding techniques and subsequent analyses.

Once all of the stakeholder responses had been open coded I sought broad themes, patterns and categories – a process known as axial coding. During this process three recurring themes in stakeholder responses became evident: (1) most agreed that there was some sort of relationship between the looting of archaeological artefacts and the demand for material; (2) all respondents had questions surrounding the efficacy of the legal market (positive, negative and undecided positions); and (3) almost all interviewees had an opinion on the recent proposed IAA initiative to sell sherds in addition to acting as the regulators of the trade (for further discussion see Kersel and Kletter 2006). While the first two themes were part of my original research design, responses about the IAA proposal to sell sherds added an interesting element to my analysis.

Each of the stakeholders approached as part of this research expressed an interest in the outcomes, for a variety of reasons. All (even the dealing and collecting communities) agreed that the destruction of archaeological sites as a result of looting was a devastating loss to our collective knowledge, but the root cause of looting was (and still is) a hotly debated point (see Kersel 2007 for further discussion), as is the relationship between demand and looting. The following section outlines the stakeholder responses to the question of the efficacy of the legal market for antiquities as a deterrent to archaeological site destruction.

Results

When asked about the relationship between the demand for artefacts and the looting of archaeological sites and thefts from museums and private collections, over 70 per cent (N=66) of the total respondents (N=94) declared that there was a causal relationship: the demand for archaeological artefacts in the legal marketplace results in the looting of archaeological sites (see Table 10.2). The table illustrates the stakeholder positions on the question of whether there is a link between demand and looting. Four of the six stakeholder (archaeologists, government employees, miscellaneous and dealers) responses supported the position that a legal market does not act as a deterrent to looting, and some asserted that the market may actually stimulate looting. The museum professional group is evenly divided over the issue. The only set of stakeholders who supported the hypothesis that a legal trade will diminish looting was the collecting community, which is an interesting comment on their ability to avoid discussions involving the origins of the artefacts they are considering for purchase.

All but one of the archaeologists interviewed (N=21) experienced some form of looting at a site with which they were associated, with all holding that

Table 10.2 Stakeholder group positions on the link between demand and looting

Stakeholder group	Yes %	No %	Total %
Archaeologists	95	5	100
Collectors	33	67	100
Dealers	54	46	100
Government employees	100	0	100
Miscellaneous	60	40	100
Museum professionals	50	50	100

the demand for archaeological material is one of the reasons why looting occurs. This group felt that demand for archaeological material in the open market has a direct impact on the looting of archaeological sites and some of those interviewed for this research provided examples which they felt illustrated this causal relationship:

> We left some pots *in situ* because it was the end of our work day and even though we covered them up and made sure there was no trace of them, the next morning they were gone. Some time later these same pots (or ones very similar, I'm not sure) were in the shop window of a very reputable dealer
>
> (Archaeologist 8)

All of the governmental employees (100 per cent; N=17) (regardless of the government: Israeli, Jordanian or Palestinian) agreed that there was a link between demand and looting. Many of them could document specific instances where material looted from a particular archaeological site then appeared in a shop inventory. Both archaeologists and government employees had, on occasion, come into contact with middlemen or even looters who confirmed that much of their illegal excavation of sites was demand-driven: 'Israeli dealers tell Palestinians where and what to dig.' Both of these stakeholder groups (archaeologists and government employees) also admitted that there might be other possible reasons why looters illegally excavate sites, but that consumer demand was the greatest driving force (see Kersel 2007). The closure of the borders between Israel and the PA as the result of the 2001 Al-Aqsa Intifada,[14] and the construction of the barrier wall along the border were often cited as reasons why looting occurs.

Of the other stakeholder categories, opinions were divided on the relationship between demand and the looting of archaeological sites. 'There must be a constant supply to meet demand, therefore a licensed dealer scheme would serve to encourage looting rather than working towards its elimination,' stated one respondent (Dealer 5). Some asserted that the current inventory (pre-1978 material) in the shops and material available through de-accessioning, chance finds and the selling off of collections were enough to satisfy consumer demand:

> There is enough material out there to satisfy everyone – tourist and high-end collector alike, there is no need for people to loot archaeological sites. People loot because it's an interesting way to spend an afternoon, not because someone in New York City wants an oil lamp with a menorah on it.
>
> (Dealer 16)

Although 46 per cent (N = 16) of the dealers interviewed felt that there was no relationship between looting and the sale of archaeological material, 54 per cent fully admitted to a connection between the two spheres of the economy:

> If a tourist comes into my store and wants a figurine from the Iron II period and I don't have one I ask some of my fellow shop owners. If they don't have one I call my 'middleman' in Hebron to ask if he has any in his storeroom. Within days I have one in my shop. I don't ask too many questions, but I do ask for the location of the find because lots of tourists want to know the name of the archaeological site that the figurine came from.
>
> (Interview, Dealer 19)

> I get the catalogues from the major auction houses and I check eBay and I monitor what is selling. Right now inscriptions are hot, anything with an inscription is a good seller, but I don't have many pieces. I am always on the lookout for inscriptions. I make sure that my contacts in the territories know that I can easily move inscriptions.
>
> (Interview, Dealer 27)

In these and other interviews, dealers relate various scenarios that confirm a tie between the demand for a particular object and its appearance in their inventory. These responses raise the question, in a truly legal (without illegal elements) market lacking an Iron II figurine, but with a consumer demanding such an item, would looting still occur to meet the demand?

Examples like this and testimony from archaeologists, dealers and government employees clearly illustrate the link between consumer demand for archaeological material and the looting of archaeological sites. The qualitative data presented as a result of this research indicate that the legal market for antiquities in Israel does not diminish looting, and may in fact contribute to greater mining of archaeological sites for saleable items. Interviewee responses indicate that the legal market is flawed, not entirely legal, and may contribute to looting, but still some sentiment remains that a trade in antiquities should be permitted.

Conclusion

Long enshrined as a method, a theoretical orientation and even a philosophical paradigm within anthropology, ethnography has recently been extended to cultural studies, literary theory, folklore, women's studies, sociology and cultural geography (Tedlock 2000: 455–6). The field of Heritage Studies may now be added to this list because heritage professionals use ethnography, interviewing and qualitative research analyses on a daily basis to inform their work. This type of research is predicated on the participation and contribution of the public. No matter how much care the heritage professional devotes to the project, its success depends on more than just individual effort. Outside social forces, including local, national and sometimes international relationships, make the research possible.

There are myriad social forces affecting the work undertaken in examining the research questions surrounding the efficacy of a legal trade in antiquities. I was confronted with ethical problems almost daily, and had to make decisions – rightly or wrongly – on how to proceed in the face of dilemmas. The underlying element of illegality in some subjects' actions determined much of how the methodology was structured, how questions were asked, and how interviews were initiated and carried out. Through trial and error, discussions with social anthropologists, heritage practitioners and professional policy evaluators, I constructed and used an acceptable, verifiable methodology to investigate the many facets of the legal trade in antiquities. It is my hope that this study produced reliable results, with supportable data that can be used in future cultural property protection policy formation in Israel and Palestine, and that my endeavours will be accepted as a meaningful contribution to the heritage field.

Acknowledgements

I would like to thank my many interviewees in Jordan, Israel and the PA; without them there would be no research. This research greatly benefited from my participation in the 'Making the Means Transparent' conference organised by Marie Louise Stig Sørensen and John Carman. I thank them for the occasion to present my preliminary results. I am indebted to the participants at that event, from whom I received many invaluable comments at a critical stage of my fieldwork. I would also like to thank Brendan Burchell, Efrat Ben Ze'ev, Paola Filippucci, Laura Jeffrey and Patricia Neu for helpful comments and suggestions. Julie Hollowell commented on an earlier permutation of the interview guide; her guidance was invaluable. This research was generously supported with grants from the Palestinian American Research Center, the W. F. Albright Institute of Archaeological Research, the Social Sciences and Humanities Research Council of Canada and the Tweedie Exploration Foundation of the University of Edinburgh.

Notes

1   Specifically Brendan Burchell, social anthropologist, Magdalene College, Cambridge; Efrat Ben Ze'ev, Professor, The Truman Institute at the Hebrew University, Ruppin Academic Center; Paola Filippucci, social anthropologist, University of Cambridge; and social policy analyst Patricia Neu, USAID. More generally, attending the Legal Anthropology module taught by various faculty members in the Department of Social Anthropology at the University of Cambridge proved an extremely beneficial experience.

2   Wolcott's (1988: 194) definition of active interview activity is 'anything that the field-worker does that intrudes upon the natural setting and is done with the conscious intent of obtaining specific information directly from one's subjects'.

3   Literally someone who guards an entrance, and in this instance it is entrance (access) to the subjects of the ethnographic enquiry.

4   Professor Efrat Ben Ze'ev, The Truman Institute at the Hebrew University, Ruppin Academic Center.

5   Patricia Neu, USAID contractor.

6   One of the fundamental tenets in the Code of Ethics of the National Association for the Practice of Anthropology (NAPA) is that 'Anthropologists will contribute to the growth of their discipline through communicating and publishing scientific and practical information about the work in which they are engaged, including, as appropriate, theory, processes, outcomes and professional techniques and methods'. The NAPA Ethical Guidelines are available at http://www.practicinganthropology.org/about/?section=ethical_guidelines.

7   Between my Hebrew and the typical mastery of English by Israeli participants there was no need to have the interview guide translated into Hebrew.

8   Kenneth Polk is Professor of Criminology at the University of Melbourne. He has written extensively on criminal aspects of the art and antiquities market.

9   This notion of informed consent is the basic principle of scientific research involving human populations. This research followed the informed consent guidelines as stated in the American Anthropological Association (AAA) Code of Ethics, available at http://www.aaanet.org/committees/ethics/ethcode.htm.

10 A subsection of the AAA. See n.6 above for the website with the NAPA Ethical Guidelines for Practitioners.

11 The research assistants posed as tourists potentially interested in purchasing antiquities. They asked in-depth questions regarding provenance, export licences, findspots, illegality or legality of their purchase. I used a total of six research assistants. None of their findings were used in my data analysis.

12 This event occurred while gathering data for a paper I was preparing on archaeological replicas for sale in the tourist shops (see Kersel and Luke 2005).

13 If I had provided the name of the unlicensed dealer it is probable that word of this incident would have spread in the dealing community and no one would then have agreed to meet me. As a result, my research (and the discipline) would have suffered.

14 In 2001, antiquities authorities on both sides of the border reported a rise of 300 per cent in incidents of tomb robbing (Ephron 2001).

Bibliography

Agar, M. (1980) *The Professional Stranger: An Informal Introduction to Ethnography*, New York: Academic Press.

Antiquities Law 5738–1978 (Israel).

Berreman, G. D. (1991) 'Anthropological Ethics in the 1980s: A Positive Approach', in C. Fluehr-Lobban (ed.) *Ethics and the Profession of Anthropology: A Dialogue for a New Era*, Philadelphia, PA: University of Pennsylvania Press, 36–71.

Bogdan, R. and S. Taylor (1975) *Introduction to Qualitative Research Methods: A Phenomenological Approach to the Social Sciences*, New York: Wiley.

Bowler, I. (1997) 'Problems with Interviewing: Experiences with Service Providers and Clients', in G. Miller and R. Dingwall (eds) *Context and Method in Qualitative Research*, Thousand Oaks, CA: Sage, 66–76.

Chambers, E. (2000) 'Applied Ethnography', in N. Denzin and Y. Lincoln (eds) *Handbook of Qualitative Research*, 2nd edn, Thousand Oaks, CA: Sage, 851–69.

Coffey, A. (1999) *The Ethnographic Self: Fieldwork and the Representation of Identity*, Thousand Oaks, CA: Sage.

deMarrais, K. (2003) 'Qualitative Interview Studies: Learning Through Experience', in K. deMarrais and S. Lapan (eds) *Foundations of Research: Methods of Inquiry in Education and the Social Sciences*, Mahwah, NJ: Lawrence Erlbaum Associates, 85–106.

Dominguez, V. (1986) 'The Marketing of Heritage', *American Ethnologist* 13, 546–55.

Elia, R. (1993) 'A Seductive and Troubling Work', *Archaeology* 46.1, 64–9.

Elyachar, J. (2005) *Markets of Dispossession: NGOs, Economic Development, and the State in Cairo*, Durham, NC: Duke University Press.

Ephron, D. (2001) 'The Tomb Raiders', *Newsweek*, 18 June 2001, 38.

Escobar, A. (1991) 'Anthropology and the Development Encounter: The Making and Marketing of Development Anthropology', *American Ethnologist* 18, 658–82.

Glaser, B. and A. Strauss (1967) *The Discovery of Grounded Theory*, Chicago: Aldine.

Hammersley, M. and P. Atkinson (1995) *Ethnography: Principles in Practice*, London: Routledge.

Holstein, J. A. and J. F. Gubrium (1995) *The Active Interview*, Thousand Oaks, CA: Sage.

Kersel, M. M. (2006) 'License to Sell: The Legal Trade of Antiquities in Israel'. PhD Thesis, Department of Archaeology, University of Cambridge.

—— (2007) 'Transcending Borders: Objects on the Move , *Archaeologies, The Journal of the World Archaeological Congress* 3.2, 81–98.

Kersel, M. M. and R. Kletter (2006) 'Heritage for Sale? A Case Study from Israel', *Journal of Field Archaeology* 31.3, 317–27.

Kersel, M. and C. Luke (2005) 'Selling a Replicated Past: Power and Identity in Marketing Archaeological Replicas', *Anthropology in Action, Journal for Applied Anthropology in Policy and Practice* 11, 32–43.

Lefkovits, E. (2005) 'Construction Workers Held for Antiquities Theft', *Jerusalem Post*, 8 March 2005, http://www.jpost.com (accessed 9 March 2005).

Lundén, S. (2004) 'The Scholar and the Art Market: Swedish Scholarly Contributions to the Destruction of the World's Archaeological Heritage', in H. Karlsson (ed.) *Swedish Archaeologists on Ethics*, Lindome: Bricoleur Press, 197–247.

Mackenzie, S. R. M. (2005) *Going, Going, Gone: Regulating the Market in Illicit Antiquities*, Leicester: Institute of Art & Law.

Marcus, G. E. (1995) 'Ethnography in/of the World System: The Emergence of Multi-Sited Ethnography', *Annual Review of Anthropology* 24, 95–117.

Marks, P. (1995) 'Antiquities Markets Should be Open and Honest', *Wall Street Journal*, 9 January 1995, A15.

Merryman, J. H. (1995) 'The Antiquities Problem', *Public Archaeology Review* 3.3, 10–11.

National Association for the Practice of Anthropology (NAPA) (1988) National Association for the Practice of Anthropology Ethical Guidelines for Practitioners, National Association for the Practice of Anthropology, http://www.practicinganthropology.org/about/?section=ethical_guidelines (accessed 16 September 2005).

Pearlstein, W. (1986) 'Claims for the Repatriation of Cultural Property: Prospects for a Managed Antiquities Market', *Law and Policy in International Business* 28.1, 123–50.

Renfrew, A. C. R. (1993) 'Collectors are the Real Looters', *Archaeology* 46.3, 16–17.
Shanks, H. (2001) 'How to Stop Looting', in N. Silberman and E. Frerichs (eds) *Archaeology and Society in the 21st Century: The Dead Sea Scrolls and Other Case Studies*, Jerusalem: Israel Exploration Society, 132–7.
Strauss, A. (1987) *Qualitative Analysis for Social Scientists*, Cambridge: Cambridge University Press.
Tedlock, B. (2000) 'Ethnography and Ethnographic Representation', in N. Denzin and Y. Lincoln (eds) *Handbook of Qualitative Research*, 2nd edn, Thousand Oaks, CA: Sage, 455–86.
Watkins, J. (2000) 'Briefing Paper on Consideration of the Potentially Negative Impact of the Publication of Factual Data about a Study Population on Such Population', *American Anthropological Association Position Paper*, http://www.aaanet.org/committees/ethics/bp4. htm (accessed 16 September 2005).
Watson, P. (1997) *Sotheby's: Inside Story*, London: Bloomsbury Press.
Wolcott, J. (1988) 'Ethnographic Research in Education', in J. M. Jaeger (ed.) *Complementary Methods for Research in Art Education*, Washington, DC: American Education Research Association, 187–206.

11

METHODS FOR INVESTIGATING LOCALS' PERCEPTIONS OF A CULTURAL HERITAGE PRODUCT FOR TOURISM

Lessons from Botswana

Susan Keitumetse

Background and introduction

While research investigating the public meaning of archaeological/cultural heritage has increased in intensity and scope over the past decades both in the USA (Little 2005; McManamon 2005; LaRoche 2005) and the UK (Merriman 2004), limited progress has been made in the African region (Keitumetse 2005). In particular, specific methods for investigating the changing attitudes that communities (or hosts, as they are referred to in tourism studies) have towards cultural heritage as it becomes a tourism product, that is, a product used in tourism transactions, are scarce. This means there is a significant lack of well-informed management strategies to guide the implementation of cultural heritage tourism projects in developing countries such as Botswana. Geographical variations, definitions and categories of cultural tourism products exist at both the local and the international level. Terms such as *cultural heritage, archaeological heritage* and *heritage tourism* are becoming global and increasingly popular due to the emerging demand for new tourism products. Consequently research that provides an understanding of the hosts' own definitions of these terms is needed. This chapter discusses how a preliminary approach based on case-study methods, combined with ethnographic research and visualisation, can be used to develop and supplement existing approaches to research on community-based heritage tourism.

Studies of material culture, as emblematic of 'traditional cultures', are gradually becoming more and more common as tourism products diversify from wildlife and wilderness to cultural and heritage resources. Earlier studies have long revealed that 'material culture is not simply a passive by-product of other areas of life. Rather, material culture is active ... produced so as to transform, materially, socially, and ideologically' (Hodder 1998: 114). Indeed in areas where cultural heritage resources are utilised in tourism, the social and ideological transformations of culture (tangible as well as intangible) are contributed to by the interactions of tourists with hosts – leading to constant change of attitudes towards heritage. For regions such as the Okavango Delta in Botswana, communities' constant change of social, cultural, traditional, religious and economic relationships results in the continuous construction of different meanings attached to both the tangible and intangible heritage. As economic conditions change, such meanings and definitions are 'packaged' and shared by the gradually emerging field of cultural heritage tourism. It is crucial to develop methodologies that can be used to gain an understanding of how such 'packages' are conceptualised, selected and interpreted prior to their dissemination to tourists in the pursuit of sustainable tourism in developing countries.

The tourism-product research method (McIntosh et al. 1995) is one approach to the study of tourism where research focuses on a particular product that is to be offered to a tourist by a host. Cultural heritage products are both tangible/ visible (such as cultural landscapes, artefacts in a museum, crafts in a village, or in situ excavation pits) and intangible/non-visible (such as song and dance, folklore, or indigenous knowledge associated with landscapes). As cultural tourism builds momentum in developing countries, product-approach research in tourism will become relevant in a bid to provide a platform for the expression of hosts' perceptions and the definition of heritage tourism products. Heritage management concepts, introduced relatively recently, such as eco-tourism, pro-poor tourism and local community participation, that are associated with the sustainable development concept (Keitumetse 2005) require that the hosts' perspectives are considered and included in sustainable tourism initiatives. Within the field of heritage management in particular, emerging international conventions, such as the UNESCO 2003 Convention for the Safeguarding of the Intangible Cultural Heritage, advocate recognition of intangible aspects of cultural heritage; this reinforces the necessity to address the needs of hosts with regard to tourism. This chapter therefore diverges from the dominant concern of tourism research with 'visitor satisfaction' (e.g. Christou 2005) to research that focuses on the hosts, or local communities[1] as they are commonly referred to in Botswana.

In developing countries communities/hosts relate directly to heritage sites, and they are often the traditional custodians of the sites, hence ethnographic approaches remain crucial in public heritage research. This essay uses research conducted in Botswana in 2003 and supplemented in 2007 to discuss methods that can be used to discern local perceptions of a heritage tourism product. The results illuminate the type of information that can be yielded from the application of alternative methodologies in cultural tourism research.

202

General methodological approaches to research
on 'local' perception of a tourism product

The origin of sociological research theory is attributed to nineteenth-century scholars such as Karl Marx, Emil Durkheim and Max Weber (Holton 1996; Kaspersen 2000), whose approaches centred on the knowing subject (or actor) as the key epistemological foundation of philosophy and social theory. In particular, Weber argued that individuals should recognise that they cannot rely on strong moral communities outside themselves to provide meaning (Holton 1996; Kaspersen 2000), an approach adopted in this chapter as it focuses on alternative ways of valuing heritage benchmarking of locals' socio-cultural attributes rather than focusing on a prescribed international approach to research methodology.

A commonly considered aspect of social science research is that of monitoring *bias* in order to achieve *value-neutrality* (Hammersley 2000). However, in this research some of the supposedly 'biased narratives' from ethnographic research are used to identify meanings, values and perceptions attached to the physical/tangible heritage. For instance, where relevant the approach to data analysis abandoned the notion of average or majority opinions as the sole or necessarily most meaningful axis of data analysis, and instead considered ways of paying special attention to what I refer to as 'knowledge storers' or those community members who guard the 'cultural capital' (Bourdieu 1993; Keitumetse 2006). In ethnographic research, such members of the community are identified from constant referral by other respondents. Most of these 'knowledge storers' are usually older people or male; their relevance to the present analysis is that they not only formulate and guard community values and perception, but they also often play central roles in formulating such views and ensure the continuous recycling of the views through time. Therefore commentaries made by selected individuals are likely to be accepted by a community as a representation of their aggregate attitudes to a particular heritage and related tourism product due to the socio-cultural status accorded certain individuals within their particular community (Keitumetse 2006). In such instances, aggregate meanings attached to a heritage are dealt with if and when they present themselves, not as an exclusive axis of data analysis.

Language or terminology is a significant factor when conducting ethnographic interviews on heritage tourism because conventional approaches to heritage management research tend to bring pre-existing and/or conventional terminologies and meanings to the research situation. Terms such as 'heritage', 'World Heritage', 'cultural' or 'archaeological heritage', 'sustainable development', 'heritage management', 'tourist' and 'tourism', to mention a few, have to be contextualised prior to commencement of the research in order to aim at what can be referred to as 'textualising the social' (Plummer 1996: 240). The use of the word 'tourist' illustrates this point.

In the two areas of Botswana and Kenya, where part of the research was conducted, locals refer to a white person as *lekgoa* or *mzungu* respectively. For locals the word *tourist* signifies a white person who is simultaneously perceived to be a tourist. Hence responses to questions of whether tourists (local or international) should pay entry fees yielded the response that *tourists* (*lekgoa* and *mzungu*) should pay higher amounts because they are not citizens of Botswana or Kenya (Keitumetse 2005). This illustrates an ingrained locals' perception of a tourist only as a white person, resulting in a lack of perception of local tourists as *tourists*. A researcher must establish such linguistic divergences prior to ethnographic interviews by engaging in observation and informal interaction and then modify the terminology used in the interview accordingly in order to achieve the desired insights and results.

Case-study method

In addition to the above, the case-study method has the potential to bring out various angles from which a particular topic can be discussed (Mauffette-Leenders *et al.* 1997; Yin 2003; Gillham 2004). Data derived through application of this method of research can cover a broad range of issues relating to the topic being investigated. The use of the case-study method is usually necessitated by the specific contexts in which management practices need to be implemented. In particular, the method can help to engender better understanding of the various factors (geographical, social, economic, political and cultural) that affect the contexts within which a particular heritage and its hosts exist, and interact. Recognising the relevance of such an approach, two different case studies are discussed in this chapter: the Tsodilo Hills World Heritage site in north-west Botswana (hereafter referred to as the Tsodilo WH site) and research conducted among junior secondary school students in Botswana (see Figure 11.1).

General factors to consider

The main aim of the research was to interview people living near to a heritage site or who interact with the cultural landscape regularly (hereafter referred to as local residents). The general categorisation of interviewees was done according to ethnic affiliation because ethnicity as an indicator correlates positively with cultural affiliation. Ethnicity is also a distinct indicator of cultural difference and connection among groups in a community. As observed by some scholars 'the roots of ethnicity lie in the original "fact" of human cultural difference' (Comaroff and Comaroff 1992: 50). In Botswana most individuals in an ethnic group share common cultural norms and beliefs, including those that are associated with their geo-cultural landscapes. However, in cases where the population investigated is relatively large (>1,000), systematic selection of interviewees has to take place. For Botswana, it is recommended that existing social groups (e.g. ethnic wards) are used in the first instance, followed by random sampling based on indicators such as age, gender, proximity to

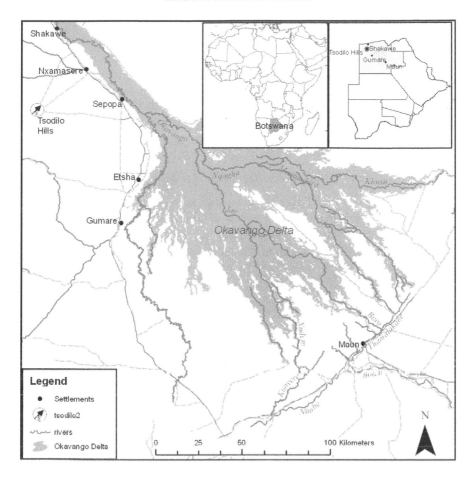

Figure 11.1 Map of Africa showing the location of Botswana with an insert showing the location of sites mentioned in the text (source: Harry Oppenheimer Okavango Research Centre)

site, or frequency of use of a heritage site/monument/group of artefacts or any form of material culture. As already mentioned, in Botswana most villages have a *kgotla*[2] (ward) system that can be used for an initial categorisation followed by either further random or systematic sampling within the *dikgotla* (wards). An example of this structure is the *dikgotla* in Kumakwane village where the missionary Livingstone's site is located. In small settlements, such as in the Tsodilo WH site or in most remote rural areas of Botswana, it is often easier to cover all homesteads in a settlement. For instance, this was the case when researching the Maasai settlements in Kenya where the *Boma*[3] system can be used as an initial category (Keitumetse 2005).

Further sampling of respondents can be either random or systematic in order to consider factors such as age, gender and education level: factors that are significant indicators of, and influences on, individuals' outlook on heritage value or their lack thereof. As an example, older members of a community are more likely to place special values on heritage compared to younger members. Furthermore, literate members of a community are more likely to possess knowledge about conventional approaches to heritage management than non-literate ones, including potentially being influenced in favour of it or against it. Sampling interviewees from varying categories will therefore increase the possibility of capturing all the divergent perspectives from the different cultural groups.

Forms of interviews, observation, heritage knowledge expression

Subsequent to sampling, informal interviews become the dominant method-ology used, particularly in rural areas such as the Tsodilo settlement in Botswana, where effective use of time and access are significant concerns. A guide questionnaire on the identified components of research is useful to ensure consistency as well as effective time management during interviews. The general objectives of the questionnaires and interviews for attitude-based research should commonly focus on the following:

- Gain insight into hosts' perceived representations of a cultural heritage product.
- Assess hosts' attitudes towards cultural resource management (identifi-cation, interpretation and representation).
- Assess hosts' level of awareness of conventional conservation approaches as these influence local responses to concerns about indigenous interaction with heritage components.

Observation: participant and non-participant observation

In addition to the various forms of interviews, both participant and non-participant methods are

> useful in discovering whether people do what they say they do or behave in the way they claim to behave during the interview. It is meant to cross-check information from interviews as well as reveal how people *perceive* what happens and not actually what happens.
>
> (Bell 1993: 109)

Figure 11.2 illustrates that observation of people's lives within a socio-cultural setting can bring out opportunities for identifying indicators that point to locals' attitudes to heritage that are not discussed explicitly by respondents during verbal interviews. The photograph shows one of the domestic dwellings at a settlement outside the Tsodilo WH site with a drawing showing one of the typical rock art images on the door. This drawing was noted by the

Figure 11.2 Dwelling in the settlement at the Tsodilo Hills World Heritage site (photo by the author)

researcher while walking through a settlement in proximity of the Tsodilo WH site (whose main heritage feature is rock art paintings), but the use of such images on domestic structures had not been mentioned in any of the interviews and was only identified through observation of the surrounding environment. In itself the drawing uses the residence as a *lieu de mémoire* (site of memory), as the actual heritage site is now a fenced-in, protected area under an international convention. At the same time, the drawing of rock art images on a residential structure indicates a form of mental interaction with the actual site that transcends the confinement of a protected, fenced-off World Heritage site. It also extends the now confined cultural heritage (rock art) to a broader cultural landscape, in the process translating the intellectual (intangible) into the visual (tangible).

Visualising perception: drawings as representations of locals' perception of a heritage product

Visualisation through drawing is one way of exploring new approaches to research in cultural heritage studies. The experiences gained from implementing this methodology show that it can be effective particularly in non-literate communities where interviews may be an alienating and unrewarding experience if people are not used to the language through which heritage is considered – for instance, that of UNESCO.

A simple methodological approach was adopted to assess people's perception. Individuals were asked to draw an image that sprung to their mind when concepts such as *archaeological heritage, cultural heritage* or *cultural tourism* were articulated by the researcher. Although individuals could respond verbally, drawing was emphasised to allow for comparison of conventional and traditional or local images depicting heritage components. It was felt that drawing, as opposed to the verbal articulation of features, indicated a certain level of connection and 'commitment' to a heritage component because it involves and hopefully captures intellectual capacity that incorporates 'logical deduction and deterministic anticipation of future events' associated with a particular heritage component (Dieterich 2004: 25).

The existing literature on visual perception is, however, dominated by discussions concerned with the dimensionality of an object (Kennedy 1974; Henderson 2005) rather than its significance as a visual symbol. This has made visual studies appear of little relevance and enticement for social science research, let alone new fields such as cultural heritage management that draw on most aspects of social science research. The drawing method has been used before by human geographers while mapping spatial information and geographical location of natural resources (Mukherjee 1993) but must be modified in order to be compatible for use wthin the field of cultural heritage management. In this chapter the objects and images drawn by the hosts are viewed and discussed as representative of definitions of certain concepts, or as visual representations of individuals' perception of a heritage product (see Figure 11.2). The emphasis is not on the physical characteristics or anatomy of an image, but rather on its cultural meaning as presented by the drawer.

Case study I: the Tsodilo Hills World Heritage site

Within the research conducted at the Tsodilo WH site, the drawing method was initially adopted as an alternative form of communication for individuals who could not read or write (Figure 11.3). However, after the analysis of several drawings, it became evident that the method could be applied as a stand-alone methodology in cultural heritage tourism research due to the characteristics outlined in the preceding sections as well as the later section. Respondents were requested to draw features that appeared in their minds when certain words, concepts or phrases, such as *cultural heritage* and *cultural tourism*, were articulated, the basic premise being that drawing enables respondents to communicate and express their responses and thoughts with less interference from the researcher but also with less pressure as compared to writing.

The sampling strategy entailed focusing on ethnic-group affiliation, followed by sampling further using indicators such as gender, age or literacy. However, due to the relatively small size of the population at the Tsodilo WH site, a 100 per cent household coverage was achieved, with at least one member from each household interviewed. The practical experience revealed that the method could be more efficient if the following steps are taken:

Figure 11.3 'Technologies of the intellect' (Goody 2000): visualising perception at Tsodilo Hills World Heritage site, Botswana (photo by the author)

1   Selecting in advance individuals who will participate in the activity. This is difficult, but much time can be wasted trying to locate individuals willing to participate. Introductions, advice and use of indirect access (popularly known as *snowballing* in social science research) through elders, relatives, traditional authorities, friends (in that order) to facilitate the location and the access to interviewees prior to the visit should be actively pursued.

2   Spending time experimenting with the equipment to be used (such as a pencil) helps to establish confidence in its use (both the researcher's equipment and the participants'). Also be prepared to replace materials or methods if the equipment fails. For instance, burnt wood or charcoal and fire ash mixed with water can be used in lieu of pencils by elder rural members of a community in Botswana due to their traditional use for writing and/or drawing purposes.

3   Staggering the interaction. In this case, it was useful to first commence drawing after a week of induction in order to establish some confidence and ease between the interviewer and the interviewee.

General challenges

The following became evident during the implementation of the method.

1   It became apparent that holding a pencil was a daunting task for several respondents because some had never had the experience and some had simply not engaged in the activity for a long time.

2   Most people do not possess drawing skills no matter how literate they are or are not. Therefore, some respondents were reluctant to engage in the activity. In addition, several individuals were initially suspicious as to why they were expected to draw when instead they could list items for the interviewer to write down.

3   The images are very difficult to manage and/or analyse once they have been acquired.

In conclusion, the method proves useful particularly where multiple stakeholders from varying cultural backgrounds participate, as their perception can be consolidated through pictures. It can bring out more results where a researcher has enough time to train participants, then implement and repeat the process. In applied tourism research, the output from the method can be used by community members to communicate the visual version of 'heritage' components which can later be showcased in an exhibition, or presented in postcard format for tourists' consumption. In this way, individual community members and hosts can be engaged directly in both research and definition of what they prefer or agree to be marketed as representative of their heritage in tourism.

Case study II: secondary school students

In addition to the 'field' approach to drawing, the drawing method was also applied in a classroom setting. In order to come up with an interview guide that encompassed components of research, a structured questionnaire that included the task of drawing was formulated and administered to a group of thirty secondary school students in Gaborone, the capital city of Botswana. This section therefore provides a brief addition to the discussion surrounding drawing as a method of research in heritage. The students' kinship affiliation is spread throughout Botswana. The structured questionnaire was administered in order to assess responses to various questions on heritage management (such as definition, description, categorisation, presentation and representation). Only those that required drawing/visualisation are addressed in this chapter. The participating students originated from various villages in Botswana, therefore their responses provide an invaluable source of information about the perception of a cultural heritage product from city residents who are affiliated with certain 'heritages' in various other parts of the country. The students' geographical origin is a significant analytical feature as it denoted students' ethnic affiliation as well as their socialised perception of what constitutes a cultural heritage product, and consequently a cultural heritage tourism product. However, achieving a focused research project would be better served by focusing on students from one village/settlement (as evident from case study I), from a common cultural affiliation or from one community so as to maximise opportunities of analysing responses on related aspects of heritage that are shared by certain groups. As indicated earlier, in Botswana it is common for a village to comprise various groups of people (communities) that share a common heritage. These communities are constituted in the wards or *dikgotla* mentioned above. For the purpose of this essay, however, the highlighted approach and results provide an example of approaching heritage tourism research in the future.

The method proved to be useful in bridging the gap between verbal and visual descriptions of heritage components. It also provided a visual definition of heritage components (Figure 11.4). The main challenge of the methodology is that a substantial amount of data is yielded, data which are difficult to manage and whose analysis is time-consuming. Computer software that can be used to analyse the images efficiently could benefit the use of the images in tourism as well as in future research.

Conclusions

Representing a different mode of communication than words, drawings become an additional aspect of visual expression, and drawing adds a medium through which respondents can define and represent their perception of a heritage product for use in tourism. The lessons derived from the two case

I.   ARCHAEOLOGICAL HERITAGE

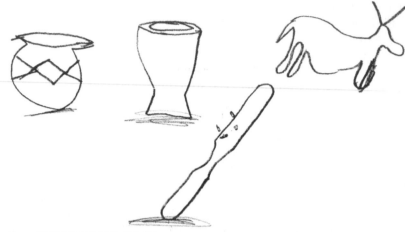

II.   CULTURAL HERITAGE

III. ARCHAEOLOGICAL TOURISM

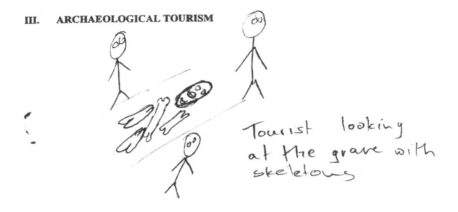

Tourist looking at the grave with skeletons

IV. CULTURAL TOURISM

Tourist looking at a pottery of Bakgatla

Figure 11.4 Defining cultural tourism: examples of drawings by students

studies indicate that combining elements of both the verbal (interview) and visual (drawing) approaches to research enhances the knowledge and understanding of how hosts interpret their cultural heritage and how they prefer it to be presented to visitors or tourists. The dynamic interplay between the verbal and visual representation of varying components of heritage complements existing methods on cultural heritage management research. Results emanating from these new approaches are relevant to international heritage eco-tourists (Spennemann *et al.* 2001) who prefer a connection with hosts' socio-cultural contexts and world-views. International conventions such as UNESCO 2003 also advocate a focus at the local or community level, which can be achieved through adoption of research approaches that incorporate characteristics outlined in this chapter. On the other hand, heritage eco-tourism advocates social and cultural sensitivity during tourism consumption as well as engagement in tourism activities that directly benefit local communities. The images produced by locals through drawing are useful for a well-informed tourism interpretation. Therefore, in addition to ethnographic interviews that solicit as well as measure people's attitudes, it is relevant to consider drawing as an applied research method in heritage tourism research. Goody rightly points out that

> verbal forms reduced to the written take on not only a visual aspect but a stationery character that enables people readily to distinguish differences and to assert similarities – or rather, to do with the new levels of accuracy because of the use of an additional instrument of measuring those differences and similarities by comparing linguistic statements visually as well as orally.

> (Goody 2000: 56)

Drawing as a sub-component substantiates this research approach by adding a layer of value to the visual output, resulting in a tangible tourism product that can be presented as emanating directly from the cultural custodians, hence sustainable. Sustainable approaches to developments are advocated through programme areas contained in Agenda 21 of UNCED's Sustainable Development manual that encourages governments to 'improve the collection of information on target groups and target areas in order to facilitate the design of focused programmes and activities, consistent with the target group needs and aspirations' in a bid to achieve sustainable development ideals (Robinson 1993: 35). The research approaches suggested for analysis of hosts' perception and attitudes do provide ideas for the development of tools that enable researchers to generate insights that are consistent with the target group's needs and aspirations. These tools should be used and implemented in a manner that involves the hosts or resident communities as collaborators because it is their perceptions and potential roles that are at stake.

Acknowlegements

Thanks to the Cambridge Livingstone Trust, the Smuts Memorial Funds, the Cambridge Commonwealth Trust and Dr M. L. S. Sørensen, University of Cambridge, the University of Botswana's Office of Research and Development (ORD) and the Harry Oppenheimer Okavango Research Centre, University of Botswana.

Notes

1   In this chapter the term 'local communities' is used to refer to individuals who live in prox-imity to a heritage site and have a significant cultural affiliation to the site as well as being involved in utilising it for heritage-related purposes.
2   The *kgotla* (singular; *dikgotla*, plural), is made up of a group of individuals in a village who conform to the same cultural traits, beliefs, norms and practices. Traditionally, members of the same *kgotla* resided in the same space within a village. However, as land-allocation powers were devolved from the Chiefs in the 1960s, members of the same *kgotla* can now reside anywhere in a village.
3   A *Boma* refers to a household made up of individuals who are related by birth or marriage.

Bibliography

Bell, J. (1993) *Doing Your Research Project: A Guide for First-Time Researchers*, Buckingham: Open University Press.

Bourdieu, P. (1993) *The Field of Cultural Production*, Cambridge: Polity Press.

Christou, E. (2005) 'Heritage and Cultural Tourism: A Marketing-focused Approach', in M. Sigala and D. Leslie (eds) *International Cultural Tourism: Management, Implications and Cases*, London: Elsevier Butterworth, 3–12.

Comaroff, J. and J. Comaroff (1992) *Ethnography and the Historical Imagination*, Oxford: Westview.

Dieterich, M. (2004) 'Reflections on the Intelligence of Natural Systems', in M. Dieterich and J. van der Straaten (eds) *Cultural Landscapes and Land Use: The Nature Conservation–Society Interface*, London: Kluwer, 25–36.

Gillham, B. (2004) *Case Study Research Methods*, London: Continuum.

Gregory, R.L. (1974) *Concepts and Mechanisms of Perception*, London: Duckworth.

Goody, J. (2000) *The Power of the Written Tradition*, Washington, DC: Smithsonian Institution.

Hammersley, M. (2000) *Taking Sides in Social Research: Essays on Partisan and Bias*, London: Routledge.

Henderson, J. M. (ed.) (2005) *Real-world Scene Perception*, Hove: Psychology Press.

Hodder, I. (1998) 'The Interpretation of Documents and Material Culture', in N. K. Denzin and Y. S. Lincoln (eds) *Collecting and Interpreting Qualitative Materials*, London: Sage, 110–28.

Holton, R. J. (1996) 'Classical Social Theory', in B. Turner (ed.). *The Blackwell Companion to Social Theory*, Oxford: Blackwell, 25–50.

Kaspersen, L. B. (2000) *Anthony Giddens: An Introduction to a Social Theorist*, Oxford: Blackwell.

Keitumetse, S. O. (2005) 'Sustainable Development and Archaeological Heritage Management: Local Community Participation and Monument Tourism in Botswana'. PhD Thesis, Department of Archaeology, University of Cambridge.

—— (2006) 'UNESCO 2003 Convention on Intangible Heritage: Practical Implications for Heritage Management Approaches in Africa', *South African Archaeological Bulletin* 61.184, 166–71.

—— (2007) 'Celebrating or Marketing the Indigenous? International Rights Organisations, National Governments and Tourism Creation', in P. M. Burns and M. Novelli (eds) *Tourism and Politics: Global Frameworks and Local Realities*, London: Elsevier, 109–22.

Kennedy, J. M. (1974) *A Psychology of Picture Perception*, San Francisco: Jossey-Bass.

LaRoche, C. J. (2005) 'Heritage, Archaeology, and African-American History', in *SAA Archaeological Record* 3.5, 34–7.

Little, B. (2005) 'Archaeologists and Interpreters', *SAA Archaeological Record* 3.5, 19–21.

McIntosh, R., R. Goeldner and B. J. R. Ritchie (1995) *Tourism Principles, Practices, Philosophies*, 7th edn, New York: John Wiley.

McManamon, F. (2005) 'The Public Meaning of America's Archaeological Heritage', *SAA Archaeological Record* 3.5, 22–3.

Mauffette-Leenders, A., J. A Erskine, M. R. Leenders (1997) *Learning with Cases*, London: Ivey Publishing.

Merriman, N. (ed.) (2004) *Public Archaeology*, London: Routledge.

Mukherjee, N. (1993) *Participatory Rural Appraisal: Methodology and Applications*, Studies in Rural Participation 1, New Delhi: Concept.

Plummer, K. (1996) 'Symbolic Interactionism in the Twentieth Century: The Rise of Empirical Social Theory', in B. Turner (ed.) *The Blackwell Companion to Social Theory*, Oxford: Blackwell, 223–44.

Robinson, N (ed.) (1993) *Agenda 21 and The UNCED Proceedings*, Third Series: International Protection of the Environment, vol. 6, New York: Oceana Publications,

Spennemann, H. R, D. W. Look and K. Graham (2001) 'Heritage Eco-Tourism in Micronesia: Expectations of Government Officials', *Cultural Resource Management* 1, 30–2.

UNESCO (2003) *Convention for the Safeguarding of the Intangible Cultural Heritage, Adopted 17th October 2003*.

Yin, R. K. (2003) *Applications of Case Study Research*, 2nd edn, London: Thousand Oaks, CA: Sage.

12

THE PUBLIC ARCHAEOLOGY OF AFRICAN AMERICA

Reflections on pragmatic methods and their results

Carol McDavid

Over the past fifteen years I have worked as a public archaeologist on two projects dealing with the historical archaeology of African America: the Levi Jordan Plantation Project in Brazoria, Texas and, recently, the Yates Community Archaeology Project, in Houston. My public archaeology work also includes ongoing consultation with other history organisations as they develop their relationships with their publics. Over this period, I have used various theoretical, philosophical and disciplinary tools to develop particular methods for specific situations, and to deal with the issues that arise from the ethical mandate to involve descendant voices in these projects – especially the multiple ways that people understand the objects and places that are under archaeological examination. My approaches have ranged from critical theory, to American pragmatism, to (more recently) Critical Race Theory and ideas drawn from the community organising/activist literature. In this chapter I discuss each approach, using examples from various projects to illustrate specific methods and strategies, some of which are drawn from my training in the parent discipline within which most American archaeology operates – anthropology. Throughout, I will attempt to evaluate each approach through a lens suggested by pragmatist philosopher William James a century ago: that theories provide instruments, not answers, and that our work must be evaluated less as a solution than as a programme for more work.

Critical theory and the Levi Jordan Plantation Project

The approach I used first, when the public outreach work at the Jordan Plantation was getting started in 1992, was critical theory – the insights from which had already found a firm place in public archaeology so they need little explanation here (Wylie 1985; Handsman 1981; Handsman and Leone 1989; Leone et al. 1987; Potter 1994). In this project, I was recruited by Kenneth L. Brown, the Principal Investigator, to try to involve descendant communities in the public interpretation of the site, the archaeology of which focused on the slave and tenant quarters. Critical theory helped me to better understand how the production of knowledge is historically situated, and to see more clearly how archaeological findings were relevant to particular social and political interests – in this case, local political interests as well as more broad-based disciplinary ones. Expanding the focus of both analysis *and* public presentation to include the lives of *all* the people who lived on a plantation, and doing so in a both/and, not either/or way,[1] helped us (the archaeologists) and our publics to reconsider our often stereotypic views of plantation life. Even more important, as we worked together to plan public interpretations, we discussed the issues that arose from this approach in explicit terms, which in turn helped all participants to internalise and act upon the idea that our understanding of the past is, in part, a function of how it is presented (Tilley 1989: 114). This was a new idea to my collaborators in Brazoria, Texas, as it was new to public archaeology when we first started in the early 1990s.

A critical approach also demanded self-reflection by each social actor (Held 1980: 191), as well as a great deal of transparency. Therefore, my methods included asking project participants to become familiar with my academic and philosophical biases and methods – even with my terms – as I attempted to become familiar with their points of view, through interviews, conversations and participant observation. The goal was to create truly participatory collaborations, with members of the public involved in every stage of the work. We did not always succeed in this, even though the effort continues (I will say more about the difficulty of creating fully participatory projects later in this chapter).

Several specific research and outreach methods were employed during this early Jordan Plantation study: fact-finding trips to other plantation sites; formal but unstructured interviews with community residents; participation in community meetings; presentations to community organisations; informal encounters with respondents; and active participation in professional associations concerned with the presentation of historical materials. The fact-finding trips took place in the summers of 1992 and 1993, and will not be addressed here except to say that they affirmed my initial impression that most public interpretations of the history of the plantation south (despite a few well-known exceptions) tend to focus almost exclusively on the owners' homes, furniture and wealth. Formal taped interviews with descendants and community residents began in October 1993 and continued into the autumn of 1994. Many informal conversations and meetings took place during this period and are, even at the time of writing, part of an ongoing research process.

I attempted to interview representatives from various publics: descendants of Levi Jordan, descendants of the African Americans who lived on the plantation, members of communities surrounding the plantation, persons interested in Texas history and tourism, and community leaders. The selection criteria for these interviews were based on my perception of family and community influence (that is, family elders, community leaders and people actively involved in historical interpretation) and on the respondent's willingness to participate.

As mentioned previously, part of my method was to state my personal and professional agendas very clearly. Interview transcripts reveal that I sometimes did almost as much talking as my respondents: explaining what I meant by a both/and approach, talking about work being done at other sites, explaining our goals in terms of community empowerment and so on. I usually revealed something of my own 'baggage' during these interactions – there were many animated discussions about what it was like to grow up as southerners in a racially polarised culture, our feelings about the Civil Rights movement, how the legacies of slavery affect people in the present and similar topics. The insights gleaned from these conversations later found their way into my more recent work on racism, as I will describe later.

These transcripts revealed extremely interactive conversations, not one-sided objective question/answer sessions. I wanted my respondents to trust me, but neither they nor I could ignore that I was a white, urban, university-affiliated outsider. If I had attempted to position myself as an insider, or to hide behind a mask of objectivity, I would have been seen as less trustworthy, not more. One African American businessman commented:

> Well, I don't want to interview *you*, but I think this has changed you
> ... your attitude about things. And I really don't know what they
> were before, but I sense that since you've been doing this thing you
> see things differently, you know, as you really search and find out the
> truth about things ... and, then, I do sense that you are sensitive,
> maybe more sensitive, to people since you've done this.
>
> (McDavid 1996: 53)

In short, my willingness to own my otherness – to talk about it openly and to reveal personal reasons for doing this research – led to more frank, open communication than would have been possible otherwise. It was sometimes essential in getting people to talk to me at all.

During this research, I always made it clear that 'we', meaning the core group of people initially involved in this project, wished to see if it would be feasible to create an inclusive, both/and public interpretation of this archaeology *at this site*. I made it clear that community members, especially descendants, would be the ones to decide whether to support such a public interpretation. If they chose not to support it, then the public interpretation, if any, would take place elsewhere (or not at all). This was the first phase of my long-term interest in community empowerment and archaeology.

Pragmatism and the Levi Jordan Plantation website Project

In the late 1990s I began my doctoral studies at the University of Cambridge and decided to study the new communication technologies, which were starting to be a subject of scholarly examination in archaeology during that period. Collaborating with the Jordan participants described above, we created an internet website about the Jordan project. My doctoral research then examined the way the website operated, and attempted to learn whether the internet could be a way to create conversations about archaeology which were open, democratic, relevant and multi-vocal (McDavid 1999, 2000, 2002a, 2002b, 2003, 2004a, 2004b).

This conversational framework was taken directly from American pragmatist philosophy, so I will first describe why I adopted that approach. After the first few years of working with the Jordan project, the critical theory approach had begun to feel a bit too top-down and pretentious, especially as my collaborators began to read my academic writing and to evaluate whether I was writing accurate accounts of our work together. Critical theorists tend to talk a lot about 'making' social agents aware of hidden coercion, 'thereby freeing them from that coercion and putting them in a position to determine where their true interests lie' (Geuss 1981: 55). The idea is that social agents can be 'deluded' and 'falsely conscious' (Geuss 1981: 60), thus requiring 'emancipation' and 'enlightenment'. The overall tone of the writing is that the theorists are the ones doing the enlightening, although this was likely not the intent of people like Habermas, Luka'cs and others. As I attempted to share critical theory ideas with my collaborators, and to do so in a transparent, open way, it felt wrong to imply that my collaborators were deluded and falsely conscious (even though I did not use the term). It struck me that we were *all* falsely conscious, and to some extent always would be. I found myself looking for a philosophical framework, a language and an approach that not only demanded self-reflection and transparency, but was also more respectful of all social agents, as well as more pluralist, open and democratic. I needed a framework in which the sort of enlightenment that critical theory called for could *emerge from* mutually empowered social interactions – in this case, during interactions which frequently took place while sitting around someone's dining-room table, with people whose ancestors enslaved, or were enslaved by, each other. Critical theory also demands that a 'final state' of emancipation and enlightenment must happen if the work is to be seen as successful (Geuss 1981: 84), and I needed a framework which could allow for more incremental change, as well as for the optimism I continued to experience as we dealt with the hurtful histories that we shared.

That is, I came to see that the *process* of creating the Jordan website was as important as the website itself, and at the suggestion of a colleague[2] I began to explore American pragmatism. Pragmatist philosophy – not to be confused with the colloquial definition of pragmatism as practicality – is a philosophy which began in the late nineteenth century with the writing of John Dewey, William James, Jane Addams and Charles Sanders Peirce and continues today with the late Richard Rorty, Cornel West, Nancy Fraser and others.[3] In contrast to critical theory, it acknowledges the contingency and fluidity of any negotiation, and is willing to suspend the goal of a final state in favour of a situated awareness of what each individual actor's beliefs are. Simply put, in pragmatism the main goal is *to keep the conversation going*. It is an optimistic, pluralistic, but not nihilistically relativist approach. In pragmatism, the small emancipations from everyday interactions can be celebrated, and small defeats are seen as a normal part of the process.

Certain themes emerge in the writings of all pragmatists, namely, all pragmatists share an anti-essentialist, anti-foundationalist and pluralist point of view towards truth and reason. All are keenly aware of the contingency of historically and socially constructed categories and practices (the 'stories we tell', to borrow Rorty's term), and share an interest in the possibility of social change. Some key ideas are that truth is *made* rather than *found*, that there are no unmediated facts and that all interpretation is value-laden. Even though these ideas are also present in the work of other philosophers, within pragmatism they take on a more active, social flavour. Pragmatists do not necessarily agree on the proper limits one should use when making truth claims, but all put a primary emphasis on the action aspects of the *making* of those claims. It is not so much that pragmatists believe that there is no objective reality, or no 'bottom of things' that can be discovered (though some do believe this), but rather that we will be better off finding our answers *within* the process of looking for them. Further, pragmatism insists that whatever answers we find are temporary, historically situated and contingent on whatever changes 'we' may agree on. It also acknowledges that the 'we' itself is contingent and fluid – as people join or leave the conversation. It does not say that critical theory's final state is a bad thing, but nor does it bemoan things when it is not attained – when a Habermasian ideal speech situation is a distant dream. It says, simply, that it is important to keep talking.

To a pragmatist, continuing the conversation is more important than continually trying to describe ourselves more accurately (to create archaeological interpretations that are more 'true'), or to get to the bottom of things. Some of the so-called neopragmatists, Cornel West and Nancy Fraser in particular (Fraser 1989; West 1989), take the pragmatist project further by insisting that we take account of this creative process (the capacity for action and cooperation) by actually doing and acting. They insist that we take the pragmatist philosophical endeavour out of the academy and into mainstream cultural critique: to use academic work to inspire social action (West 1989: 234). This view situates contemporary action within its historical antecedents. It takes a long view of history and applies it to an action plan for the future – a future which can create alternative stories about who and what we are. Common to all pragmatist writing is the idea that the value of any work, philosophical or otherwise, is best evaluated by looking at its results. What are the practical consequences of our work?

To examine this question, I will describe some of the methods we used in the Jordan website project to create and evaluate the website and its operation. The Jordan excavations took place in Brazoria, Texas, a small rural Texas town. Many of the people I worked with in this community are descendants of the people whose material lives were being studied. They included the community-defined elders – the gatekeepers – and their voices were (and are) an important part of both past and present in these communities. However, many of these same people had little or no interest in purchasing or using computers. To many, the internet was something that one heard about on occasional television programmes, not something which one had personally experienced. Despite this, I needed to create a website (a conversation) which would include these important community voices.

To do this, I first met with some of these key individuals and conducted oral-history interviews with them. These interviews were transcribed and portions of the transcripts were included on the website, and linked to other parts of the website that came up during these offline conversations. Usually another family member and I conducted the interviews together, and frequently I found that family members asked most of the questions. These jointly led interviews led to inter-family discussions about history, genealogy, etc. that would not have occurred if the interviews had not taken place. Transcripts of the interviews were given to the family members involved and subsequent meetings were held to clarify information, approve the interview segments used for the website, obtain pictures and the like.

Second, we adopted a policy of using some interviews to ask permission – even when we did not legally have to – to put certain kinds of information on the website. Much of the material we wanted to use was from public records, but we did not do so without explicit permission from at least some of the family's descendants. Doing this had two positive results. First, it assured descendants that we respected their own and their families' privacy, and it reinforced our position as collaborators, not authorities with some right to use their families' histories for our own purposes. Second, it opened avenues for additional information – this new information has not only enhanced our understanding of the past, but it has also helped contemporary people to see their ancestors in ways they had not before (McDavid 1999, 2002a).

These two strategies helped us to develop interactive content from the ground up, and to include people who did not own computers in that process, but we also needed to find ways for people without computers to actually see and use the website. So we held a series of online internet workshops for students and members of the public in the computer labs of local schools and libraries. I was present to help people who had not used computers before, and to gather information about how people interacted with the website, with me and with each other while the workshop was going on. During these workshops I encouraged them to use the online interactive elements, such as the discussion forums, feedback forms and questionnaire (McDavid 2002a, 2004b). In addition, we also arranged for several computers to be donated to the local community library. These provided another public access point, and, in return, the library promoted the website and mentioned it in signage located near the public access computers.

We also developed a participants' section of the website, which included short biographies of descendants, academics, students and other participants, as well as links to information they wished to put on the site under their own names. Whenever possible, the biographies were written by the individual participants, and sometimes they used their own pages to publicise information about various community causes. On these participant pages, archaeological and local agendas merged in mutually empowering, reciprocal ways and the website project became more firmly situated within the social context of the local community, even though it was accessible to people all over the world.

The Jordan archaeological site is now owned by a large state bureaucracy instead of local descendants (McDavid 2004a, 2004b, 2007a). The original Jordan website is archived at www.webarchaeology.com, and is now an artefact of the past, although still accessible in the present. I still work with the local group, though not as actively as before. Time, funding and energy permitting, we will work together to update the site, and when that happens a different sort of conversation will no doubt emerge.

Pragmatism and the Yates Community Archaeology Project

More recently, I have discovered the limits of this pragmatic conversational approach when dealing with my current project, the Yates Community Archaeology Project. This project is located in Freedmen's Town, an urban African American neighbourhood in Houston, Texas. In the Jordan context, even though there were different understandings of history among the different players, the archaeological project was seen by most people in Brazoria as an opportunity for community enrichment. There were obviously 'hurtful histories', especially given that the archaeology had to do with the archaeology of slavery and the post-Civil War Reconstruction period, but in Brazoria we were able to locate individual collaborators who approached the idea of a new public archaeology project with open hearts and minds. For the most part, they *wanted* to undertake the often difficult conversations that the work initiated, and their individual contributions to the success of the project cannot be underestimated.

The Freedmen's Town project is very different. Stakeholders hold diverse, entrenched and often hostile political positions, and there is a decades-long history of hurt and betrayal between different groups. These groups include grassroots community members, historic preservationists, people in city government (including a succession of mayors), bureaucrats in various agencies, opportunistic property developers and, more recently, new residents who have no interest in embracing the history of the community in which their new, gated, expensive homes are being built. The historical landscape itself is highly endangered – to the point that many say that the battle to save Freedmen's Town has already been lost (Franks 2007). The neighbourhood was built by previously enslaved people right after the Civil War, and has been a major hub of black life in Houston since then. When it was listed on the National Register of Historic Places in 1986, it included over 530 historical structures, many of which were occupied at that point by the poor and elderly (although most had been built by professional-class black Houstonians in the late nineteenth to early twentieth century). According to recent survey data, fewer than thirty of those original structures remain (Rutherford B. H. Yates Museum, 2005). What has happened in Freedmen's Town embodies the abuses of insensitive gentrification at its worst.

Trying to enact pluralist, democratic and open conversations in this fraught setting has been very difficult. We have had to learn to see these difficulties as data, and we *attempt* to approach situations philosophically, not personally. One set of problems has revolved around the fact that some of our archaeological goals (which spring not only from pragmatism and critical theory but also from the larger discourse about inclusive public archaeology around which African American archaeology in the United States has developed (McDavid and Babson 1997; Leone *et al*. 2005)) are to support community agendas. We believe that indigenous grassroots people have the right to decide for themselves which strategies and programmes should take place in their community, and if this means that they also have a degree of control over our archaeological programme, all the better. However, the historic house museum which makes our work possible (through funding, provision of lab space and support of our time-consuming contextual methods) has historic preservation as its main mission. It is difficult to argue with this agenda, given the rate at which historic structures are being demolished, and while we do support it, sometimes its 'preservation first' agendas are at odds with community goals. The museum group is diverse with regard to ethnicity, age, gender, class and skill, and it shares a strong commitment to the ancestors of Freedmen's Town and the need to preserve and celebrate the neighbourhood's history. The group is, however, composed largely of people who live outside the community.

One example will illustrate how this affects our ability to have a *community* archaeology project. Early on in our association with it, the museum insisted that the best way to preserve the area's historic brick streets – which could be quite significant archaeologically – was to pedestrianise them. Most local community members wanted to preserve the streets too, and had been trying to persuade the city government to do so for some time. However, to them certain infrastructure improvements needed *under* the streets were just as important, and they were willing to accept a city plan that would renovate (but not fully restore) the streets and repair the infrastructure at the same time. Because of its mission, the museum campaigned for an ambitious plan which would close the streets to all vehicle traffic. This plan included a number of features, such as parks, which it argued would benefit the community. While a few members of the community agreed with the museum's plan, several major leaders did not. More to the point, they were insulted that the museum was campaigning for pedestrianisation without *their* agreement. They maintained that pedestrianisation would affect *their* day-to-day lives in a significant way. Some saw the museum's proposal as an elitist, even racist notion, one that outsiders had no right to pursue. My co-director and I found ourselves at odds with our museum sponsors, because we felt that the community should make the decisions about how, or whether, to pedestrianise the streets. We felt that community choice and empowerment should trump preservation, but for the museum, it was the other way around.

Underlying this situation is the sad reality that both the community and the museum have met systematic and ongoing opposition to their efforts to save the historic landscape of Freedmen's Town.[4] Despite the museum's position as a major property owner in the neighbourhood (and its status as a legitimate not-for-profit institution under US tax laws), its representatives have been excluded from both local planning committees and state-mandated consulting procedures. They have been denied restoration permits of various sorts (requiring constant, costly appeals) and have been denied tax exemptions on their properties (also requiring costly litigation). In short, both official and unofficial attempts to block the museum's efforts have been deliberate and continuous. Likewise, attempts to displace the grassroots (mostly African American) community have been ongoing. Elderly tenants are displaced by outsider landlords with no regard for their long-term tenure in the community. Low-income homeowners have been evicted because of tax delinquencies, which are driven by increased land values, driven in turn by gentrification. Local activists have characterised these attempts as 'cultural genocide' (Johnson 2003; House 2006). Whereas in Brazoria I was able to successfully advocate a stance of openness, pluralism and transparency as a productive way to begin to deal with 'hurtful histories', in Freedmen's Town I have been told that this approach is 'too honest' and 'naive'. When I have attempted to bring insights about outreach and community work learned from other projects – insights informed by philosophy, training and ethics – these efforts are frequently rejected. This is not surprising, given the challenges that both the museum and the community have had to deal with, but it does make public archaeology difficult.

A pragmatic approach requires that different parties bracket their distrust and long-term agendas in favour of attempting to find solutions to short-term problems, and unfortunately the absolutist thinking which drives much of the discourse in Freedmen's Town does not lend itself well to this. Frequently people have misunderstood my willingness to be open and transparent as a willingness to compromise on important issues. Pragmatists may well have lines in the sand beyond which we will not cross, but we actively seek other ways around these lines. We do not believe that one truth is as good as another, but we avoid slipping into a nihilistic relativism by seeking conversations with those with whom we disagree, still expressing our own voices and opinions. Pragmatism does not offer easy answers, but it does provide a mechanism for keeping communication lines open. However, as is clear from the examples above, power, discrimination and unequal access to resources are part of the problem in Freedmen's Town, and some scholars have noted that pragmatism does not account for power as well as it might (Fraser 1998: 157).

In methodological terms, in addition to looking at the above situation as data (not simply as a source of personal frustration) I have come to realise that in Freedmen's Town we are not running a community-*based* programme, which had been our original intent. Instead, we are running a community-*placed* programme (Ervin 2000). We have had to realise that we exist *in* the community, but we were not *of* it. And because of our association with the museum, our idealistic public archaeology agendas about shared community power and open conversation have sometimes been compromised. We have had to find ways to acknowledge and deal with this.

First, we have had to separate ourselves from some of the larger policy objectives of our sponsors, while being loyal to their overall historic preservation effort (to their credit, once we began to discuss the situation, museum leaders understood the difficulty of our dilemma). With the museum's knowledge, we began to communicate more directly with some of the more vocal community members that insofar as our *archaeology programme* was concerned, we 'worked for' them as much as we 'worked for' the museum (this is in fact true; we are consultants to the museum and are paid only when funding permits, and our work for community leaders has, thus far, been pro bono). We also developed new brochures, displays, public talks, tours and other communications materials which discuss our desire for community input and involvement. Even when these are not immediately forthcoming, we are vigilant in asking for them and in creating as many opportunities for them to emerge as possible. These materials are, of course, all typical public archaeology strategies, but our texts are as open and transparent as possible about who pays us and what our agendas and motivations are. We are also careful to avoid public disagreements with either sponsor or community. When we disagree about a matter of policy – pedestrianisation, for example – we attempt to work quietly from the inside to effect change.

We have also begun to conduct more ethnographic interviews with community leaders, focusing not just on oral history, but on understanding more about the community's priorities regarding both past and present. I have presented analyses of this data at professional conferences and shared them with the community members I interviewed, offering opportunities for them to change or clarify my texts. To date all players seem to respect my intellectual freedom to say what I wish, especially in professional venues, but if they do object I would deal with it on a case-by-case basis (in a pragmatic fashion, I do not attempt to solve such problems ahead of time, but only if and when I need to) (Mouer 2000).

226

Another way to operationalise the idea of pragmatic conversation has to do with a seemingly mundane matter – project administration. By this I refer to simply taking care of business in an efficient manner, and paying close attention to the sorts of things that executives hire secretaries for (but which funding for public archaeology rarely provides). This includes sending thank-you notes and reminders, making follow-up phone calls before important meetings and sending prompt and accurate meeting notes afterwards, and calling people promptly when a business card is stuck in one's pocket at a community event. At the Levi Jordan project, we have taken this approach a bit further. We found it necessary to execute a formal agreement (a 'Memorandum of Understanding') with the new state agency owners in order to ensure continued community involvement, because of business-as-usual bureaucratic procedures which made this difficult (McDavid 2007a). While some will disagree with me for elevating these sorts of activities to the status of method, I would argue that attention to project administration and the formalities of consultation (even when this consultation is not legally mandated – there is no NAGPRA for African American archaeology[5]) communicates something very clearly to local communities. It tells them that we take the time *they* spend working with *us* seriously – that it matters to us just as much as essays like this do. I maintain that what some jokingly refer to as 'administrivia' is not trivial at all.

Over time, using these sorts of methods has yielded good results. For example, an important community leader (one who had been the angriest about the pedestrianisation issue) asked us to do some archaeological testing on property planned for use as a community centre. We did the testing for free, as part of a field school. We did the work on time, we wrote a proper report by the promised date, we treated this leader as the respected client she was and we were able to provide a useful service. The museum supported our efforts, even though it took time and supplies away from doing archaeological work on their property (it has also attempted to help this leader find funding to build the community centre, although at the time of writing funding is still being sought). The museum also decided to back off from some of its original positions, such as pedestrianisation, and is now acting in a more respectful, inclusive way towards key community leaders – even leaders with whom it disagrees on some matters. It too is taking care not to disagree in public about community issues, and is listening more to what the community wants – even while still working hard to save as many historic properties as possible. A key recent development was the museum's successful effort to help several local historical churches form a new 'Coalition of Pastoral Leaders'. At the request of these churches, the museum provided the funding and expertise to get this group off the ground, and as a result the museum is now seen by these important stakeholders as an ally. In turn, this Coalition is providing community-*based* advocacy for preservation that some powers-that-be are starting to listen to. Even though the overall situation in Freedmen's Town is still threatened, these small victories are important.

Critical Race Theory and the public archaeology of African America

Making archaeology matter, in a pragmatic sense, has been the focus of my most recent work, so I have become very involved in the recent activist archaeology discourse which sees civic engagement as a primary reason for doing archaeological work in the first place (McDavid 2007a, 2008). In the context of African American archaeology, being an activist archaeologist means using our work to deconstruct racism and white privilege in the present, even as we try to understand how these things occurred in the past. I have found that a body of work known as Critical Race Theory (CRT) can be useful in doing this.

Introduced to archaeology by Terry Epperson (Epperson 1999, 2004), CRT (also known as 'race-crit') represents a wide body of legal, political and more recently educational research, mostly conducted by scholars of colour, that critically examines the role of race as a social construct that organises both everyday and institutional interactions. A major tenet of CRT is to centre the study and understanding of racism as something which continues to be tightly knit into the fabric of society (Bell 1995) – it reminds us that racism is the common, everyday experience of most people who are not white. It is enacted not just through individual acts of prejudice, but, more insidiously, through the everyday taken-for-granted realities of white privilege (Jensen 2002a, 2002b; McIntosh 1988; Sleeter 2000/1; Wise 2002).

CRT rejects so-called liberal approaches to racism, such as neutrality and colour-blindness. Neutrality implies that whiteness is the norm, and part of white privilege means having the luxury, in most situations, to simply not be aware of one's race. Colour-blindness is equally problematic because, despite our best intentions, most *people* cannot practise true colour-blindness – we notice each other's colours whether we want to or not (McDavid 2007a). The CRT critique points out that because colour-blindness is *presumed* to fully incorporate racial justice ('justice for all') it has not allowed American society to develop a concept of justice that takes account of racial difference. Another issue raised by 'race-crits' is that of 'false empathy', which Richard Delgado (Delgado and Stefancic 2001) argues is the mistake some people make when they believe they can discern the feelings, thoughts or opinions of another person. This caution against false empathy is important in public archaeology, as race-crit also demands that we find ways to actively involve the lived experiences of people of colour in the ways that we both do and publicly present archaeological work.

In terms of method, CRT provides a framework to insist on this sort of involvement despite occasional accusations of reverse discrimination. For example, we do not shy away from telling prospective employees or volunteers that, yes, we *do* seek African Americans (and members of other ethnic groups) to take specific positions with our project (we are white). We problematise our own whiteness, and we take issues of cultural competency seriously, even when we cannot solve them. We work *purposefully* towards a future reality in which our staffs, board members, volunteers and audiences are diverse with respect to both race and class. We use CRT to theorise about race and white privilege even as we try to think carefully and intentionally about how knowledge is created and controlled, and then act upon what we learn.

An awareness of CRT allows and encourages us to approach race very frontally. We talk about it, we critique how it operated in the past (as illuminated by the archaeology) and we discuss how it continues to operate in the present. The specific methods are frequently the same as those I have already described – interviews, public talks, brochures and the like – but when we do these things with a clear anti-racism agenda, the relevance of our work becomes more evident. Many times, after doing a talk about the archaeology in which I include comments about white privilege, people of colour will comment with surprise, 'I've never heard a white person talk about this stuff before.' Being willing to be both critical (and self-critical) about race makes our work *about* race more credible and meaningful. Obviously we could do those things without CRT, but the theoretical work does put the issues in relief and makes them easier to identify.

Community organising approaches

Yet another body of work has informed much of my public work in the past few years. I refer to the literature of community organising and participatory research, and in particular the work of Randy Stoecker.[6] Stoecker points out that there are three different ways that academics usually engage with communities: 'The *Initiator*', 'The *Consultant*' and 'The *Collaborator*' (Stoecker 1997).

The *Initiator* is someone who comes up with a research or project idea and invites the community to participate. In these cases, the process can become more and more participatory, *if* the researcher is willing to learn community organising skills, and if the community is willing to develop its own skills and resources. This is the type of interaction into which the Levi Jordan Plantation Project has evolved – I started as an Initiator, but now the community directs my actions there, even as they welcome my input on most – though notably not all – issues.

In the *Consultant* scenario, the community commissions the research and the academic is accountable to it. This is where the Yates Community Archaeology Project may be moving, as I described above, although we began as Initiators. However, there is a danger that using our expertise may 'reinforce knowledge inequality and dependence'; as Stoecker points out, 'What if the media shows up and they only want to talk to us about our research instead of the community?' (Stoecker 1997). Therefore, while we are willing to deploy the public's interest in archaeology to get (for example) media attention, we try to focus this attention on community agendas whenever we can, after learning what these issues are with the strategies outlined above.

Our desire would be to act in the third role, as true *Collaborators*, with equal participation from empowered community partners to define and direct the research. This poses problems too, however. In the ideal sense, in this scenario the community would help to formulate research questions, analyse results and so on. But the reality is that people have their own lives to lead and collaborative research takes a huge amount of time – time for meetings, time for reading (to be on common ground with respect to research questions, theories and so on) and time to work out the conflicts which inevitably arise. Stoecker reminds us that while 'we' – the archaeologists – may be willing to devote large chunks of time to a project, this is because we see this as our 'job'. Local and indigenous community members may not have that luxury, especially when they have to go to their real (paying) jobs every day. Over the past fifteen years, with two different projects, I have found few participants who are willing to be true research partners.

Not surprisingly, communities sometimes prefer to call upon the experts to work *for* them – and why not? After all, corporations and the rich hire consultants to do things for them, and I would argue that indigenous people should have access to the same sort of expertise, and have the same sort of power with regard to work that takes place in their community. In addition, as a practical matter, a report with a PhD's name on it may serve community interests more than one which does not (Stoecker 1997). So, even though I continually seek mutually empowered collaborative relationships, and welcome them when they emerge, I am not surprised when they do not.

The last point I want to bring in from Stoecker's work is that we also need to problematise the whole notion of thinking that participatory projects are 'research'. Even though I have characterised my observations in this essay as data, the projects I work with are, at the core, community organising and/or development projects, of which my research is only one piece. When we think of participatory research in this way, we can define our roles in terms of a larger context in which our work 'matters' in a different way.

Conclusion

In this chapter I have described specific methodological examples derived from a variety of approaches, theories and philosophies, and these examples are organised more or less in the order I have used them over time. It is important to realise, however, that the work itself does not operate in such a linear, orderly fashion. I return to old tools when they suit, even while exploring new ones, and am comfortable with a fair amount of theoretical eclecticism. Therefore I still try to be critical and reflexive, as well as watchful for masked ideologies, even though I do not rely directly on critical theory as much as I once did. Likewise, I still attempt to frame my interactions with the public as pragmatic, open-ended, pluralist conversations, even when my collaborators and clients choose not to do so. I learn what I can from Critical Race Theory about working within a society still infected by race and class privilege, and I use insights from community organising activists to find ways for my work to matter to one particular community.

Archaeology does have a useful role to play in society, although discovering what that *is* is a messy process – we will make mistakes, we will be criticised and sometimes our work will be misunderstood. So, to return to pragmatism, we have to remember that our continued experiments will benefit from re-evaluating old approaches, even as we stay open to new ones. In pragmatic terms, we still have much work to do.

Notes

1   That is, we attempted to talk about *both* black history *and* white history in the plantation south, without talking about either at the expense of the other. A both/and approach provides a framework to explore the interaction of dominant and non-dominant groups, and rejects simplistic definitions of non-dominant individuals as 'victims who react, negatively motivated by dominance, without any positive viewpoints or ideology of their own' (Spencer-Wood 1992: 4). It also rejects definitions of all dominant individuals as oppressors and villains.

2   I have Victor Buchli to thank for this introduction, and for many conversations later which also included Lynn Meskell, Emma Blake and Suzanne Spencer-Wood.

3   Pragmatism emerged as an identifiable strain of philosophical thought in America in the late 1880s. It was first identified as such by mathematician, physicist and philosopher Charles Sanders Peirce (Peirce 1878) and psychologist William James (Bird 1995; James 1996). However, glimpses of ideas that Peirce and James identified as 'pragmatic' were anticipated in the writings of Ralph Waldo Emerson (Emerson 1995; West 1989). Shortly after Peirce and James, pragmatism was taken up by educational theorist John Dewey, who took it in a more action-oriented, social and political direction (Dewey 1916). During this early period Dewey's pragmatism was influenced by Jane Addams and other female domestic reformers (Addams 1961), although the contributions of these women to pragmatist writing have only been acknowledged recently (Seigfried 1996; Spencer-Wood 1997). My own research tends to draw most heavily on the work of some of the later 'neopragmatists', most notably Richard Rorty, Hilary Putnam, Nancy Fraser and Cornel West. These later writers, while all identifying themselves as pragmatists, engage with and have been variously influenced by the work of Marx, Heidegger, Nietzsche, Derrida, Quine, Foucault, Habermas, the later Wittgenstein, Du Bois, Davidson and others. The sort of down-to-earth pragmatism I employ does not require a detailed analysis of the many differences between the 'classical' pragmatists and more recent writers. I refer readers wishing to explore such matters to any good reader (e.g. Goodman 1995) or to the many volumes in which these pragmatists engage with each other and with other philosophers (e.g. Fraser 1989; West 1989; Saatkamp 1995; Mouffe 1996; Mounce 1997).

4   My description of these events is based on personal knowledge.

5   The Native American Graves Protection and Repatriation Act, passed by the US Congress in 1990, which provides some measure of Native control over some types of archaeological remains.

6   I thank Fred McGhee for introducing me to this body of work (McGhee 2000).

Bibliography

Addams, J. (1961) *Twenty Years at Hull-House, with Autobiographical Notes*, New York: New American Library. Originally published (1910), New York: Macmillan.
Bell, D. (1995) 'Who's Afraid of Critical Race Theory?', *University of Illinois Law Review*, 893–910.
Bird, G. H. (ed.) (1995) *William James: Selected Writings*, London: J. M. Dent.
Delgado, R. and J. Stefancic (2001) *Critical Race Theory: An Introduction*, New York: New York University Press.

Dewey, J. (1916) 'Does Reality Possess a Practical Character?', in *Essays, Philosophical and Psychological, in Honor of William James*, New York: Longmans, Green and Co., reprinted in R. B. Goodman (ed.) (1995) *Pragmatism: A Contemporary Reader*, New York: Routledge.

Emerson, R. W. (1995) 'Circles', in R. B. Goodman (ed.) *Pragmatism: A Contemporary Reader*, New York: Routledge.

Epperson, T. W. (1999) 'The Global Importance of African Diaspora Archaeology in the Analysis and Abolition of Whiteness', paper presented at World Archaeological Congress 4, Cape Town, South Africa.

—— (2004) 'Critical Race Theory and the Archaeology of the African Diaspora', *Historical Archaeology* 38, 101–8.

Ervin, A. M. (2000) *Applied Anthropology: Tools and Perspectives for Contemporary Practice*, Needham Heights, MA: Allyn & Bacon.

Franks, J. (2007) 'Texas District Built by Freed Slaves Fades Away'. Reuters.

Fraser, N. (1989) *Unruly Practices: Power, Discourse and Gender in Contemporary Social Theory*, Minneapolis: University of Minnesota Press.

—— (1998) 'Another Pragmatism: Alain Locke, Critical "Race" Theory and the Politics of Culture', in M. Dickstein (ed.) *The Revival of Pragmatism: New Essays on Social Thought, Law and Culture*, Durham, NC: Duke University Press.

Geuss, R. (1981) *The Idea of Critical Theory: Habermas and the Frankfurt School*, Cambridge: Cambridge University Press.

Goodman, R. B. (ed.) (1995) *Pragmatism: A Contemporary Reader*, New York: Routledge.

Handsman, R. G. (1981) 'Early Capitalism and the Center Village of Canaan, Connecticut: A Study of Transformations and Separations', *Artifacts* 9, 1–21.

Handsman, R. G. and M. Leone (1989) 'Living History and Critical Archaeology and the Reconstruction of the Past', in V. Pinsky and A. Wylie (eds) *Critical Traditions in Contemporary Archaeology*, Cambridge: Cambridge University Press.

Held, D. (1980) *Introduction to Critical Theory: Horkheimer to Habermas*, Berkeley: University of California Press.

House, G. (2006) 'Houston Destroys Largest Black Historic District in United States: Empowerment of Grassroots Blocked while Gentrification Grows'. *EURweb.com*.

James, W. (1996) *A Pluralistic Universe*, Lincoln: University of Nebraska Press. Originally published (1909), New York: Longmans, Green and Co.

Jensen, R. (2002a) 'More Thoughts on Why the System of White Privilege is Wrong', in C. Rose (ed.) *STAR: Students and Teachers Against Racism*, http://www.racismagainstindians.org/WhitePrivilege/WhitePrivilegeResponse.htm (accessed 8 May 2009).

—— (2002b) 'White Privilege Shapes the US', in C. Rose (ed.) *STAR: Students and Teachers Against Racism*, http://www.racismagainstindians.org/WhitePrivilege/WhitePrivilege.htm (accessed 8 May 2009).

Johnson, L. (2003) 'Street Closure in Freedmen's Town', in N. P. Collins (ed.) 'Houston, TX', email communication copied to several people.

Leone, M. P., P. B. Potter, Jr and P. A. Shackel (1987) 'Toward a Critical Archaeology', *Current Anthropology* 28, 283–302.

Leone, M. P., C. J. Laroche and J. J. Babiarz (2005) 'The Archaeology of Black Americans in Recent Times', *Annual Review of Anthropology* 34, 575–98.

McDavid, C. (1996) 'The Levi Jordan Plantation: From Archaeological Interpretation to Public Interpretation.' Master's Thesis, Department of Anthropology. University of Houston, University Microfilms.

—— (1997) 'Descendants, Decisions, and Power: The Public Interpretation of the Archaeology of the Levi Jordan Plantation', *In the Realm of Politics: Prospects for Public Participation in African-American Archaeology*, special issue of *Historical Archaeology* 31.3, 114–31.

—— (1999) 'From Real Space to Cyberspace: Contemporary Conversations about the Archaeology of Slavery and Tenancy', *Internet Archaeology* 6, special theme: digital publication. http://intarch.ac.uk/journal/issue6/mcdavid_toc.html.

—— (2000) 'Archaeology as Cultural Critique: Pragmatism and the Archaeology of a Southern United States Plantation', in C. Holtorf and H. Karlsson (eds) *Philosophy and Archaeological Practice: Perspectives for the 21st Century*, Lindome, Sweden: Bricoleur Press.

—— (2002a) 'Archaeologies that Hurt, Descendents that Matter: A Pragmatic Approach to Collaboration in the Public Interpretation of African-American Archaeology', *World Archaeology*, special issue 'Community Archaeology' 34, 303–14.

—— (2002b) 'From Real Space to Cyberspace: The Internet and Public Archaeological Practice'. Doctoral Thesis, Department of Archaeology, University of Cambridge.

—— (2003) Context, Collaboration and Power: The Public Archaeology of the Levi Jordan Plantation, in L. Derry and M. Malloy (eds) *SAA Community Partnership Handbook*, Washington, DC, Society for American Archaeology.

—— (2004a) 'From "Traditional" Archaeology to Public Archaeology to Community Action: The Levi Jordan Plantation Project', in P. Shackel and E. Chambers (eds) *Places in Mind: Archaeology as Applied Anthropology*, New York: Routledge.

—— (2004b) 'Towards a More Democratic Archaeology? The Internet and Public Archaeological Practice', in N. Merriman (ed.) *Public Archaeology*, London: Routledge.

—— (2007a) 'Beyond Strategy and Good Intentions: Archaeology, Race, and White Privilege', in P. Shackel and B. Little (eds) *An Archaeology of Civic Engagement and Social Justice*, Lanham, MD: AltaMira Press, 67–88.

—— (2007b) 'The Death of a Community Archaeology Project? Ensuring "Consultation" in a Non-mandated Bureaucratic Environment', paper presented at World Heritage: Global Challenges, Local Solutions conference, Ironbridge Institute, Birmingham.

McDavid, C. and D. Babson (eds) (1997) *In the Realm of Politics: Prospects for Public Participation in African-American Archaeology*, special issue of *Historical Archaeology* 31.3.

McGhee, F. (2000) 'From "Engaged" Archaeology to Participatory Research', paper presented at the Annual Meeting of the American Anthropological Association, San Francisco, California, November 2000.

McIntosh, P. (1988) *White Privilege and Male Privilege: A Personal Account of Coming to See Correspondences Through Work in Women's Studies*, Wellesley, MA: Center for Research on Women, Wellesley College.

Mouer, D. (2000) 'Comment: Can there be a Pragmatic Archaeology?', in C. Holtorf and H. Karlsson (eds) *Philosophy and Archaeological Practice: Perspectives for the 21st Century*, Göteborg: Institutionen för arkeologi, Göteborgs universitet.

Mouffe, C. (ed.) (1996) *Deconstruction and Pragmatism*, London: Routledge.

Mounce, H. O. (1997) *The Two Pragmatisms: From Peirce to Rorty*, London: Routledge.

Peirce, C. S. (1878) 'How to Make our Ideas Clear', *Popular Science Monthly* 12, 286–302, reprinted in R. B. Goodman (ed.) (1995) *Pragmatism: A Contemporary Reader*, New York: Routledge.

Potter, P. B., Jr. (1994) *Public Archaeology in Annapolis: A Critical Approach to History in Maryland's Ancient City*, Washington, DC: Smithsonian Institution Press.

Rutherford. B. H. Yates Museum (2005) Research notes on file in museum archives.

Saatkamp, J. H. (ed.) (1995) *Rorty and Pragmatism: The Philosopher Responds to His Critics*, Nashville: Vanderbilt University Press.

Seigfried, C. H. (1996) *Pragmatism and Feminism*, Chicago: University of Chicago Press.

Sleeter, C. (2000/1) 'Diversity vs. White Privilege: An Interview with Christine Sleeter', Rethinking Schools Online.

Spencer-Wood, S. (1992) 'Introduction to Critiques in Historical Archaeology', *Annual Meetings of the Society for Historical Archaeology*, Kingston, Jamaica.

—— (1997) 'Pragmatism and Feminism', paper presented at the Annual Meeting of the American Anthropological Association, Washington, DC, November 1997.

Stoecker, R. (1997) 'Are Academics Irrelevant? Roles for Scholars in Participatory Research', *American Sociological Society*. http://comm-org.wisc.edu/papers98/pr.htm.

Tilley, C. (1989) 'Archaeology as Socio-political Action in the Present', in V. Pinsky and A. Wylie (eds) *Critical Traditions in Contemporary Archaeology*, Cambridge: Cambridge University Press.

West, C. (1989) *The American Invasion of Philosophy: A Genealogy of Pragmatism*, Madison: University of Wisconsin Press.

Wise, T. (2002) 'Honky Wanna Cracker?' in C. Rose (ed.) *STAR: Students and Teachers Against Racism*, http://www.racismagainstindians.org/WhitePrivilege/HonkyWannaCracker.htm (accessed 8 May 2009).

Wylie, A. (1985) 'Putting Shakertown Back Together: Critical Theory in Archaeology', *Journal of Anthropological Anthropology* 4, 133–47.

Part IV

HERITAGE METHODOLOGIES: INVESTIGATING THINGS

13

THE USE OF GIS
IN LANDSCAPE HERITAGE
AND ATTITUDES TO PLACE

Digital deep maps

Matthew Fitzjohn

Introduction

This chapter addresses the ongoing development of information and communication technologies (ICT) as tools in archaeological research, cultural resource management (CRM) and Heritage Studies. The term ICT covers a wide range of new media and technologies, including, but not limited to, the use of computer game software or virtual environments for the production of digital versions of cultural heritage sites like Stonehenge or Thebes, social networking software, and cross-media interaction where these media are all merged. ICT offers enormous potential for the recording, documenting and archiving of cultural materials and sites, enabling new forms of analysis and reconstruction. They can also provide new modes of communicating and presenting information that would not otherwise be possible (Giaccardi *et al.* 2008; Malpas 2008).

Importantly, ICT media are not merely tools for recording, reproducing and publicising heritage. They can further the development of heritage practices, and help us to think about how we document and present sites, materials and intangible heritage in ways that were previously unimagined. In doing so, ICT can help to capture the value of heritage, raising awareness of the importance of cultural heritage for our sense of the past and our sense of place (Giaccardi *et al.* 2008: 195–6). These media can enable new forms of engagement with place by drawing upon neglected sensory modalities or by bringing to the fore aspects of the place that are difficult to access or have gone unnoticed. Despite these possibilities, we have to ask ourselves whether a sense of place can be separated from the location to which it otherwise belongs: can we appreciate place without being in place (Malpas 2008)?

It is surprising that Geographical Information System (GIS), with its ability to locate data in their spatial context, has not been taken forward as a means to recreate heritage while maintaining its geographical specificity, albeit in a digital environment. Perhaps it is because despite the dramatic rise in the utilisation of GIS as a way to manage and visualise our data, we routinely display our representations of cultural heritage as maps. We transform the real world into a manageable and understandable form, representing the world from the top down, with symbols, lines and polygons representing our heritage data. Even within the digital environment of the GIS, our representations are often flat, failing to convey a real sense of the space that we are trying to represent.

My position here is that GIS can actually allow new ways of approaching heritage in space, as part of a landscape. This means we can examine our data in place, but only if we see the medium as a dynamic platform with which we can be creative when expressing and investigating both our data and ideas. I also suggest that to do this requires us to reconsider how our instruments, data and media are mixed intimately into our practice (the method, recording, analysis and output). Rather than regarding each element as a stage of a discrete practice and interpretation, I see them as constituent parts in an ongoing process of place construction and a means to enrich and illuminate our understanding and experience of the heritage of a place.

The discussion will be illustrated with an example of the ongoing development of a GIS for the Troina Project, a landscape project based on and around the town of Troina in Sicily. The project is an interdisciplinary study incorporating multiple methodologies and ways of examining the long-term history of Troina. For Troina, we have been collating contemporary, historical and archaeological data – juxtaposing text, image and sound. Within this discussion, I will focus on a number of the methods we have used to create an environment within which we can collate our different datasets to contrast and complement each other in order to create what Pearson and Shanks have referred to as a kind of 'deep map' (2001), in this case in a digital environment.

GIS in archaeological research and cultural resource management

The majority of data that we are interested in is either spatial in nature or has a spatial attribute; artefacts, structures and sites are all located in space and typically we record their coordinates to place them in context. Knowing the location and context of our data helps us to understand the significance of the archaeological record as well as how to monitor and manage the cultural resources in terms of development and environmental impact. In the past few decades, the quality and volume of our data have increased dramatically: continued surveying and the ever-expanding inventory of archaeological sites and cultural resources require the creation of systems to store and maintain the data. GIS is now regarded as the essential tool for the effective management of spatial records and has become ubiquitous in archaeological research and cultural resource management. However, the storage of increasingly large datasets of archaeological sites and historic information should not be the only aim for the creation of a GIS, just as with other types of ICT. As important as data management and retrieval are, it is the ability of GIS to perform spatial and attribute analysis that has been key to its widespread adoption. Within GIS it is possible to examine spatial relationships between sites of different period or type, to create predictive models to determine the probability of encountering certain types of sites on a given unit of land, and even to query the number of known sites within a kilometre of a proposed land development. Furthermore, GIS can provide visualisation of our records and different analyses to enable communication to a wide range of stakeholders on a project team or to the associated groups in the environmental, planning, development or political sectors.

Despite the widespread uptake of GIS, extensive discussions and innumerable publications on the subject, they are not revolutionary in technical terms (Wheatley 2004). GIS simply comprises a variety of hardware and software including database management systems and computer-aided design and mapping. As such there has been a tendency for GIS visualisations of archaeological or cultural material to take the form of distribution maps that are offered as representations of particular cultural landscapes. The creation of a map links a predetermined territory of interest with features and attributes that have been selected by the mapmaker. Despite claims to neutrality, neither paper nor digital maps are inert records of topography or passive reflections of the world of objects. They are socially constructed forms of knowledge that represent a way of conceiving, articulating and structuring the world (Daniels and Cosgrove 1988; Harley 1988). The creation of a map distances the observer from the landscape that it represents: simplifying reality for disciplinarian purposes of inspection.

Inevitably, all maps embody their author's prejudices and partialities, and the map reveals not the 'world' but the agency of the mapmaker. Thus, preferences of the mapmaker determine what is included or excluded from the representation of reality. The mapmaker's attention will focus upon, classify and represent what they perceive to be of interest; in contrast, what they deem to be uninteresting or irrelevant is excluded. Thus there are 'silences' on maps that ultimately have consequences; they exert as much influence on the viewer as the features that are depicted (Harley 1988: 290–2).

For this reason, critics have questioned the suitability of GIS for analyses of how we understand place; arguing that it perpetuates the problems of standardised cartography, causing us to continue to gaze at our data in a particular way (Thomas 2004: 200; Webmoor 2005; Witmore 2006). Within geographical information science these problems have long been recognised (Longley et al. 2001; Rambaldi et al. 2006). Actually, practitioners of GIS rarely consider their outputs as definitive representations of a reality; they are more frequently used in a suggestive manner (Sturt 2006). Rather than assuming, as Thomas (2004: 200) and others have done, that there is a conflict between the use of GIS and investigations of cultural landscapes and place, I argue that GIS provides an ideal context in which we can move beyond simply looking at our data from the top down. We can turn our ideas of our data and the appropriate uses of GIS on their head by combining a wider range of landscape and heritage elements that represent different understandings, memories and emotions of place.

The potential of GIS is already recognised within geographical information science, in particular in the realm of CRM in developing countries. Participatory GIS (PGIS) (whether in digital and physical cartographic or model form) has been developed to integrate people's spatial knowledge and diverse forms of information (quantitative and qualitative) in order to represent the existence of multiple realities of a place. Geo-referencing and visualising Indigenous Spatial Knowledge (ISK) help communities to promote their claims for the control over ancestral lands and cultural resources (including traditional knowledge), as well as to engage in two-way communication with higher-level government and economic bodies (Rambaldi et al. 2006).

One of the most recent and well-developed examples of PGIS is a joint Cambodian and international programme that has been developing collaboration policies, monitoring approaches and GIS for site management of the Angkor World Heritage site in Cambodia (Fletcher et al. 2007). A wide range of traditional and non-traditional datasets have been gathered within this programme. Remote sensing data including aerial photography, radar and high-resolution satellite imagery have been gathered to monitor land-use practices and landscape change. These data have been combined with existing records of the archæological sites and intensive ground survey to assess the impact of development and land-use change on the World Heritage site. Semi-structured interviews with local villagers were carried out to provide local meanings for the natural and cultural features of the landscape. Local terms and place names have been used to document indigenous conceptions and memories of the landscape.

These different sources of data have been incorporated into the site PGIS to ensure that different local, regional and international perceptions are effectively represented in decision-making on heritage and development through participatory planning. GIS data-structures are being developed to assemble images, local-knowledge maps, traditional place names and other forms of knowledge to be linked to spatial locations. The PGIS is intended to address the conceptual and methodological problems of managing the entangled relationship of heritage, environment, development and social life at Angkor.

PGIS has provided a new forum through which people can express their ideas of place and be involved in the development and management of resources. The strategies of PGIS, including the integration of disparate datasets and the inclusion of different perceptions and representations, have great relevance for the development of GIS in archaeological and heritage research.

In archaeology and among archaeologists, different data types are not ascribed the same scientific value (Webmoor 2005: 56). There is a distinction between primary and supporting evidence. Photographs, for example, are a means to record sites and artefacts but are not a primary data source; this distinction is credited to the section drawing or site plan and map (Shanks 1997: 74). In contrast to such hierarchisation of archaeological data, PGIS reveals the benefit of using a wide variety of media to inform the understanding of a landscape. Contrary to what some critics might think, we can explore spatiality, archaeological evidence and cultural heritage by using GIS to integrate, analyse and visualise traditional data together with the less familiar data that are often regarded as supplementary to 'real' interpretation.

In this sense, GIS could provide the perfect medium for the creation of what Pearson and Shanks have called deep maps:

> rich collations and juxtapositions of the past and the contemporary, the political and the poetic, the factual and the fictional, the discursive and the sensual; the conflation of oral testimony, anthology, memoir, biography, natural history and everything you might want to say about a place.
>
> (Pearson and Shanks 2001: 64–5)

Pearson and Shanks were concerned originally with narrative or some form of storytelling in performance or art installation. Building on this idea, Shanks and his colleagues have rightly suggested, in their collaborative project through Stanford University, that these modes of articulation and engagement can develop through web-based social software forums such as Traumwerk, a website where various media, online publication and comment have been brought together. The following sections introduce a GIS project on Troina that builds upon work in PGIS and in ICT environments such as Traumwerk to explore how we can make use of cultural material to make sense of place.

Troina

Troina is a small town in the southern limits of the Nebrodi mountain range in the Enna province of Sicily. Located on the Monte di Troina, between the twin peaks of Monte Panteon to the west and Monte Mugana to the east, Troina is the highest inhabited town in Sicily at about 1,120 metres. Once the capital of Roger II's Norman kingdom in 1063, the town and region were the site of one of the most famous battles in the 1943 confrontation in the fight for Sicily. In the past fifty years Troina has been the focal point for the Oasi, an international research centre and hospital (Figure 13.1).

As a result of the Oasi's development and construction programme, parts of the town have been the subject of detailed archaeological and historical research that has documented Troina's existence as a Hellenistic town through to the

Figure 13.1 Troina: map of the town and area of archaeological research. Field survey units are marked on the regional map, which was created using ArcGIS.

consequent Roman (Militello 1961; Scibona 1980: 377–86; Ragusa 1995: 33–7), Saracen and Norman occupation.

Since 1997, the Troina Project, which is directed by Drs Caroline Malone and Simon Stoddart, has developed interdisciplinary landscape research to investigate the occupation of the town and upland valley system from prehistory through to the modern period. The project has four main components: excavation (Ashley *et al.* 2007; Malone and Stoddart 2000a, b; Malone *et al.* 2003), geomorphological study of landscape development and degradation (Ayala 2004; Ayala and French 2003, 2005), intensive archaeological field survey (Ayala and Fitzjohn 2007), and historical research in the town and of the regional land-use practices (Ayala 2004; Walker 2007).

The Troina GIS

At the inception of the project, GIS was developed to provide, on one level, the means with which all of the members of the project could input, manage and integrate the disparate datasets produced by each of the small studies within this overarching project. A secondary aim was to use the GIS as a means to visualise the location, spatial extent and density of the data (predominantly archaeological material) across both individual sites and the entire survey region.

We have been using ESRI's ArcGIS to manage and analyse our data. The GIS has been created in a similar way to that on many other archaeological landscape projects. We have a mixture of raster and vector layers that represent a wide range of information ranging from topography and geology (raster layers) to field survey units (vector layers). Each of these layers has associated data ranging from artefact information attached to the layer of field survey units to attributes of the different geological types (Figure 13.2). At this level, the Troina GIS offers what most other archaeological project GIS does. It has proved to be an invaluable way to visualise and investigate the material recovered in the different surveys. For example, the individual who is interested in the location of all prehistoric sites in the region can visualise the total distribution of prehistoric artefacts that were recovered in the field survey. If they want further information, they can categorise these locations according to the typology of recovered artefacts or perform a quantitative analysis to recover the number of survey units from a particular period in prehistory and according to the number of artefacts. These data can also be examined in relation to other sources of information such as topography or other datasets ranging from the local geology to the elevation.

While the GIS has provided a range of possibilities to visualise and interpret our data, it could be used to produce little more than maps of concentrations of finds. In this way, it could produce the digital version of a traditional

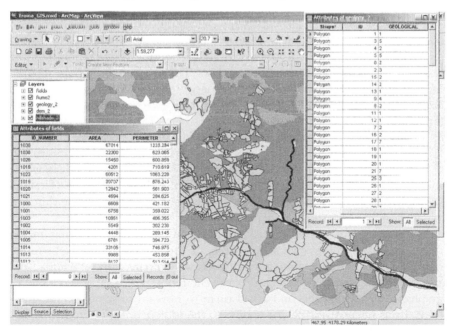

Figure 13.2 Screen shot of digital geology map overlain by field survey units and the river, with their associated data represented in the open spreadsheets

distribution map. It may allow us to see patterns in our data more easily but often we end up visualising our material in a rather traditional way, perpetuating what Thomas and others have objected to (e.g. Thomas 2004) rather than enabling new forms of engagement and understanding of place. However, the Troina GIS does not only provide a way to visualise the usual forms of archaeological landscape data. The Troina Project represents a collaboration of scholars who have been involved in a range of interconnected activities, ranging from archaeological and historical research to oral history and photographic documentation, that have produced a variety of data types, including but not limited to spreadsheets, text, illustrations, photographs, video and audio footage. Our GIS is the place where many of these disparate forms of data are finding a home.

One of the main ways that we have been collating and accessing these data is by using the often underutilised hyperlink tool to connect photographs, drawings and spreadsheets to our more traditional data. One of the clearest examples of the use of this tool is the way that we can access the conversations with farmers and members of the local community, which were an essential component of the archaeological field survey and geoarchaeological research. These conversations provided an invaluable source of information on historic land-use change and the location of locally known archaeological sites. Furthermore, the interviews began to reveal the complexity of what we, as archaeologists, may have referred to as the Troina landscape.

There were two levels of work with the local population. The first often happened in an *ad hoc* fashion as we were walking the fields of the valley system or buying bread at the local *panificio*. A second form of conversation took the form of a series of semi-structured interviews. The structured component of the interviews was based upon the use of a variety of visual media to discuss life in the mountains (see Andrews (chapter 8) and Sørensen (chapter 9) in this volume for studies using semi-structured interviews). Here, I will focus on two aspects of the interviews: a photo elicitation study and a drawing task (see chapter 14 (Lillehammer) in this volume for another example of the use of drawings) and their visualisation within the GIS (Fitzjohn 2007a). I have discussed elsewhere the possible ways that we could interpret and use these interviews (Fitzjohn 2007a, b); what is important in this discussion is the way that the different datasets can be accessed, visualised and analysed within the GIS.

The photographic elicitation task was based on a series of twenty-four images that I had taken in the town and territory of Troina. The photographs represented an equal number of images that I felt were intrinsically 'of Troina', and also those that I felt were not. During the elicitation task, I showed the photographs to the participants and asked them to respond to some specific questions. I was interested in their response to the subject of the photographs, not their perception of the aesthetic quality, the importance or value of the scene, or even whether they could identify where it was or what it was of. In the first instance, I was interested to see if they felt that the photograph was 'of Troina'.

Later on in the interviews, after we had looked at each of the photographs and the participants had offered their initial response to them, they were invited to discuss their ideas and impressions of the images in more detail.

The results of the photo elicitation study were then digitised as a means to view how those interviewed responded to the images. We created one vector layer that contained twenty-four polygons that correspond to the panorama in the relevant photograph. For example, the polygon that related to photograph number one represented how much space in the survey universe could be seen in photograph number one. Polygon 1 was also hyperlinked so that it is possible to view the photograph that it represents. The responses to the photo elicitation were input into a spreadsheet, which was then joined to each of the polygons. Doing this enables the user to compare the responses of the interviewees, by viewing how many photographs each person had recognised, and to evaluate which photograph was recognised as being the most or the least as 'of Troina' (Figure 13.3).

However, the identification of a photograph on a GIS map does not adequately capture the sometime contradictory meanings and interpretations of that photograph in the broader discussion. Without information regarding the reason why it was a valued image, it is difficult to read any real significance into the respondents' reactions to the photograph. In our GIS, the linked spreadsheet recorded all the descriptive responses to the photographs, so that

Figure 13.3 Three photographs from the photo elicitation study. The point from which the photographs were taken is represented on the map as a pair of glasses. The polygons correspond to the panorama represented in the photographs.

245

it is possible to evaluate why particular images were valued or seen as representative of Troina. The most obvious example of the importance of this kind of qualitative data was photograph twenty-four, which was of the sign that welcomes people travelling into Troina from the south and the east. The sign is located at the end of a straight section of the otherwise winding mountain road; it appears to have been located at this specific point in order to maximise its impact as a marker to the town. If the GIS was used to identify how many people felt that the photograph was of Troina, it would reveal that this was the second most recognised photograph, whereas the text file would reveal very different interpretations of the scene. The majority of the interviewees talked about the image in terms of its significance as the entrance to the town, but no one focused upon the road sign, which one might assume gives the image its significance. Instead, they talked about other aspects of the photograph: the bend in the road; the tree on the bend; or the view of the valley when one travels along the road.

The second issue, highlighted by both the photographs and the sketches, concerns how archaeologists construct their ideas of place and how those are projected upon the interpretation of both archaeological landscapes and the importance of heritage in a region. We often ascribe historic or cultural significance to objects, sites or locales that are not even seen or valued by others. The interviews in Troina showed that even those features that were highly visible and seemed valuable to us, the academics (and also outsiders), were not necessarily the most significant places for others. The places that were most commonly referred to by the interviewees, which resulted in the most discussion, and which appeared on the sketches that people drew of the landscape of Troina, did not have monumental markers. Moreover, only some of the sketches featured sites that are of archaeological significance. Most of the important places in the region were not visible to me – or if I had seen them, I had attributed to them a different meaning to that given by the interviewees. These were, for example, the places that produced the most delicious mushrooms or asparagus, were the favourite playgrounds of their childhood, or were the shortcuts to work or the best views for the sunrise. The significant locales in the landscapes of the Troinese were related to memories of the past and experiences of the everyday; they did not need to be defined by a monumental marker or be associated with what we may classify as cultural resources or sites of historic or cultural value. The visualisation and analysis of both the photographic elicitation task and the sketch maps illustrate how GIS has considerable potential as a platform where varied types of public participation with both qualitative and quantitative data can be collated, layered and evaluated to help us to think and speak about place. The privileged status of visual perception can be perpetuated within digital studies of landscape because ready-made tools exist within most GIS software for the analysis of visibility and inter-visibility (Gillings and Goodrick 1996: section 1.4). While many studies of visibility within GIS have proved to be invaluable for our understanding of the past, there have been very few that have incorporated sound; Mlekuz (2004) and Mills (2005a, b) are notable exceptions. Aside from the images and maps that we have been creating and bringing together, we have been recording audio and movie files of Troina.

The past twenty years have seen a growing interest in the archaeology of the senses, and in particular auditory experience. The importance of sound and auditory experience in our lives is without question; it is powerful in signifying existence, generating a sense of life and place. With sound we are always at the centre of both localised and more distant auditory spaces (Rodaway 1994: 103). Sound gives important information about the distinctive character of a location at different times of the day and in different seasons (Rodaway 1994: 106).

The majority of archaeological research into sound has dealt with acoustic properties or resonance of tool use, the acoustic properties of a place such as a megalithic tomb, or studies of musical instruments such as bells (Lawson 1999; Lawson *et al*. 1998; Watson and Keating 1999). Sound as a fundamental quality of everyday life has not been examined to the same extent, probably because of its ephemeral nature. It is temporal, continually coming and going, so typically we fail to consider the sounds or experiences of the valley system – what Schafer (1994) and others after would refer to as the soundscape, the sonic environment surrounding a person.

In contrast to archaeology, there are a number of web-based heritage sound and image archives, such as the Smithsonian Global Sound, the *Museo virtuale della memoria collettiva* (MUVI) and the *Silence of the Lands* at the University of Colorado, which have invited participants to record and map their soundscapes in urban and natural environments (Giaccardi and Palen 2008). In a similar vein, we have been identifying the different auditory characteristics and activities of the various areas of the Troina valley – for example, the sounds of the river, of walking, of the animals and the bells – and inserting them in the GIS. As the GIS user moves through the digital environment investigating the sights of the valley, they can click on a hyperlinked point and listen to audio clips that might make up an individual's soundscape.

We have not been limited to the sounds of the landscape alone. The landscape and all actions within in it are multi-sensual experiences (Gibson 1968: 31; Merleau-Ponty 2001: 233). We are open to include all types of qualitative and quantitative data from all of the different aspects of research. A perfect example of this is *La festa dei rami e della ddarata a Troina*, a month of festivities held annually in May in honour of San Silvestro, a Basilian monk and patron saint of Troina. The main focus of the festivities are two pilgrimages, *La festa dei rami* (by foot) and *La ddarata* (by horse), to the forest of Troina, which is 40 kilometres to the north in the Nebrodi mountains. As part of the historical research we have been digitising accounts of the festivals and identifying key locations of activities. This is supported with digitised routes of the processions to the forests; photographs of the costumes and the traditional Troinese food; and audio files and text documents of the traditional festival songs (Figure 13.4).

Figure 13.4 Screen shot of ArcGIS software in use. The question marks represent locations at which multimedia data were recorded. In this illustration: two photographs and audio file of *La festa dei rami e della ddarata a Troina* that can be viewed or heard in a media player.

A GIS user is able to investigate the history and activities of the festivals and examine other types of data such as different cost surface analyses. These methods were devised to incorporate principles of movement to understand the difficulty of processing from Troina to the northern forest, where difficulty of movement is based on the friction principle that it is more difficult to walk on an incline than on flat ground (Bell and Lock 2000; Harris 2000; De Silva and Pizziolo 2001). Furthermore, it is possible to investigate the points of the processional route that receive the highest and lowest temperatures during an average May, and thus which may have been more or less pleasant to walk along during the day or sleep out in the open during particular times of the festival. The GIS is enabling us to say things about the festivals, not only when and where they take place but also related to those who participate and their potential sensory experiences.

Conclusions

The Troina GIS began and continues to be a way for us to manage, investigate and visualise our data. The archaeologists are able to examine and make sense of the locations and distributions of both sites and artefacts, while the geomorphologists can study landform change. It has also become something more. The festival and the data from the semi-structured interviews are but two examples of the ways in which we are experimenting with our GIS. Influenced by PGIS, the development of our GIS is an ongoing process of what Pearson and Shanks may refer to as 'deep map' creation: a process through which we can remove the distinction between our different datasets, from maps of soil types or medieval mills to the sound recordings of flocks and festivals, as well as remove the distinction between the different media with which we may record and visualise our data.

The different datasets do not solely provide a way for us to understand the past. As I have stressed in previous work (Fitzjohn 2007a, b), the perceptions presented in the semi-structured interviews are not those of people in the past. The Troinese do not occupy or make sense of the world in the way that those who occupied the region in the Bronze Age or the medieval period did. However, for a project such as ours that is studying long-term landscape history, the sounds that we have recorded, tastes that we have documented (admittedly only through photographs) and knowledge that we have identified within the GIS are as valuable to our understanding of Troina as the distributions of Roman pottery or Iron Age tombs. They tell us about how this landscape is used, and manifest something of the complexity and temporality of this place.

Furthermore, the development of the Troina Project GIS has illuminated several important themes that may be of use to others who are working on archaeological and heritage projects. In the first instance, GIS is not just a tool to create maps. It has the potential to tie different parts of the same project together, to enable dialogue between those who are involved in archaeological research and those who are involved in more heritage-based research. It provides an environment where our varied types of archaeological, historic or even public participatory data can be collated and juxtaposed, evaluated and layered with the non-traditional data so that we can start to think and speak about place in new ways. Second, hyperlinking, an underutilised tool in GIS, can be used to provide access to field notes, audio files, photographs and personal memories; this increases the value of each dataset as it makes it possible for the different members of the project to read, view or listen to the data in its spatial context.

There are possibilities for developing GIS to run as web-based software, which would enable a wider range of people to become involved in the project, submitting and sharing their own sounds, sites and memories to our data. In this sense, our GIS would be similar to the web-based software of the *Silence of the Lands* (Giaccardi and Palen 2008), and would encourage an engaged and collective way of not only listening to but also viewing, discussing and thinking about all aspects of what makes the place that is Troina.

The creation of our inclusive GIS is removing the distinction between our data of the past and our data of the present. By doing this we hope to challenge the assumed understandings and practices of space; to offer a way to understand what Lefebvre (1991) has defined as the trialectics of lived space. In this view, the first space is the perceived time/space of everyday life, which is often represented in GIS in the form of the accumulation and mapping of the 'factual' knowledge about places and their relational properties; the second space is the conceived time/space of cognitive maps and conceived and imagined geographies; the third space is, in Soja's words, a 'rememberence-rethinking-recovery of spaces lost ... or never sighted at all' (Soja 1996: 81). Our GIS offers a third space which distinguishes it from the traditional binary mode of looking at place and heritage from either a material/real-world perspective or an imagined perspective; instead it allows us to look at Troina as a lived space in both the past and the present.

Bibliography

Ashley, S., J. Bending, G. Cook, A. Corrado, C. Malone, P. Pettitt, D. Puglisi, D. Redhouse and S. Stoddart (2007) 'The Resources of an Upland Community in the Fourth Millennium BC', in M. Fitzjohn (ed.) *Uplands of Ancient Sicily and Calabria: The Archaeology of Landscape Revisited*, Accordia Specialist Study on Italy, London: Accordia Research Centre, University of London, 59–80.

Ayala, G. (2004) 'Landscape/Land-use Change in North-central Sicily: A Geoarchaeological Approach'. PhD Thesis, Department of Archaeology, University of Cambridge.

Ayala, G. and C. French (2003) 'Holocene Landscape Dynamics in a Sicilian Upland River Valley', in A. J. Howard, M. G. Macklin and D. G. Passmore (eds) *The Alluvial Archaeology of North West Europe and the Mediterranean*, Rotterdam: Balkema, 229–39.

——— (2005) 'Erosion Modeling of Past Land-use Practices in the Fiume di Sotto di Troina River Valley, North-central Sicily', *Geoarchaeology* 20.2, 149–67.

Ayala, G. and M. Fitzjohn (2007) 'To Be Seen or Not to Be: Interpretations of Survey Data and Questions of Archaeological Visibility in Upland Sicily', in M. Fitzjohn (ed.) *Uplands of Ancient Sicily and Calabria: The Archaeology of Landscape Revisited*, Accordia Specialist Study on Italy, London: Accordia Research Centre, University of London, 99–113.

Bell, T. and G. Lock (2000) 'Topographic and Cultural Influences on Walking the Ridgeway in Later Prehistoric Times', in G. Lock (ed.) *Beyond the Map: Archaeology and Spatial Technologies*, Amsterdam: IOS Press, 85–100.

Daniels, S. and D. Cosgrove (1988) 'Introduction: Iconography and Landscape', in D. Cosgrove and S. Daniels (eds) *The Iconography of Landscape: Essays on the Symbolic Representation, Design, and Use of Past Environments*, Cambridge: Cambridge University Press, 1–10.

De Silva, M. and G. Pizziolo (2001) 'Setting up a "Human Calibrated" Anisotropic Cost Surface for Archaeological Landscape Investigation', in Z. Stancic and T. Veljanovski (eds) *Computing Archaeology for Understanding the Past, CAA 98: Computer Applications and Quantitative Methods in Archaeology; Proceedings of the 28th Conference, Ljubljana, April 2000*, Oxford: Archaeopress, 279–86.

Fitzjohn, M. (2007a) 'A Cognitive Approach to an Upland Landscape', in M. Fitzjohn (ed.) *Uplands of Ancient Sicily and Calabria: The Archaeology of Landscape Revisited*, Accordia Specialist Study on Italy, London: Accordia Research Centre, University of London, 143–55.

——— (2007b) 'Viewing Places: GIS Applications for Examining the Perception of Space in the Mountains of Sicily', *World Archaeology* 39.1, 36–50.

Fletcher, R., I. Johnson, E. Bruce and K. Khun-Neay (2007) 'Living with Heritage: Site Monitoring and Heritage Values in Greater Angkor and the Angkor World Heritage Site, Cambodia', *World Archaeology* 39.3, 385–405.

Giaccardi. E. and L. Palen (2008) 'The Social Production of Heritage through Cross-media Inter-action: Making Place for Place-making', *International Journal of Heritage Studies* 14.3, 281–97.

Giaccardi, E., E. M. Champion and Y. Kalay (2008) 'Editorial', *International Journal of Heritage Studies* 14.3, 195–6.

Gibson, J. J. (1968) *The Senses Considered as Perceptual Systems*, London: George Allen & Unwin.

Gillings, M. and G. Goodrick (1996) 'Sensuous and Reflexive GIS: Exploring Visualisation and VRML', *Internet Archaeology*, 1. http://intarch.ac.uk/journal/issue1/gillings_toc.html.

Harley, J. B. (1988) 'Maps, Knowledge, and Power', in D. Cosgrove and S. Daniels (eds) *The Iconography of Landscape: Essays on the Symbolic Representation, Design, and Use of Past Environments*, Cambridge: Cambridge University Press, 277–312.

Harris, T. (2000) 'Moving GIS: Exploring Movement within Prehistoric Cultural Landscapes Using GIS', in G. Lock (ed.) *Beyond the Map: Archaeology and Spatial Technologies*, Amsterdam: IOS Press, 116–23.

Lawson, G. (1999) 'Getting to Grips with Music's Prehistory', in A. F. Harding (ed.) *Experiment and Design: Studies in Honour of John Coles*, Oxford: Oxbow Books.

Lawson, G., C. Scarre, I. Cross and C. Hills (1998) 'Mounds, Megaliths, Music and Mind: Some Thoughts on the Acoustical Properties and Purposes of Archaeological Spaces', *Archaeological Review from Cambridge* 15.1, 111–34.

Lefebvre, H. (1991) *The Production of Space*, trans. D. Nicholson-Smith, Oxford: Blackwell.

Longley P.A., M. F. Goodchild, D. J. Maguire and D. W. Rhind (2001) *Geographical Information Systems and Science*, Chichester: John Wiley.

Malone, C. and S. Stoddart (2000a) 'A House in the Sicilian Hills', *Antiquity* 74, 471–2.

—— (2000b) 'A Contribution towards the Understanding of Serraferlicchio', *Sicilia Archeologica* 33, 97–103.

Malone, C., G. Ayala, M. Fitzjohn and S. Stoddart (2003) 'Under the Volcano', in *Accordia Research Papers*, London: Accordia Research Centre, University of London.

Malpas, J. (2008) 'New Media, Cultural Heritage and the Sense of Place: Mapping the Conceptual Ground', *International Journal of Heritage Studies* 14.3, 197–209.

Merleau-Ponty, M. (2001) *Phenomenology of Perception*, trans. C. Smith, London: Routledge.

Militello, E. (1961) 'Troina: Scavi effettuati dall'Istituto di Archeologia dell'Università di Catania negli anni 1958 e 1960', *Notizie degli Scavi di Antichità* 15, 322–404.

Mills, S. (2005a) 'Sensing the Place: Sounds and Landscape Perception', in D. W. Bailey, A. Whittle and V. Cummings (eds) *(Un)settling the Neolithic*, Oxford: Oxbow, 79–89.

—— (2005b) 'Auditory Archaeology at Çatalhöyük', Çatalhöyük 2004 archive report. http://www.catalhoyuk.com/archive_reports/2004/ar04_40.html.

Mlekuz, D. (2004) 'Listening to Landscapes: Modelling Past Soundscapes in GIS', *Internet Archaeology*, 16. http://intarch.ac.uk/journal/issue16/mlekuz_toc.html.

Pearson, M. and M. Shanks (2001) *Theatre/Archaeology*, London: Routledge.

Ragusa, G. M. R. (1995) *Insediamenti antichi in territorio di Troina*, Catania: Università degli Studi di Catania.

Rambaldi, G., A. P. Kwaku Kyem, P. Mbile, M. McCall and D. Weiner (2006) 'Participatory Spatial Information Management and Communication in Developing Countries', *Electronic Journal on Information Systems in Developing Countries* 25.1, 1–9.

Rodaway, P. (1994) *Sensuous Geographies: Body, Sense and Place*, London: Routledge.

Schafer, R. M. (1994) *The Soundscape: Our Sonic Environment and the Tuning of the World*, Rochester, VT: Destiny Books.

Scibona, G. (1980) 'Troina 1: 1974–1977, Nouvi dati sulla fortificazione ellenistica e la topografia del centro antico', *Estratto da Archivo Storico Messinese* 31 (series III): 349–89.

Shanks, M. (1997) 'Photography and Archaeology', in B. L. Molyneaux (ed.) *The Cultural Life of Images: Visual Representation in Archaeology*, London: Routledge, 73–107.

Soja, E. W. (1996) *Thirdspace: Journeys to Los Angeles and Other Real-and-Imagined Places*, Oxford: Basil Blackwell.

Sturt, F. (2006) 'Local Knowledge is Required: A Rhythmanalytical Approach to the Late Mesolithic and Early Neolithic of the East Anglian Fenland, UK', *Journal of Maritime Archaeology* 1, 119–39.

Thomas, J. (2004) *Archaeology and Modernity*, London: Routledge.

Walker, L. (2007) 'Populating the Medieval Upland Landscape of Troina: A Review of the Published Documentary Sources for the 9th–15th Centuries', in M. Fitzjohn (ed.) *Uplands of Ancient Sicily and Calabria: The Archaeology of Landscape Revisited. Accordia Specialist Study on Italy*, London: Accordia Research Centre, University of London, 115–42.

Watson, A. and D. Keating (1999) 'Architecture and Sound: An Acoustic Analysis of Megalithic Monuments in Prehistoric Britain', *Antiquity* 73.280, 325–36.

Webmoor, T. (2005) 'Mediational Techniques and Conceptual Frameworks: A Model in Mapwork at Teotihuacan, Mexico', *Journal of Social Archaeology* 5.1, 51–86.

Wheatley. D. (2004) 'Making Space for an Archaeology of Place', *Internet Archaeology*, 15. http://intarch.ac.uk/journal/issue15/wheatley_index.html.

Witmore, C. L. (2006) 'Vision, Media, Noise and the Percolation of Time: Symmetrical Approaches to the Mediation of the Material World', *Journal of Material Culture* 11, 267–92.

14

MAKING THEM DRAW

The use of drawings when researching public attitudes towards the past

Grete Lillehammer

An approach to conflicts in space

The spatiality of cultural heritage in the landscape is frequently the cause of dispute and outrage involving local communities. On a global scale conflicts in the landscape form part of social, economic, political and religious struggles between groups who have different interests with regard to the cultural heritage. It is a debate about identity and values, the vulnerable core of qualities that make up the contradictory attitudes of those who either cherish or despise the thought of having to live with the cultural heritage. Some would even consider dissonance to be a characteristic feature of the relationship between resource management and cultural heritage (Turnbridge and Ashworth 1996). My case study of such present-day conflicts, where two types of professional landscape management regimes were investigated (Lillehammer 2007, 2005, 2004, 2001), developed a particular method in order to overcome the dissonance between the two groups.

The overall objective was to investigate public attitudes towards cultural heritage in a rural district of south-western Norway (Figure 14.1), and to explore how these attitudes influenced the environmental management of the landscape. Notably, in this case the conflict between the two management groups was harsh and heavy, and had been so for a long time, which meant that the development of new methods suitable for analysing the hot social and political climate was required. The uncomfortable situation of dissonance in the landscape management made me decide on a research procedure from the phenomenological point of view of the practitioner. In order to stick to the practical side of the object of study, this is also how I will here present the process of searching for a suitable method.

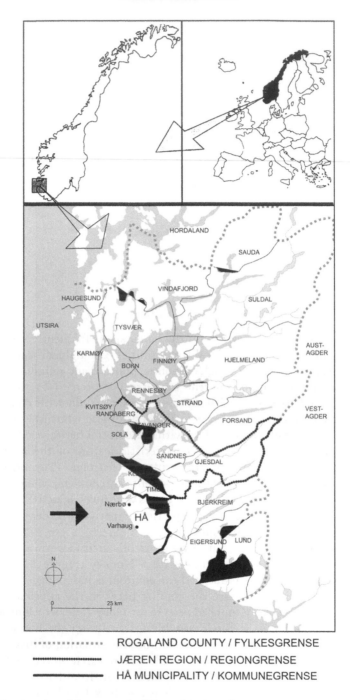

Figure 14.1 Location of the case study, Hå municipality of the Jæren region, Rogaland county, south-western Norway (source: Museum of Archaeology, University of Stavanger)

To start with my own point of departure, the initial idea, which remained influential throughout the study, was to use my qualification as an archaeologist and my early training as an undergraduate in art history and ethnology in the research. Apart from discussing phenomenology in the process of practising it (see Lillehammer 2005, 2004), my aim was to find an approach which could set aside problems already known to exist between the management groups. I expected the approach would open up new avenues for exploring the uneasy field of strained power relations between them, but which in the analytical process would need and allow a reflexive analysis to follow the investigation.

The approach was a matter of finding methodological applications suitable for this purpose, because in my case some of the means were already there. I had been awarded a scholarship from the Norwegian Research Council in support of the project which I had already initiated (Lillehammer 1996). General questions about the conflict had been formulated as a joint venture between two types of managers (Groups 1 and 2, i.e. farmers and environmental bureaucrats (including archaeologists)). Now, I was looking for theoretical and methodological approaches that could be used to study this in-between relationship of the two groups. I was sponsored by the Department of Archaeology, University of Cambridge, and was happily located in the University Library. Day by day I contentedly handled and systematically recorded books of interest. One day I found myself in the geography section of the library, and it was there that I found what I was looking for. What it was that I discovered on the shelves, I will return to later.

The project

The research of this case study was to investigate 'Landscape conflicts: cultural heritage and cultural perception. "Fairy ring" monuments, out-lying fields and heath-land in Hå municipality of Rogaland, SW-Norway' (Lillehammer 2007). This is a theoretical and empirical study of how management of the cultural heritage and the environment is perceived by the two different interest groups of bureaucrats and farmers in the local society. The study is limited to a district where much of the cultural heritage and the environment surrounding it are often in conflict with agricultural land use and are therefore cleared away unintentionally or illegally by farming activities. The analyses include archaeological, palynological and geological investigations of a particular type of protected monument, which has been singled out to represent the cultural heritage specific to the rural district. To meet the demands of this scientific analysis, the category of monument had to be non-distinct in the environment and on the surface. To spot it, the managers need a special interest in the past landscape or specialist knowledge of its function and place in the cultural environment. Also, for preservation purposes the monuments and their environment must be vulnerable and threatened by specialised farming practice and land use adapted to the local environmental conditions (Lillehammer 2007, 2005, 2004; Lillehammer and Prøsch-Danielsen 2001; Prøsch-Danielsen 2001; Prøsch-Danielsen and Simonsen 2000a, b).

The monuments chosen to fit these requirements are a group of mysterious earthworks (Figure 14.2a–b), the so-called 'alvedans', in English 'fairy-circles', or in Orkadian 'fairy rings' (Lillehammer 2005:103, fig. 3a–b). The earthworks had been recorded, investigated and debated as favoured objects of local folk belief and superstition since the 1820s. The monuments consist of an enclosure defined by a bank and a circular, oval, rectangular or U-shaped ditch in loose deposits. These are linked with a specific type of environment, the coastal heath-lands of south-western Norway, which has an Atlantic distribution (Steinnes 1988: 8–9; Kaland 1979; Skogen 1974). The set-up of the study was two-sided. It aimed firstly to increase the knowledge about the age, function and context of the earthworks in relationship to the environment, and to answer the question of continuity–discontinuity in the past landscape compared to the present-day landscape. Second, the aim was to gain a wider understanding of the cultural perceptions and attitudes among present managers of the rural landscape towards the protection of these monuments and their environment.

The interdisciplinary investigation revealed that the monuments selected for examination were the bases of haystacks in the marginal land of outfields dating to between the end of the Early Iron Age (cal. AD 410–50) and recent periods (AD 1835–c. 1970) (Lillehammer 2007, 2005, 2004; Lillehammer and Prøsch-Danielsen 2001; Prøsch-Danielsen 2001). It also showed that knowledge of the fairy myth tradition as well as that of the long and enduring tradition of original use was now extinct or almost dying out among the local farmers. The findings supported the information which was collected regarding attitudes towards the preservation in the landscape. There is a difference in cultural attitude between farmers and bureaucrats. The two professions of landscape managers represent interests that have the potential for conflicts in the future. Their perspectives differ; they have a different time perspective, both 'backwards' and 'forwards', as expressed in how they perceive farming as either a long or short history, in choice of value and in their perception of the landscape (Lillehammer 2007, 2005).

The idea of drawing landscapes

Here I shall not dwell on the details of this interdisciplinary collaborative study, but focus on the methods, which were used to carry out the second part of the study. In the first part I had asked about the pre-modern background to the historic relics, their environment and change of use (Lillehammer 2005: chapter 5; 2004). Now, however, I was looking for methods that could link the first part with the second part of the research. I was asking about the attitudes which formed the modern background for the preservation or destruction

(a)

(b)

Figure 14.2 Fairy rings: (a) Fairy ring in grassy field at summertime (photo: Lisbeth Prøsch-Danielsen), (b) Fairy ring in pasture at wintertime. A large stone is situated in the ditch (photo: Lisbeth Prøsch-Danielsen).

257

of the monuments in these people's environment. In particular I wanted to catch the cultural gaze of farmers towards outfields and outland (Lillehammer 2007) and to use this as the basis for understanding their attitudes towards environmental management, which the public perceive as most properly carried out by bureaucrats.

The initial plan was to interview both farmers and bureaucrats about their knowledge of the historic relics and their views on the management of the cultural environment which aim at preventing it from being further cultivated. The challenge was how to approach the problem of testing these recordings in relation to attitudes towards the marginal landscape of outfields and outland. As mentioned previously, I had brought myself as far as the shelves in the geography section of the University Library. I was browsing through an American handbook on human geography for planners of land use (Lowe and Pederson 1983). One chapter dealt with the issue of perceiving environments. Another chapter discussed the partitioning of space and the allocation of land in non-capitalist economies compared with the allocation of profit maximisation and competition in modern capitalist economies.

The outline in the handbook suited my approach well enough for dealing with a continuity/discontinuity pattern of land use which differed between a pre-modern and a modern landscape. In the handbook, I discovered six illustrations of cognitive mapping and understandings of the environment which caught my attention. Among these were two sketch maps of the city of Sunderland, England, two mental maps of Idaho Falls, in the USA, one map of crop distribution on a farm in central Spain and one model on the idealised zones of agricultural land use (Lowe and Pederson 1983: 34, figs 2–11; 36, figs 2–12; 224, fig. 11; 238, figs11–14). In the end, I decided to copy some of the relevant pages and put them among the collection of 'bright ideas' I gathered systematically while doing the literature study.

Making them draw

Back in Norway, while making preparations for the round of interviews with the managers, I decided to give the handbook collection a second thought. I figured out that making the informants draw landscapes would combine well with the situation of interviewing them. Each interview should end with a free invitation to draw, but I had to consider what type of landscape. As the focus of analysis was on marginal land management, an approach that might get it all in one shot was to concentrate on a single motif. This type of motif had to be more or less familiar to both groups of managers. A motif showing the typical farm in the rural district, the so-called 'Jæren farm', would tie the whole land property of each farmstead together, including the marginal areas in the outfields and outland. The motif would also cover aspects laid down and marked on the official ordnance maps (Økonomisk Kartverk). The general task of both groups should be to draw 'Jæren farm' as they saw it, and to name the inventory in the landscape. Their specific task should be to mark the location of cultural heritage remains, including fairy circles, and to mark the centre of the farm. In this way I expected the test to reveal their knowledge about the landscape distribution of ancient monuments and fairy circles and their perceptions of spatial locations most vital to the agricultural running of 'Jæren farm'.

Since the overall method was that of practising phenomenology (Lillehammer 2005, 2004), there would be no rules laid out for me to follow in this procedure. I did not know beforehand whether the procedure would be feasible or the results would end in complete failure. I decided to carry it out according to the above description in an experimental manner with both groups. I restricted myself to considering only the explanations given in the copies of reference literature on perceiving environments and partitioning space. These concerned the examination of distance as a dimension of images and the distance relationships that determine the arrangement of spatial schemata and the structure of mental maps (Lowe and Pederson 1983: 29). Cognitive maps are products of the mind's ordering of information. In general the conflicts of cultural heritage management often arise when farmers have initiated new plans for expanding the use of agricultural areas at the farms. The outcome of dealing with these plans is the result of outside decision-making by the heritage management. Therefore I anticipated various sets of landscape schemata in the mental ordering of the diverse conditions in the agricultural landscape, such as the distribution of buildings, land use, and natural and cultural resources in the landscape. However, I chose not to conduct an extensive critical reading about environmental knowledge with regard to theories, research and methods involved in such processes in preparation for the task. Instead I chose to make my way through the whole operation as freely and openly as possible to see what happened.

Nearly 80 per cent of the participants responded positively to the task of drawing the landscape of 'Jæren farm'. Only a few withdrew reluctantly from the task, giving excuses that ranged from being a bad draughtsman to being uninterested. Others were quite enthusiastic, performing the task at once, without any hesitation, and even producing three-dimensional images. Some of the participants sketched maps without even asking. Others stopped while struggling with the problem of solving the task given to them. When they discussed it with me, I made some suggestions about their own preferences, pointing at options such as sketching or mapping landscapes. The result came out as 97 per cent sketch maps (exemplified by Figure 14.3a), 2 per cent zone models (as seen in Figure 14.3b) and 1 per cent landscape sketches (Figure 14.3c). The sketch maps were rough drafts of landscape plans similar to the construction of ordinary maps. The zone models were drawings of principal landscape structures according to a zonation from the centre to the outskirts of the agricultural land. The landscape sketches were drawings of three-dimensional landscapes (Lillehammer 2005: 199, fig. 55A–F). While carrying out an evaluation of all the documentation (such as interviews, tapes, transcripts, notes, reports) collected for analysis, I noticed that the most representative record according to person and gender was actually the drawings made by the two groups. I decided therefore to use the drawings as the main source of study, and to include the interviews as supporting evidence in the analysis.

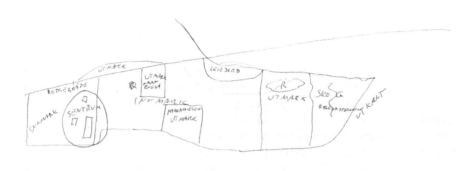

(a)

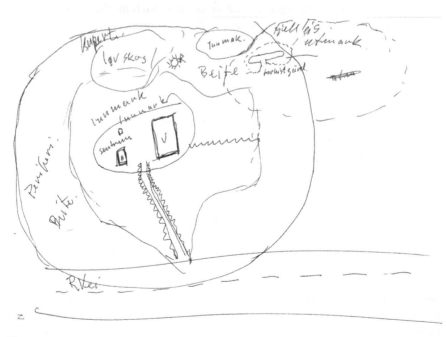

(b)

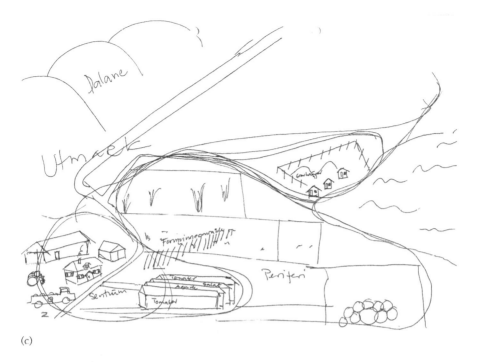

(c)

Figure 14.3 Three landscape drawings of 'Jæren farm': (a) Sketch map, (b) Zone model and (c) Landscape sketch

Beneath the surface

At this stage in the process, I was not clear about what else to do with the drawings. I concentrated firstly on getting the interviews into a readable shape in order to prepare the material for the analysis. Second, I looked through the copies of reference literature from the University Library seeking methodological advice, or at least I was hoping for some ideas that could serve as a way to continue with the research work. As the overwhelming majority of the drawings were sketch maps, I went back to the handbook and dwelled on the following passage:

> The mental map of one's immediate environment evolves to guide daily behaviour. Other mental maps evolve as organisational structure to arrange haphazardly acquired but potentially useful locational information. Both type of maps have behavioural implications. The mental map of one's immediate environment is used in day-to-day decision making ... Mental maps of more distant areas serve a number of purposes: motivation, decision making and spatial search.
>
> (Lowe and Pederson 1983: 36)

While reading the passage I recognised a distinctive structure of spatial schemata which could separate mental maps into different types in terms of their relation to human behaviour in the landscape. This meant that based on their spatial schemata the drawings could be divided into two distinct groups: (1) a type of map for daily use in the immediate environment, that is, the domestic landscape near to a habitat or the habitat itself, and (2) a type of map for organisational information purposes, that is, the landscape of surveillance far from the habitat. In short, there could be at least two different cultural images presented on mental maps. Maps are likely to be characterised in terms of their origin and date, their position in the development of techniques for surveying and production, and their geographical accuracy. They are also assessed as historic documents with hidden meanings (Delano-Smith 2001; Harley and Laxton 2001). When analysed critically in their proper context, the mapping practice could link the information presented upon drawings to the management of a cultural landscape and the legitimisation or transaction of power over the land. Deliberate distortion or manipulation of map content for political or other purposes by individuals, state bureaucracy or the market can be traced through the history of maps (see Harley and Laxton 2001: 60–5). These factors become evident when maps are considered to show ownership to property, property rights and the relationship between territorial divisions of land and long-term structural changes in the agricultural transition from pre-modern to modern landscapes (see Lillehammer 2007).

While pondering the construction of perspectives in the landscape drawings, I decided to spread out the whole collection, and to look it over in order to see whether I could sense some lines and forms of patterns. I recognised some similarities and differences between the drawings, which were difficult to single out without the application of a more refined method. I then returned to the interviews and concentrated on defining the managers as draughtsmen more closely. I had prepared a questionnaire for each group beforehand (Lillehammer 2005: 252–5; 2004) which I had used as a mental guide to support me during the interviews. The sessions had been taped, and a short report on the atmosphere and setting together with an abstract of the essential keynotes in the conversation had been summarised right after each interview. Afterwards, transcripts of the tapes had been typed, then sorted out and filed together with the drawings.

Now I would continue by analysing systematically the social background of the managers and their relationship to place and farmsteads in the landscape. I went repeatedly through the whole series of questions focusing on keywords in the questionnaire, such as 'farming', 'being a farmer', 'cultural heritage', 'landscape protection', 'preservation of outfields', 'outland'. By looking for those elaborations of subtle and intersecting factors that converge to form a particular interview (Briggs 1986: 22–3), I could engage with the interviews in a way that deepened my understanding of the patterns and see them as the index of an ethical relation between conflicting and competing elements (Lillehammer 2005: 178; Levinas 1996). I found that the two groups of professions had different social and practical lifestyles. However, except for a very small minority of bureaucrats, all shared a similar blending of official and private interests in their attitudes towards managing the landscape. The finds were disturbing from an ethical point of view. I had expected the bureaucrats to take a more objective stand to these questions than the farmers, and the results made me ask if some of these preferences were shown on the landscape drawings.

Next, I therefore decided to return to the drawings, looking in particular for spatial schemata in the landscape in order to compare the two groups of managers with each other. The drawings of the landscapes had been constructed as sequential arrangements of elements from a bird's-eye view without my instructions (see Figure 14.3 a–c). As the focus of the case study was on the preservation of cultural heritage remains in outfields and outlands, all the elements marked on the drawings were registered and ordered systematically, starting with the outskirts of the farm, followed by the outland/outfield, the infield, and then ending with the farmyard (Lillehammer 2005: 256–7; 2004).

The common references on the drawings by both groups turned out to be social, economic, legal, historic and geographic elements of the rural landscape (Lillehammer 2005: 200, table 10; 2004: 204, table 10). On the other hand, the landscapes differed from each other with reference to variation in details, such as place names, location of crop distribution, natural conditions and topography. Therefore, each group of managers had drawn landscapes that were distinct from each other (Lillehammer 2007, 2005, 2004). The analysis confirmed that the farmers had a more intimate relationship to their homesteads compared to the references of the bureaucrats, who – being outsiders – were more distant from the farms and had presented the landscape drawn from afar.

The strategy to follow from here was to define the landscape of 'Jæren farm' more precisely using the method of visual perception. I looked in particular for focal points in the landscape in correlation with the rectangular shape of the drawing sheet (Lillehammer 2005: 202–4, tables 11–15; 2004). The selection of focal points was based on two traditional models of integrated farming systems which included a centre and where the different economic, social and cultural parts complemented each other (Lillehammer 2007: 164–7). These focal points of interest were accommodated to include the draughtsperson's placing of farmyard, agricultural resource areas and archaeological heritage monuments in the landscape drawing of 'Jæren farm'. This included therefore locating and marking the perceived centre of the 'Jæren farm' as indicated by the draughtsperson's use of the paper size. In practice this was done by placing a grid system over the drawing and locating the centre at the crossing of the grid lines (Figure 14.4). It also involved locating the viewing position of the draughtsperson to establish whether a close or distant viewpoint was imagined when he or she was sketching the landscape (Figure 14.5).

Finally, the results were tested against the location of economic production areas and the distribution of archaeological heritage in comparison with the official ordnance maps (*Økonomisk Kartverk*), looking in particular for the

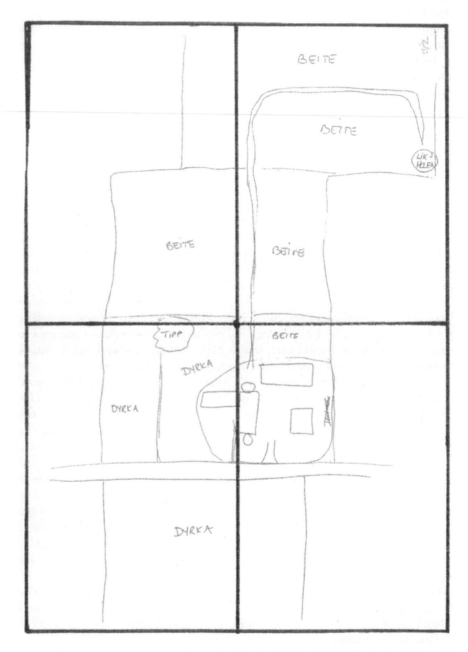

Figure 14.4. Marking the centre at 'Jæren farm' in the drawing of a sketch map according to a partitioning grid system

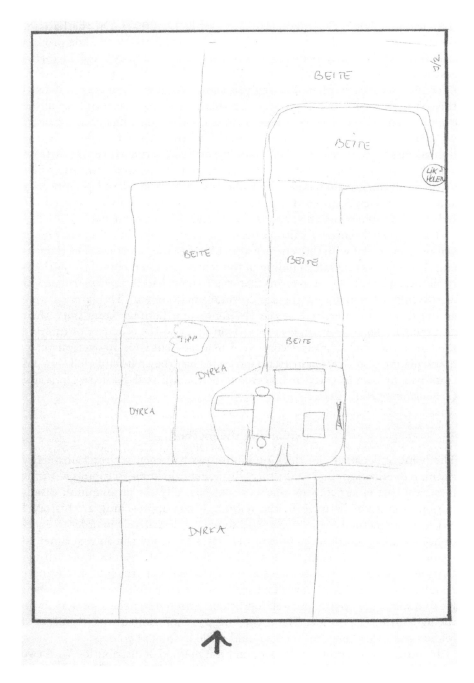

Figure 14.5 Location of the viewpoint position of the draughtsperson (position indicated by arrow) when producing a sketch map of 'Jæren farm'

distribution of cultural heritage remains in the drawings of the farmers (Lillehammer 2005: 207, table 16; 209, table 17; 2004). On the basis of these analyses I found that the two groups had cognitive landscape profiles that differed distinctly between economic–aesthetic and cultural historic–aesthetic values (Lillehammer 2005: 205, fig. 56; 2004), and that these were in conflict with each other. The analysis showed that the farmers rarely used the courtyard as the central point, but rather placed it at the periphery of the drawing. At the same time, whereas most of their drawings used a nearby viewpoint, the courtyard is perceived as the centre of the far. In contrast, the bureaucrats, if they centred their drawing on the courtyard, viewed it from afar or, more commonly, from another viewpoint. There were some examples of them producing drawings where the courtyard was placed peripherally and a nearby viewpoint used, but the majority of their drawings placed the courtyard peripheral on the page and used a viewpoint from afar.

The perceived centre of cultural heritage management in the environment was not concurrent with the centre of agriculture in the landscape. The bureaucrats had a far better understanding of the central requirements of the agricultural management of 'Jæren farm' than the farmers had in their management of the cultural remains in the agricultural environment. The farmers were ambivalent or uninterested in the environmental heritage issue since their cultural gaze lay elsewhere. Focusing strongly upon the economy of running the farms, they had a far more consistent management style of practical-pragmatic planning of a bio-industrial landscape than the environmental bureaucrats had in planning the management of the cultural heritage landscape (Lillehammer 2007, 2005, 2004).

Explaining the method

The point of departure for drawing landscapes had been my early university training in ethnology and art history. Ethnology aided me in coping with the historical part of agricultural phenomena, especially the geographical distribution of cultural heritage in the region. When approaching art history I rediscovered methods which were used somewhat intuitively in order to experience what happened in the process. This was carried out in an experimental fashion, and from my point of view the method was plain and simple sailing. Critically speaking, the approach was less conscious than the interdisciplinary research method featured in the first study of the 'fairy ring' monuments, their localities and the environmental conditions surrounding the monuments in the agricultural landscape. The procedure was more suited to the process of forcing one's backbones to come out and rattle in front of you.

In retrospect, I combined the geographical method of distribution with two central methodological traditions in art history. One was the formalistic tradition derived from Heinrich Wölfflin (Wölfflin 1957), which expressed itself in the comparative analyses of surface patterns from the lines and volumes in the drawings. The other was the iconographical tradition derived from Erwin Panofsky (1939), reflected in the emphasis on studying the underlying principles of the drawings in order to reveal the persuasion condensed in one work.

In this context I will comment on the second method, linked as it is with the first. In art history iconography developed as a method of looking at painting forms as a mode of literary representation. Due to the influence of the philosopher Ernst Cassirer, who wrote about symbolic forms, symbolic values were analysed in terms of what they imply within the imagery of a painting (Daniels and Cosgrove 2003: 1–4). Initially, I had begun my research by reading Cassirer (1994) to focus on the subject of cultural conflicts in the landscape. While writing this essay I was reminded of this particular relationship. How Cassirer influenced the approach of 'making them draw' is hard to tell in retrospect, except for his approach of 'reading what we see', and his symbolic thinking lingered in the deep recesses of my mind as a pre-thought. What I draw from the experimenting experience is that in the end the research method became my own accomplishment. Cassirer's thoughts made me look for structures underlying the patterns which governed the formal outlines of the drawings. This led me to interpret the symbolic levels embedded in the lines and forms of the landscapes, and to proceed even further by reaching for the areas governing the cognitive landscape of the managers.

Conclusion

In the end the results of the study suggest that both means and methods were successful. It is evident that the journey to Cambridge was worth all the time, money and energy invested in the visit. I actually found what I was looking for: a method that was easy to carry out for the participants. While examining the context I was working on I also discovered that my aim could be easily achieved in the analytical part of the research procedure. Thanks to the practice of the phenomenological approach, I had turned to the application of drawings more openly and freely than I would have in another more formal setting. I was working independently and on my own.

By linking the interviews with the methodological traditions of analysing landscapes in art history, the approach of formal and iconographic applications used on the collection of drawings is comparable to that of a diagnostician or the inspector in a criminal plot. The idea of maps as the manipulated form of knowledge of an empowerment of land use made it possible to approach the cultural practice of informants from a new angle, and to widen the scope of analysis. Not only did the method of drawing landscapes supplement the interviews, but it became the practical vehicle to look for meanings that were hidden on the surface, or difficult to reach only through the interviews.

In situations of strong spatial conflicts, such as between the agricultural and cultural heritage management on Jæren, the relationship between specialist professions is a paramount consideration. The lessening of tensions by having fun together opens new avenues for transgressing the protective boundaries of cultural intimacy (Herzfeld 1997). The practical method of drawing landscapes has obtained far more general theoretical implications on landscape perception and power relations than was expected at the beginning of the research investigation. Evidently the outcome of the study demonstrates the close link between theory and method in being an innovative process of transformation. The potentiality of applying methods generated from the theory of different disciplines stresses the importance for Heritage Studies and archaeology continuing to explore and even further extend its means of investigation.

Acknowledgements

Thanks to Marie Louise Stig Sørensen and the Department of Archaeology and Anthropology, University of Cambridge, for being my sponsor, the Norwegian Research Council for financing of the project, Bjørn Myhre for scientific advice, Lotte Selsing for administrative support, my workplace, Museum of Archaeology, University of Stavanger, for all the necessary support for the research project, and Ingegjerd Holand for the English corrections of the first draft of the essay.

Bibliography

Briggs, C. L. (1986) *Learning How to Ask: A Sociolinguistic Appraisal of the Role of the Interview in Social Science Research*, Studies in the Social and Cultural Foundations of Language series, Cambridge: Cambridge University Press.

Cassirer, E. (1994) *Kulturvitenskapenes Logikk. (Zur Logik der Kulturwissenschaften. Fünf Studien)*, Oslo: Pax Forlag.

Daniels, S. and D. Cosgrove (1988) 'Introduction: Iconography and Landscape', in D. Cosgrove and S. Daniels (eds) *The Iconography of Landscape: Essays on the Symbolic Representation, Design and Use of Past Environments*, Cambridge: Cambridge University Press, 1–10.

Delano-Smith, C. (2001) 'The Hidden Meanings of Maps', *Nature* 411, 133–4.

Harley, J. B. and P. Laxton (2001) *The New Nature of Maps: Essays in the History of Cartography*, Baltimore: Johns Hopkins University Press.

Herzfeld, M. (1997) *Cultural Intimacy: Social Poetics in the Nation-State*, London: Routledge.

Kaland, P. E. (1979) 'Landskapsutvikling og Bosetningshistorie i Nordhordlands Lyngheiområde', in R. Fladby and J. Sandnes (eds) *På Leiting etter den Eldste Garden*, Oslo: Universitetsforlaget, 41–70.

Levinas, E. (1996) *Den Annens Humanisme, Thorleif Dahls Kulturbibliotek, Det Norske Akademi for Sprog og Litteratur*, Oslo: H. Aschehoug and Co.

Lillehammer, G. (1996) 'Kontakt-Konflikt: Kulturminnevern og Kulturforståelse, Analyse av Utmarksmiljø i Hå Kommune i Rogaland', *Frá Haug ok Heiðni* 4, 30.

—— (2001) 'Alvedans-Haugtussas Syn eller en Gåte i Hverdagen?', *Frá Haug ok Heiðni* 1, 45–53.

—— (2004) *Konflikter i Landskapet. Kulturminnevern og Kulturforståelse: Alvedans og Utmark i Hå Kommune i Rogaland, SV-Norge*, Stavanger: AmS-Varia 42.

—— (2005) *Konflikter i Landskapet. Kulturminnevern og Kulturforståelse: Alvedans og Utmark i Hå Kommune i Rogaland, SV-Norge*, Stavanger: AmS-NETT 1, 2005 (http://www.am.uis.no).

—— (2007) 'The Past in the Present. Landscape Perceptions, Archaeological Heritage and Marginal Farmland in Jæren, South-Western Norway', *Norwegian Archaeological Review*, 40.2, 159–78.

Lillehammer, G. and L. Prøsch-Danielsen (2001) 'Konflikt som Kontakt. Kulturminnet Alvedans på Jæren', in B. Skar (ed.) *Kulturminner og Miljø. Forskning i Grenseland mellom Natur og Kultur*, Oslo: Norsk Institutt for Kulturminneforskning, 35–63.

Lowe, J. and E. Pederson (1983) *Human Geography: An Integrated Approach*, New York: John Wiley and Sons.

Panofsky, E. (1939) *Studies in Iconology: Humanistic Themes in the Art of the Renaissance*, New York: Oxford University Press.

Prøsch-Danielsen, L. (2001) 'The Environmental Aspects and Palyonlogical Signals of the "Fairy-Circles" – Ancient Earthworks Linked to Coastal Heathland in South-Western Norway', *Environmental Archaeology* 6, 39–57.

Prøsch-Danielsen, L. and A. Simonsen (2000a) 'Paleoecological Investigations towards the Reconstruction of the History of Forest Clearances and Coastal Heathland in South-Western Norway', *Vegetation History Archaeobotany* 9, 189–204.

—— (2000b) *The Deforestation Patterns and the Establishment of the Coastal Heathland of South-western Norway*, Stavanger: AmS-Skrifter 15.

Skogen, A. (1974) 'Den Vestnorske Lyngheien – et Kulturlandskap i Endring', *Forskningsnytt* 19, 4–6.

Steinnes, A. (1988) *Vern og Skjøtsel av Kysthei i Rogaland*, Ås: Økoforsk Rapport (1988): 1.

Turnbridge, J. E. and G. J. Ashworth (1996) *Dissonant Heritage: The Management of the Past as a Resource Conflict*, Chichester: Wiley.

Wölfflin, H. (1957) *Konsthistoriska Grundbegrepp: Stilutvecklingsproblem i Nyare Tidens Konst*, trans. B. G. Söderberg, Stockholm: Scandinavian University Books, Svenska Bokforlaget/Norstedts.

15

THE HERITAGESCAPE

Looking at heritage sites

Mary-Catherine E. Garden

Introduction

For those engaged in studying heritage, the notion of the 'heritage site' presents one of the most fundamental paradoxes in the discipline. On the one hand heritage sites are highly familiar spaces that tend to be readily recognised; on the other, after nearly twenty years our understanding of just what heritage sites 'do' and how they 'work' remains incomplete. This is not for lack of trying. Over the past twenty years considerable effort has been directed to investigating the myriad of places that fall under the heading of 'heritage site'. Yet, despite a widespread and almost innate familiarity with these places, a number of fundamental questions continue to be unanswered.

There are a number of reasons why so many issues remain unresolved but one of the most significant is that, to date, there is no agreed-upon or even widely used methodology which might be applied to heritage sites. Indeed, even the vocabulary we use and the sets of terms coined are by no means pervasive. Such is the extent of this trend that, despite an intuitive sense of what a heritage site is, currently there is no common or agreed-upon understanding of these places. Apart from the more obvious difficulties created by this omission, the impact runs much deeper and affects our understanding of the larger notion of heritage (Garden 2004).

Among the points upon which most researchers agree are the importance of heritage sites in the creation of identity (e.g. Smith 2006: 68) and in the development of a sense of 'the past' (Corbin 2002: 225; Little 2007: 139). Heritage sites are both tangible places, that is, bounded physical space, and cultural constructs – unique and highly experiential social spaces – and it is here that the paradox begins to emerge. As physical places – sites on the landscape – heritage sites are relatively easy to identify, yet as cultural constructs they are much more difficult to grasp. These qualities mean that in order to develop a means of analysis that will allow a better understanding of these unique social spaces, the methodology must be replicable and transparent, but it must also be able to capture a sense of heritage sites as both tangible and intangible spaces and also as places 'of the past'. This chapter will consider this challenge and will offer a new method – the *heritagescape* – as a means of addressing some of the problems currently surrounding heritage sites.

The key to the heritagescape is an acceptance of the notion that *all* heritage sites are landscapes. Thinking of a heritage site as a landscape has the important outcome of locating a site within its larger environment – offering a more integrated sense of these spaces within their surroundings. Another benefit of this is that we are able to draw on methods and theories arising from research in landscape archaeology, enabling us to better capture the complexities of a heritage site.

Research to date

Heritage sites are distinct spaces that make up some of the most familiar and tangible elements of 'the past'. Occupying a space on both the physical landscape and within the landscape of memory these places can act as markers or way-stones for individuals to connect to a wider sense of heritage and to locate themselves within the larger group and existing identities. As cultural constructs we know that heritage sites can be key to locating ourselves in time and space (Corbin 2002: 225; Davis 1999: 5, Harris 1995: 5; Teather and Chow 2003: 93; Walsh 1992: 105). As landscapes that take in both the tangible elements of a landscape of heritage and also the intangible, experiential qualities, heritage sites are less well understood.

Until quite recently a look at the index of most heritage-themed texts would have failed to produce even a single entry for 'heritage site'. Instead, one would find countless other terms, including 'heritage visitor attractions' (Leask and Yeoman 1999), 'heritage centres' (Carman 2003; Hems and Blockley 2006; Howard 2003; Walsh 1992), 'heritage experiences' (Millar 1999; Prentice 1991; Walsh 1992) and 'heritage properties' (UNESCO: http://whc.unesco. org). In the past few years 'heritage site' has begun to find its way into the indices of textbooks, readers (e.g. Corsane 2005) and monographs (Smith 2006); however, once again most of these are concerned with issues (e.g. interpretation or performance) at heritage sites rather than the sites themselves. This all might seem a pedantic splitting of hairs – particularly the listing of alternative terms which, after all, clearly refer to what most people would immediately recognise as a heritage site. However, I suggest that this profusion of terms is symptomatic of the much deeper issue of a lack of understanding of what qualities characterise heritage sites. Not only do we lack the means to investigate, we also lack the words to discuss these spaces.

The investigations that have been undertaken today can be characterised in terms of a few significant trends that have in turn influenced the current, accepted understanding of heritage sites. In the absence of a widely accepted or overarching methodology much of this early work still holds as the benchmark for new research.

One of the simplest, yet most fundamental, impediments to a more complete sense of heritage sites is a continuing failure to agree upon a collective list of those places which are most often described as 'heritage sites'. What may for one researcher be an obvious candidate as a heritage site may be something quite different for another.[1] In an attempt to resolve these and other issues surrounding heritage sites, many researchers have previously relied upon methodologies which are based upon a rigidly defined set of criteria. Using this tactic – essentially a 'laundry list' approach – sites have been compared using the presence or absence of key elements (e.g. Stone and Planel 1999). Typically, this entails using a template site, which often results in one heritage site being 'read' off another. What often happens in these cases is that the individual qualities – the personality – of a site are lost as we impose a veneer of 'sameness' on heritage sites.

Because it has long been the trend to *define* heritage sites based upon specific elements and/or imposed criteria, there has been a tendency to compare sites that appear to be similar. Thus it may be that while, intuitively, we recognise that, for example, not all museums are similar or operate in the same way, the inclination to group sites with the same titles together means that the understanding of their differences becomes hazy. Equally importantly, it can craft a false hierarchy of sites where one well-known or established site is set up as an exemplar; in this way a site like Stonehenge becomes the shorthand for all ancient monuments and the Swedish open-air museum Skansen stands in for all open-air sites. Once again this may lead to like being grouped with like, threatening to seriously limit any discourse. Usually it also means that any one analysis will cover only a very narrow range of sites.

Another important feature of the work undertaken to date is that much of this research has been polarised, with one set of studies focusing on how individuals react to, use or interpret a site, and another set concentrating on the material components of a site. The first approach is usually weighted towards the perceptions of the visitors and often fails to fully acknowledge the role of the landscape in creating those experiences. Others who choose to look at the messages being conveyed by heritage sites have focused their analyses on the tangible components of the site, viewing structures or other material elements as objects through which meaning is filtered. A common oversight here is a failure to consider the empty spaces in between the buildings/structures. More critically, this focus may result in the blurring of a critical distinction between objects as conveyors of meaning in display-based environments and those at a more experiential site. Ultimately neither of these two approaches is able to sufficiently account for the multiple functions of heritage sites, which can have important roles as interactive social spaces along with their more traditional roles of conserving, marking or preserving the past. This polarisation has prevented a comprehensive and coherent understanding of the complexities and the multiple processes that make up a heritage site.

One issue that has not yet been discussed is the role of change and other processes that occur at a heritage site. These notions remain underexplored and poorly understood. No doubt the long-held habit of viewing heritage sites as 'frozen' or 'static' (e.g. Cooper 1997: 157; Laenen 1988; Shanks and Tilley 1992: 85) has stood in the way of developing a fuller sense of the heritage site as a landscape. Without this it has been difficult to recognise the heritage site as a protean space, 'not so much artefact as in process of change' (Bender 1993: 3), and this has made it difficult, if not impossible, to identify the many processes that accompany a heritage site over time. In the 1980s and early 1990s there was a strong inclination to explore heritage sites as they were in the process of change from private or individual heritage to a public or group past. This was generally referred to as a process of transformation. This is of immense value, but it is not the same as understanding extant heritage sites and how they evolve and change over time. In those instances where the process of change explicitly has been included in an analysis, the attention was on the changes that occurred within the strategies of interpretation in the face of changing social mores and an evolving historiography (Gable and Handler 1996; Handler and Gable 1997; Knell et al. 2007; Lowenthal 1998: 135; Rowan and Baram 2004; Uzzell and Ballyntyne 1998).

Recent research suggests that many of the older ideas and influences that have directed the way that heritage sites are understood and analysed are, at long last, beginning to be replaced by a more nuanced and coherent understanding. In the process, accepted notions such as authenticity are being questioned. Rather than focusing on whether a site is 'real' we are beginning to understand that the 'vividness' of the experience is as important as whether it is 'real' (e.g. Holtorf 2005: 112). It is the way in which the site (and 'the past') is being conveyed and the resonance of the experience of the heritage site that ultimately will determine the strength of the sense of place. It is only more recently that we have come to fully realise that heritage sites are much more than undifferentiated space (Bagnall 2003; Mason 2005).

Looking back at these approaches, it quickly becomes apparent that to begin to grasp the notion of the 'heritage site' and to develop a coherent, replicable and transparent methodology, we need to acknowledge that these are protean spaces which are at the same time both distinct from and fully integrated into the larger landscape. Heritage sites operate both as places 'apart' and as places of 'the past'. While many authors have clearly comprehended this point, few, if any, have acknowledged it as a key feature of heritage sites or as a quality which impacts on the sort of experience offered by an individual site. Instead, most tend to get mired in the discussion of whether a site is 'real' or not. This quality of 'real' is rarely defined but most often ends up as an evaluation of authenticity. Although authenticity may be operating as a form of shorthand for other equally or more complicated notions, in practice it has come to obscure more nuanced ideas of place at heritage sites. I suggest what is needed is a duality of understanding and approach which will allow us, first, to develop a stronger sense of the individual heritage site and, second, to comprehend these sites as part of a larger network of heritage sites.

The heritagescape

The heritagescape as a method addresses many of these issues (Garden 2004). First, it is structured enough that it offers a replicable and transparent means of analysis, yet it is also flexible enough that it is able to accommodate the particular 'personalities' of individual heritage sites. Rather than being over-whelmed by the differences, this methodology looks for underlying qualities that characterise these places. Second, the heritagescape is not meant to provide a single incontrovertible answer. Any analysis of heritage and/or heritage sites needs to offer room for a variety of perspectives and interpretations and must be able to identify and account for the role of change. Thus, rather than creating a set definition, the heritagescape offers a measure – a constant – against which individual sites may be evaluated both as specific places and in relation to other sites. Inevitably disagreement will remain among scholars but critically the heritagescape provides a common vocabulary. Because it is based on a constant it is possible to use the heritagescape to evaluate how and why conclusions were reached both in the analyses of individual sites and in their comparisons. In the past not only did the methods vary from one analysis to another, often the criteria varied within the same analysis (see Shanks and Tilley 1992: 69). This made it virtually impossible to evaluate results or to compare sites with any sort of coherence. Finally, the flexibility of the methodology means that the heritagescape has an open-ended quality and can therefore easily accommodate other forms of analysis (e.g. visitor surveys) to supplement the information yielded from the application of the heritagescape methodology.

Although the idea of a heritage site as a landscape is not new[2] even the most developed of these ideas (in particular the geographer Rodaway's work (1994: 164) with 'themescapes') fails to grasp completely the complexity and the individuality of heritage sites as unique social spaces. Most work to date, including that considering the physicality of space and layout in museums (e.g. MacLeod 2005), has either not been universal enough or else it has been unable to adequately account for important and ongoing processes. Somehow, even when the idea of the heritage site as a landscape has been considered in an analysis, it has tended to be as a synchronic concept rather than a diachronic approach.

What is novel about the way I want to think about the heritage site as a landscape is the way in which the analytical concept of landscape as a social construction is applied to the question of what qualities affect the heritage site as a coherent and convincing entity. It must be remembered that this model is predicated first on the understanding that *every* heritage site (including enclosed spaces) is a landscape, and second on the assumption that there are universal processes which may be found at these sites. When thinking about the heritagescape it is important to recognise that it is both a method and a concept. As a concept it is a means of describing and thinking about those specific landscapes that make up a heritage site. While the heritagescape incorporates some of the basic constructs of landscape theory, it is a particular idea that relates wholly to heritage sites. It is distinct from but at the same time an integral part of the larger landscape in which it is located. Like the larger landscape, the heritagescape is more than the sum of its physical components, and while centred on the site itself, it may not necessarily be restricted to the physical limits of the place.

As a method the heritagescape, based upon a set of *'guiding principles'*, allows us to identify the components that make up a heritage site and to recognise the nature of the heritagescape as it is manifested at an individual site. This is a critical aspect of the methodology as, like in any other landscape, it is the set of individual components that, together, create a particular place. These elements play key roles in identifying the underlying processes and significantly highlight the process of change where it most often first occurs.

In this method, three guiding principles allow sites to be evaluated against a constant. Each of the principles, based around ideas of (1) boundaries, (2) cohesion and (3) visibility, together make up the heritagescape. It is the relationship and interplay of these three principles together that is a key component of this methodology. Thus, while all three must always be present (in order to have a heritagescape) it does not necessarily follow that they will always operate in exactly the same way or assume the same resonance relative to each other. As such, a site will have a 'robust' or a 'strong' heritagescape when all three of these principles are operating and in approximately equal proportions. What this means in terms of a landscape and its character is that an open-air museum with a 'robust' heritagescape will appear as a distinct, yet integrated space: a landscape. For the visitors this will translate into an experience that offers a sense of the site being both a place 'of the past' and a place 'apart'. This notion of the three guiding principles is intrinsic to the idea of the heritagescape because it is the means by which the individual and commonplace site components (e.g. the signs, the nature of the entrances and the paths) that make up the landscape of each site are first identified and later analysed and evaluated. The framework of the guiding principles remains as a constant, yet its ability to also accommodate the individual variations that occur at the site level is a fundamental aspect of understanding the heritagescape.

The guiding principles, in turn, are identified by applying them to tangible features – the *site criteria* – that are found at each site. These features consist of basic elements including fences, signs, objects and pathways that make up all sites. As there is no set list, however, the evaluation of the presence and/or nature of the site criteria remains at the level of the individual site where they can be identified and considered on their own. It is the second step, the application of the site criteria against the constant of the guiding principles, that makes it possible to evaluate sites within the larger context of heritage sites and to assess their relationship with other sites. Focusing on the site criteria as a first step means that attention is drawn to the individual components at a particular site. This is important for many reasons, but perhaps one of the most critical is that it aids in identifying change where it first occurs and where it is most apparent to visitors and others who interact with the site.

Before discussing some case studies in order to explore how the heritage-scape works in practice, it is useful to spend a bit of time looking very briefly at the three guiding principles.

Boundaries

The fencing-off, demarcating or acknowledgement of the landscape of heritage is a seminal act that defines the site. Entrances (into a site) are key components. Boundaries are an important aspect of the ongoing and original size, shape and appearance of the site. Comprehending the boundaries, how they subsume change and what they represent underlies the methodology of the heritagescape. While the physical boundaries of the site must not be dismissed, the significance of the envisioned and/or understood limits of the site must be underscored. It is very likely that this latter set of limits may turn out to have greater resonance than their tangible counterparts.

Cohesion

Simply put, cohesion is how the site 'holds together'. It is this feature that imparts a sense of 'place' to the site. This seemingly elementary statement may indeed be the most complex of the three guiding principles. At one level, cohesion refers to how the site works together in a physical sense (and here it is most closely linked to the concept of boundaries). In order to be cohesive, there must be a recognisable link that ties the individual components together. The point of this statement is not that the elements are similar; in fact, it is the very point that they are dissimilar that is a hallmark of cohesion. Central to the idea of cohesion is that all components – visible and invisible – of a site are interconnected.

Visibility

Visibility has two components: physical visibility and cultural (in)visibility. Beyond the more obviously physical visibility (i.e. what we see) there is the idea of cultural (in)visibility which refers to the way that tangible elements within the landscape may assume a greater or lesser presence depending on their roles and whether they are recognised or have been designated as 'heritage'. Cultural (in)visibility tends to emerge out of a changing vision of the past. Physical visibility is the means by which we recognise the tangible features that create a cohesive site and it is the way in which we identify the physical limits of a site. Importantly, visibility also encompasses the idea of a view or a gaze, and it is a critical aspect of visibility to consider where and how the line of sight is employed at a particular heritage site.

The actual analysis begins with site visits where the tangible components of the landscape are identified and assessed. These will be made up of ordinary and omnipresent elements such as the fences that define the edge of the site, the means by which to enter, and the signs and maps that direct visitors through the space. The public interpretative material (including guidebooks, maps, audiovisual presentations) also reveals the way that the institution perceives and/or hopes to portray the site to those who interact with it. Likewise, sources such as newspaper accounts, local authority or institutional documents (including management plans) or even interviews with staff will all give a sense of how the site is perceived from within and without. In the end, it is by recording the physical features and evaluating them against the envisioned site (as presented by the interpretative material and the staff) that it becomes possible to begin to identify how the guiding principles may be applied to the individual components present. In turn, by understanding the various strengths of the guiding principles a sense of the heritagescape begins to emerge. This means that not only is a site being analysed on its own merits, but because it is reliant upon the constant of the guiding principles it is possible to compare any number of sites using a single, coherent and overarching method. It no longer matters that the individual elements that make up one site are quite different to those making up another because, ultimately, it is the constant of the three guiding principles that will be used as a means of comparison.

Heritage sites, such as open-air museums, ancient monuments, 'traditional' display-based museums or any of the vast and varied places that have, as their primary mandate, a portrayal of the past by one means or another, do not exist as a single coherent entity. Rather, they are the result of often quite different, heterogeneous elements and, importantly, processes that over time create dynamic and changing landscapes. An important component of many heritage sites is the sense of the creation of a place of 'the past', and the tangible landscape usually reflects this. However, they are also visitor attractions, and thus the space making up a heritage site will, in addition to those devices that help to create a 'past' place, also include a variety of elements that are necessary to provide a visit and a landscape that is safe and amenable for visitors. Among the elements that need to be accommodated through specific measures are modern spaces such as car parks, toilets, workspaces, cafes and shops. Each of these features is a necessary component of a site; each one allows the site to function and also provides critical amenities for visitors and staff. As such they are a critical part of the experience. They are at the same time a challenge to the nature of the site and the difficulty comes in integrating these clearly modern and defined spaces or features into a landscape of 'the past'. The notion of the 'heritagescape' enables us to concentrate first on these individual elements (structures, artefacts or the spaces in between) as components of a larger landscape in order to study the material and experiential qualities of heritage sites.

By studying heritage sites as landscapes we can focus upon the boundaries, cohesion and visibility of the sites: elements that combine to create the 'heritagescape'. This is particularly important because there is a broad implicit assumption that sites categorised together do or should operate in a similar way. This has left no context in which to explore the disparities between sites. The case studies below will demonstrate that it does not follow that similar spaces will always function or use the past in exactly the same way and, in turn, will provide the visiting public with different experiences. Until now, there has been no means by which to explore such differences. The heritagescape as a means of analysis is able to overcome this.

Case studies

Given that the heritagescape is rooted in notions of landscapes, open-air museums and other outdoor sites are, at first glance, the most obvious candidates for analysis. The first case studies below – all open-air sites – illustrate the sort of information that may emerge from the application of the heritagescape.

The tradition of open-air museums is long-established within Europe, which is home to what is usually recognised as the oldest of these sites: *Skansen*, located on Djurgården, an island close to Stockholm's city centre. Founded in 1891 by Arthur Hazelius, Skansen is often cited as both the template and the exemplar for other open-air museums. Advertising itself as 'Sweden in Miniature', Skansen represents 400 years of folk traditions and portrays traditional houses and buildings relocated from all over the country – many of which are from farms or rural settlements – and grouped into a number of areas representing different regions of Sweden. Skansen also includes an aquarium, a children's area, a modern-style zoo and a natural heritage museum.

Inside Skansen there are very 'strong' areas where an encounter with the past is particularly vivid. Yet partly because of the size of the site and partly because of the variety of different roles that Skansen performs, the site does not hold together very well. The spaces between the main interpretative areas are empty, causing visitors to often lose track of 'the past', despite the fact that in the farmsteads and around some of the interpretative areas there is considerable stage setting (milk churns sitting beside the road, bicycles leaning against fences etc. (Figure 15.1)). Because of its great size the visual clues need to be strong, but in many cases not only are they weak, they are absent. Furthermore, several of the areas at Skansen have been given over to modern functions so that as a visitor one is constantly moving 'in and out of the past'. One minute the site appears like a public park, the next like a fair and the next like something of the past. Simply put, Skansen fulfils too many different roles to be a cohesive and defined heritage site. Indeed, because Skansen is not only a museum and a zoo but also a place for picnics and outdoor concerts, it does

Figure 15.1 Filling 'empty' spaces: Skansen Open Air Museum, Stockholm (photo by author)

not really even fully exist as a place apart. The sense of Skansen as a distinct place works to varying degrees and is best seen by considering the boundaries. While the limits of the site in the recreated areas tend to be marked by low fences, enabling a view of the city that helps to locate the landscape of Skansen within its larger environment, at the main entrance the boundaries are quite different. Here, the striped awning and illuminated signs are reminiscent of the Tivoli (amusement park) located around the corner, and rather than marking Skansen as a distinct place the places blend together to such an extent that recognition of the site limits becomes blurry. So, although Skansen occupies an important place in the hearts and minds of Swedes and acts as a cultural and folk icon, in fact, on the ground, it melts into its surroundings and takes on the appearance of just one more among the many attractions on the Djurgården.

The Danish open-air museum *Den Gamle By* offers an opportunity to look at a site which is apparently quite similar to Skansen. Although considerably smaller, Den Gamle By emerged from the same tradition of preserving and collecting the folk traditions that produced Skansen and was established soon afterwards in 1914. Like Skansen, it occupies a large urban site, but here there is a much stronger sense of being 'elsewhere'. Because the museum considers that 'the streets are rooms too' (B. Kjær, personal communication, 2001), the outside spaces become much more than the means to move from one place to another. As one moves through the site one can see and recognise the layout of town squares, city streets and even miniature neighbourhoods, all of which work together to create cohesion. Critically, at Den Gamle By one tends to remain within the past. The physical limits of Den Gamle By are not marked in a substantial way; in most cases the edges are marked simply by low (often wooden) fences allowing the area 'outside' the site limits to be seen. In contrast to the impact of the fences at Skansen the site is readily recognised as a distinct place that is also connected with its larger environment. This is due to the strong sense of place – brought about by each of the three guiding principles operating roughly equally and robustly. At Den Gamle By the surroundings complement rather than detract from the sense of place and from the experience of being 'in' the past.

Den Gamle By also offers the opportunity to look at the role of change within a heritage site. In 1998 the site added a large structure – the Mintmaster's Residence – into the Town Square, the heart of their interpretative area. This very large and imposing structure was slotted into the site, necessitating the removal of a significant portion of the hillside (which formed one of the boundaries of the site) as well as the relocation of two other buildings. As a familiar landscape for Den Gamle By's many visitors, it would be logical to assume that an intrusion like this into the centre of the site and into one of its central interpretative areas would have serious ramifications. Critically, it appears that this was accomplished without taking away from the essential identity of the site: the boundaries changed but the site did not. Both visibility and the marked, physical boundaries were altered, yet the site seems to have remained as a cohesive entity and the new structure has been assimilated into the landscape of the past at Den Gamle By. The threat posed by change has been subsumed by the strong identity of the site.

It would be a mistake to assume sites that appear to have a 'robust' heritagescape, and which operate simultaneously as a place 'of the past' and a place physically 'apart', necessarily have landscapes with few visible modern elements. Den Gamle By, which as noted has a notably robust heritagescape, marks all of its buildings with easily visible modern blue and white signs. Likewise the Belgian open-air museum *Bokrijk* (in northern Belgium) and the English open-air museum *Beamish* in County Durham, England (Figure 15.2), have areas that offer a vivid experience and yet have obvious modern metal signs, security systems and other modern devices. In these instances the signage does not dominate, probably because the strength of the heritagescape means that the experience of the past and of the place is enough to incorporate these modern elements as part of a multidimensional landscape (Garden 2004). This does not always work, and is dependent on a site being cohesive with a strong sense of place.

Greenfield Village, part of the Henry Ford Museum in Dearborn, Michigan, is one of the United States' older open-air museums. Originally conceived of as an outdoor educational institute, Henry Ford opened the site to the public in 1933. Deliberately located within the heart of his automotive empire, Greenfield Village invites visitors to 'experience three hundred years of history as the sights, sounds and sensations of America's past comes alive' (www.thehenryford.org).

Figure 15.2 Beamish Museum, Co. Durham (photo by the author)

At this site most of the buildings come with a pedigree and in one place visitors can see a courthouse where Abraham Lincoln practised, a Victorian sweet shop (originally a jewellers in London), a seventeenth-century Cotswold cottage and shops, and workshops and homes owned by American luminaries including Thomas Edison, the Wright brothers and Noah Webster, to mention but a few. Applying the heritagescape to Greenfield Village reveals that there is very little cohesion. The spaces between the buildings are just that – spaces – and there are few street signs or other stage-setting devices that create a sense of a place of the past. Compounding this is signage that is so variable that it is impossible to achieve a visual sense of connectedness. Rather than being subsumed into the larger landscape as in the above examples, at Greenfield Village some of these signs assume a prominence within the landscape and tend to feel like giant labels on displays (Figure 15.3).

Because the cohesion is so weak at Greenfield Village it is difficult to identify (visibly or otherwise) what is or is not the site. There is little sense of this site as a place. Although the site boundaries (in the public areas) are marked by a prominent red brick wall, the weak cohesion and the absence of a sense of place mean that when one regularly glimpses the Ford plants situated beyond the limits of the site and the apparently strong physical boundaries, the awareness of the boundaries tends to fade and the site as a discrete entity tends to blur. No doubt the emphasis on the individual building rather than the site as a whole is at the root of this lack of cohesion; while this focus on structures and their particular past is a hallmark of this institution it may also be that it is a

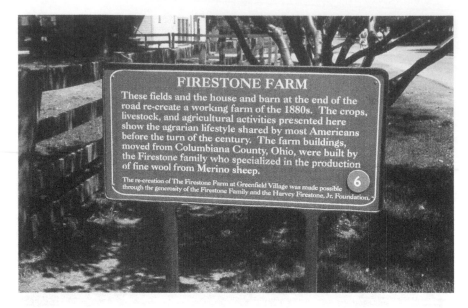

Figure 15.3 Greenfield Village at the Henry Ford Museum, Dearborn, Michigan (photo by the author)

strong factor standing in the way of an experience of 'the past'. This also means that Greenfield Village becomes more of a 'museum of buildings' (Howard 2002: 67) than a unified heritage landscape.

Two other sites – both located in Ontario, Canada – likewise demonstrate that the role of an open-air museum within its larger surroundings may be both complex and, in some instances, unexpected. *Historic Fort York*, a smaller outdoor museum located in downtown Toronto, Canada, was constructed by the British in the late eighteenth century as a defence against the Americans. It is now virtually dwarfed by the landscape of a modern city (Figure 15.4). Although few tangible remnants of the historic landscape remain, the lost landscape clearly figures prominently in the interpretation and the experience of this site. On first glance the limits of this site would appear to be well defined and bounded by the stone walls which surround the property. In fact, the surroundings have an active role in the interpretation and understanding of the site. The interpretative materials (including, but not limited to, signs and maps) and the interpreters themselves all evoke the nineteenth-century town of York as the predecessor of the modern city of Toronto. This is notable for a couple of reasons. First, it draws the view *away from* the tangible fort landscape to a now-hidden town site, visible only in the themed street signs that presently mark the area. Second, by adopting this tactic, the line of sight is deliberately directed towards the twenty-first-century vista of the skyscrapers of downtown Toronto. In essence the landscape of the invisible town of York plays at least as important a role as the much closer and very much more visible

Figure 15.4 Fort York National Historic site, Toronto, Canada (photo by the author)

Commons and cemetery that sit adjacent to Fort York. Yet, somehow in terms of visibility at this site the skyscrapers are either invisible and/or incorporated as part of a very large and diverse heritagescape.

Like Fort York and Greenfield Village, *Ste Marie Among the Hurons* is surrounded by a prominent wall (in this case a high wooden palisade) but operates quite differently to either of the two examples discussed above. Ste Marie is a recreated seventeenth-century Jesuit mission located on its original site with a clear historical link to its surroundings. Located just north of Toronto, it sits in an area noted for its qualities as an unspoiled wilderness; however, in this case the visibility is almost entirely centred on the site, with the view drawn inwards to the site itself. Given that Ste Marie sits in a virtually unaltered landscape, it might have been expected that the heritage-scape would extend well beyond the walls and that the relationship between the site and the larger environment would be well integrated. Yet this is not so. Despite strong and important links with the physical surroundings of Ste Marie, the wider landscape figures in very little of the interpretative material offered to visitors. The guide map shows only the area contained within the reconstructed palisades (walls) surrounding the main interpretative areas. The museum staff identify the area within the palisades as the 'whole site', providing a vivid sense of the past, allowing visitors to 'walk where the Jesuits walked'. That the interpretative material and the staff perceptions are so strongly directed inwards is even more notable because of the historic connec-tions with the more modern Martyr's Shrine[3] clearly visible from the reconstructed area. Staff indicated that they considered the Shrine 'outside' the site limits and 'quite distant'. Even more notable is that, under agreement with the Society of Jesus, the Jesuits' part of the Ste Marie site (the reconstructed chapel and grave site) must remain open and accessible to all visitors. In effect, this part of the site 'belongs' not to the museum but to the Martyr's Shrine. For many of Ste Marie's visitors the Shrine and the reconstructed mission at Ste Marie together figure prominently on a much larger landscape. For them the heritagescape clearly incorporates the Shrine, while for staff it is a much smaller and more discrete entity centring on the visible limits marked by the palisades.

While the heritagescape to date has been applied most often to built sites, it also offers potential for sites that possess few or no built remains but which are recognised spaces (e.g. battlefields (Carman and Carman 2006: 226, and this volume, chapter 16)). Preliminary work at *Culloden Battlefield* near Inverness, Scotland, suggests that the heritagescape concept has much to offer this type of heritage site (Figure 15.5). Considering this site as a heritagescape draws attention to the use of boundaries, cohesion and visibility. Here the sense of place is palpable, with the surrounding hills and peaks of the Scottish Highlands providing a frame around the views over the battlefield. The main area of the site is held together primarily through a set of

Figure 15.5 View of battlefield, Culloden Battlefield site, Scotland (photo by the author)

standard signs and by a tarmac path that runs throughout. The site is marked out by fences (both for management and for safety purposes); however, it is clear that the museum sees the site extending beyond the physical boundary. In more than one instance, visitors' eyes are drawn purposefully out of the site, across the main road to the (now) forested area that played a role in the Battle of Culloden. It is possible, therefore, that some of the most important elements at Culloden rest in the visual aspects and most particularly the view. No doubt further work will offer important clues to the role of visibility at sites such as this. This case study speaks to the growing interest and recognition of the role that the 'setting' plays at heritage sites (e.g. Cowley *et al.* 2005; ICOMOS 1999; Council of Europe 2000). As a postscript to the original analysis at Culloden, the new Visitor Centre which opened in April 2008 shows strong evidence that the designers and curators took into account the role of the landscape and the experiential qualities of the battlefield itself. The Centre, built with windows facing onto the battlefield, now draws the exterior landscape into the interior spaces, making the two landscapes much more coherent and connected. This notion of bringing the outside in continues in their 'Night March' corridor – a darkly lit corridor with recordings that replicate the activities of both armies on the eve of the battle. By means of the soundscape of the corridor visitors are drawn both outside and into the past.

On the battlefield itself, the visitors are now guided by handheld audio devices and, interestingly, these may be contributing to a new sense of space. The location of the site means that the reception is poor and, thus, the audio devices frequently fail as one moves further away from the Visitor Centre. In this way, the site limits are being redefined as visitors adjust their movements to the areas of the site that enjoy good and/or consistent reception. Quite clearly the landscape of Culloden Battlefield site is very much a work in progress, and the strength of the heritagescape – as a method – is that it enables us to 'capture' moments in time and identify change in a heritage site.

Having so far discussed outdoor sites, it seems likely that sites which lie within firm boundaries would also appear to conform to the definition of a heritagescape, that is, they are at once unique and at the same time part of their larger surroundings. In interior sites such as traditional indoor museums, the structure of the surrounding walls can often mean that, once inside, there is very little sense of being in a larger landscape. This was for many years the experience offered by most museums. Among these was the *British Museum*, which presents almost impermeable boundaries in the form of its walls. Even the addition of the Great Court in 2000, bringing in the exterior via the glass roof, and the incorporation of the formerly exterior spaces surrounding the library, has ultimately only served to focus the view inward away from its surroundings. In contrast, the *Museum of London* is an early example of a museum that deliberately linked the interior museum space to the exterior environment. Constructed with a large bank of windows and accompanied by signage, the museum invites the extant

Roman walls (located outside the modern museum) into the display and landscape of the interior. The archaeological remains and the view beyond to the City of London help locate the museum within its landscape, strengthening the visibility and making the interior and exterior landscapes work together as a much more cohesive space. A number of newer museum projects (e.g. Riverside, the new Museum of Transport planned for Glasgow, Scotland) suggest that many 'traditional' display-based museums are now seeking to locate themselves firmly within their larger landscape. A recent project at Jamestown Island, Virginia, is just one example of this. Here, the *Archaerium*, a museum opened in 2006 to display artefacts and to interpret the story of America's first English Settlement at Jamestown, has been constructed with a glass wall that faces onto the island landscape and towards the ongoing excavations in order to 'connect' the interior display space and '[integrate] the historic landscape into the interpretative experience' (Kostelny 2007).

Still more recently, the Michael Lee-Chin Crystal, a new addition (2007) to the *Royal Ontario Museum* (ROM), has deliberately located itself within the urban landscape of downtown Toronto (Canada). Recognising that for many years the museum has sat apart and isolated from its wider landscape, the 'Crystal' was intended to establish a link to the older 'heritage' buildings and at the same time acknowledge and draw attention to the exterior surroundings in order to 'creat[e] a landscape of desire, inviting people inside' (Browne 2008: 24). Although the idea of the building as a landscape was clearly in the mind of the original architects and curators,[4] alterations which had taken place had resulted in windows being painted over and the formerly grand spaces being divided up into smaller galleries. The recent work has acknowledged the outer spaces of the ROM and has seen the long-blocked-up windows and walls opened up, forming extended lines of sight and incorporating the exterior vistas into the new galleries. Tucked in between the heritage buildings, the Crystal was designed by architect Daniel Libeskind to embrace the outside spaces, enhancing a new entrance and creating a connection with the pavement so that it 'transforms the secretive and fortress-like character of the ROM, turning it into an inspired atmosphere dedicated to the resurgence of the museum as the dynamic centre of Toronto' (Royal Ontario Museum 2002). From within the galleries of the Crystal, visitors not only have a strong sense of the surrounding city and its landscape, there are also directed views back onto the heritage building, firmly locating the new structure as part of the museum's heritagescape (Figure 15.6). Out of these changes the heritagescape of the ROM, for years firmly locked into the physical confines of the building, has begun to expand beyond the walls both to locate the museum within its surroundings and to bring the outside into the museum (e.g. ROM Foundation 2003a: 3). We now see that the three guiding principles are operating in much more equal fashion.

Figure 15.6 View directed back to the Heritage Building: Royal Ontario Museum, Toronto, Canada (photo by the author; courtesy of the Royal Ontario Museum)

Conclusion

Through these wide-ranging examples, I have sought to demonstrate how the idea of the 'heritagescape' and its methodology, based on the three guiding principles of cohesion, visibility and boundaries, makes it possible to explore both the individual characteristics of a site and also the nuances of the relationship between a site and the landscape in which it is located. Thinking about these sites as distinct, yet integrated landscapes allows us to begin to comprehend the heritage site not just as a specific place; it also offers us a method for exploring the phenomenon of the heritage site. As both a method and a concept, the heritagescape seeks to offer an inclusive framework in which to locate a dialogue about many different types of heritage sites, as well as providing a means to evaluate heritage sites – capturing both the tangible and the intangible aspects of these landscapes, their experiential quality and how they may change over time. The creation of an experience is a fundamental component of a heritage site and to do this a sense of place must be evoked. Visitors must be able to move from the present to the past – to 'step back' – in a recognisable and, ideally, vivid way. In this fashion, expectations of the site are set up, with visitors prepared for the experience of 'the past' that lies inside the entrance. This experiential quality of heritage sites is fundamental to their nature and is what makes them such a prominent medium for conveying 'the past'.

Any methods used to investigate these places must take into account their complex and protean nature. Heritage sites, like other landscapes, are 'never inert' and are subject to constant reworking by those who interact with them (Bender 1993: 3). The heritagescape is able to accommodate these qualities. Importantly, instead of asking whether an open-air museum is 'real' or an 'authentic' version of the past, the heritagescape considers a more useful and rewarding question of how a site uses the components of its tangible landscape to create a distinct place of the past. Considering heritage sites as landscapes serves to remove the discussion from the site level and allows intriguing new information to emerge.

This chapter has aimed to consider how ideas of landscape can inform our understanding of these unique social spaces. Among the key questions facing heritage sites today is the idea of change and the notions of a place of 'the past' and a place 'apart'. Using the heritagescape to analyse sites has highlighted the need to dismiss the erroneous and superficial notion of heritagescapes as static or frozen spaces. Heritage sites are dynamic, evolving spaces, and the introduction of a flexible yet coherent methodology not only makes this apparent (at the site level), it offers the means to account for changes that may occur over time and helps to clarify the relationship between change – as a process – and heritage sites. A place of 'the past' and a place 'apart' are both related to a sense of place – a widely recognised notion that has been discussed earlier and which is an important component of the unique experiential qualities and space of heritage sites. While neither of these ideas is new, what is novel and unusual within this chapter is that both have been considered explicitly and individually and by doing so we are better able to recognise the relationship between them and at the same time note their unique qualities. Most importantly the heritagescape as a concept provides a common language and offers the means to discuss these places in a coherent and transparent fashion. As a method, it moves the dialogue away from the individual heritage site and in this way the focus is drawn to the relationship with its larger landscape and with other sites.

The heritagescape allows issues like these to be identified, evaluated and discussed and, in doing so, highlights the complex workings of these heritage landscapes both as distinct places and as intrinsically linked to the mental and material landscape(s) in which they are located. Heritage sites are complex social spaces and beginning the process of taking them apart to view their inner components in order to start to understand how they 'work' is an intricate endeavour. By considering these spaces as landscapes in and of their own right and by drawing upon ideas inherent in the study of cultural and natural landscapes the heritagescape is able to offer a radical new approach for analysing heritage sites, allowing us to expand and deepen our understanding of heritage places.

Notes

1   Among Millar's list of more conventional sites, including 'open-air museums, heritage centres and historic centres', she also includes 'garden centres, casinos and marinas' (1999: ix).
2   The 2005 UNESCO University and World Heritage Education Forum took this notion as a central theme and it has also been adopted by researchers in a variety of disciplines.
3   The Martyr's Shrine is the repository for the bones of the Jesuit priests who were killed by the Iroquois who attacked the mission at Ste Marie. The grave site of one of these martyrs is still marked within the reconstructed mission. There is a strong thematic and historic link between these two sites.
4   Descriptions of the interior space of the 'heritage buildings' (built 1906 and 1931) refer to 'grand vistas' and incorporate the notion of a view and a sense of connection (ROM Foundation 2003b: 4). Clearly, these spaces are acting as a landscape.

Bibliography

Bagnall, G. (2003) 'Performance and Performativity at Heritage Sites', *Museum and Society* 1.2, 87–103.

Bender, B. (1993) 'Introduction: Landscape – Meaning and Action', in B. Bender (ed.) *Landscape: Politics and Perspectives*, Oxford: Berg, 1–17.

Browne, Kelvin (2008) *Bold Visions: The Architecture of the Royal Ontario Museum*, Toronto: Royal Ontario Museum Toronto, Canada.

Carman, J. (2003) *Archaeology and Heritage*, London: Continuum.

Carman, J. and P. Carman (2006) *Bloody Meadows: Investigating Landscapes of Battle*, Stroud: Sutton.

Cooper, M. (1997) 'The Representation of Time at Two Shaker Village Sites', *International Journal of Heritage Studies* 3.3, 157–67.

Corbin, C. (2002) 'Representations of an Imagined Past: Fairground Heritage Villages', *International Journal of Heritage Studies* 8.3, 225–45.

Corsane, G. (ed.) (2005) *Heritage, Museums and Galleries: An Introductory Reader*, London: Routledge.

Council of Europe (2000) *European Landscape Convention*, Florence: Council of Europe (European Treaty Series No. 176), http://conventions.coe.int/Treaty/en/Treaties/Html/176.htm.

Cowley, D., J. Downes, M. Edmonds and Landscape Group (2005) 'Researching the Landscape', in J. Downes, S. M. Foster and C. R. Wickham-Jones (eds) *The Heart of Neolithic Orkney World Heritage Site: Research Agenda*, Edinburgh: Historic Scotland, 35–6.

Davis, P. (1999) *Ecomuseums: A Sense of Place*, London: Leicester University Press.

Gable, E. and R. Handler (1996) 'After Authenticity at an American Heritage Site', *American Anthropologist* 96.3, 568–78.

Garden, M. C. E. (2004) 'The Heritagescape: Exploring the Phenomenon of the Heritage Site'. PhD Dissertation, Department of Archaeology, University of Cambridge.

Handler, R. and E. Gable (1997) *The New History in an Old Museum: Creating the Past at Colonial Williamsburg*, Durham, NC: Duke University Press.

Harris, R. (1993) 'The Shallow Screen: Open-Air Museums and the Heritage Crisis'. Unpublished manuscript.

Hems, A. and M. Blockley (2006) *Heritage Interpretation*, Abingdon: Routledge.

Holtorf, C. (2005) *From Stonehenge to Las Vegas: Archaeology as Popular Culture*, Walnut Creek, CA: AltaMira Press.

Howard, P. (2002) 'The Eco-Museum: Innovation that Risks the Future', *International Journal of Heritage Studies* 8.1, 63–72.

—— (2003) *Heritage: Management, Interpretation, Identity*, London: Continuum.

ICOMOS (1999) *The Burra Charter: The Australia ICOMOS Charter for the Conservation of Places of Cultural Significance*, Burra: International Council on Monuments and Sites (ICOMOS), http://icomos.org/australia/burra.html.

Knell, S. J., S. MacLeod and S. Watson (2007) *Museum Revolutions: How Museums Change and are Changed*, London: Routledge.

Kostelny, E. (2007) *The Archaerium*, http://historicjamestowne.org/visit/archaearium.php.

Laenen, M. (1988) 'The Integration of Museums and Theme Parks: The Example of Bokrijk', in D. Uzzell, L. Blud, B. O'Callaghan and P. Davies (eds) *The Leverhulme Report: A Strategy for Interpretive and Educational Development*, Telford: Ironbridge Gorge Museums Trust.

Leask, A. and I. Yeoman (eds) (1999) *Heritage Visitor Attractions: An Operations Management Perspective*, London: Cassell.

Libeskind, D. (2002) 'Renaissance ROM. Extension to the Royal Ontario Museum: The Crystal', http://www.daniel-libeskind.com/projects.

Little, B. J. (2007) *Historical Archaeology: Why the Past Matters*, Walnut Creek, CA: Left Coast Press.

Lowenthal, D. (1998) *The Heritage Crusade and the Spoils of History*, Cambridge: Cambridge University Press.

MacLeod, S. (2005) 'Re-thinking Museum Architecture: Towards a Site-specific History and Use', in S. MacLeod (ed.) *Reshaping Museum Space: Architecture, Designs, Exhibitions*, London: Routledge, 9–25.

Mason, R. (2005) 'Nation Building at the Museum of Welsh Life', *Museum and Society* 2.1, 18–34.

Millar, S. (1999) 'An Overview of the Sector', in A. Leask and I. Yeoman (eds) *Heritage Visitor Attractions: An Operations Management Perspective*, London: Cassell, 1–21.

Prentice, R. (1991) *Tourism and Heritage Experiences*, London: Routledge.

Rodaway, P. (1994) *Sensuous Geographies: Body, Mind and Sense*, London: Taylor and Francis.

ROM Foundation (2003a) 'Supporting Heritage: The Heritage Restoration at the ROM', Philosophers' Walk, Toronto: Royal Ontario Museum, 3 December, http://www.rom.on.ca/renaissance.

—— (2003b) 'Supporting Heritage: The Heritage Restoration at the ROM', Queen's Park, Toronto: Royal Ontario Museum, 12 December, http://www.rom.on.ca/renaissance.

Rowan, Y. and U. Baram (eds) (2004) *Marketing Archaeology: Archaeology and the Consumption of the Past*, Walnut Creek, CA: AltaMira.

Royal Ontario Museum (2002) Press Release 'Final Architect for Renaissance ROM Announced', 26 February, http://www.rom.on.ca/releases.

Shanks, M. and C. Tilley (1992) *Reconstructing Archaeology: Theory and Practice*, 2nd edn, London: Routledge.

Smith, L. (2006) *The Uses of Heritage*, London: Routledge.

Stone, P. J. and P. G. Planel (eds) (1999) *The Constructed Past: Experimental Archaeology, Education and the Public*, London: Routledge.

Teather, E. K. and C. S. Chow (2003) 'Identity and Place: The Testament of Designated Heritage in Hong Kong', *International Journal of Heritage Studies* 9.2, 93–115.

Uzzell, D. and R. Ballantyne (eds) (1998) *Contemporary Issues in Heritage and Environmental Interpretation*, London: Her Majesty's Stationery Office.

Walsh, K. (1992) *The Representation of the Past: Museums and Heritage in a Post-Modern World*, London: Routledge.

16

THE INTANGIBLE PRESENCE

Investigating battlefields

John Carman and Patricia Carman

'Historic battlefields' represent a particular category of encultured place. Battles as events are frequently the main focus of attention for military historians of all periods (e.g. Hanson 1989; Keegan 1976; Weigley 1991), and the study and preservation of historic battlefields has also become an expressly archaeological concern over the past few years, partly because of a revived interest in archaeologies of warfare throughout the world (e.g. Haas 1990; Carman 1997; Keeley 1996; Carman and Harding 1999; Parker-Pearson and Thorpe 2005; Otto *et al.* 2006; Haldon 2006) but also because battlefields themselves have become the focus of archaeological work (Scott *et al.* 1989; Freeman and Pollard 2001; Doyle and Bennett 2002; Pollard and Banks 2006; Scott *et al.* 2007). The object of battlefield preservation – a point made strongly by a number of commentators, especially Foard (2001) – is usually the memory of the now unrecoverable event itself rather than the material evidence of that event which may be present in that space; in other words, these places matter as the place where a historic event took place, rather than as archaeological sites. Hence one reason, we think, for the general lack of discussion of the ontology of such places in the archaeological literature (although for an exception see Carman 2005) is that what they represent is not the places themselves or the objects they contain, but instead the way they serve to evoke a past event.

This chapter will discuss the work of the Bloody Meadows Project (Carman and Carman 2001, 2006a and b, 2007a and b) as an approach to the study of historic battlefields both as places where particular kinds of events took place in the past and as contemporary places of experience. It is simultaneously an exercise in the kind of 'landscape archaeology' which investigates the past and an exercise in contemporary 'heritage studies'; in combination these two elements ultimately focus on the historicity of certain kinds of places.

A 'phenomenological' approach to landscapes of the past

Battlefields as historic places

[What] is clear [from the ethnographic record] is the symbolic, ancestral, and temporal significance of landscape [to peoples]. The landscape is continually being encultured, bringing things into meaning as part of a symbolic process by which human consciousness makes the physical reality of the natural environment into an intelligible and socialised form ... It [is accordingly] evident ... that the significance of landscape for different populations cannot be simply read off from the local 'ecological' characteristics of a 'natural' environment.

(Tilley 1994: 67)

Looking at the two-dimensional plane of the modern topographic map with sites plotted on it, it is quite impossible to envisage the landscape in which these places are embedded. The representation fails, and cannot substitute for being there, being *in place*. [The] process of observation requires time and a feeling for the place.

(Tilley 1994: 75)

Cultural markers [such as monuments] are used to create a new sense of place .... An already encultured landscape becomes refashioned, its meanings now controlled by the imposition of [a new] cultural form.

(Tilley 1994: 208)

A 'phenomenological' approach to the study of landscapes as taken by archaeologists has generally been limited to the monumental 'ritual' landscapes of later European prehistory. The approach is, however, also of more general relevance to any encultured space, especially any marked as a particular kind of space. Drawing upon Tilley's approach, the primary data source used in the Bloody Meadows Project is the physical landscape of the place where warfare was practised. Overall, the project seeks to contribute to current debates upon the nature of war by developing an understanding of changes in warfare practice over the long term. In operation, it is an exercise in the comparative study of battlefield landscapes from all periods of history and, ultimately, in all parts of the world. In doing so, we focus upon the landscape of individual battle sites to ask specific questions that are designed to aid in describing the particular qualities of the space, including:

• how clearly bounded is the battlefield space (does it have clear boundaries, such as impassable ground or a water obstacle)?
• is it high or low ground relative to the surrounding space?
• what kind of use (other than for war) was the site put to, if any?

- is it near to or distant from a settlement?
- is it visible from a settlement?
- does the ground contain particular types of landscape features – natural or built – which play a part in the battlefield action?
- what features present in the landscape (if any) played no part in the battlefield action?
- was the battlefield subsequently marked by a monument or memorial in any way?

In approaching the landscapes that are our object, we use what we call 'the archaeologist's eye' – that is, the capacity of an experienced landscape archaeologist to interpret space and to identify features in landscapes – to reach an understanding of the spaces of battle. By approaching such sites with a structured set of questions and by recording data in a standard format it becomes possible to recognise both what such sites have in common and how they differ from one another. This in turn allows the identification of the types of location favoured as battle sites in particular periods of history, and these can be related to other aspects of the battle as recorded by historians – including the type of participants, the nature of the conflict of which the battle is a part and the flow of the action. Overall, it presents an opportunity to gain a direct insight into the ideological factors guiding warfare practice in that period and to compare them with those guiding warfare practices in a different period.

The Bloody Meadows Project therefore looks very specifically at the *kind* of place where a battle was fought. The majority of archaeologists working on battlefields spend their time looking at the ground, trying to find the material left behind by the action. We instead spend time looking up and around us, at the shape of the space itself. In particular, we seek to identify those features not present on the day of the battle, those present but now lost and those present but not identified as 'useful' on the day, which give a valuable insight into how those involved perceived the landscape around them. Our 'embedded' approach allows a comparison to be made between spaces of battle in ways that battlefield plans do not. Using these, we can compare battlefields of one period or battlefields across time to identify what kinds of places were selected as battlefields in the past. Differences of choice across space and through time thereby become evident (see Table 16.1).

Investigating battlefields as places in the present

The interest of the Bloody Meadows Project in the way battlefields are subsequently marked – whether soon after the battle or a considerable time later – is reflected particularly in the following research question:

- was the battlefield subsequently marked by a monument or memorial in any way?

Table 16.1 The shapes of battlefields through time

Battle	Date	Country	Battlefield landscape-type							Period
			Coastal or estuarine	High ground (4)	Urban (2)	Visible from urban space	Defensive structures	Low ground (1)	Featured ground (3)	
Marathon	490 BC	Greece	•			?				Classical
Thermopylae	480 BC	Greece	•			•				
Plataea	479 BC	Greece				•		•		
Levktra	371 BC	Greece				•		•		
Philippi I & II	42 BC	Greece				•		•		
Maldon	991	UK	•					•		Early medieval
Assandun (4)	1016	UK	•					•		
Stamford Bridge	1066	UK		•						
Bouvines	1214	France		•		•		•		Medieval
Courtrai	1302	Belgium					•			
Aljubarotta	1385	Portugal		•			•			
St Albans I	1455	UK			•		•			
Northampton	1460	UK		•	•	•	•	•		
St Albans II	1461	UK		•		•				
Tewkesbury	1471	UK		•		•				
Bosworth	1485	UK		•						
Stoke	1487	UK		•		•				
Roundway Down	1643	UK						•		Early modern
Cropredy Bridge	1644	UK						•		
Naseby	1645	UK								
Linton (5)	1648	UK			•		•			
The Dunes	1658	France	•							

Table 16.1 (continued)

Battle	Date	Country	Battlefield landscape-type							Period
			Coastal or estuarine	High ground (1)	Urban (2)	Visible from urban space	Defensive structures	Low ground (1)	Featured ground (3)	
Sedgemoor	1685	UK						●		Early modern
Oudenaarde	1708	Belgium						●		
Fontenoy	1745	France		●				●		
Quebec I	1759	Canada				●	●			
Quebec II	1775	Canada			●	●		●		
Valmy	1792	France				●			●	Modern
Rolica	1808	Portugal				●			●	
Corunna	1809	Spain							●	
Sorauren I & II	1813	Spain							●	
Laon	1814	France				●			●	
Reims	1814	France				●			●	
Vionville-Mars la Tour	1870	France							●	
Gravelotte – St Privat	1870	France							●	
Sedan	1870	France				●			●	

Notes
1 Relative to surrounding land
2 i.e. fought within an existing urban space
3 Containing recognisable landscape features which are used during the course of battlefield action
4 The most likely – and generally accepted – site has been chosen for inclusion
5 Technically a skirmish or civil disorder, but nevertheless included here because it has sufficient 'battle-like' attributes

We take note of all such markers on or near the site itself, contemporary with the battle or later, and are particularly interested in asking:

- where is it in relation to the battle site?
- what form does it take?
- who or what does it commemorate?
- who raised it?
- when was it raised?
- is there any indication of the specific audience it is intended to address?
- what does it say about the relations of commemorator or commemoratee to the battle site?
- are links made with other sites or to other events?

We are always fully conscious that marking a site is not the only measure of its importance or interest. Failure to mark a site can itself constitute a statement; sometimes this will simply represent a failure to recognise any importance or significance the site may carry for certain people, but other times it can be a positive omission with a purpose to it. By looking closely at such sites and the monuments and other marks they bear it is possible to come to an understanding of the meanings they carry in our own time.

These marks are also reflected in the purposes for which such sites are used. Battlefields from the past rarely offer much in the way of an obvious physical legacy. Where earthwork defences were constructed, or the fighting resulted in significant changes to the shape of the land, these traces may persist to become part of later uses. In those cases where archaeological investigation has been carried out, the archaeology has most often consisted of human remains buried at the site (do Paço 1962; Cunha and Silva 1997; Fiorato et al. 2000). More recent researches have revealed the presence of scatters of material across the battlespace – most typically for battles of the firearms era, bullets and bullet casings (Scott et al. 1989; Foard 1995; Haecker and Mauck 1997); for earlier periods, attachments to clothing which may have been torn off in the struggle (Sutherland 2000). Since such remains are generally invisible to the naked human eye, however, the landscape of such places has been seen as 'empty' of archaeology and therefore available for other uses. These uses may extend to the provision of park and amenity spaces, the historical significance of the location giving it an extra attractiveness to visitors. At the battlefield of Northampton, for instance, the place of the battlefield has been converted into the municipal golf course; at Quebec in Canada the site of the conflict of 1759 has been used as a site of recreation since the beginning of the twentieth century (Mathieu and Kedl 1993).

Accordingly, we also ask of all such sites:

- to what use(s) has the battlefield been put, and what is it used for today?

From this we can ascertain the various uses over time to which the space has been put – other than, or at least as well as, for warmaking – and from this gain some insight into the level of significance the place has acquired over time.

Insights 1: what we have achieved

It is clear from our research that the places where people fought in the past are subject to changes in use and appropriation. In the past, particular types of people came with a particular purpose in particular sets of circumstances. The memory of that past event has since been used to support contemporary causes and to create modern meaning; but it is important to recognise that the memory and the event are connected but are not the same; and the form of the memory often does not reflect the form of the event at all. In visiting battle-fields today, one can look at these issues as changes in three areas: the ownership (or claimed ownership) of the site; the realm of modern discourse within which the treatment of the site is located; and the modern experience of being at the site (Table 16.2).

Ownership

The majority of battles involve the active occupation of ground and a determination to hold it against assault; on occasion this also includes the construction of physical barriers to assault. In circumstances where forces meet by happenstance rather than by planning, the ground itself is disputed as both sides move to occupy it. Accordingly, the act of claiming possession of a piece of ground is central to the act of battle. It is the subsequent outcome of the battle that may determine ownership – or at least recognised and acknowledged claims of ownership – today. Frequently where victory was achieved by the forces of the state in whose territory the battlefield is located, it is that nation state which makes the claim, using the event as part of its own claim to legitimate existence. Where national forces were defeated, the battle may not be adopted by the host nation, but by others. Where the battle was fought between forces from places alien to the host territory, a more local and regional association may be forged, although at some such sites no particular claim of ownership is made. Where all the combatants were natives of the home state (especially in civil conflicts) a local claim seems to be the most common, and this kind of association may also be made where there was a specifically local involvement in the battle.

Discourse

The notion of 'discourse' is defined as 'the communicative practice in a specific domain of knowledge' (Gray 1997: 95), so that rules of discourse 'establish who can be listened to, and who can't, as well as conventions that mark out

Table 16.2 Battlefields from past to present: from event to memory

| Battle | Past | | | | | Present | |
	Conflict & battle type	Combatants	Landscape type	Ownership / claim	Discourse	Experience
Aljubarotta 1385	International, attack on prepared position	Professional	Open, high, rural, defences	National	Nationalist	Monumental
Assandun 1016	International, mutually agreed	Warriors	Open, low, riverside	None	N/A	Personal
Bosworth 1485	Civil war, mutually agreed	Professional	Open, high, rural	Private	Commercial	Tourist
Bouvines 1214	International, mutually agreed	Professional	Open, high, rural	National	Trans-historical	Monumental
Corunna / Elviña 1809	International, mutually agreed	Professional	Featured, high, rural	Local & regional	Future-oriented	Monumental
Courtrai 1302	Rebellion, mutually agreed	Volunteers, professional	Open, low, urban	Local & national	Nationalist	Monumental
Cropredy 1644	Civil war, encounter	Volunteers	Open, low, rural	Local	Historical	Tourist
The Dunes 1658	International, attack on prepared position	Professional	Open, coastal	Local	Trans-historical	Monumental
Fontenoy 1745	International, attack on prepared position	Professional	Open, low, rural, defences	Other national	Nationalist	Monumental
Gravelotte – St Privat 1870	International, attack on prepared position	Professional	Featured, rural	Other national	Memorialisation	Memorial
Laon 1814	International, mutually agreed	Professional	Featured, low, near town	None	N/A	Personal
Levktra 371 BC	Inter-polity, mutually agreed	Citizen soldiers	Open, low, rural	National	Nationalist	Monumental

Table 16.2 (continued)

Battle	Past			Ownership / claim	Present	
	Conflict & battle type	Combatants	Landscape type		Discourse	Experience
Linton 1648	Rebellion, attack on prepared position	Volunteers, professional	Urban & rural	None	Historical	Personal
Maldon 991	International, mutually agreed	Warriors	Coastal	Local & national	Historical	Tourist
Marathon 490 BC	International, mutually agreed	Citizen soldiers versus professional	Coastal, low	National	Nationalist	Monumental
Naseby 1645	Civil war, mutually agreed	Professional	Open, low, rural	National	Historical	Tourist
Northampton 1460	Civil war, attack on prepared position	Professional	Open, low, near town	National	Historical	Personal
Oudenaarde 1708	International, encounter	Professional	Open, low, rural	None	None	Personal
Philippi I & II 42 BC	Civil war	Professional	Open, low, near town	None	None	Personal
Plataea 479 BC	International, mutually agreed	Citizen soldiers versus professional	Open, low, rural, near town	None	None	Personal
Quebec I 1759	International, night assault	Professional	Open, high, near town	National	Historical	Memorial
Quebec II 1775	International, assault on prepared position	Professional	Low, urban	National	Nationalist	Monumental
Reims 1814	International, night assault	Professional	Urban	National	Nationalist	Monumental
Roliça 1808	International, attack on prepared position	Professional	Featured, high, rural	Visitors	Common	Natural

Table 16.2 (continued)

Battle	Past			Present		
	Conflict & battle type	Combatants	Landscape type	Ownership / claim	Discourse	Experience
Roundway 1643	Civil war, mutually agreed	Volunteers	Open, low, rural	Local	Historical	Natural
St Albans I & II	Rebellion, attack on prepared position	Professional	High, urban	Local	Historical	Historical
Sedan 1870	International, mutually agreed	Professional	Featured, near town	National	Nationalist	Memorial
Sedgemoor 1685	Rebellion, attack on prepared position	Rebels, professionals	Open, low, rural	Local	Memorialisation	Memorial
Sorauren I & II 1813	International, attack on prepared position	Professional	Featured, rural	None	None	Personal
Stamford Bridge 1066	International, attack on prepared position	Warriors	Open, high, rural	Local & national	Historical	Monumental
Stoke 1487	Civil War, mutually agreed	Professional	Open, high, rural	National	Historical	Historical
Tewkesbury 1471	Civil War, mutually agreed	Professional	Open, low, near town	National	Historical	Monumental
Thermopylae 480 BC	International, assault on prepared position	Citizen soldiers versus professional	Coastal	National	Nationalist	Monumental
Valmy 1792	International, mutually agreed	Citizen soldiers versus professional	Open, high	National	Nationalist	Monumental
Vionville-Mars la Tour 1870	International, mutually agreed	Professional	Featured, rural	Other national	Memorialisation	Memorial

permitted areas for discussion, and those [that are] forbidden, and rationales that allow certain questions to be asked but not others' (Gray 1997: 95–6). In the context of the study of war, these rules need not limit themselves to words: what 'warriors and soldiers do with their bodies is more important than what they say. Weapons, rituals, traditions and techniques are all parts of the discourse of war' (Gray 1997: 95–6). In looking at battle, these rules concern who may take part and how they should be treated, and where it may take place and in what form. These things are the content of a particular 'discourse' of battle.

In the past, on the day(s) of the battle, the realm of discourse within which the site was located was always that of war: and the site chosen reflected what was expected and allowed in terms of the rules dictating warfare practice at that time. Our research (Table 16.1) indicates that in medieval times the preference was for sites either on high ground, or adjacent to or even within urban centres, or both (see Figure 16.1); that in the seventeenth and eighteenth centuries the preference was for sites on low ground away from major settlements (Figure 16.2); and that by the nineteenth century the preference was for sites containing a number of different kinds of features (Figure 16.3). Once the battle is transferred to the realm of memory, however, the appropriate realm of discourse is no longer that of past war but of contemporary purposes (see Table 16.2). Where a straightforward national ownership is claimed, the discourse is generally that of nationalism (Figure 16.4). A variation is rung on this theme

Figure 16.1 The battlefield at Bouvines, 1214, typical for its period, showing the relative height above surrounding land by the rooftops of a nearby village

Figure 16.2 The battlefield at Oudenaarde, 1708, showing the flatness of the ground and how it rises gently away from the battlefield

Figure 16.3 The battlefield at Sorauren, 1813, a highly featured landscape containing a stone-built village, high and low ground and major rivers with bridge crossings

Figure 16.4 The modern monument at Thermopylae, glorifying Greek arms

at Fontenoy (Figure 16.5), where the Irish claim on the site is a nationalist one, but the site itself is inside the territory of France. At others the site is treated as a place for commercial interaction with tourists. Sedgemoor (Figure 16.6) is a site occupied by memorials to the dead of all wars, while other sites have been forgotten except as past events, thereby relegated to history. These contrast with those places where the forging of specific links with later events at that place renders the discourse one that works across historical periods. At Corunna (Figure 16.7), the identification of the battle site with a place for the education of future generations not only crosses historical periods but takes us beyond our own time into that future.

Experience

The experience of battle is one of violence and terror: physical features in the battlefield – if any – are examined in terms of the potential threat or possible safety they offer. By contrast, the experience of that place today will be one of peace and tranquillity. Nevertheless, due to the different claims of ownership made upon the place and the modern field of discourse in which it is located, the modern experience of the historic place of battle will vary from site to site (see Table 16.2). For many sites, the modern experience is that of confrontation with a monumental past, frequently represented by one or more built monuments. This is particularly the case where one is dealing with nationalist sites or where links to other historical times are being asserted (see Herzfeld 1991: 5–9) At others, the monumental experience is transformed into one

Figure 16.5 The monument at Fontenoy raised by the Irish Military Historical Association in 1888 to commemorate the Irish troops fighting for the French

Figure 16.6 Monuments at the site of Sedgemoor

Figure 16.7 The university built on the site of the Battle of Corunna (known locally as Elviña), 1809

primarily of memorialisation by the presence of monuments specifically to the dead. Where commercial or visitor interest is paramount, the experience is very much one of tourism. At others the site has lost its close historical associations and will be experienced primarily as a natural landscape.

Methodology

It will be clear that we think our approach (in some sense) 'works'. By focusing on sites of battle in the past specifically as landscapes we believe we are accessing a resource for understanding aspects of the past generally left untapped. We believe that our results so far represent types of knowledge that others interested in battlefields and indeed historic landscapes generally (who use different techniques and approaches) have not been able to acquire. In particular, this relates especially to the patterning of landscape choices made in different periods of history and the range of current treatments deemed appropriate for such sites in the present. On this basis, we believe that our approach is reasonably consistent in its application, that it allows us to understand aspects of places and events widely different in space and time, and that in so doing it allows us to make meaningful comparisons between one site and another and different sites from different historical periods. We believe that it can also be used in conjunction with other techniques of battlefield investigation. There is no reason, for instance, why archaeologists concerned with the study of artefact patterning on sites or with the excavation of mass graves (e.g. Freeman and Pollard 2001; Pollard and Banks 2006; Scott *et al.* 2007) should not also be able to apply our approach to understanding the locations where these are found. At the same time, geologists more concerned with understanding the role of the physical terrain of battlefields (e.g. Doyle and Bennett 2002) should also cast their eyes up and around them as well as below their feet. In terms of the ways in which sites are marked, memorialised and managed, our work may help elucidate some of the issues addressed by responsible agencies (e.g. English Heritage 1995; Hewitt 2001).

We believe that any value our work contains is due to its three key aspects: that it represents an entirely material culture-based approach; that in taking such an approach it applies ideas from phenomenology without being sidetracked too heavily by philosophy; and that it uses this basis to consider its objects of enquiry in a comparative frame of reference. We are less concerned to relate what we encounter to the literature of the battles fought there, than to identify those features present and absent and especially their physical relations to one another. Although taking a broadly phenomenological approach, we are not constrained by its limitation to the specificity of so many 'postprocessual' archaeologies (see Hodder *et al.* 1995: 5): instead, by considering those places we study, the objects they contain and the relationships between them in an overtly comparative frame of reference – of site with site, and of period or geographical region with other periods or geographical regions, and especially in terms of differences of apprehension between periods, regions and today – we are able to come to more general statements about what these places are like, how they may have been understood in the past and how they are understood in the present.

Having said this, we also believe that our approach must be applied with a concern for specifics. It is not sufficient to take in the general lie of the land or rely on contemporary testimony of battlefield observers as to significant features. Instead, the approach relies upon a capacity to 'see' the space very clearly for oneself, to identify features that are present, and to distinguish what is present today from what was present in the past. Where sources are used – as indeed they will be – it is important not to be 'reading' the landscape in their terms but in one's own: it is the difference between an experience by a present visitor and that of a past visitor that allows a new understanding of the site to develop. It is necessary to approach the site from a number of different directions in order to gain a sense of the space from various locations within it and from the perspectives of those in the past who may have passed through it in differing ways and with differing purposes. Since we rely heavily upon our own cultural norms to 'read' the space, the approach is relatively simple: but because of the need to be constantly alert to the difference of a modern reading from past readings, and indeed differences in reading by different individuals in the present, it is not necessarily easy. Accordingly, as the project develops we have found the need to revisit some of the sites covered, to note new developments and to reconsider them in the light of further work.

Insights 2: limitations

One of the key activities of research is always to review its own progress and to reconsider earlier findings in the light of new data or alternative explanations. In the same way, one of the main purposes of research is always to generate new sets of research questions and reconsider old ones. In the case of the Bloody Meadows Project, this means a constant review of our aims and methods, and taking our approach into new areas and new historical periods.

Places

Our work so far offers only a small sample of the total number of known sites of battle across the globe: a mere 38 out of an estimated 7,000 (approximately 0.54 per cent). Any broad conclusions we have reached – about sites, about ideologies of war, about understandings of landscape, and about memorialisation and remembrance – must remain provisional until more work has been done. All our sites have also so far been limited to Europe (except for a single visit to a single site in North America), where a high degree of cultural interaction can be both assumed and demonstrated: any patterning we can infer is likely to be the result of that cultural interaction. It is also of course our own cultural background that we have been investigating: certain of the assumptions we make – and of which we may be unaware – can therefore be relied upon to hold true. We can perhaps expect that this will not be the case with battles fought elsewhere and under very different political and cultural conditions. This is one of the issues that Jeremy Black (1991, 2000, 2002) has concerned himself with, and in particular the Eurocentricity of much of the discussion of military affairs. If the 'culture of war' changes over time within a relatively small geographical zone (as from our work it seems to) then presumably the changes will be consequently greater over wider geographical space and larger spans of time. In particular, the style of fighting in colonial or other contexts may well turn out to be very different from that in Europe. This is an aspect we have yet to explore. The problem may be compounded if the attitude towards war taken in that region is also significantly different from that in Europe (e.g. those drawn upon by Keegan 1993).

The idea of 'battle'

A particular question that may arise as we extend our coverage into new regions and periods is how we should cope with cultures of war that do not involve battles as we understand them. We have excluded from our coverage actions such as civil disorder, sieges and military manoeuvre without fighting, as well as issues of logistics. If, however, we encountered a cultural context where these were the only types of warlike activity, it would hamper our ability to make any comment upon it apart perhaps from noting the lack of battles. To some extent we have already gone beyond our own bounds, by including in our coverage so far several actions fought as part of uprisings rather than battles as more conventionally understood: two of these were nevertheless ascribed the status of 'battle' at the time.

A specific example of where this issue may particularly emerge as we extend our geographical coverage is in the military history of China. 'Battles' (e.g. those discussed by Tao 2000) are very large in geographical scale and involve actual fighting only as part of much wider manoeuvres: in the Western tradition these would more likely be referred to as 'operations' or even as 'campaigns' rather than as battles proper. Quite how we would deal with them in our scheme is problematic. As an issue it is one that must remain open and the questions it raises unanswered for the time being. It may be that we shall be reduced to acknowledging the fundamental difference of the ancient Chinese approach to war from the European tradition, and that therefore we shall have nothing to say except that no events that we can call battles took place. Otherwise we may be able to identify those warmaking activities that are not battles as we define them but involve fighting and are yet not sieges, skirmishes or responses to civil disorder. In this respect, we would identify those activities which perform the same functions as battles in the Western tradition and treat them accordingly.

Methodology

We have yet to fully develop our merging of interests in both landscapes in the past and their role as heritage in our present. These remain quite separate in terms of the issues covered and the manner of approaching them. Other researchers are also interested in places as various kinds of historic landscape, however, and it may be possible for us to combine some of our interests with theirs to the benefit of both. One approach in particular may prove enlightening: modern 'heritagescapes' (Garden 2006, this volume, chapter 15) are considered in terms of three parameters – those of boundaries, cohesion and visibility – which have some affinity with aspects of our own work. One of the interesting aspects of such a 'heritagescape' approach is its ability to distinguish 'places [with a sense of] of the past' from 'places apart' (from the rest of modernity); these differences are assessed in terms of the experience they offer. This will clearly offer something to our own work as it develops; it may also serve to address other areas of uncertainty as they emerge.

Battlefields as 'heritage'

Part of the transformation of battlefields to 'heritage' places is often a process whereby they become memorialised in some manner: this is most obvious by the erection of a physical structure on or near the place of battle to mark it as significant. When this takes place – either soon after the event or later in the site's history – we are able to comment upon it in terms of its form, its location relative to the site of battle, its dedicator and its dedicatee. Where no such structure exists, however, we can do little except note its absence in comparison with those more formally marked. Shelby Foote in his discussion of American sites of tragedy and violence calls this process of non-marking 'rectification' (1997: 23), whereby the site gains only 'temporary notoriety' and is then reabsorbed into the everyday.

The problem for our approach, however, is knowing whether such sites achieved even temporary notoriety in any meaningful sense. Instead, it may be that armies in the past moved in, fought and moved away without noting in particular the location where they met, and without leaving behind them any feeling of the significance of their passing. 'Rectification' in Foote's (1997) sense of the term requires a measure of notoriety or fame, however short-lived after the event that inspired it. Rectification is for him one of a set of responses that assumes sanctification, designation and deliberate obliteration as legitimate and proper responses to places of trauma: rectification is the positive absence of these. We have noted, however, battles from periods where it seems memorialisation (whether sanctification or designation in Foote's terms) is not a norm. Accordingly, battles from the seventeenth and eighteenth centuries (in particular) that remain unmemorialised and unmarked may represent something other than 'rectification' in the sense used here. In our age, and in the centuries preceding early modernity, the marking of battlefields as special places seems to have been a cultural norm: the form differs in the medieval period from the modern, and most probably the specific audience and purpose, but there is some similarity of practice. Such places do not appear to require any kind of marking in the intervening period, however, suggesting that a very different set of cultural imperatives is at work. Without any material legacy to consider, it may prove difficult if not impossible for us to say very much about those very different cultural traditions of remembrance.

For us to study battlefields as a part of our heritage it is necessary for them to be treated as part of that heritage. Where remembrance is lacking, that 'heritage' status is effectively withheld. Modern attitudes to sites of historic conflict are different from those in the past, but inevitably include the evidence for those past understandings. Where no such evidence exists, it is possible that we shall need to be silent apart from noting the lack of remembrance, and leave it to others to consider the specifics of that particular cultural choice.

Conclusions

This chapter has been a critical review of the work of the Bloody Meadows Project so far. It has reviewed our results and those areas we may need to address further as the project continues. It has suggested areas where the project may not be able to make any clear statements about the objects of enquiry we specifically address. There are, however, areas where we feel we can make a contribution.

The main students of historic battlefields are military historians and military, battlefield or conflict archaeologists (the terms used vary). Our work derives directly from the latter concerns and it is to these that the most direct contribution can be made. We think our work may have three distinctive values, all relating to the limitations of the standard military historical discourse. First, we represent an approach to battlefields neither grounded in nor deriving from military history but instead directly from archaeology, allowing us to offer insights about battles and battlefields that a military historian simply cannot. This is not to demean military history as such, but we believe that an overreliance on military history as a source discipline prevents the emergence of the full value of the material culture approach that is central to archaeology. Second, we believe that our work may have some predictive value where scholars are seeking to locate a battle from the past: by using our 'typology' for that period (Carman and Carman 2007b) some places may appear more likely and others less so. Third, because we highlight not functional rationality in decision-making but the unstated assumptions that lie behind choices in the past, we also help to undermine the contemporary myth of war as a rational activity and an appropriate response to perceived threat (Carman and Carman 2007a). Our work goes some way towards demonstrating that the way wars are fought is not grounded in rationality but in cultural beliefs, and that these vary across time and across space. Our work reveals some of this variation for further investigation by both military historians and military archaeologists.

Our second audience is students of landscapes from the past, especially those in our host discipline of archaeology. We believe that our work demonstrates the utility of an approach to landscapes based upon phenomenology: moreover, by applying this approach to historic landscapes we show the usefulness of the approach beyond the study of prehistory. Our approach is based entirely upon the notion that attitudes towards and expectations of landscape in the past are different from those held by people in the twenty-first century: if they were not different we would have nothing to say. We believe our approach seeks out and identifies those differences by using an explicitly Western mode of investigation of space and comparing that with the use of that space made by people in the past. It is from noting the manner in which objects are used, or any failure to use them as we would today, that these differences emerge. We can also compare the uses of space in one historical period with those of another, revealing other differences in attitude and expectation. Where objects that were present in the past and would be available for use in the present – especially for military purposes, such as facilitating or impeding movement, for concealment or for protection – but were not used for these purposes, it can be inferred that the objects were not seen as useful. This in turn indicates a measure of difference between the past and the present. We believe choosing to examine landscapes that were used for a very particular kind of purpose in the past makes the identification and examination of these differences in attitude and expectation – as revealed by differences in use – more reliable, and that they therefore reveal real differences between various periods of history. These can then be taken up by others who are interested in understanding the use and attitudes towards space of people in the past.

Finally, as students of the remembrance of historic places, we aim to contribute to studies of modern 'heritage' and of social memory. Here, we record the actual means by which places were marked and memorialised in the present and in the past: where no such marking is evident, we record that too. Accordingly, unlike so many of those interested in these areas, we do not start from the premise that the marking and commemoration of battlefields (among other places) is a universal cultural norm, but that they are one form of cultural practice in which we can be interested. From our work the differences in style of marking between the medieval and modern periods emerge; as does also the apparent hiatus in commemoration from the end of the medieval period to the nineteenth century. This is something apparently not remarked upon by other researchers (see Borg 1991; Hewitt 2001; Yarrington 1988). Our work therefore serves to assist those who wish to challenge the assumptions so often made about what is right and proper in relation to social memory, and instead to establish the forms of that memory as an object of study in their own right. It offers to us as something strange our own cultural practices and accepted norms of behaviour. It may serve to raise questions about our own modern attitudes to war and remembrance in the same way that work such as ours raises questions about the rational basis for decision-making in war.

Ultimately, as is so common with much contemporary research work, our project is not really about the past but about our own attitudes and understandings in the present. It lays before us our beliefs and practices as a set of ideas that do not hold true in all times and places and are different from those in the past. It causes us to question our values and expectations by revealing how historically shallow those values and expectations are. We hope it tells us about the past, but we also hope it tells us about the present and gives indications to a different, perhaps better, way of thinking about issues of war and violence more generally. We certainly hope it encourages our readers to think about these things.

Bibliography

Black, J. (1991) *A Military Revolution? Military Change and European Society 1550–1800*, Studies in European History, London: Macmillan.

—— (2000) *War: Past, Present, and Future*, Stroud: Sutton.

—— (2002) *European Warfare, 1494–1815*, London: Routledge.

Borg, A. (1991) *War Memorials: From Antiquity to the Present*, London: Leo Cooper.

Carman, J. (ed.) (1997) *Material Harm: Archaeological Studies of War and Violence*, Glasgow: Cruithne.

—— (1999a) 'Beyond the Western Way of War: Ancient Battlefields in Comparative Perspective', in J. Carman and A. Harding (eds) *Ancient Warfare: Archaeological Perspectives*, Stroud: Sutton, 39–55.

—— (1999b). 'Bloody Meadows: The Places of Battle', in S. Tarlow and S. West (eds) *The Familiar Past? Archaeologies of Later Historical Britain*, London: Routledge, 233–45.

—— (2005) 'Battlefields as Cultural Resources', *Post-Medieval Archaeology* 39.2, 215–23.

Carman, J. and P. Carman (2001) 'Beyond Military Archaeology: Battlefields as a Research Resource', in P. Freeman and T. Pollard (eds) *Fields of Conflict: Progress and Prospects in Battlefield Archaeology, Proceedings of a Conference Held in the Department of Archaeology, University of Glasgow, April 2000*, Oxford: BAR International Series 958, Archaeopress, 275–81.

—— (2006a) 'Ancient Bloody Meadows: Classical Battlefields in Greece', in T. Pollard and I. Banks (eds) *Past Tense: Studies in the Archaeology of Conflict*, Leiden: Brill, 19–44.

—— (2006b) *Bloody Meadows: Investigating Landscapes of Battle*, Stroud: Sutton.

—— (2007a) 'From Rhetoric to Research: The Bloody Meadows Project as a Pacifist Response to War', in M. Palus, A. Piccini and L. McAtackney (eds) *Encounters Between Past and Present: Proceedings of the First CHAT Conference 2003*, Oxford: BAR International Series, Archaeopress, 109–114.

—— (2007b) 'Mustering Landscapes: What Historic Battlefields Share in Common', in D. Scott, L. Babits and C. Haecker (eds) *Fields of Conflict: Battlefield Archaeology from the Roman Empire to the Korean War*, vol. 1: *Searching for War in the Ancient and Early Modern World*, Westport, CT: Praeger Security, 39–49.

Carman, J. and A. Harding (eds) (1999) *Ancient Warfare: Archaeological Perspectives*, Stroud: Sutton.

Cunha, E. and A. M. Silva (1997) 'War Lesions from the Famous Portuguese Medieval Battle of Aljubarotta', *International Journal of Osteoarchaeology* 7, 595–9.

Doyle, P. and M. R. Bennett (eds) (2002) *Fields of Battle: Terrain in Military History*, Dordrecht: Kluwer.

English Heritage (1995) *Register of Historic Battlefields*, London: English Heritage.

Fiorato, V., A. Boylston and C. Knusel (2000) *Blood Red Roses: The Archaeology of a Mass Grave from the Battle of Towton AD 1461*, Oxford: Oxbow.

Foard, G. (1995) *Naseby: The Decisive Campaign*, Whitstable: Pryor Publications.

—— (2001) 'The Archaeology of Attack: Battles and Sieges of the English Civil War', in T. Freeman and A. Pollard (eds) *Fields of Conflict: Progress and Prospects in Battlefield Archaeology, Proceedings of a Conference Held in the Department of Archaeology, University of Glasgow, April 2000*, Oxford: BAR International Series 958, Archaeopress, 87–104.

Foote, S. (1997) *Shadowed Ground: America's Landscapes of Violence and Tragedy*, Austin: University of Texas Press.

Freeman, P. and T. Pollard (eds) (2001) *Fields of Conflict: Progress and Prospects in Battlefield Archaeology, Proceedings of a Conference Held in the Department of Archaeology, University of Glasgow, April 2000*, Oxford: BAR International Series 958, Archaeopress.

Garden, M.-C. (2006) 'The Heritagescape: Looking at Landscapes of the Past', *International Journal of Heritage Studies* 12.5, 394–411.

Gray, C. H. (1997) *Postmodern War: The New Politics of Conflict*, London: Routledge.

Haas, J. (ed.) (1990) *The Anthropology of War*, Cambridge: Cambridge University Press.

Haecker, C. M. and J. G. Mauck (1997) *On the Prairie of Palo Alto: Historical Archaeology of the US–Mexican War Battlefield*, College Station: Texas A&M University Press.

Haldon, J. F. (ed.) (2006) *General Issues in the Study of Medieval Logistics: Sources, Problems and Methodologies*, History of Warfare 36, Leiden: Brill.

Hanson, V. D. (1989) *The Western Way of War: Infantry Battle in Classical Greece*, Oxford: Oxford University Press.

Herzfeld, M. (1991) *A Place in History: Social and Monumental Time in a Cretan Town*, Princeton and Oxford: Princeton University Press.

Hewitt, N. (2001) 'The National Inventory of War Memorials: Profile of a National Recording Project', in J.-M. Teutonico and J. Fidler (eds) *Monuments and the Millennium: Proceedings of a Joint Conference Organised by English Heritage and the United Kingdom Institute for Conservation*, London: English Heritage, 13–22.

Hodder, I., M. Shanks, A. Alexandri, V. Buchli, J. Carman, J. Last and G. Lucas (eds) (1995) *Interpreting Archaeology: Finding Meaning in the Past*, London: Routledge.

Keegan, J. (1976) *The Face of Battle*, London: Hutchinson.

—— (1993) *A History of Warfare*, London: Hutchinson.

Keeley, L. H. (1996) *War before Civilization: The Myth of the Peaceful Savage*, Oxford and New York: Oxford University Press.

Mathieu, J. and E. Kedl (1993) *The Plains of Abraham: The Search for the Ideal*, Sillery, Quebec: Septentrion.

Otto, T., H. Thrane and H. Vandkilde (eds) (2006) *Warfare and Society: Archaeological and Social Anthropological Perspectives*, Aarhus: Aarhus University Press.

Paço, A. do (1962) 'Em tormo de Aljubarotta. I-O Problema dos ossos dos combatentes da batalha', *Anais da Academia Portugesa da História* 2.12, 115–63.

Parker-Pearson, M. and I. J. N. Thorpe (eds) (2005) *Warfare, Violence and Slavery in Prehistory: Proceedings of a Prehistoric Society Conference at Sheffield University*, Oxford: BAR International Series 1374, Archeopress.

Pollard, T. and I. Banks (eds) (2006) *Past Tense: Studies in the Archaeology of Conflict*, Leiden: Brill.

Scott, D. D., R. A. Fox, M. A. Connor and D. Harmon (1989) *Archaeological Perspectives on the Battle of the Little Big Horn*, Norman and London: University of Oklahoma Press.

Scott, D., L. Babits and C. Haecker (eds) (2007) *Fields of Conflict: Battlefield Archaeology from the Roman Empire to the Korean War*, vol. 1: *Searching for War in the Ancient and Early Modern World*, Westport, CT: Praeger Security.

Sutherland, T. (2000) 'The Archaeological Investigation of the Towton Battlefield', in V. Fiorato, A. Boylston and C. Knusel (eds) *Blood Red Roses: The Archaeoogy of a Mass Grave from the Battle of Towton AD 1461*, Oxford: Oxbow, 155–68.

Tao, General Hanzhang (2000) *Sun Tzu's Art of War: The Modern Chinese Interpretation*, trans. Yuan Shibing, New York: Sterling Publishing.

Tilley, C. (1994) *A Phenomenology of Landscape*. Oxford: Berg.

Weigley, R. F. (1991) *The Age of Battles: The Quest for Decisive Warfare from Breitenfeld to Waterloo*, Bloomington and Indianapolis: Indiana University Press.

Yarrington, A. (1988) *The Commemoration of the Hero 1800–1864: Monuments to the British Victors of the Napoleonic Wars*, New York and London: Garland Publishing.

Part V

COMMENTARIES

HERITAGE AND METHODOLOGY

A view from social anthropology

Paola Filippucci

As a social anthropologist, my field encounter with 'heritage' was disconcerting and somewhat frustrating. In 2000, in the context of an archaeological project in a rural area of France, I was charged with investigating perceptions of the area's past and archaeological remains in view of the 'valorisation' of its heritage, identified in regional and national public policy as the most promising growth sector in an economically weak and marginal area. Ethnographic fieldwork revealed a population voicing a marked attachment to place but who did not consider place and identity to be embodied in what policy-makers called 'heritage', which was instead associated with an inauthentic, makeshift relationship with local reality, exemplified by tourism. In a context of depopulation and economic decline, the sorts of claims normally associated with 'heritage' (about authenticity, continuity, identity and attachment) were instead associated with ordinary surroundings and practices not necessarily linked with the past: with functional, habitable village houses, with the presence of people in the street, with going to the bakery or the post office, with attending a local school instead of commuting. Ethnography revealed a sense of 'heritage' centred on continuity into the future as much as or even more than continuity from the past, which did not match local policy-relevant notions of heritage as material or indeed immaterial traces of the past. Moreover the narratives I collected were diverse and sometimes contradictory, so that in practice it proved impossible to translate them into recommendations to public policy agencies charged with developing 'local heritage'. Ethnography had identified a mismatch between public policy and local perceptions and agendas, but not the means to redress it. From my point of view, the category 'heritage' was a straitjacket into which I struggled to frame and contain my findings and which ultimately denied them practical if not theoretical value. The report I eventually wrote was much praised by the commissioning agency but, to date, has not had any practical results.

Since then, I have come to realise that conducting qualitative research in relation to heritage poses particular challenges, particularly from a methodological point of view. As the introductory chapters to this volume argue, heritage is an interdisciplinary, 'in-between' field not only because it engages scholars from different subjects but also because the object itself is inherently diverse, incorporating as it does 'people, things and texts' (Sørensen and Carman, chapter 1). From the point of view of a social anthropologist this creates particular theoretical and methodological challenges. For instance, in the case of my research in France, I see now that the disappointing outcome can partly be attributed to the fact that French public policy enshrines (or enshrined at the time) a particularly narrow and inflexible definition of heritage more centred on things than on people, and on certain stereotyped ideas about rural areas and tradition (see Filippucci 2004). This may be an interesting finding in itself, but this example also raises to my mind the question of why we employ qualitative methods in the investigation of heritage. While not all heritage research is aimed at generating policy, should it be assumed that methods such as participant observation are inherently valuable in this field? Just because they work in another discipline, should they be adopted by others without further methodological reflection? This is what I would like to address in the rest of this essay with regard to qualitative methods of enquiry.

Qualitative research and heritage

As this volume demonstrates through many of its contributions, ethnography and more broadly qualitative methods have become a central methodology in heritage research in recent years. This responds to what arguably is the most interesting and intellectually productive contribution of Heritage Studies since its inception, the idea that heritage is not, as posited in policy and popular views, an assemblage of things: items, mostly material, that have historical value for a collectivity and that can be catalogued, listed, protected and so forth. Instead 'heritage' has been convincingly redefined as a field concerned first and foremost with people. Scholars now theorise heritage as a diverse range of social practices, processes and experiences through which people invest things, sites and practices with value and sentiment, and claim them in collective ownership or guardianship to affirm continuity, authenticity and identity; this investigation also frequently examines the ways in which such processes are institutionally 'managed' through policy and legislation.

The use of qualitative methods of investigation is a corollary of this way of conceptualising heritage, as qualitative methods are used to document and analyse perceptions, attitudes and motivations of those involved in the heritage process. These methods are drawn from disciplines specialising in the study of 'people', such as sociology and social anthropology, and can be deployed productively to advance our understanding of the phenomenon we call heritage. Contributors in this volume use the 'highly disciplined subjectivity' enjoined by this method for recognising implicit, unspoken attitudes to heritage (Keitumetse, chapter 11); for 'accessing and interpreting the cultural dynamics that underpin the creation and maintenance of identity' in the context of heritage tourism, and 'understanding the experience' of tourists and of heritage more widely (Palmer, chapter 7, Andrews, chapter 8); and 'to immerse myself in the world of the tourist and to explore issues of meaning and interpretation' and to elicit and create new meanings and understanding of the heritage (Palmer, chapter 7, Keitumetse, chapter 11). Ethnography is also a valuable method for eliciting comment on 'sensitive' issues and navigating the boundary between legality and illegality in the heritage field (Kersel, chapter 10). More broadly, as Kersel notes, heritage professionals use ethnography, interviewing and qualitative research all the time because this type of research is predicated on participation and contribution of the public.

Indeed, these methods, particularly the classic anthropological one of participant observation (see e.g. Andrews, chapter 8, Kersel, chapter 10), are invaluable for revealing the nuances and richness of people's perceptions and lifeworlds. However, as my example above suggests, they can reveal 'too much' nuance and richness: too much for the purposes of policy but also for advancing our understanding of 'heritage'. Even in national and policy contexts where eliciting 'local attitudes' is a routine aspect of policy (perhaps particularly where this is the case, as in instances where 'public participation' is required), conducting unreflecting qualitative research risks becoming a way to tick the boxes of protocol that does not advance either policy (cf. McDavid, chapter 12) or theory. The researcher is in danger of taking for granted that case studies are useful and of omitting basic questions such as: why, exactly, do qualitative research? What is one trying to find out by it and what exactly does it reveal? How does one make data so derived relevant to how we conceptualise heritage as a phenomenon in the contemporary world? In other words, even in a field centrally concerned with 'people', the richness of qualitative data does not speak by itself: it must be made to speak by being related to a framework of analysis.

In social anthropology, the framework in which localised, qualitative studies have classically been made to 'speak' is the so-called 'comparative method'. This method reflects and advances the central aim of anthropology: to grapple with the problem of the diversity of human social and cultural life, while assuming the fundamental unity of humankind (see e.g. Carruthers 1992). It posits that generalisable insights about human phenomena may be derived from comparing and contrasting case studies. The history of the discipline shows the potential pitfalls of this method: it can degenerate into what Leach famously called 'butterfly collecting', losing itself in creating typologies at the expense of analysis; or, as with post-modern relativism, lead to an almost exclusive focus on local meanings denying the possibility of generalisation (cf. Carsten 2004: 22). In spite of these extremes, the method arguably retains the potential of enabling empirically grounded generalisations about human phenomena, exploiting the tension between uniqueness and generality that characterises them (Eriksen 2001: 6). In the case of heritage, seen as a contemporary human phenomenon, comparison can come into play at a number of different levels that can enrich and valorise the use of qualitative methods in this field.

Comparison in heritage research

As Sørensen and Carman note (chapter 1), the qualitative case study has become a 'trope of publication' in the heritage field in recent decades, so the first, most obvious axis of comparison which may be suggested is that between case studies. This entails not simply publishing collections of case studies but also systematically designing, conducting and analysing case studies in a comparative framework. In a self-consciously comparative approach, case studies are not simply designed to document diversity and variety in the experience of and attitudes towards heritage, but also to answer questions about the reasons for variation or indeed for similarity across cases. While attending to the intricacies of the individual case, the aim is also always to compare and contrast it with others in a search for patterns and regularities. In this way comparison helps to clarify questions to guide further empirical observation, such as: what does and what does not become heritage in a given case? Who does and does not engage with it? How do things become repositories of temporality and authenticity, by what material and symbolic manipulations? How do different institutional worlds influence and shape how heritage is defined and 'lives' in a given society? How does 'heritage' relate to cultures of management and policy, definitions of citizenship and public, notions of property and claim, and notions of culture in a given society?

Asking such questions also leads one to analyse heritage-related behaviour comparatively against other sorts of social and cultural behaviour, for instance with other ways of knowing the past and claiming identity and authenticity. Thus at another level, case studies of how the concept and practice of heritage plays out in individual cases can be compared with ethnographic evidence and analytical discussions about other ways in which societies construct and relate to the past. In heritage this has already been done on a historical plane, charting the emergence and differentiation of 'heritage' from other societal ways of knowing the past such as myth, history and tradition (e.g. Lowenthal 1985; Nora 1989). However, in order to fully understand and analyse the phenomenon it is also important to compare and contrast 'heritage' with other modes of knowing the past within and between contemporary societies, both those within the Euro-American 'core', where the notion of 'heritage' is indigenous (see e.g. Hartog 2003), and beyond it, in societies now embracing or engaging with the international idiom of 'heritage' as a recent and imported cultural influence (cf. e.g. Kalinoe and Leach 2004). The comparative study of heritage in relation to other ways in which societies imagine, materialise and make the past known and visible to themselves and claim it in processes of identity formation helps to refute the idea, mentioned earlier in this volume (see Carman and Sørensen, chapter 2), that 'heritage' is an inferior, ideologically suspect way of approaching the past. Instead it shows heritage to be one of the modalities by which societies approach their past and construct identities around it. This links Heritage Studies to the anthropological study of 'social memory', to which

Heritage Studies could validly contribute in the empirical and theoretical study of *modern* social memory, a burgeoning interest in anthropology and the humanities more broadly (e.g. Rossington and Whitehead 2007). Similarly, the institutional frameworks of 'heritage' could also be studied comparatively: not only historically (see Swenson 2007) but also in relation to other contemporary policy and property forms contributing to the wider study of modern institutional, policy and property cultures (cf. Pottage and Mundy 2004).

A comparative approach to case studies also helps to refine our understanding of the nature and significance of the 'local' and therefore of the 'local knowledge' collected using qualitative methods, leading us to better evaluate its contribution to our understanding of heritage. As anthropological work on place has shown, there is a danger of reifying and romanticising local knowledge as encapsulating some essential and primordial set of meanings and understandings (see e.g. Gupta and Ferguson 1997). This is often encouraged by policy that includes a survey of 'local attitudes', thereby characterised as a self-contained, unified set of meanings that pre-exists the heritage encounter and that is juxtaposed to policy as a 'management' of, again, pre-existing resources. This assumption ignores the fact that, first, 'locals' are often internally divided and embrace different and contrasting viewpoints (cf. McDavid, chapter 12), and second, that the 'local' is not isolated from but emergent in wider contexts so that 'local' knowledge usually includes and engages with many influences. 'Local' people may mobilise a complex blend of school- and media-derived knowledge and images, policy-derived categories originating in policy, and more localised understandings as they attach value to heritage things and sites. On another level, policy-makers and other authorities conventionally opposed to 'local' communities are also often simultaneously themselves 'locals' and may position themselves as such contextually. By adopting a comparative mindset the 'local' is seen more clearly as an emergent and dynamic field, a location adopted as various constituencies stake their claim to the heritage. This helps to enrich and deepen our understanding, advocated by Andrews (in chapter 8), of 'heritage as an experience'. This last can be broadened beyond the subjective perceptions of 'users' and 'policy-makers' to a more comprehensive picture of a field of engagement in which discourse and action about 'heritage' are an aspect of the formation and crystallisation of 'communities' and interest groups: to see that by doing and speaking 'heritage' people form communities, and claim identities, including 'local' ones.

The final axis of comparison for qualitatively based case studies in heritage that I would like to suggest is disciplinary. As the introduction to this volume makes clear, the heritage field does not only include people but also, importantly, things and texts. This has methodological implications: while qualitative methods can generate valuable insight in heritage research, in some cases quantitative methods might be more appropriate; or also methodologies (such as those developed to study material culture) that take into account the 'thingness' of heritage and the way in which material representation generates a particular 'force field', its own sort of 'meaning' not reducible to symbolic, linguistically mediated meaning (see Pinney 2005: 261). It is the interplay between people and things (including texts) that makes the field of heritage so unique and theoretically exciting. In order to fully do justice to this quality of heritage, a sustained 'comparison' or dialogue between qualitative and non-qualitative methods is in order, helping to develop methodologies for connecting qualitative with quantitative data. As Fitzjohn (chapter 13) and Garden (chapter 15) both show, tools can be developed for integrating ethnographically derived knowledge with 'harder' definitions of heritage as quantifiable spaces, objects and/or sites. Both authors use the notion of landscape as a template to frame the cultural, intangible knowledge gained ethnographically and combine it with other knowledges. In particular, Fitzjohn's hyperlink model shows how it is possible to relate these different knowledges without each losing its particular character or being privileged over the others, but instead relating them in such a way that each is a context for the others. It also creates a model of reality that can be replicated or compared across local contexts, helping to analyse them, and so to discern patterns without abandoning uniqueness. As Fitzjohn also suggests, such models can enable various stakeholders and members of the public as well as researchers both locally and beyond to interact with the virtual 'heritage site' so created. By fostering interaction and debate beyond the actual heritage site, and so to speak extending the heritage site into virtual space, such a model can contribute as much to the analysis of heritage as to its creation.

Conclusions

More broadly, the image encapsulated by Fitzjohn's model of interacting and mutually contextualising knowledges is apt to describe a field like heritage, in which many different disciplinary approaches can meet and institute a fruitful dialogue. This possibility is inscribed not only in the heterogeneity of its object, but also in an aspect that underpins many of the contributions in this volume and is relatively unique to the heritage: the fact that heritage research can be and often is conducted by teams of scholars, each bringing different expertise and disciplinary backgrounds. On hindsight, a mistake I made in my investigation in France outlined above, partly also to blame for some of its failures, was that I did not sufficiently plan and develop my methodology in conversation with the archaeologists also involved in the project. Such interdisciplinary confrontation and comparison is rare or indeed absent in social anthropology, in which the lone researcher dominates, and is in my view a strength of the heritage field that has enormous potential for the methodological as well as theoretical advance of the field. As the history and sociology of science demonstrate, new methods and ideas are not (or not only) born through comparison and confrontation in the recesses of a researcher's own mind but also crucially in and through social encounter, dialogue and collaboration between scholars. By the heterogeneity of its object, the heritage field facilitates such encounters and collaborations. This makes it a privileged site for methodological reflection and innovation, as this volume clearly demonstrates.

Bibliography

Carruthers, M. (1992) *Why Humans Have Cultures: Explaining Anthropology and Social Diversity*, Oxford: Oxford University Press.

Carsten, J. (2004) *After Kinship*, Cambridge: Cambridge University Press.

Eriksen, T. H. (2001) *Small Places, Large Issues: An Introduction to Social and Cultural Anthropology*, London: Pluto Press.

Filippucci, P. (2004) 'A French Place without a Cheese: Problems with Heritage and Identity in Northeastern France', *Focaal – European Journal of Anthropology* 44, 72–86.

Gupta, A. and J. Ferguson (eds) (1997) *Culture, Power and Place*, Durham, NC: Duke University Press.

Hartog, F. (2003) *Regimes d'historicité: présentisme et expériences du temps*, Paris: Seuil.

Kalinoe, L. and J. Leach (eds) (2004) *Rationales of Ownership: Ethnographic Studies of Transactions and Claims to Ownership in Contemporary Papua New Guinea*, Wantage: Sean Kingston Publications.

Lowenthal, D. (1985) *The Past is a Foreign Country*, Cambridge: Cambridge University Press.

Nora, P. (1989) 'Between Memory and History: Les lieux de mémoire', *Representations* 26, 7–25.

Pinney, C. (2005) 'Things Happen, or, From Which Moment Does that Object Come?', in D. Miller (ed.) *Materiality*, Durham, NC: Duke University Press.

Pottage, A. and M. Mundy (eds) (2004) *Law, Anthropology and the Constitution of the Social: Making Persons and Things*, Cambridge: Cambridge University Press.

Rossington, M. and A. Whitehead (eds) (2007) *Theories of Memory: A Reader*, Edinburgh: Edinburgh University Press.

Swenson, A. (2007) 'Conceptualising Heritage in Nineteenth- and Early Twentieth-century France, Germany and England'. PhD Thesis, Department of History, University of Cambridge.

WHERE IS THE DISCIPLINE IN
HERITAGE STUDIES?

A view from environmental psychology

David Uzzell

Charlotte Andrews in her opening paragraph (chapter 8) states, quite rightly, that 'Heritage Studies does not yet offer a set of established methodologies to choose from, [so] researchers are challenged, but also free, to employ novel lines of enquiry towards our aim of a more complex and satisfying under-standing of heritage'. This is hardly surprising since Heritage Studies is the lovechild of a multitude of relationships between academics in many disci-plines, and then nurtured by practitioners and institutions. There is no discipline as such as heritage; this is reinforced by the fact that we give it the catch-all term 'heritage studies'. The fellow travellers we find on the way are geographers, sociologists, archaeologists, psychologists, historians and many others – many of these disciplines are represented in this book. What these researchers share in common is a fascination with the past, a yearning for a deeper understanding of it not least because although the past is elusive it has a critical effect on the present and the future. It sits somewhere 'out there', a tangible resource and source of inspiration, meaning and identity as well as commercial profit. It is a physical reality that is more than just the fabrication in our minds that Lowenthal (1998) suggests. But it is clearly 'in here' as well, in the minds of the observer; it is a social construction, an empty box, waiting to be filled with our values, beliefs, desires. Its func-tional role, however, is more nuanced than simply suggesting it adds a repository and framework for meaning. The meaning of the heritage will vary over time and for different groups of people. It serves social, cultural and political functions. But the heritage during this process does not remain static and unchanged. It also becomes a piece of clay ready to be moulded into something we want it to be. We use the heritage in the creation of our own individual, group and national identities (Devine-Wright and Lyons 1997; Anteric 1998; MacDonald 2003). We construct meanings from the heritage and we construct ourselves from it as well.

This is not the place for an extended discussion of the nature of heritage and its function for individuals, groups and society (for this, see the collection of readings by Smith (2007) and Fairclough *et al.* (2008)). The opening paragraph of this contribution does, however, suggest that how we access the heritage is far from straightforward, an issue made more complicated by the fact that heritage is not the preserve of one discipline but many. We are all familiar with L. P. Hartley's opening lines from *The Go-Between* (1953): 'The past is a foreign country: they do things differently there.' Indeed, the quotation is cited endlessly in studies of the heritage, and is the title of Lowenthal's seminal book (1999). But a little more self-reflection might lead researchers to see that no less foreign an experience are the academic disciplines into which all of us stray invariably as researchers of 'the heritage'. The heritage is the meeting ground of many disciplines, and it is on that meeting ground that we are confronted with issues which as researchers we give scant regard. One of these issues is methodology.

The purpose of this brief essay is to discuss the importance of methodological awareness and the need for the imagination in the development of new methodologies and methods for understanding the heritage in the context of interdisciplinary collaboration. Heritage Studies is, as a consequence of its mixed parentage, the archetypal interdisciplinary study area. Methodologies are important in Heritage Studies because they are the hand which guides us into the past from the present. They show us how to look and see. But they should also come with a health warning.

O'Brien (2008) recently conducted a small study examining the positive and negative aspects of interdisciplinary collaboration, questioning researchers from at least eight different natural and social science disciplines working on a three year ESRC/RELU (Rural Economy and Land Use) programme. There was a positive response to interdisciplinary working. It was seen to lead to: a better understanding of how other scientists work, enabling new areas of work to be developed and incorporated into a holistic project; different points of view; new insights, new angles and techniques brought to topics of common interest; learning from other perspectives and understanding different epistemologies; broader questions being addressed and other methods and approaches included; opening up of different literatures; the encouragement of applied and policy-oriented research which may be more likely to address the problems under investigation and be more meaningful to the research client.

The negative features of interdisciplinary collaboration were: it is time-consuming and sometimes frustrating; the approaches to and standards of evidence in some disciplines are sometimes questioned by those in other disciplines; the language differences (i.e. jargon) in different disciplines; publishing in single discipline journals can be difficult if it includes theories from other disciplines; the length of time taken to achieve certain outputs can be considerable due to time taken to accommodate different interests.

Although these findings are derived from a study assessing and communicating animal-disease risk for countryside users, their significance is no less relevant for those working in Heritage Studies. It is noteworthy that most of the issues surrounding interdisciplinary working focused on methodology, the subject of this book. In the remaining pages I would like to discuss further methodological issues which are not always so readily apparent and may be overlooked when disciplines come together.

There are no methods without theory

Whether the heritage is 'out there' or 'in here' there is a relationship between 'it' and 'us'. There are various ways of thinking about and analysing our relationship with the physical world. Moscovici (1972), in the context of analysing different approaches in social psychology, names these relationships as 'taxonomic', 'differential' and 'systematic'. The relationships are sufficiently generic to be of relevance for researchers of the heritage as they all relate to the relationship between people and their physical world. The 'taxonomic' is concerned with investigating the nature of the variables which might account for the behaviour of an individual. Social stimuli are seen to affect the processes of judgement, perception and the formation of attitudes. The independent variables are either people or groups of people, or they are physical objects – the environment or the heritage (?) – which have social value. In practice this might be how the social value of the cultural heritage confers and sustains national identity. The environment is ascribed psychological characteristics, and social phenomena are in turn treated as natural objects. The emphasis is on reaction to the social and environmental rather than the relationship with the environment.

The second set of relationships is the 'differential', in which the subject of research is classified and differentiated according to whatever social and psychological criteria we are interested in – for example, social categories such as curators *versus* the public, scientists *versus* lay people, landowners *versus* non-owners, or according to the position they may take, for example possessing pro- or anti-environment attitudes. The properties of the environment are of little interest as the focus of attention is on the role the individual occupies and the consequent effect that the social role has on attitudes and behaviour in respect of, for example, heritage. The aim in this form of social psychology is to find out how different categories of people or positions respond when faced with a particular problem such as the destruction of heritage.

In the 'systematic', there is an interdependence of people/groups in relation to a common physical or social environment. The relationship of the individual to the heritage is mediated through the intervention of another person or group such as archaeologists or exhibition designers. This can lead to two types of studies. The focus of attention in the first is on changes in the behaviour of individuals participating in the interaction and the developing nature of the relationship. The second approach focuses on the effects of the relationship

– on the individuals, their relationship with each other and their relationship with the heritage.

This classification, and the methodologies it suggests, might be a useful way for researchers to think about future heritage research.

Methodological assumptions and the model of the person

All methods have embedded within them sets of assumptions about the relationship *between people* and *between people and their physical environment and their relationship to the past*. The assumptions reflect different models of the person. The model of the person assumed (but not necessarily articulated) by those working in one discipline (e.g. architecture or archaeology) may be different from that assumed by those working within another discipline and with whom they are collaborating (e.g. psychology). In practical terms what this means is that one group may be working with a set of assumptions which are inherently individual and behaviourist, whereas another discipline may be working within a more social or relational model framework.

Israel (1972) suggests that three models of the person[1] have been assumed in social psychology – the behaviouristic, the role and the relational. Behaviourist theories are oriented primarily to the individual, who invariably is in passive mode. For example, social learning theory explains the processes by which an individual acquires attitudes and behaviours through interacting with another individual. In exchange theory, the emphasis is on the rewards, costs, outcomes and comparison levels of the individuals involved in the exchange rather than the dyad as a social system. Cognitive theories are heavily oriented towards the individual, with little recognition of the social context in which individuals operate and the role and influence of the social group and collective thought and action. Behaviourist theories suggest that by controlling the environment it is possible to control the individual. If we can understand the effect of environmental (and temporal?) events on people's behaviour it may be possible, it is argued, to anticipate their influence, even plan for that influence and gain control over events. Such a view lies at the heart of environmental and architectural determinism (Lee 1976), a position which suggests not only that the environment is highly influential on (and in some cases deterministic of) people's behaviour, but that it is possible to design the environment to achieve particular social outcomes.

Israel's second model of the person that has been dominant in social psychology is the *role model*. Role theory has been described as follows:

> Man has certain positions within the social system and related to these positions are normative expectations concerning the individual's behaviour and concerning relevant attributes. Positions are independent of a specific occupant.
>
> (Israel 1972: 140)

In contrast to behaviourist/cognitive theories, role theory assumes that the individual will submit passively to the influence of social and political constructions. While it allows the individual to break rules and act out other roles, and although it has a strong social orientation, it tends to minimise the individual's own perceptions, preferences, norms and interests.

Israel's third model is a *relational model* of the person which is represented by the work of George Herbert Mead and the symbolic interactionists. Mead wrote: 'a self can arise only where there is a social process within which this self has its initiation. It arises within that process' (Mead 1956: 42). Within this model, Stringer writes:

> Man is not seen as a bundle of traits, or an individual simply responding to rewards and punishments, but as his social relations. Man is the sum of his social interactions through constant interactions with others, the self is constantly changing; interaction is fully reciprocal as neither the individual nor social processes are given priority.
>
> (Stringer 1982: 58)

The relational approach recognises that all action takes place within a social and historical context. Although acts may appear to be individual acts, at various levels they inevitably implicate other members of the group or society; they also have a past or a history. Unlike both behaviouristic and role models, the relational model of the person assumes a more psychologically and socially aware person who plays an active role in their own development and in their relationship with the rest of society.

What is the relevance of this to heritage studies? We are aware that the way questions are asked will affect the kind of answers one receives. We typically think of this as a problem in relation to biased questioning. But the implications of question-framing extend beyond issues of bias. The way we ask questions will influence if not determine the kinds of analysis of and the explanations we can infer from the data. Framing questions which assume a behaviourist position will invariably lead to individualistic and reductionist interpretations of people's behaviour; questions framed within a more relational model of the person will enable more socially contextual interpretations.

Interdisciplinary research in an ethical context

Each discipline develops its own ethical standards. Ethical standards are important as they provide a normative framework for professional courses of action and rules of conduct. Each profession's ethical standards are developed over many years in the light of practical experience. Research methodologies in general and specific methods in particular have ethical implications and requirements. Very little attention is often paid to those situations where a methodology from one discipline is used in another. When a research method, even one so ubiquitous as interviewing, is employed by those who are not taught such a skill as part of their own disciplinary repertoire, it is easy for those borrowing the technique to treat it mechanistically and ignore the ethical assumptions, implications and requirements which accompany its use.

An example can be provided outside the area of Heritage Studies but which illustrates the problem well; indeed, it is not difficult to think of such a situation arising in research being conducted on heritage. This example involved two groups of architecture and psychology students working together on a collaborative field trip (Romice and Uzzell 2005). The purpose of the field trip was to bring these two groups together so that they could learn from each other, see the world through the others' eyes and share methodologies for the understanding of urban space and place.

Simple observation of each group revealed that the two groups perceived the public quite differently. While walking through residential areas, the architects were more willing to peer into people's houses, call out to residents, ask passers-by questions and try and get invited into locals' houses or flats in order to see their internal layout and space provision. The psychologists were much less willing to engage in these types of behaviours. The psychology students, having been inculcated into the mores of the psychology profession and the ethics of research, placed greater importance on the privacy of the residents. The psychologists felt that the residents had a 'right' to be left alone; the idea of shouting up to a resident several floors above violates most principles of anonymity of participants. For the psychology students anything that smacks of data collection automatically puts one in a researcher/respondent relationship. It may have been that the architecture students did not see themselves in a professional relationship with the residents; the architects justified their behaviour in terms of being casual enquiries which the residents could have declined. The presence of large numbers of inquisitive students on the housing estate could have led to the residents feeling pressured to respond, or being made uncomfortable in their own homes and settings, which again raises ethical questions of how we treat members of the public who may neither have been asked nor have consented to participation. The architecture students simply did not feel the same burden of an ethic of care towards the public as the environmental psychology students did. This is not a criticism, but it does serve to illustrate quite graphically how the adoption of methodologies in an interdisciplinary context also requires the adoption of the ethical standards which are assumed to accompany their employment.

Conclusion: feeling the elephant

Heritage Studies is a rich and stimulating area of research precisely because it requires a multidisciplinary and, even better, an interdisciplinary approach. This is its great strength but also its potential weakness. The problems of interdisciplinary work are often epitomised in books on methodology by reference to John Godfrey Saxe's poem 'The Blind Men and the Elephant'.

It was six men of Indostan
To learning much inclined,
Who went to see the Elephant
(Though all of them were blind),
That each by observation
Might satisfy his mind.

As Heat comments on the men from Indostan who each feel a different part of the elephant: 'They seize, literally, on various features of the elephant, its legs, trunk, tail and so on, and then come to blows over what the elephant is "really" like. Their investigations revealed many things about the elephant, but "elephantness" eluded them' (Heat 1974: 182).

And so these men of Indostan
Disputed loud and long,
Each in his own opinion
Exceeding stiff and strong,
Though each was partly in the right,
And all were in the wrong!

This is supposed to illustrate how people from different perspectives will see only one aspect of a phenomenon. But, of course, we are all blind when it comes to understanding the totality of what we research. We might like to think we understand the phenomenon under investigation but our understanding is always situated whether because of where we stand, how we observe, or how we interpret. Theorising the heritage is always a site of discursive struggle (Hall 1999). Notwithstanding this, one of the reasons why we undertake interdisciplinary research is to communicate and engage with others in order to develop and employ methodologies in an imaginative and informed way in order to understand the heritage, whether it is 'out there' or 'in here', and, indeed, capture the quality of 'elephantness'.

Note

1   Israel, as was the practice of the time, refers to 'models of man', as do subsequent commentators. This has been changed in the present essay to reflect current practice when possible (i.e. not within specific quotations).

Bibliography

Anteric, M. (1998) 'Contested Heritage in the Former Yugoslavia', in D. Uzzell and R. Ballantyne (eds) *Contemporary Issues in Heritage and Environmental Interpretation: Problems and Prospects*, London: The Stationery Office, 172–84.
Devine-Wright, P. and E. Lyons (1997) 'Remembering Pasts and Representing Places: The Construction of National Identities in Ireland', *Journal of Environmental Psychology* 17, 33–45.

Fairclough, G., R. Harrison, J. H. Jameson and J. Schofield (eds) (2007) *The Cultural Heritage Reader*, New York: Routledge.

Hall, S. (1999) 'Whose Heritage? Un-settling "The Heritage", Re-imagining the Post-nation', *Third Text* 46, 3–13.

Hartley, L. P. (1953) *The Go-Between*, Harmondsworth: Penguin.

Heat, T. (1974) 'Should We Tell Children about Aesthetics, or Should We Let Them Find Out in the Street?', in D. Canter and T. Lee (eds) *Psychology and the Built Environment*, Tonbridge, Kent: Whitefriars Press, 179–83.

Israel, J. (1972) 'Stipulations and Construction in the Social Sciences', in J. Israel and H. Tajfel (eds) *The Context of Social Psychology: A Critical Assessment*, London: Academic Press, 123–211.

Lee, T. (1976) 'Psychology and Architectural Determinism', *Architects' Journal* 154, 253–62, 475–83, 651–9.

Lowenthal, D. (1998) 'Fabricating Heritage', *History and Memory* 10.1, 5–24.

—— (1999) *The Past is a Foreign Country*, Cambridge: Cambridge University Press.

MacDonald, S. J. (2003) 'Museums, National, Postnational and Transcultural Identities', *Museum and Society* 1.1, 1–16.

Mead, G. (1956) 'The Problem of Society – How We Become Selves', in G. Mead (ed.) *George Herbert Mead on Social Psychology*, Chicago: University of Chicago Press, 19–42.

Moscovici, S. (1972) 'Society and Theory in Social Psychology', in J. Israel and H. Tajfel (eds) *The Context of Social Psychology: A Critical Assessment*, London: Academic Press, 17–68.

O'Brien, L. (2008) 'Results 2008 Questionnaire on Interdisciplinary Working', unpublished paper from RELU Lyme Project: Assessing and Communicating Animal Disease Risk for Countryside Users, Alice Holt: Forest Research.

Romice, O. and D. Uzzell (2005) 'Community Design Studio: A Collaboration of Architects and Psychologists', *CEBE Transactions* 2.1, 73–88.

Smith, L. (eds) (2007) *Cultural Heritage: Critical Concepts in Media and Cultural Studies*, London: Routledge.

Stringer, P. (1982) 'Towards a Participatory Psychology', in P. Stringer (ed.) *Confronting Social Issues*, vol. II, London: Academic Press, 45–64.

INDEX

Lightning Source UK Ltd.
Milton Keynes UK
UKOW06f1042171115

262899UK00005B/36/P